ARTHUR BERRIEDALE KEITH
1879–1944

1 Arthur Berriedale Keith, Kensington Gardens, *c*. 1938. Photograph by
Michael J S Dewar and used with his permission.

ARTHUR
BERRIEDALE
KEITH
1879-1944

THE CHIEF ORNAMENT OF
SCOTTISH LEARNING

Ridgway F Shinn Jr

ABERDEEN UNIVERSITY PRESS
Member of Maxwell Macmillan Pergamon Publishing Corporation

First published 1990
Aberdeen University Press
© Ridgway F Shinn, Jr 1990

The publisher acknowledges subsidy from the Scottish Arts Council towards the publication of this volume.

The publisher also acknowledges subsidies from Rhode Island College: the Office of the Dean of Arts and Sciences, and the Faculty Research Fund.

British Library Cataloguing in Publication Data

Shinn, Jr, Ridgway F
    Arthur Berriedale Keith (1879–1944): 'the chief ornament
    of Scottish learning'.
    1. Scotland. Keith, Arthur Berriedale, 1879–1944
    I. Title
    941.1081′092′4

ISBN 0 08 037737 8

Typeset and printed by AUP Glasgow/Aberdeen—A member of BPCC Ltd.

For
CLARICE WAGNER SHINN,
With great gratitude and abiding affection

Contents

List of Illustrations

Preface

Since the task of reconstructing a life from such materials as may exist is scarcely easy, one who undertakes the writing of a biography must explain to readers why one chose to study a particular person. In my case, I must confess to a long-standing query, raised in my mind, I suppose, about 1942 when I first encountered the writings of Arthur Berriedale Keith on constitutional aspects of the British Empire. I noted with great curiosity and interest that beneath his name on the title page of several of his books was this:

> Of the Inner Temple, Barrister-at-Law, and of the Scottish Bar; Regius Professor of Sanskrit and Comparative Philology, and Lecturer on the Constitution of the British Empire at the University of Edinburgh

How, I asked myself, was it possible for one person to be engaged in law, both English and Scottish, in languages and the study of language, and in constitutional studies all at the same time? Could one person work in all those fields productively and with integrity?

Some years later, I undertook a study of the ways in which the emergence of the right, or claim, of secession by the dominions, especially argued by the Union of South Africa and the Irish Free State at Imperial Conferences in the 1920s, helped transform the constitutional basis of the British Commonwealth of Nations in the interwar period. For that, I had to study virtually all of Keith's published writings on the constitution of the British Empire. And the more I read, the more the query persisted! At that point, in the late 1950s, I decided that, at some future time, I would attempt to find an answer. When, therefore, opportunity arose in the last decade, I went to work pursuing the query and, in the process, attempting to understand Keith's life. This biography is the result.

Obviously, I came to work on Keith out of my interest in issues related to the history and development of the British Empire and the British Commonwealth of Nations, rather than from studying Sanskrit. In my undergraduate and graduate days, I was stimulated to study about imperial matters by four extraordinary teachers and first-rate scholars: Howard Robinson at Oberlin College, Robert L Schuyler and J Bartlet Brebner at Columbia University, and Charles L Mullett of the University of Missouri. My indebtedness to each is life-long. I am grateful for the opportunity I had to learn under their direction; I treasure the ways I came to enjoy the rich rewards of good stories, engaging conversation, and on-going scholarship.

In the course of preparing a study such as this, one becomes indebted to numerous persons for their interest, response to inquiries, and help. In the paragraphs which follow, I note some persons of especial help while I indicate others in footnotes. If, inadvertently, I neglect to mention a name, I apologise; such omission may simply be a defect in my judgement or memory.

Two persons are of central importance: Michael J S Dewar and Mrs J Walcot Burton, 'Bill'. Brother and sister, children of Nan B Keith Dewar, they are nephew and niece of Arthur Berriedale Keith. Both have been extraordinarily generous in granting access to family materials which they hold and equally generous in responding to all sorts of questions about the family. I was able to gather information which could not be found in any other way. Perhaps I experienced the most delightful aspects of research with them: a wonderful weekend with Michael and his wife, Mary, at their home then in Austin, Texas, and several lunches, teas, talks in the garden with 'Bill' in London. I hope that I have used the information they shared in a fair and faithful manner.

On the basis of my long-standing query about Keith, I was able to enlist major support from my own institution, Rhode Island College. I acknowledge with gratitude the kind assistance of the late David Sweet, President of Rhode Island College, who helped in ways he could not have anticipated; of David L Greene, Dean of Arts and Sciences who, among other ways, found funds to assist in publication; of successive chairmen of the Department of History—the late Ronald B Ballinger, David S Thomas, and Norman W Smith. All these responded affirmatively to my requests for time and funding to pursue this study. The major portion of this book was completed in Edinburgh while I was on leave during the spring and summer of 1985. My colleagues in the Department of History heard segments of this book as I presented several papers in departmental colloquia and, out of discussions, offered numerous suggestions. Countless discussions with my colleague, Kenneth F Lewalski, have been fruitful as they covered a wide range of historiographical issues and of the challenges of writing biography. The staff of the James P Adams Library helped with response to queries and with securing materials on inter-library loan while that of the Audio-Visual Department reproduced photographs for me. Further, I acknowledge with appreciation the grant made from the Faculty Research Fund to help with costs of publication.

Pursuit of research materials about Keith took me to Edinburgh. I am deeply grateful for the warm hospitality given me by many persons at the University of Edinburgh. In the summer of 1981, I was privileged to be a Fellow at the Institute for Advanced Studies in the Humanities, then directed by Professor David Daiches with whom I had several helpful conversations as he, from his youth and student days, recollected some of the stories about Keith. Over many years, the staff of Edinburgh University Library has been gracious. My first inquiries were made when Charles Finlayson was still heading the special collections department. More recently, Dr John T D Hall directed that department and, with his colleagues Marjorie Robertson and Margaret Brown, supported the work as I catalogued the Keith Papers and Correspondence and used the Keith Collection. The help of that department reflects the on-going interest of Brenda Moon, Librarian, and Peter Freshwater, Deputy Librarian. Paul Dundas of the Sanskrit Department has been gracious and helpful in person and through correspondence. Professor Gordon Donaldson shared his recollections of Keith and, as well, assisted me in tracing the Keith family through the Scots Ancestry Research Society.

Also, he suggested I contact one of his student contemporaries, Mrs Neil Bayne who studied with Keith in the mid 1930s. I deeply appreciate correspondence and conversation with her. She read the course on constitutional history of the British Empire and had helpful recollections of the course and of Keith as a person.

To know where Keith lived a major portion of his life in Edinburgh, I am profoundly indebted to Dorothy Bull and the late Harry Bull for their extraordinary generosity in receiving me, several times, in their home at 4 Crawfurd Road, Keith's house from 1920 to his death in 1944. The first owners after Keith, they were able to recall how the house was used when they purchased it in 1945. Graciously, they permitted me to photograph throughout the house. They guided me to talk with Stuart McArthur whose mother had known the Keiths, especially Nan Dewar, and the neighbourhood.

Many persons helped me understand the special place of Royal High School. Dr Farquar Macintosh, Rector, and Mary M Urquhart, Archivist, provided access to school records and materials. Gilbert Watson, at ninety-six years of age in 1979, talked with me one long evening about his experiences as a student there, as well as about numerous things Scottish. Dr J H Barclay answered some of my questions about the school, as well.

To get some sense about the house Keith's mother had built in Dunbar, I received access and permission to wander throughout the house by the kindness of Michael O'Donnell, Secretary-Treasurer, Winterfield Golf and Sports Club. St Margaret's, as it was called when built, is now the central building for that club. Further, T W Spencer, a member of the Club, kindly arranged for Jacki Morton to take the photograph which appears on page 118.

Above all, I must express great and warm appreciation to George Albert Shepperson, William Robertson Professor of Commonwealth and American History, University of Edinburgh. When he learned of my interest in and queries about Keith, he urged me onwards in most emphatic ways. He is a worthy successor to Keith in imperial studies at Edinburgh! Through continuing conversations and correspondence with him about Keith, the University, Scotland, the Commonwealth, and the like I have been able to flesh out numerous details.

In addition to Edinburgh and Scotland, research took me to many other places in Britain. I was directed to Cambridge where, at St John's College, I spent a full day in conversation with John Brough, Professor of Sanskrit. His initial study in Sanskrit was done at Edinburgh with Keith and he shared recollections of the teaching style, course content, examinations, and the University as well as of Keith personally. Moreover, he looked at a listing of all Keith's published works in Sanskrit and oriental studies and provided a critical review and comment, indicating which are still of importance and which are 'dated'. From that critique, I confirmed the continuing importance of Keith's scholarly contributions to the field, a point I noted, subsequently, as various presses in India continue to reprint his principal works.

In London, I spent several long periods to pursue Keith's work at the Colonial Office. Various institutions were hospitable, especially the Institute of Historical Research of the University of London, and the Public Record Office. Staff in both places were helpful. I used other libraries and collections, and am grateful to those who staff and fund them: the Bodleian at Oxford University; the Institute of Commonwealth Studies, London; the India Office Library, London; the British Library; the Foreign and Commonwealth Office Library, London, Miss E C Blayney, Library and Records Department; Archives, Balliol College, Oxford, John Jones, Archivist; Archives, Oxford University Press, Oxford, through the kindness of Peter Sutcliffe. Several persons responded to inquiries: Sir Robert Armstrong, HM Management and Personnel Office, in regard to Keith and the Civil Service Examination in 1901; W W S Breem, Librarian, Inner Temple, about Keith's being called to the Bar; Peter W H Brown, Secretary, British Academy, about Keith's resignation from membership; Dr Richard Pankhurst, Royal Asiatic Society, about Keith's relationship to the society and, also, to E Sylvia Pankhurst on Abyssinian issues; Mrs K Vevers, Vice-Chancellor's Office, University of Leeds, about Keith's honorary degree; Sir Kenneth Wheare, Oxford University, about his knowledge of Keith for the notice in the *Dictionary of National Biography*.

It is important, as well, that I acknowledge the kind interest in and skilled attention to this work given by Mr Colin MacLean of Aberdeen University Press. I am grateful that he secured funding from the Scottish Arts Council in support of publication. He and his associates have effectively translated manuscript into print, and I appreciate their work.

Yet, with all those numerous contributions acknowledged, I must name the unusual and important role played by my wife, Clarice Wagner Shinn. Her role went beyond interest and general support, although those were always present. She actively participated in gathering materials as, in effect, a research assistant, taking notes, tracking materials, preparing lists, gathering bibliographical details, and the like, to say nothing of her help in reflecting on and talking through what we learned about Keith, his life, and his correspondents. To say that this study could not have been completed without her help and investment of energy is absolutely true! And, I am, therefore obviously, deeply in her debt.

With all the help and support I have received, I must point out that none of those persons carries any responsibility for the narrative or for the interpretation; that responsibility is solely mine. I offer this study as my answer to the query about how one person could be productive in so many different fields. It is my hope that this study of Keith may set him and his extensive production in several fields appropriately in the familial, intellectual, educational, social, and political context in which he lived and worked.

Ridgway F Shinn, Jr
Rhode Island College
Spring 1990

CHAPTER 1

Keith and his Times

If, at the summit of Arthur's Seat, that great brooding crag which looms over Edinburgh, there were a pantheon to honour Scots of extraordinary genius, a special niche, or perhaps two, would have to be reserved for Arthur Berriedale Keith. Born in 1879 in the shadow of that landmark and living until the latter part of 1944, he was, in his time, one of the world's leading authorities on the constitution of the British Empire and the British Commonwealth of Nations, an outstanding scholar in Classics, Sanskrit, and Oriental Studies, a writer about and practitioner of English and Scots law, and, as well, a public figure whose work with various organisations involved him in significant issues and whose letters to many newspapers in Britain and throughout the Empire, especially, were influential in helping to criticise, interpret, define, and shape public policy on numerous matters. The wide range of his work, represented by more than fifty books and hundreds of scholarly articles among these fields, made it difficult for his contemporaries and, indeed, interested persons in more recent years to see his life and work as a whole. Statesmen, public officials, and politicians knew his writings on the constitution of the British Empire; Sanskrit and Oriental scholars knew his contributions in those areas; readers of *The Scotsman*, *The Times*, and other newspapers became familiar with his views and comments on public issues through his letters; persons who wrote to him to raise queries in relevant subject matter welcomed his critiques and suggestions; some native Africans even looked to him for assistance in carrying appeals to the Judicial Committee of the Privy Council. Yet, each tended to see Keith in but one dimension of his work while he, in fact, functioned in all these areas simultaneously.

Certainly, he was unusual as a man naturally endowed with an authentic and a wide range of mental abilities. Based on those talents, he was moulded into a unique intellectual through his rearing, his education, and his work. He lived his life essentially in the triangle formed by Edinburgh, Oxford, and London. In his later life, he was characterised as an 'ornament of Scottish learning';[1] to become that, he had most certainly been polished brilliantly. To be sure, during his lifetime and subsequently, he had his share of critics even as he had many more persons who understood, acknowledged, and appreciated his unique gifts and contributions.

The very nature, the wide range, and the sheer volume of his published works raise questions about his genius, mental capacities, and methods of work, about the sort of support he received from family and others, and about

1

the kind of person he actually was. In addition, the years which frame his life stretch from the seeming placidity of the later Victorian world of the nineteenth century into the horrors of the Second World War in the mid twentieth century and raise questions about the ways in which profound changes in the British Empire, in Britain itself, and in the international sphere, influenced his work and provided the context within which he felt it necessary to respond.

While one can only begin to approach an understanding of Keith and his works through a careful study of his life and career, it is possible, in a general way, to indicate something about Keith's nature and about the shape of the years comprising his life span. Such a view will set the stage and provide the backdrop for more detailed analysis.

Keith's Nature

It is always difficult, indeed risky, to undertake the task of reconstructing the nature of any person; yet, this is precisely the task which every biographer must face. What is the essence of an individual's personality? What did the person look like and how did the person appear? What are the principal elements for explaining a person's behaviour? What are the ingredients which account for someone's achievements, or lack of them? What made the person 'tick', as it were? Even if that person is still alive, it is hard to know precisely which features provide the best clues to understanding that person. The task becomes even more formidable when that person is Keith with his wide natural gifts, with his many-faceted interests and concerns, and with his published works, almost overwhelming in their quantity and variety.

The task of describing Keith's nature is further complicated both by the presence and the absence of materials: numerous letters remain and provide a degree of insight into Keith's personality; a great quantity of material which he handled at the Colonial Office remains and is of help; many of the notes he made about various aspects or episodes in his life remain and are vital; minutes and documents from school, universities, and various organisations are available to answer certain questions; his published works, of course, exist and are essential; some members of the family have recollections; some former students have notes or can recall classes. All these available materials are useful and of importance. But even with a few photographs of Keith at different stages in his life, all these materials only provide the basis for inferential insight into his nature.[2] Materials which would give more direct insight into his nature appear not to exist: there remains no diary which he kept and to which he confided his hopes, dreams, fears, and frustrations, or even his daily activities; there was no close confidant, no Boswell, to leave notes; there are no diaries and no extensive letters from his mother, his wife, or his younger sister who, apparently, were the persons closest to him.

Yet, from materials that are available, it is feasible to infer and to sketch certain aspects of Keith's nature. One obvious aspect of anyone's nature has to do with the physical frame and endowment which nature and genetics provide. Here, for Keith, it is possible to proceed with considerable assurance since photographs, certain letters, and recollections of persons who knew him directly all remain. Perhaps the most distinctive feature he possessed was an impressive, squarish, commanding head, clearly a feature he shared especially with his brothers as part of the Keith inheritance. When he was grown, he was of moderate height, perhaps about 5 feet 8 to 9 inches tall. He possessed a stocky frame and always had a tendency to be somewhat overweight, even as a child; 'portly' might be the appropriate word to use when he was older. He had penetrating eyes which, with the frequent set of his mouth in a manner approaching a smile, gave him a rather quizzical or whimsical expression. He dressed in styles suited to his times and his work: university dress when he was there, uniform of the Civil Service when he was on the staff at the Colonial Office in London, morning coat for appropriate occasions, dinner jacket for evenings. Stiff collar, four-in-hand cravat, and waistcoat were all usual attire. Often, in his later years, he wore a jumper for warmth in place of the waist-coat. When he went out to classes or for a walk, he carried a handsome, knobbed stick and wore a wide-brimmed hat and overcoat, depending upon the weather. In a letter to his mother, he described himself dressed for a reception in May 1911, in conjunction with the Imperial Conference of that year:

> I was clad in my beautiful new frock coat (which fits admirably), in my pretty waistcoat & a pair of my new trousers, which are really too smart for words. The pattern is a joy forever, and I was much admired.[3]

In that same letter, there is further evidence about his appearance, most significantly that it was servants who did his shopping and provided him with whatever he needed to wear.[4] This may account for the term used by one of his students from 1934–5 when she characterised Keith as appearing to be 'cosseted', that is, always cared for, sheltered, protected, perhaps even pampered. That same student described him as being 'elderly, grey-haired, pale, plumpish, reticent and extremely courteous. He seemed to feel the cold and was always well wrapped-up, sitting beside a well-stoked fire ...'[5] In all, an observer would scarcely be filled with awe by his physical presence; rather, an observer might be filled with awe by knowledge of the unusually distinctive intellect and the complex person contained in that relatively indistinctive physical frame. That awe led some persons to conclude that Keith was quite unapproachable.

Another aspect of any person which is of great importance is speech and language. While Keith developed detailed knowledge of classical western languages, Greek and Latin, of modern languages, French and German with an occasional use of Russian and Spanish, and of classical Indian languages, Sanskrit, Pali, and others, his principal language was, of course, English. He set numerous translations into English. During his years at the Colonial Office, he gradually developed a rather bureaucratic style of writing prose: he numbered paragraphs and sections of a book or an article or a letter. As a result, his prose frequently moved forward with greater mathematical precision than with felicity of expression. When he spoke, both in selection of vocabulary and in accent, he always reflected that he had been reared in Scotland. Even with many years of studying and working in England, he never lost that pronunciation, nor is there any indication that he wished to deny his Scots origins at any point. Scots-born, Scots-bred, Scots-educated, he valued that aspect of his life. In speaking, apparently, he made his points clearly and forcefully. His spoken language was as clearly ordered as his written. When he completed his training in law, he often asked questions precisely along legal lines of enquiry where each question led logically to the next, where a line of argumentation was broken into component parts. He reflected in speaking the same agility of mind that appeared in his writing. Apparently, he could vary, if he wished, the breadth of inflection when he felt the occasion warranted it, 'Peterborough' in *The Daily Telegraph* reported an interesting story, after Keith's death, under the caption, 'Floored Examiners', about, at least, one important occasion where he chose to use English with a strong Scots twang:

> An old Oxford man was telling me a story of that great scholar, Dr Arthur Keith, whose death has occurred at Edinburgh, where he was Regius Professor of Sanskrit.
>
> Dr Keith—who afterwards passed first into the Civil Service—carried everything before him, and was at one and the same time the despair and admiration of the examiners.
>
> These found the greatest difficulty in deciphering his handwriting, and then an equal difficulty in not giving him the highest possible marks.
>
> After his Greats papers had all received an alpha plus, the examiners decided to get a little of their own back by giving him a gruelling 'viva'. The young Keith, however, is said to have answered in such broad Scots that the examiners could not understand his replies.[6]

Information about language adds to the picture of Keith. It is clear that he wrote and produced his numerous works in English although he had a wide command of many other languages. As he knew them thoroughly, so also he knew English. It is clear, as well, that he spoke English with the regional variation found in the Edinburgh area. On more than one occasion, and one can almost imagine a twinkle in his eyes and a slight smile creasing his face, Keith could broaden that accent to achieve a certain desired effect on his listeners.

With some sense of his appearance and his language, it is possible to use two accounts of his bearing in the presence of family or friends or students to add to an understanding of his nature. A niece tells about being present at one time when Keith was visiting his younger sister, Nan Dewar in the 1930s. A few persons were gathered in the lounge of Nan's flat in London, there engaged in conversation. The door opened. The shy, somewhat diffident, whimsical genius entered. He moved slowly and deliberately to his sister, bowed low, smiled, and greeted her with the words, 'My venerable sister'. It is virtually possible to feel his repressed humour in the salutation and, as well, his desire to make the occasion pleasant.[7]

The other account comes from a student who, after Keith's death, paid tribute in a letter to *The Scotsman*. In this, after acknowledging Keith as 'a very great teacher and a still greater scholar', N Chaudhuri described his bearing:

> Precisely at the stroke of two, the small, rather drooping, figure of the professor would appear round the corner with a genial, 'Good afternoon, gentlemen.' Sitting round a roaring fire, we had the privilege of studying a great authority on various subjects at close quarters. To me who was taught Sanskrit in the land of its origin, it was a source of pardonable surprise to me to find the great gift of interpreting the nobility of the language in Professor Keith. ... He was the most retiring and individualistic personality I have ever had the privilege to study under.[8]

Appearance, language, bearing, all these provide some indication about Keith's nature. In addition, it is also possible to indicate some of the traits of his personality. He certainly possessed a sense of humour, a sense of the comic in the situations of life, in general, and, on occasion, in his own particular situation. During his years on the staff of the Colonial Office, he often wrote terse, sarcastic, and witty comments on the files which he handled. Among others, he used these phrases: 'Now what does all this mean & what is the use of it?[9] ... This is really a peculiarly comic production.[10] ... I am not particularly enamoured of this.[11] ... Rather funny[12] ...' He saw the humour in some of the situations in the colonies: 'Remarkably dreary even for Tasmania'[13] he wrote on one occasion. On another one, this, too, while he was in London, he wrote to his mother in Dunbar explaining how he had been invited to a reception. In order to make clear his humorous understanding of the phrase 'to bring me along', he created a cartoon (see p 6) so that his mother could get the full import.[14] He thought the phrase, and, indeed, the situation in which he found himself to be amusing.

In addition to a sense of humour, he possessed a strong streak of contentiousness. Whatever the particular circumstance, if he took a position and developed what to him were the logical arguments for supporting it, he held that position firmly and had caustic remarks for those who did not concur with him. This was as true of his personal correspondence as it was of his public. Patrick Ford noted this trait quite publicly in a poem published in 1938 in *The Scotsman* which dealt with various distinguished and notable people of Edinburgh, especially those who had appeared, for one reason or another, in the columns of that paper. When he wrote 'As Spring Draws Near', Ford devoted the largest number of lines to Keith:

> As Spring draws near
> And gets in gear,
> *The Scotsman's* columns are a riot—
> While on the page

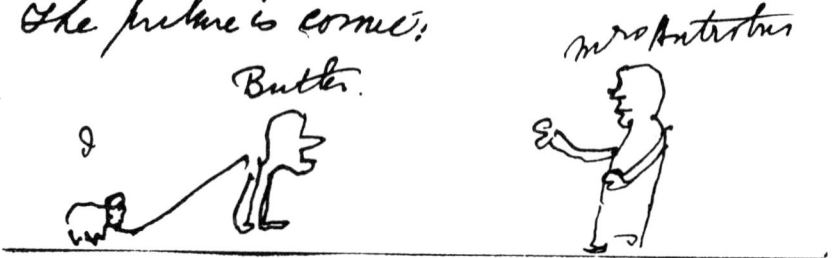

2   Arthur Berriedale Keith's cartoon of invitation.

Where factions rage
B Keith is eager to inherit
The place that once—
And he no dunce—
Professor Laurie dominated.
From day to day
Keith has his say,
And though to Sanskrit consecrated,
Lays down the law
In words of awe
On rights and treaties desecrated.[15]

The words require little explication: Ford knew that Keith was vigorously contentious in arguing for positions he held.

All who knew Keith indicated him to be a complex person. Fundamentally, he was a shy, somewhat retiring, very reserved individual. This is an interesting characteristic since it resulted in a reticent demeanour. That may have given others the impression that he was unapproachable. In addition, Keith had, as one person phrased it, a 'low level of boredom'.[16] Perhaps this resulted from his intellectual brilliance and his ability to see through to the heart of complex matters quickly, decisively, and definitively, at least in his own terms. Such a trait would be consistent with the considerable cerebral power that Keith possessed. Further, whatever the combination of elements might have been, as soon as he was able, he became an omnivorous reader. He read everything he could get his hands on, initially children's books and books around the house, later on complicated, abstruse Sanskrit or Pali manuscripts, articles in any of the languages which he commanded, newspapers, government documents, parliamentary debates, mystery stories. He liked mysteries and would certainly have read those of popular writers which came out during his lifetime. In fact, it is often in relation to mystery stories that Keith's amazing intellectual prowess is tied. He possessed that rare capacity to carry on two different mental activities simultaneously as, for example, working on the manuscript for an article or review or book and listening to his wife or, later, his sister read a mystery book. Could he really do these two things at the same time? Could he prepare a manuscript and follow the complexities of a mystery plot? There is conclusive evidence that, indeed, he could, and did.[17]

One other characteristic of his personality was his helpful nature. Scarcely an extrovert, he was, however, interested in persons who wanted to know about any of the numerous matters he pursued. He was approachable and was genuinely of assistance to many persons. In his years as Professor at Edinburgh University, he took an interest in several of his students and was helpful in writing testimonials for them and following their careers.[18] In those years, professors were on a pedestal and appeared distant. Yet, students who wished to talk with him, certainly found him accessible. After Keith's death, one former student wrote:

> ... my own studies under his guidance will always remain a happy memory. After I left the university in 1930, the relationships as between Professor and pupil ripened into a warm friendship and I always felt at liberty to approach him as I often did on personal and national matters. ... There [at meetings in Keith's home] we saw the varied character of the man—his wide interests in the community in which he lived. Indeed at no time did he ever forget the importance of human relationships.[19]

On many occasions, he participated in various studies carried out by the Government. As a writer in the *Daily Sketch* put it, in 1923, 'When any knotty constitutional problem puzzles Downing Street a reference to Professor Keith is invariable. By some diabolic mental agency he can explain in a flash what jurists fret and fume over for weeks together'.[20] In his correspondence, he was invariably useful in answering questions and enquiries from statesmen in Britain, the British Empire, and the British Commonwealth of Nations to say nothing of his help to scholars and students in Sanskrit and Oriental Studies. Perhaps, one person summed up this aspect of Keith's personality well: 'But, individualist as he may have been, he was ready to encourage the humblest student in the vast field where he was so great a master'.[21] While that referred specifically to Sanskrit, it is an appropriate comment about Keith's helpful nature.

The clues about Keith's nature in terms of appearance, language, bearing, and personality provide an initial base upon which one can build some understanding of his life and work. Certainly, he had a more complex personality than that indicated here. Equally certainly, he had motivations in addition to the obvious intellectual ones. And, certainly, he was shaped and influenced by his family and his education and, as well, by the times in which he lived.

The World during Keith's Life Span

No one chooses the time in which one lives. The fact that Keith's life started in the later years of Victoria's reign and ended in those of her great-grandson, George VI, simply reflects the happenstance of the family and of the generation into which he was born. In his early years, that is until he was twenty-two, he experienced, along with everyone else in the United Kingdom, the presence of Queen Victoria, her golden and diamond jubilees, her death in 1901. The accession of Edward VII which followed was simply one change in the monarchy, among many, that Keith witnessed since, in fact, he lived during the reigns of five different monarchs.

For the sixty-five years when he lived, Keith's life divided, interestingly enough, into two principal blocs, each bounded by wars: his London years at the Colonial Office from 1901 to 1914 and his Edinburgh years as Professor at the University from 1914 to 1944. Those four decades of the twentieth century were times of profound change for Britain domestically, imperially, and internationally.

Certain striking points of contrast mark the differences between 1901 and 1914. When Keith started his years in London in October 1901, the South African War was still proceeding in its unhappy way, with atrocities on both sides, towards a truce, or a stalemate, that would not be achieved until the late spring of 1902; when Keith left in the fall of 1914 after the First World War had started, South African troops were raised on behalf of the King, led by former Boer generals, and organised to gain the earliest Allied victories. When Keith entered the Colonial Office, Joseph Chamberlain, radical turned Tory opposing home rule for Ireland and one of those knowledgeable about plans for the Jameson Raid that eventually led to the South African War, was Secretary of State for the Colonies in Lord Salisbury's Conservative-Unionist Cabinet, perhaps the most powerful Colonial Secretary ever; when Keith left in 1914, Lewis Harcourt was Secretary of State for the Colonies in the Liberal Cabinet. The start of the Great War in August 1914, marked what, in retrospect, is now seen as the decisive turning-point for the world, dividing the Victorian and Edwardian period from that of the twentieth century where changes in the structures of international power led to the end of the *Pax Britannica* and to fundamental changes in Britain's role.

During those first decades of the new century, Edwardian Britain experienced dramatic change in the distribution of power within the British government as well as in the role of the government in relation to social needs. Those were the years when the Conservative-Unionist party, suffering under the ineffectual leadership of A J Balfour, lost control of the government in December 1905 and in the election of 1906; and was replaced by the Liberals with a solid majority and a radical programme. Henry Campbell-Bannerman led the party but, when his health deteriorated, gave way to H H Asquith who dominated the era. Yet, in those years before the First World War, the dynamic for political change was in the hands of David Lloyd George as Chancellor of the Exchequer who, through the People's Budget of 1909, presented an unequivocal challenge to the equal power of the House of Lords. Two elections in 1910 resulted in no party holding a majority but with the Liberals continuing to govern while dependent on Irish nationalist votes. Yet, budget changes did go through and clearly laid the basis for the twentieth-century welfare state in Britain through graduated income taxes, escalating death duties, and sharp expansion of old age pensions and survivors' benefits. The Parliament Act of 1911 ended the power of the House of Lords to block legislation and reduced its power to that of delay. From that time on, effective political power clearly rested in the House of Commons. Ironically, one of the pieces of legislation to come into effect under the new constitutional provisions was the Third Home Rule Bill for Ireland which, after a tortuous passage, became law in September 1914, only to be suspended for the duration of the war. What years of ferment and change inside Britain under the Liberals![22]

Another way to consider the thirteen years that Keith was at the Colonial Office is with respect to the nature of the British Empire. Under Joseph Chamberlain, the British Empire reached its apogee: nothing comparable to it existed in the world in terms of area, population, and complexity. While some territory would be added later, particularly under the mandate system created in 1919, the basic shape of the Empire was formed by the time Keith entered the Colonial Office. Then, under the authority of the Crown, Britain controlled, in some manner or other, an area that comprised about one-quarter of the land surface of the earth. The Empire included territory on all continents, in all latitudes, in all kinds of climatic settings, in all sorts of terrain, in areas of rich mineral resources, in areas of poor mineral resources, and in regions with extensive raw materials. The Empire represented great wealth, yet, at the same time, contained regions of great poverty. Britain controlled all the principal points for shipping lanes round the world. Coaling stations and, increasingly, petroleum stations were essential to trade, commerce, and defence. One-quarter of the world's people, or some 4 to 5 hundred million, lived under British aegis. These millions included only some 60 million whites so that the overwhelming majority of British subjects were persons of colour, with the single largest group located in the subcontinent of India under the supervision of the India Office and the Government of India. The Empire embraced virtually every known cultural and linguistic group, a veritable babel when representatives gathered together, although, throughout the Empire and by design, the language for communication was English.

When Keith entered the Colonial Office, the Dominion of Canada, the premier and sole dominion, created as a federal union in 1867, was joined by Australia then in the first year of operating its federal system among the six states under the Commonwealth of Australia; by the time Keith left, dominion status had been extended, as well, to New Zealand and to the Union of South Africa, a centralised union created in 1910 as a calculated gamble. Military initiatives by South Africa in the War of 1914 seemed clear evidence to the Liberals that the gamble had paid off.[23] When Keith entered the Colonial Office, Britain carried sole responsibility for the defence of the Empire; when he left, defence, although still heavily dependent on Britain, was accepted by all the dominions as a collective responsibility even as individual dominions differed on the degree of direct, as opposed to British, control to be exercised.

When he entered, meetings involving premiers from the various colonies were styled as the Colonial Conference; by the time he left, both style and concept had been changed to Imperial Conference with the Prime Minister of Britain one among the premiers. Substantial changes in imperial relationships, indeed.

If Keith wanted to know about the political, geographical, cultural, economic, and linguistic varieties existing throughout the world, he could learn that at no better place than his desk in the Colonial Office. And, if he wanted to know in some detail about changes in relationships among Britain, the dominions, and the colonies, he was situated at the best possible place right in the Colonial Office.

Given his intellectual attainments and his unusual abilities, he acquired unique preparation for his studies on the constitution of the British Empire. While details of that work are discussed below, it is useful, here, to note, in general, the sorts of matters to which he had regular access. His actual handling of despatches from a wide variety of colonial governments gave him daily experience with learning how the central government responded to concerns raised in parts of the Empire. He was able to understand the main issues of colonial and imperial policy and to learn the ways by which persons at various levels in the Colonial Office made decisions, or avoided making them. He clearly understood, and this within a matter of the initial months, the processes through which the Colonial Office operated, especially in relationship to the Foreign Office, Treasury, and other departments of government. In time, he participated in the secretariat for the conferences which brought leaders together from the colonies and dominions; he knew the issues and concerns addressed at those conferences. He came to know dominion statesmen and officials on a personal basis and earned their respect for his work and contributions. As well, he became acquainted with many Britons who went as governors to the colonies; he carried on a personal and an unofficial correspondence with many of them that, in several instances, continued for years, long after he had returned to Edinburgh. Consequently, his works on the constitution of the British Empire were informed through direct experience and knowledge.

Imperial change and domestic change went along together in those years. Keith although non-political as a civil servant was a Liberal by persuasion and made use of the National Liberal Club, from time to time. He admired Lewis Harcourt and supported Asquith. He must have seen and noted all the various changes through Liberal eyes. Keith was in a position to observe, to understand, and to assimilate all these changes and, then, to reflect on them in his writings.

Political change, constitutional change, imperial change, international change, all these occurred during those years when Keith was in London. In the fall of 1914, he left the Colonial Office to take up his relationship with Edinburgh University which, as it turned out, continued for the rest of his life.

In those thirty years, a profound transformation occurred in Britain's role in the world and, concurrently, in the nature of the British Empire. Keith, of course, removed from direct information which was available in the Colonial Office became increasingly a person who spoke to the issues and changes of the day from his professorial position. Those years include the completion of the First World War with victory for Britain and the Allies, joined late in the war by the United States. But, although the victory was won through heroic deeds, great expense, and human sacrifice, the world scarcely was made safe for democracy. The aftermath of the First World War progressively revealed the characteristic features of the twentieth century: international instability; a world economy increasingly enmeshed so that the economic destinies of all countries were entwined; sharply conflicting ideologies; angst, existentialism, and psychodynamics; radio and the potential of mass communications; aspirations of various national and subnational groups to achieve political self-determination; and 'backward' peoples, anxious to cast off the image of being 'half-devil and half-child',[24] eager to join the process of modernisation. The economic consequences of the Peace of Versailles[25] led to the near collapse of the entire Western world by 1929 and the depression of the 1930s gave way to recovery only when the clouds of war loomed on the horizon as that decade ended.

While, by any measure, Britain remained one of the great powers in the world during those years, clearly her role and position altered. Instead of holding the debts of the world, Britain now had to deal with the United States as creditor for the principal war debts. Instead of being able to conduct relations with Europe along the lines of the balance of power as in the nineteenth century, Britain faced an almost continuously shifting structure of power inside the largest continental countries and, at the same time, the emergence of two new ideological forces in the theory and reality of communism and fascism. Instead of being pre-eminent and virtually alone in naval power, Britain had to accept the emergence of the United States and of Japan to positions of near comparability. Instead of being the world's leading industrial power, Britain could only claim to be the world's oldest since industrial leadership had passed to the United States and Germany, actually before the First World War.

With her world role changing, Britain found herself, at the same time, confronting almost intractable domestic problems. The emergence of well-organised trade unions, the shift of energy sources from coal to petroleum, the expansion of the electorate to universal adult suffrage, the continuation of the Irish question in new forms, the continuing need to restructure industry—and the list continues at length, all these posed serious problems for Britain and her leaders. Weakened economically, competing on the premise of free trade in a protectionist world and then abandoning that premise, unable to find the magic formula to achieve post war recovery, coping with industrial strife, and committed to an expanding level of state support for social services, Britain was weakened at its domestic core. Yet, it contained the world's most responsive, daring, and democratic political system.[26]

In many ways, changes in the empire during these same years were directly related to domestic issues. The principal change, of course, was the emergence of the British Commonwealth of Nations, an association reflecting changed relationships among Britain and the dominions. The term came into use during the course of the First World War and more particularly in the rapid evolution and transformation of dominion status during the 1920s.[27] That change, ultimately, resulted in a definition of dominion status enacted in the Statute of Westminster, 1931, which made each of the dominions equal with Britain in relationship to the Crown. Ironically, in view of the history of their relationships to Britain, it was the Irish Free State and the Union of South Africa which were the principal dominions, together with support from Canada, who successfully pressed for that change in status.[28] Was Britain's participation in the process which achieved that change simply altruistic or did it reflect the altered circumstances of British power? Did Britain have any other options, especially in view of the extraordinary contributions the dominions made to winning the First World War? Perhaps Britain's response to initiatives for change was a combination of altruism tempered by hope and a realistic assessment of alternatives.[29] Perhaps nothing so dramatically underscored the fundamental changes that had occurred as the declaration of neutrality by Eire, as the Free State was then styled, when war broke out in 1939; uncomfortable though it was, Britain had no alternative but to accept that neutral position.[30]

Keith saw the relationships among domestic issues, international affairs, and imperial concerns. He knew that the old order was passing even as he was unhappy about that prospect. By the summer of 1939, Britain faced a different challenge as, once again, she was plunged into another great war where, a year later after the fall of France in June 1940, she faced the forces of Hitler virtually alone and unaided. Keith died before that war ended but not before he wrote a book in which he outlined his views on why it had occurred, *The Causes of the War.*

These, then, are some of the themes and issues which outline the six and a half decades during which Keith lived. They provide the context for understanding many aspects of his career, work, interests, and publications. Of course, one must consider all these aspects of context, as well, in relation to his basic nature and personality in order to begin to comprehend him.

PART ONE

Formative Years, 1879–1901

CHAPTER 2

Portobello, Edinburgh, and Oxford, 1879–1901

Like all human beings, Arthur Berriedale Keith owed much to the particular circumstances of his birth and his rearing. Early, the family identified his particular gifts of genius and nurtured him with care. It is likely, too, that the school mistress who first taught him recognised those same gifts. His intellectual promise and achievements led to extensive formal education where he earned honours and prizes at all levels. On the basis of an exceptional record of achievement, he entered into his formal careers, first as civil servant and later as university professor. Especially in his earlier years, he developed patterns and methods of work that made it possible for him to produce extensively in diverse fields during his lifetime.

Family: Portobello and Joppa

Arthur Berriedale Keith, customarily called by his middle name or a shortened form of it, was born in Portobello, Scotland, on Saturday, 5 April 1879,[1] the fourth child and third son of Margaret Stobie Drysdale and Davidson Keith. His parents had married seven years earlier in July 1872 at a time, according to the weather reports, of intense, unusual heat. Perhaps that augured a complex relationship to come in their marriage. Their wedding was held in a pleasant informal setting 'at the home of the bride's uncle, David Stobie, Esq, Solicitor' in Dunbar.[2]

Keith's parents came from substantial middle-class families. Margaret, or as the family referred to her, MSK, was a younger daughter in her family and grew up in Dunfermline where her father was a linen manufacturer. Early, she displayed the power, determination, independence, and endurance which were to characterise her personality during her life. For example, she insisted on her own room when she was still a child. At the time of her marriage, she was twenty-one years old.[3]

The marriage must have appeared a good one to MSK for the Keiths were an old Scots family with roots and relatives in Caithness. Davidson was eight years older than MSK when they married. A tall, well-dressed man, he was already engaged in a successful career as one of the first comprehensive advertising agents in Edinburgh. 'Keith & Co' with offices on George Street provided, according to their advertisement, all sorts of services related to advertising including design and production of materials, placement of infor-

15

3   Margaret Stobie Drysdale Keith, 1851–1911. Reproduced courtesy of Mrs J Walcot Burton.

mation in newspapers, cuttings from newspapers, circulation of newspapers from throughout the kingdom, and the like.[4] Davidson's brother, Peter, one of the witnesses at his wedding, was Factor to the Earl of Caithness. Thus, Davidson and his young family often spent holidays in the far north of Scotland visiting Uncle Peter.

That his parents' wedding took place in Dunbar is of significance, for MSK, apparently, viewed Dunbar with particular favour. It is, of course, naturally scenic and delightful near the water but, for her, it was where her maternal relatives lived, relatives whom she viewed with affection and valued as being of some influence and standing.

After Margaret and Davidson's marriage, children came quickly: William John, the eldest, in 1873; Jean Ramsay, a year later; three years after that, a second son, Robert Charles Steuart; in 1879, Arthur Berriedale; a second daughter, Annie (Nan) Balfour, in 1880; and the youngest, Alan Davidson, in 1885.[5] In all, six children were born over a twelve year span, four sons and two daughters.

At the time Berriedale was born, the family lived on Abercorn Terrace in Portobello. Portobello was, then, still an independent town although the city of Edinburgh with its businesses, offices, stores, schools, societies, and university could be reached easily by a half-hour's trip on train or tram.[6] Abercorn Terrace simply continued the main street of Portobello easterly for a few blocks. On one side, the street was lined with Victorian terrace houses neatly arranged behind fences and hedges. Opposite were neighbourhood shops: chemist, greengrocer, dry goods, bakery, and so on. House 'No. 3' where the Keith family lived differed from adjoining houses only by being located at the end of the row and nearest to the centre of town. Two storeys high plus an attic and surrounded by a garden, it was constructed of the solid grey stone widely used in that region of Lothian with a prominent, typical three-sided window at the front on two of three storeys.[7] For the family with moderate means, it provided suitable living space in proximity to Davidson's business in the city and, as well, to shops, parks, and beaches. As the children became old enough to go to school a local 'dame school' was available, while Royal High School, at the east end of Princes Street in Edinburgh, was quite accessible.

After Nan's birth, the family moved from Abercorn Terrace to 8 Brunstane Road, Joppa.[8] This move did not involve the family in any significant dislocation for, in fact, the boundary line of Joppa was but a few blocks east, a short walk from Abercorn Terrace. The time to the centre of Edinburgh for work and schools was extended only by a few minutes. The house on Brunstane Road where Keith lived throughout his school and university years was similar to the one the family had left. Constructed of the same grey stone and as solidly built, it possessed certain distinct advantages. It provided more space for the family, now with five children. It was a semi-detached house rather than being located in a long terrace. It stood on a side street away from the noise and traffic of the main road. It was a few steps to church, shops, and sea front. Perhaps of particular significance to MSK, it was somewhat closer to Dunbar where she regularly visited relatives. In her view, these

Sir William John Keith, 1873–1937.   Robert Charles Steuart Keith, 1876–1919.

Alan Davidson Keith, 1885–1928.

4   The Keith Children. Photographs reproduced courtesy of Mrs J Walcot Burton.

Jean Ramsay Keith Adamson Groom, 1874–1969.

Nan Balfour Keith Dewar, 1880–1973.

advantages could be construed as helping her rise in social status, just a little.

Keith's early years, therefore, were centred in a large, active family living in reasonably comfortable houses in the suburbs, yet, being in regular contact with Edinburgh. The physical setting in which he was reared emphasised the links between suburb and city. The waterfront of Portobello and Joppa faced the south shore of the Firth of Forth as it continued easterly from Edinburgh's busy harbour at Leith; ships were always nearby and on the horizon. Yet, it was possible from several points in Portobello or Joppa to look to the south up one of the streets, there to catch a glimpse of Arthur's Seat and to be reminded of the proximity of Edinburgh. For MSK, the setting also gave constant reminders of Dunbar as the railway trains stopped en route to and from Edinburgh and as she viewed the peaks of North Berwick near Dunbar in the far distance across Portobello Bay.

When Keith was a child, he certainly joined his father and brothers, perhaps the whole family, in trips to Edinburgh. The complexity of the city provided the boy with fantastic, profound contrasts to the small town. At an early age, he must have absorbed indelibly a sense of the beauty, drama, and awe that Edinburgh provided, and still provides, in its aspect, best seen from any point on Princes Street: Arthur's Seat reaching for the nearest cloud at one end of a ridge and, at the other, the high walls and towers of Edinburgh Castle. At the base of these two heights existed a curious array of Greek and Roman style temples; castellated hotels; Victorian Gothic monuments and memorials; sweeping gardens; a classical fragment, a tower, and the Doric façade of the Royal High School on Calton Hill; a nondescript, below street level railroad station named for Scott's Waverley; houses and wynds climbing the slopes to the old city; and the lantern dome of St Giles' Cathedral etched on the skyline. Looking at this view, he must have experienced, as well, the industrious tone of the city with bustling crowds queuing for trams, going into shops, banks, and offices, yet, with gentility, taking time to exchange greetings. A visit to his father's offices must have underscored the range of activities in the city and helped him to understand his father's business. Likely, too, it impressed him with the role and importance of newspapers in the life of the city. Keith learned something of the history, sombreness, excitement, and distinctiveness that characterised the Athens of the North. As Robert Louis Stevenson, a son of Edinburgh and a contemporary of Keith's parents, expressed his enchantment:

> the lamps begin to glitter along the street, and faint lights to burn in the high windows across the valley—the feeling grows upon you that this also is a piece of nature in the most intimate sense; that this profusion of eccentricities, this dream in masonry and living rock is not a drop-scene in a theatre, but a city in the world of everyday realities, connected by railway and telegraph-wire with all the capitals of Europe.[9]

Keith valued this heritage and, in spite of his many years of residence in England, never rejected it.

His more immediate heritage, of course, was within the family where he was reared. It is hard to know about actual details of the relationships that exist in any marriage. This is especially true in the instance of Davidson Keith and MSK since no letters or diaries or papers remain, apparently, to substantiate clues that can be inferred from the sequence of events.[10] What seems to be the case is that the marriage proceeded without major disruption for nearly twenty-five years, or until Keith was about eighteen years old. During that time, the children were born and raised. Yet, there are indications that, even in those years, MSK and Davidson would go in different directions, she, for example, to take the children to visit relatives in Caithness or Dunbar while he remained in Joppa and Edinburgh, presumably because of work.[11] How serious these separations were is hard to tell. But, by late 1897 or early 1898, MSK had left Davidson, taking Nan and Alan with her as she moved the household to Oxford where Steuart and Berriedale were students. From that time on, MSK and Davidson lived distinctly separate lives. She went on to live in London and Dunbar while he remained with the business in Edinburgh until, after its eventual sale, he moved to London where he remained until his death.[12]

All indications are that MSK possessed a dominant, determined, and, to a considerable extent, detrimental personality. She made the major decisions for herself and her family. She ran the household and supervised the domestics who cared for the family. Her strong personality and her ingratiating manner resulted in her gaining her own way. She used a variety of techniques. She might resort to considerable persuasion, or she might exude an overpowering charm, a 'fatal fascination', or she might fall back upon her unusual physical condition, a hole through her heart, which made her life precarious as a choice specimen of medical curiosity.[13]

By contrast, Davidson appears to have been a meticulous person, an interested father, and a very successful businessman. That he was able to order his affairs with the advertising firm in an effective manner is obvious. Further, it was he, evidently, who took the primary lead in insisting on good education for all the children and who gave them particular encouragement and support. Even the two girls had schooling considered appropriate for the time in which they lived.[14]

The complexity of the relationships between Davidson and MSK affected the children variously. It is striking that five of them, all but Berriedale, spent major portions of their adult lives in Burma or India, far distant from Scotland and maternal influence. It seems that none of the children maintained any extensive relationship with their father after their parents separated; yet, all were in regular correspondence with their mother. Berriedale, alone, remained directly under the aegis of MSK. The evidence indicates that the attachment was deep and that he was devoted to her. Not surprisingly, in Keith's papers that remain and are available, there are numerous endearing references to his mother but none at all, not even a single reference, to his father.[15]

Formal Studies: Edinburgh

Whether it was maternal or paternal genetic inheritance, or the accident flowing from the combination, all the Keith children were infused with a streak of intellectual brilliance. While Berriedale stood out early with the marks of genius, he was not alone in academic success. He followed his older brothers who led the way and set the pace by winning honours and prizes for their achievements. They attended 'Miss Douglas's Classes' in Joppa, the local 'dame school', before entering the Royal High School. The preparation must have been sound for all the boys followed this route and were successful applicants for the Royal High School. In that earliest formal setting for learning, they acquired the basic intellectual skills of reading, writing, and arithmetic. Was it in that first schoolroom, or earlier at home, that Berriedale was found to possess his unusual and uncanny ability to give full attention to two different areas or activities of learning simultaneously and equally well? How disconcerting that discovery must have been for his teacher! It was at that school in Joppa where, as he finished the course, Berriedale earned his earliest prize for excellence, on that occasion for 'grammar, writing, and arithmetic', a book, *Paws and Claws: Being True Stories of Clever Creatures.*[16] He was eight years old and ready to join his brothers in going to school in the city.

As soon as he was able to, he read everything in sight. He had an unusual ability to remember and recall fine detail. He used his intellectual prowess to amaze and amuse the family. The story is told that, among the many things he devoured in reading were the timetables for various routes and lines around the United Kingdom. When he had put the tables away, members of the family would tease him by asking him to plot trips from Edinburgh. Promptly, he would respond, accurate to the last detail with necessary train numbers, connections, changes, and times.[17]

With such distinctive intellectual skill, especially the ability to memorise, sort, and recollect, he easily won a series of medals, prizes, and honours, and, as well, set record scores on examinations during his years at the Royal High School from 1887 to 1894. This included going one better than his oldest brother and instead of once being Dux of the school, that is, the top scholar, he held that distinction in each of his two final years.[18]

Dating from its origins in the twelfth century, the Royal High School had an extraordinary history as the 'tounis scule'.[19] Surviving under various forms of civic control through the political and religious changes of mediaeval, reformation, and Stuart periods and being moved to available buildings in different parts of the old city, it was finally relocated on the south side of Calton Hill in 1829 in an impressive set of new buildings specifically planned for school purposes. The architectural design, appropriately enough, in view of the main programme of studies of the time, took its inspiration from the symmetry, proportions, harmony, and grace of classical Greece. In a visual sense, the school set on that height, appeared as an intellectual acropolis for the city, in fact remaining at that location until 1968. Over the years, it established a deserved reputation for academic excellence as one of the finest schools in the realm, enrolling sons of distinguished and important families, including HRH the Prince of Wales under the tutorship of the Rector in the late 1850s. Yet, true to the civic spirit of its founding, the school always welcomed young men of intellectual promise from all levels of society. The boys of the Keith family were definitely welcomed.

The core of its curriculum was rooted in classical and religious studies. But, by the later nineteenth century, the school had expanded from that base to offer, as well, work in both French and German, in book-keeping and drawing, in a considerable range of laboratory sciences, in many levels of mathematics, and in the study and use of metals. Additional space built in 1885 provided for a new gymnasium and swimming pool to make physical training more readily available to develop sound bodies for classically educated minds. Indeed, for that time, the Royal High School was exceptionally comprehensive in its offerings.[20]

This, then, was the school that Keith entered. Following the model of his brothers, he pursued the classical curriculum which gave, according to the *Prospectus* for 1893–4, 'thorough preparation for Bursary and Scholarship competitions'.[21] Clearly, that programme was designed for students who had the ability and who intended to continue studies in pursuit of an Arts degree in one of the universities.

The seven year classical programme was rigorous with required studies in Latin, Greek, Mathematics, English, and French. The range of work, to be evaluated through regular examinations, was extensive. For example, the Latin sequence carried students through Caesar, Ovid, Livy, Horace, Cicero, Terence, and Virgil, both the *Aenead* and the *Georgics*. Grammatical studies paralleled the literature while concurrent studies in Roman history provided the context for literary works. The Greek sequence was equally thorough with readings and exercises drawn from Xenophon, Homer, Thucydides, Euripides, Plato, and Aristotle as well as large amounts of the New Testament in Greek. Again, grammatical and historical studies paralleled the literature. The programme in Mathematics covered all stages and aspects of arithmetic, geometry both plane and solid, algebra, and trigonometry. The course of study in English was considerably broader than the label, at first, might seem to indicate. It was the general classification for studies in the English language, grammar, literature, writing, and spelling. Also, it included studies in Scottish and English history, in British, European, and world geography, and in substantial portions of the Scripture, this time in English translation. To complete this programme, students had to read widely in significant writing from Chaucer to Shakespeare to Milton to Goldsmith to Tennyson and in all genres of prose, poetry, and drama. With the required work in classical languages and religious texts, students were well-equipped to understand literary allusions drawn from the history, literature, and philosophy of Greece, Rome, and Israel and, also, from Christian thought, theology, and institutions. The French programme started with simple grammatical exercises, readings, and conversation and proceeded progressively to more complex aspects including a study of significant eighteenth- and nineteenth-century literary works.[22]

By the time Keith completed this programme of studies, he had acquired the foundation suitable not only for the next immediate steps in his intellectual life but also for his future, significant scholarship. His work in Latin, Greek, English, and French gave him solid grounding in the structural and formal side of language: grammar, vocabulary, philology, syntax, and phonology. His work in the literature written in those languages gave him equally solid grounding in the categories and terminology for literary criticism. His unusual genius permitted him to master, understand, retain, recall, and use an almost infinite number of specific items. He learned a great deal from the masters during his years at the Royal High School and his mind was well-trained by the time he left. In his final year there, in addition to being Dux of the school he was, at the same time, the highest ranking student in English, Latin, Greek, and Mathematics. In 1906, looking back on the record of those school years, he summed up his prizes:

> winning gold metals for Latin (twice), Greek (twice), English, Mathematics (twice) and a special prize for the best English essay. I also obtained the prizes for Ancient and Modern History and the India Prize for Indian History.[23]

An incredible record earned by a young man with incredible capability! He was fifteen years old when he finished at the Royal High School.

With his extraordinary qualifications and his outstanding record on examinations, it was logical that he should follow his brothers in the next stages of formal education and pursue the Arts Curriculum at the University of Edinburgh. On 15 October 1894, he completed the necessary steps for matriculation: registering his name in the Matriculation Album, filling out the Matriculation Form, and paying the fee of £1. 1s. required for that academic year.[24] In addition, matriculation involved his signature on the *Sponsio Academica* by which he pledged, in his case somewhat superfluously, to be a faithful, diligent student, an obedient scholar, and avoider of dissidence and disruption, and a grateful supporter of the University. He was one of 738 students enrolled in 1894–5 in the Faculty of Arts and one of the youngest students starting that autumn.[25]

Edinburgh University was unique among Scottish universities in that its roots, like the Royal High School, were civic and public rather than religious.[26] Formally organised under a royal charter granted in April 1582, with actual instruction commencing in the following year, its original faculties in Arts and Theology continued to be of central importance. By the time that Keith matriculated, the University had added distinctive work in many fields beyond those two traditional ones. For him, of course, the primary focus was on the resources the University had available in Arts: its teaching staff, professors and lecturers, and its library. Although in the 1880s, the University started its process of expansion to the southwest with the construction of the New Quadrangle for the Faculty of Medicine, the centre of the University remained at the corner of South Bridge and Chambers Street in the grand buildings designed by Robert Adam and William Playfair and constructed between 1798 and 1815. For Keith, the move to the elegant, neo-classical lines of the University from the Doric harmonies of Royal High School must have strengthened his sense of the pervasiveness and endurance of the classical world, right in the centre of Edinburgh. Might not that transition in the location for his studies have seemed to him simply a natural progression from the splendours of Greece to the more extensive glories, wonders, and heights of Rome? The University block embodied an extraordinary, classical architectural conception. Its power to compel attention remains. Leaving the drabness of South Bridge, one enters a great courtyard through a dramatic and noble archway located under the tower centred on the east façade. Around the courtyard are grouped, in carefully proportioned arrangement, striking porticoes, finely detailed pediments, gracious stairways, open ambulatories, and circular colonnades, all of these placed on balanced and pleasing elevations. It seems as if one has entered a great forum where the muses of academe dwell in temples of appropriate splendour and where all issues of the intellectual world will be dissected and debated. If newly matriculated students comprehended and understood these elements of the architectural design, they would perceive in a profound way the primary reason for the role and the existence of the University as the sole institution of society dedicated to intellectual activity in all its forms: lecturing, tutoring, studying, discussing, examining, researching, writing, publishing. Serious students in the University had regular access to instructors and, as well, to the library, the heart of any university, with its collection of books, periodicals, and manuscripts. The Upper Library Hall must be William Playfair's masterpiece: its sweeping double storeyed height, its magnificent vaulted ceiling, its spaciousness and gracefulness, its collection and display of objects of art, and, above all, its shelves, alcoves, and corners filled with books.[27]

When Keith matriculated, he entered into this stimulating intellectual environment. His studies required him to seek out materials in that grand library. Classes, tutorials, and conferences held in many parts of these buildings meant that he came to know the different settings for scholarly activity very well.

By the time he started at the University, a newly approved programme was available which allowed a successful student to complete an Honours MA, the principal degree, in three years, rather than four. The programme in Classics required work in Latin and Greek language and literature, with optional subjects such as comparative philology, ancient philosophy, or classical archaeology. In addition, work was required in at least five subjects including one each in language and literature, mental philosophy, and science. He followed this rigorous programme of studies to a successful conclusion.[28]

During those years, he came under the tutelage of a distinguished, effective group of instructors, especially Samuel Henry Butler, Professor of Greek from 1882; William Ross Hardie, Professor of Humanity (Latin) from 1895; and Julius Eggeling, Regius Professor of Sanskrit and Comparative Philology from 1892.[29] Keith, in 1907, provided a summary of his studies in Classics when he applied for the Lectureship in Ancient History at Edinburgh:

In October, 1894, I entered Edinburgh University, gaining the Sibbald Bursary.

I attended the Senior Classes in Latin under Professor Goodhart, Greek under Professor Butcher, Logic and Psychology under Professor Seth Pringle-Pattison, Mathematics and Natural Philosophy under Professor Tait, and the Honours Classes in Latin under Professor Hardie, Greek, and Greek philosophy under Mr R P Hardie, and gained seven Class medals, besides special prizes for Latin and Greek literature, Critical Work in the Classics, etc. I also gained the Dunbar Prize for Greek, the Bruce of Grangehill and Falkland Bursary for Second Year Students, the Vans Dunlop Scholarship in Classics, and the Guthrie Fellowship in Classics. In April, 1897, I took the degree of Master of Arts with First Class Honours in Classics, Ancient Philosophy being my optional subject.[30]

But that was not all. He undertook studies in Sanskrit, as well, although he did not commence them until his last year. His extraordinary progress and facility in that field were attested to by Professor Eggeling:

I have known MR KEITH since October, 1896, when, as a highly distinguished student of our Classical Honours School, and Holder of the Vans Dunlop Scholarship in Classics, he joined my Sanskrit class. His progress whilst reading with me was the most astonishing I have ever met with. Starting with the alphabet at the beginning of the five months' session, he read the *Meghadūta* with *Mallinātha's* Commentary—practically Honours work—at the end of it. In view of his exceptional attainments in languages, I took him separately from the very beginning, and his genial and enthusiastic manner made it quite a pleasure for me to read with him.[31]

Keith readily acknowledged that special contribution to his education: 'Professor Eggeling took me separately and spared no pains to give me a sound knowledge of Classical Sanskrit.'[32]

Yet, his primary work was in Classics. Extensively grounded in the range and substance of Latin and Greek languages and their literature, he was often asked about points of fine grammatical detail by his instructors. For example, Professor Hardie put a query about Greek grammar in a note which remains of 19 February 1897: 'Someone laid it down as a recognised canon that neuter substantives in the plural take the plural verb if they designate *animals*. Is there any foundation for this?'[33] At an early age, then, Keith began that correspondence which would continue throughout his lifetime with persons who wished to draw upon his extraordinary mind and his exceptional fund of knowledge.

He compiled an outstanding, unique record at Edinburgh. His superior attainments were recognised not only in Classics but also in other related fields. He continued studies in French language and literature. He pursued studies of higher mathematics. And, in the final year, he laid the substantive base for his long career in Sanskrit. The total curriculum at Edinburgh provided, for students who completed it, solid preparation in all fields of the Arts. By the time he sat the round of examinations for the MA at the end of March in his last year, Keith had developed a deserved reputation for intellectual brilliance. His knowledge of languages, in all their detail, and of literatures, in all their wonderful variety, had been widened and deepened.

The knowledge he had mastered at the Royal High School was extended as he matured, studied more, and added to it. His unusual ability to comprehend, retain, and recall detailed information served him well in every set of examinations he wrote. Certainly, his learning was cumulative with little, if anything, ever forgotten. He was a young man of unusual talent and genius, and recognised as such by his instructors, examiners, and fellow students. One of the first students to finish under the three year option, he took his first academic degree on 10 April 1897.[34] Five days earlier, he had his eighteenth birthday.

Continued Studies: Oxford

His excellence in Classics provided the necessary base which permitted him to undertake the next stage of his academic preparation. There had been no doubt where that step would take him since he had written the examinations for Classical scholarships at Balliol College, Oxford, in the autumn of 1895, at the start of his second year of university when he was only sixteen years old, and, as he explained, 'though not taking the papers in Latin and Greek Verse and Divinity, obtained the third place in the open competition'.[35] In the autumn of 1897, then, he went up to Balliol as a Scholar. That same autumn he wrote the examinations to win the Ferguson Scholarship in Classics, open to all graduates of the four Scottish universities. That scholarship provided him with an additional £80 of support each year.[36] To these two scholarships, he added the Boden in Sanskrit and, as well, the Guthrie. Clearly, he was well supported financially through these various awards which he earned on the basis of his splendid achievements and his rare mind.

In going to Oxford, he followed, again, the pattern set by his older brothers. Will, taking the Indian Civil Service examination in 1895 and scoring at the head of all examinees, had returned to Christ Church College for further study and preparation prior to taking the first of his many assignments in Burma in the autumn of 1896. In that same autumn, Steuart had gone up to Trinity College where he was to continue his studies for several years. Eventually, Alan, too, would come along to join the rest of his family in Oxford with a scholarship to Wadham College in 1901.[37] Intellectual brilliance, honed at the Royal High School and Edinburgh University, shone through the accomplishments of all the brothers at Oxford. Yet, Berriedale's record shone most brightly. In part, this may reflect the help he received in the transition to Oxford from Will and Steuart who had knowledge and experience about the various resources, traditions, expectations, and requirements of the University. Yet, in the main, it resulted simply from the fact that he undertook more by reading for several degrees in his four years there and, with his exceptional ability, obviously scored and achieved more.

What a contrast Oxford must have presented to Keith, the bright youth from Joppa! If his move from the Royal High School to Edinburgh University reflected continuities in classical architectural styles, he must have found Oxford truly amazing: no coherent classical harmonies here but, rather, a wondrous array of architectural delights, in all styles and all periods, a storehouse for the history of English architecture, religious and secular, private and public. Each college with its own peculiar mixture of architecture reflected shifts in patronage and taste as well as in development and history. As Keith simply walked the streets of Oxford and went to visit his brothers and friends in different colleges, he experienced everything from Norman and early mediaeval foundations in Christ Church and Merton to the neo-classical symmetry of Wren's Sheldonian Theatre right on to the controversial brick patterns of Keble. And, unlike Edinburgh, Oxford was a city whose primary focus in those days was to house and service the most renowned university in the kingdom, although some at Cambridge, and elsewhere, were always prepared to dispute that claim.

For a young, brilliant scholar, what an exciting place Oxford must have been. There, the most gifted undergraduates had been collected from the realm, and beyond. There, one of the finest groups of thinkers, writers, and scholars had been assembled. There, the very atmosphere exuded scholarship, studiousness, and learning. Oxford, with its spires and steeples, its quadrangles and gardens, its Scholars and Fellows, was to be a central focus of Keith's life for years.

In many ways, his entry into Balliol College was singularly appropriate. From its origins in the thirteenth century as one of the first foundations at Oxford, it maintained strong associations with the north of England and, especially, with Scotland.[38] At the time Keith entered, the Scottish connection was readily apparent. The Master, Edward Caird, was a Scot. Keith's second cousin, W David Ross, later to become Provost of Oriel College and Vice Chancellor of the University, although born in India of Scottish parents, had come up to Balliol the preceding year through the same route of the Royal High School and Edinburgh University. In fact, five of the fifty-three men who started there in the fall of 1897 were Scots.[39] The principal Sanskrit Scholar at Oxford, A A Macdonell, was from Perthshire; he became Boden Professor of Sanskrit in 1899 and a Fellow of Balliol College in 1900. Keith was to work closely with Macdonell during the years at Balliol and later on, as well. Keith's change from Edinburgh to Balliol was undoubtedly eased through his acquaintance and study with William R Hardie since Hardie, another Scot, had gone from Edinburgh to Balliol where he remained to become a Fellow in 1884, a position he held until he returned to Edinburgh as Professor of Humanity in 1895. Keith must have felt that all these Scottish connections made Balliol quite the right place to be.[40]

Moreover, by the time he entered, Balliol had acquired a deserved reputation for being one of the more intellectually stimulating and rigorous of the colleges at Oxford. That had been true, at least, from the days that the great Benjamin Jowett had been Master between 1870 and 1893. Balliol had a splendid set of tutors, the elite of Oxford, who helped create and sustain the heady academic atmosphere.[41]

In addition, Balliol was the college where a considerable number of men who were successful candidates for entry into the Indian Civil Service came for their two years of probationary study prior to going out to India, Burma, and the East.[42] If Keith desired to follow his brother Will's example and try for the Civil Service, he certainly had men at Balliol with whom he could talk and who could give him information about the nature of that service.

From many perspectives, then, Balliol was the logical place for Keith: its Scottish connections, its intellectual core, its strengths in Classics and Sanskrit, and its links to the Indian Civil Service. The fact that his brothers were Oxford men helped him make the move successfully. After he arrived in October of 1897, he wrote to his mother. Only a fragment of that letter survives, but it gives insight into the ways in which he actually started his life and studies at Oxford and, in addition, into his attachment to MSK:

> 22 Wellington Square, Oxford
> October, Sunday

My darling Mother;

> Pardon for not writing sooner but I have never had a moment to myself till now and Steu is expecting me even at this very moment. I trust dearest you were not ill during Nan's departure. I fear however you must have been. But I know dearest Nan will do her best to aid and help you. Now I am convinced you want me to tell you all and I will do so as well as I can tho' I am no great hand at letter writing and am in addition writing this letter ... preparatory to consoling Steu whose spirits are at a very low ebb. Jean will have told you of the packing and of our departure. We went quietly on to Carlisle, Preston ($\frac{1}{2}$ hour late), Crewe (35 min), Rugby (45 min). At Rugby we had neither time nor inclination to do any eating. At [Banbury; writing is illegible] I became convinced we had left our luggage behind but could think of nothing which we could then do. Just as we were sitting in deep despondency suddenly little Macgregor flashed up and by his humour amused us and kept us in good [spirits] till the appointed time of our arrival at Oxford. Then I went & secured a cab, while Steu and Macgregor sought for the luggage. As I was in the cab Edge came up and wanted me to take lodgings with him and Dale but I rather cooled him off that idea, quite rightly, too. ... Then Macgregor came and told me there was no luggage of ours on the train. We then (i.e. Mac & I) drove to our lodgings—i.e. Mac's first where he ordered supper for 2. Then we walked to Balliol and inquired of the porter for my lodging's who politely gave me it, and then went to my lodgings where I interviewed my good landlady and told her I didn't want no supper. Then I went to Mac's rooms and had supper ... a very nice little meal. Then I went to the railway station—Macg-showing me the way—[interviewed] an inspector and tipped him liberally and was promised the sending of them as soon as they arrived to Trinity College and 22 Well. Square. Then we went first to Mac's lodgings 51 John Street then I tripped to Well. Sq. and sat disconsolately reading a list of regulations—beastly strict ones—of Balliol which had been sent to my rooms till 11 o'clock and then went to bed at 11.30. A ring came and a cab drove up with my luggage which I took in and semi unpacked thereafter bolting to bed.

> Sunday
> I awoke about 7.30 lay till 8.5 when my hot water was brought, got up, dressed very slowly till 8.45 when I went with Mac to Steu's rooms. Steu gave Mac and I a fair breakfast ... Then we wandered out and looked up Dunbar and Macpherson who both happened to be out much to my pleasure for I don't like

either at all much. Then we looked up Dud also out and Martin who amused us much and D Ross who invited us to tea on Monday at 4.30 o'clock ... As we were walking about under the trees of Balliol Smith, one of the fellows came up to me and said, 'how do you do?' So I asked him what I was to do and he told me to go to my tutor, Paravicini tomorrow morning. I should have been up on Saturday and he told me that I should have to 'salt Mr P's tail' a most extraordinary sentence! I suppose it means 'cool him down'. About 12.45 I left and lunched at my lodgings all right.[43]

Thus, Keith commenced his long years of association with Oxford University.

He did not live long in the rooms at Wellington Square for, in the year that he went up to Oxford, MSK left Davidson, took the two younger children, and relocated herself in Oxford. No evidence remains about the terms, if any, of this separation, but she never returned to live with her husband although he maintained the house in Joppa until 1902-3. The house on Iffley Road which MSK took and to which she directed both Steuart and Berriedale to move was situated a short distance from the centre of Oxford.[44] At the turn of the century, the neighbourhood of terraces would have been a little more isolated than it is at present. Yet, the colleges and libraries where the Keith brothers needed to be for lectures, tutorials, and studies were easily accessible either by foot or by tram. For Keith, the time to walk from Balliol, up the High, over Magdalen Bridge, and out on to Iffley Road would have taken no more than twenty to thirty minutes; the time by tram would have been considerably less. The Keiths lived in a large, brick, three-storeyed semi-detached house located on the southern side of the street; the house provided ample space for them. Then, as now, parks, playing fields, and the botanical gardens were nearby towards town, while meadows lining the banks of the Thames, or Isis as it is known in that section, were downhill a few blocks away. Altogether, the location on Iffley Road provided a pleasant, convenient, and comfortable place for MSK to live and to supervise her sons and family during term time.

These arrangements lasted through the years that Keith studied at Balliol. He was exceptional in not being part of the residential college and in subscribing only to the Musical Society.[45] By the time he left in 1901, Keith had earned several degrees and added numerous honours. His time in formal study at Oxford was longer than normal because he had to wait until he was twenty-two years old to meet the minimum age requirements for writing the civil service examinations.[46] In a handwritten memorandum of 1900 entitled, 'Berriedale Keith's "List of Successes" ,', he summarised his career to that date:

Oxford University: (1)   Scholarship at Balliol ...
(2)   Boden Scholar (Sanskrit) 1898
(3)   1st Class Classical Honours Moderates 1899
(4)   1st Class Oriental Final School (Sanskrit & Pali) 1900
Graduated BA in 1900 ...
The Dean's respect for my character & abilities is laid down ... infra[47]

To these, he added a first class *Literae Humaniores* in 1901. For any man to complete that body of work in that length of time was extraordinary by any measure. With his exceptional mind, Berriedale took it all in his stride. Through these studies, he expanded his knowledge in classical languages, in Greek and Roman philosophy and history, as well as in the language and literature of Sanskrit and of Pali. To the breadth of studies required for the various degrees, he added substantial work in principles for the comparative study of religions, a grounding to stand him in good stead in his later works on religions of India.

In pursuing this programme of studies, he showed independence of mind and a clear sense of what he desired to master in his years at Oxford. In 1906, he reflected upon that programme, of course, with the benefit of a few years' distance:

> After discussion with my tutor, I decided, against his advice, not to follow the usual course of study of a Classical Scholar at Balliol—which involved the devotion of much time to the writing of Latin and Greek verse with a view to competition for the Hertford, Craven, and Ireland Scholarships—but to divide my time fairly evenly between the critical study of Latin and Greek Literature, Palaeography and Textual Criticism on the one hand and Sanskrit on the other. I studied Textual Criticism under Professors Ingram Bywater and Robinson Ellis, and obtained a First Class in Classical Moderations in 1899. Sanskrit I studied under the Boden Professor, Arthur Antony Macdonell, and in 1898, after competition with a native of India, I obtained the Boden Scholarship in Sanskrit (£50 for 4 years). Thereafter I requested, and with some difficulty received, the permission of my College to devote the third year of my course to taking a Final School in Oriental Languages, thus reducing the time for preparation in Roman and Greek History and Philosophy, the subjects of the Final Examination in *Literis Humanioribus*, to one year. I obtained a First Class, the first for eleven years, in Sanskrit and Pali in 1900.[48]

In all the examinations, he achieved unusual success. In his own time, his prodigious learning became a legend at Oxford. Various professors, tutors, and examiners expressed amazement at the depth, breadth, and substantiveness of his learning and knowledge:

> I had already heard a great deal of his extraordinary powers and immense industry in a great variety of lines, especially as a student of Sanskrit Literature. In the occasional opportunities which I had of conversing with him all that I had heard was amply confirmed and justified. His reading both in Latin and Greek is very extensive, but it forms part only of his multifarious learning.[49]

> ... a man of quite exceptional powers of mind, and I have never known any young man of more extensive knowledge, or with his knowledge more ready at command.[50]

> ... I have never been privileged to teach a scholar of such brilliant promise or of such mature knowledge in as many directions as MR KEITH. ... by his very remarkable powers of work, intelligence, and memory, he stood far above his contemporaries.[51]

> I ... have a very distinct remembrance of the extraordinary excellence of his work. He was without question the most learned man of his age I have ever met.[52]

... Already as an Undergraduate he was distinguished for his erudition.[53]

I do not remember any other undergraduate in recent years who showed such a capacity for learning in many subjects. ... He never seemed to forget anything he was taught, and he showed remarkable ability in dealing with the subject.[54]

In addition to compiling this brilliant record through completing the formal requirements and writing the examinations for degrees, he commenced activity in two other areas that were to characterise his life and career: he published his first article in a scholarly journal, and he undertook studies in law with a view to being called to the Bar.

That article appeared in the *Journal of the Royal Asiatic Society* in the issue of January, 1900: 'The Nīti-Mañjarī of Dyā Dviveda.'[55] It was Macdonell's impetus that directed Keith into this aspect of his life as a Sanskrit scholar by encouraging him to draw upon the world of academic study to move into the larger world of published scholarship and of professional associations. In the preceding year, 1899, when he was twenty years old, he had been elected into membership of the Royal Asiatic Society.[56] This brought him into contact with scholars interested in Sanskrit, specifically, and Oriental Studies, more broadly, beyond those whom he knew at Oxford. Further, this brought him into association with public figures, many of whom were, or had been, in the civil service at work for the Government of India or in the India Office or in the Colonial Office. Many had had experience as governors or administrators in Burma, India, and other parts of the British Empire in the East. For example, Lord Reay, President of the Royal Asiatic Society from 1893 to 1921, had been Governor of Bombay between 1885 and 1890, and was, at the time Keith first met him, one of the important British members instrumental in the organisation of the International Colonial Institute based in Brussels. Thus, at the outset of his public career, Keith came to know, and to be known by, a variety of important individuals interested in one of his primary fields. His published article was simply the first of a long series in that journal, and he quickly became recognised as a young scholar with wide and precise knowledge in the field of Sanskrit and with certainty in the correctness of his views.

The published article reflected the unusual confidence that Macdonell had in him. Indeed, Macdonell acknowledged Keith's importance when he paid public tribute to him in the preface to *A History of Sanskrit Literature* in 1899:

To my pupil Mr A B Keith, Boden Sanskrit Scholar and Classical Scholar at Balliol, who has read all the final proofs with great care, I owe not only the removal of a number of errors of the press, but also several valuable criticisms regarding matters of fact.[57]

Beyond this, Macdonell, in 1900, recommended that Keith undertake the complex task of completing the catalogue of Sanskrit manuscripts held in the Bodleian Library.[58] That work had been started by Professor Theodor Aufrecht in 1859 but had never been resumed after Aufrecht left to take up an appointment at the University of Prague. Keith not only commenced from the point where Aufrecht left off but, in addition, included a catalogue of all the manuscripts deposited in the library in the intervening years. Cataloguing is a sophisticated task at best. In this particular instance, it required extensive, accurate knowledge of the language of Sanskrit, of styles of calligraphy, of persons writing in that language, and of the context in which the works most likely would have been written. No small task for a twenty year old! However, during 1900 and 1901, while completing courses, degrees, and examinations, Keith finished the primary task of cataloguing those manuscripts, a significant scholarly achievement for anyone, but especially so for such a young man.

Besides seeing his first article in Sanskrit into print and undertaking the preparation of a catalogue of manuscripts, Keith took initial steps in yet another area of his life. He received permission from appropriate authorities at Oxford to start legal studies. Authorities at the Inner Temple in London permitted him, as well, to start keeping terms there, commencing in 1900. Although he admitted that he 'was not able to spare time to read for the Bar Examinations', until he was later employed in London, the direction was clear: he would add law to his scholarly bases in Classics and Sanskrit.[59] Just as he related his interests in ancient Greek religions to studies about classical Indian religions, so he would study law to become equipped with the vocabulary and concepts in order to undertake studies comparing legal systems in the western classical world to those in ancient India.

Still one other aspect of his years at Oxford needs to be mentioned. His associations with Balliol, particularly, and with Oxford, more generally, brought him into a network of important and influential persons. Through that extensive network, he was related to a large group of men who preceded him, who were his contemporaries, and who followed him. There certainly was, and is, advantage in the Oxford connection. For example, one member of the group entering Balliol with him in 1897 provided a link which was to be important to Keith in future years: Raymond Asquith, older son of H H Asquith, who became, eventually, the Liberal Prime Minister. It is of interest, as well, to note that William Beveridge, later Director of the London School of Economics and chief architect of the schemes to provide social welfare and full employment for Britain after 1945, was also a member of that group which entered Balliol in the autumn of 1897. Acquaintance with the young Asquith meant that, when later he played an important and active role in the Liberal Party in Scotland, Keith had a personal connection with the Asquith family.[60] Or, again, when he entered the Colonial Office, Keith found that several of his colleagues and superiors were Balliol men including, for instance, Sir Charles P Lucas, one of the principal administrators in that office. Oxford ties ran deeply and widely throughout all of Keith's life.

Civil Service Examination

At some point in his last years at Oxford, Keith determined to follow the route taken by his older brothers and seek entry into the Civil Service. For young

5 Arthur Berriedale Keith, *c.* 1901. Courtesy of Mrs J Walcot Burton.

Scots, or, indeed, for young men from any part of the kingdom, the Civil Service offered substantial rewards in terms of interesting and important work, reasonable working hours and conditions, likelihood of promotion based upon meritorious performance, an assured salary, and ample vacation time.[61] Of course, such work required residence usually either in the London area where the general governmental offices were located, or, for the Indian Civil Service, in the East. The examinations themselves reflected the principles of the Trevelyan-Northcote Report of 1854 as they were put into effect by an Order-In-Council on Civil Service of 1870.[62] That required recruitment for government service on a professional level through competitive examinations. Applicants needed to be among the academically most able men educated in the liberal arts at the universities. The examinations required performance in a variety of subjects and, of course, the more subjects an examinee could offer successfully, the more he was likely to increase his score. In those days, Sanskrit was one language expected for the Indian Civil Service just as Greek and Latin were expected for the Home Civil Service. Obviously, servants of the Crown at the centre of the world's greatest empire were to be latter-day Augustans.

Having arrived at the minimum age required—and he became twenty-two in April—Keith completed all the formalities of application and sat the examinations in August of 1901.[63] Then, all his preparation at Edinburgh and Oxford came into focus. When the results were released to the public in September by the Civil Service Commissioners, a jubilant telegram was despatched to his family in Edinburgh: 'Berr first by 1259.'[64]

That difference meant that he headed the list for the Home Civil Service, the Indian Civil Service, and the Eastern Cadetships by a margin which established a new record for those examinations, an achievement that never was matched or neared during the years in which that particular form of examination was given.[65] The wide range of subjects Keith covered in the examination and the skills he had mastered in recalling and utilising a phenomenal body of information accounted for his success. Out of a maximum of 7,600 points possible, he scored 5,382, distributed among these areas:

English Composition	343
Sanskrit	378
Greek Language and Literature	563
Latin Language and Literature	516
English Language and Literature	336
Greek History	380
Roman History	293
English History	379
Logic and Philosophy	266
General Modern History	338
Moral Philosophy	296
Political Economy and Economic History	376
Political Science	350
Roman Law	319
English Law	249[66]

The examinee who came next in the list, although more than a thousand points behind Keith, scored an impressive total of 4,123 marks.[67] Clearly, the examination did test the sort of classical learning Keith had acquired. Writing in 1947 about the Colonial Office staff and the intellectual brilliance of the men assigned there, Sir Cosmo Parkinson alluded to Keith's success:

> There had been a time when a man could secure a high place in the examination list, perhaps even first place, if he had specialised and did very well in an out-of-the-way subject like Sanskrit (out-of-the-way, that is, for the common man), provided that he was up to standard in his other subjects. There is no more reason to object to Sanskrit as a possible subject for the examination than to Latin or any other of the humanities—on the understanding that the Sanskrit scholar's handwriting is not so illegible as to lead to the belief (this was held to have happened in one such case) that his English and Sanskrit scripts have become mixed.[68]

Since the scores were reported to the press, the public was informed about Keith's achievement. Several persons wrote to congratulate him, and most anticipated that he would follow his brothers into service in Burma, or, alternatively, go directly to India. The late Principal of Edinburgh University, Sir William Muir, wrote to him along those lines:

> 30 September 1901
> Dean Park H, Edinburgh
>
> My dear Sir,
>   I cannot allow the notice of your Distinguished position, entering the IC Service to pass, without writing a line to say how proud I feel at the honour conferred on our University by the place you have taken.
>   I conclude that you will go to Upper India, which for nearly 40 years I loved.
>   I feel an additional interest in you as one of three [brothers] similarly honoured—seeing that I went out similarly as one of four. I am sure that you will adorn the service and that Divine Providence may prosper you in your works is the prayer of
>
>   Yours sincerely,
>   W Muir
>
> PS Perhaps you may remember the portrait of my eldest brother Dr J Muir the Founder of the Sanskrit Chair in our University who was also a CS in the NWP. When anytime in Edinburgh, I should be very glad to see you.[69]

To the surprise of many, Keith did not enter the Indian Civil Service but rather took an appointment in the Colonial Office. Some years later, he described his decision in terms that suggested it to be rather a matter of chance:

> One great fault in the existing system is the mode in which the candidates are allowed to choose their offices: in my case no notice was given of Colonial office vacancies until the moment when I was asked to choose: I knew nothing of the comparative merits of the two offices, Colonial and Indian: I asked the man

there at the Commission which was supposed to be the better: he said the Colonial, and I took it. Of course I acted in good faith, and I recognise he had no responsibility in advising, but I do not see what fairness there is in a system like that.[70]

Yet, it is clear from his determination to pursue legal studies, expressed in his days at Oxford, that his principal motive was to be in one of the government offices in London where he would have ready access to the Inner Temple. Of course, he could have served on the staff of the India Office and achieved that same goal just as well as being at the Colonial Office. It seems unlikely that he gave serious consideration to an overseas posting. In a letter to Sir Montagu Ommanney, Under-Secretary of State in the Colonial Office, Keith, as he accepted appointment and indicated the date on which he would be available to start, requested that his superiors approve of his continuing to keep terms at the Inner Temple on a regular basis: 'I suppose the Department will have no objection to my doing so with a view to be formally called to the Bar.'[71] Clearly, he would have been unable to pursue legal studies had he been posted to India or Burma or any place outside London and, just as clearly, he was eager to add formal study and training in law to his array of academic knowledge.

So it was that Keith, reared in Portobello and educated in Edinburgh and Oxford, and having already achieved distinct recognition in many different ways for his unusual and exceptional scholarship, commenced the next stage of his life. He started work at the Colonial Office as a Second Class Clerk. In that position, he was to serve in various parts of the Office; at the same time, he continued his scholarship in Sanskrit, completed his preparation in law both by being called to the Bar at the Inner Temple and by taking a BCL at Oxford. He also produced his first works on the nature of responsible government in the dominions. For the next thirteen years, he centred his life primarily on London.

PART TWO

Colonial Office, 1901–1914

CHAPTER 3

Initial Year at the Colonial Office, 1901–1902

With the completion of his first degrees at Oxford and with his great success in the Civil Service Examination, Keith was prepared to shift the centre of his attention from that of being a full-time student to that of being a full-time member of staff even as he continued his studies and his scholarship. His time in London spanned thirteen years.

During those years, he lived at several places on the south bank in the area of Battersea Park. Obviously, until her death, his mother, MSK, selected the specific residence in each instance. Initially, he lived at 2 Prince of Wales Mansions, an address to which he returned from 1906 to 1909 as well. In 1904, MSK moved the household to Albert Bridge Road where the moves were merely up and down the street from No. 49 to No. 75. After MSK's death, Keith and his wife remained on that same street but moved to No. 107.[1] Each house in which the Keiths lived faced the park. The view from the entry door or from the front rooms of each of these houses must have been pleasant for MSK and members of the family. While the houses fronted on busy streets, acres of green, tended, delightful park with lawns, trees, and flower gardens were directly opposite. What a pleasing place to stroll and take the air!

In that section of the greater city, all the buildings were of mid-Victorian vintage, multi-storeyed, attached, and brick. Individual houses were narrow and high. Only a variation in the colour of the front door might distinguish one of the houses from any other in the row. Interior space would have been sufficient for MSK and her household and would have provided adequate space, as well, for Keith to continue his studies and writing. The location had two primary assets: the park, itself, with its sense of spaciousness, airiness, and gentility, and, then, the ease of access by tram to Whitehall. Keith would have taken a tram along the south bank to get off near Westminster Bridge and, from there, walk the short distance to the Colonial Office nearby. The excellence of the city's transportation system in Edwardian times provided Londoners with an easy way to enjoy Battersea Park with its open areas, while persons living near that park had a sense of country living, yet they were near to work in the City, the West End, or Westminster. It was a good location for the Keiths.

Entrance to the Staff of the Colonial Office

Keith's entry to the staff of the Colonial Office followed the established procedures. After he achieved the record score in the Civil Service examination in August 1901, the Civil Service Commissioners sent him appropriate notification about the vacancies for Second Class Clerks from which he might select an appointment; he chose the Colonial Office.[2] Then, on 7 October, they sent the Civil Service Certificate to the Colonial Office; that attested to his fitness for service in terms of age, physical condition, character, and knowledge. At the same time, they informed him of that action and advised him to make a direct enquiry about the actual date for starting work.[3] On 9 October, on the letterhead of Balliol College, Keith wrote to the Secretary of State for the Colonies to indicate that he was ready: 'I should be very much obliged if you could let me know on what date I am required to join. I am, of course, prepared to do so at once.'[4] Sir Montague F Ommanney, Permanent Under-Secretary of State, responded to that letter on 12 October. In his response, Ommanney repeated that the starting salary would be £200. per annum and indicated, as well, that Keith might be required to be one of the two Second Class Clerks who occupied rooms in the Colonial Office to attend to telegrams and communications that arrived outside normal working hours; as it turned out, Keith was not assigned that duty on any continuing basis. Ommanney also enclosed documents which specified the other terms of the position: a two year probationary period, a six day work week but with a half-holiday on alternate Saturdays, vacation time of thirty-six weekdays in the first ten years of service but with forty-eight thereafter, sick leave of two days with a medical certificate and up to four months leave in normal course with discretion by the Secretary of State to extend it further, retirement provisions at sixty years of age but mandatory at sixty-five, and a requirement to sign an attendance book on entering or leaving the office.[5] Keith replied to Ommanney's letter on 13 October and indicated that he was prepared to start work on the following Monday. With characteristic forthrightness, he also asked permission to continue keeping terms at the Inner Temple in preparation for being called to the Bar. While some of the staff handling his correspondence had reservations about that request since they were dubious about 'a man combining the two occupations', he did receive formal permission on the day he started to work: 'There will be no objection to your continuing your legal studies provided that they do not interfere with your attendance at this office.'[6]

So it was that on the morning of Monday, 21 October 1901, Keith, the young man of twenty-two who, in time, would become one of the primary interpreters of the constitution of the British Empire, made his way along Whitehall to turn into King Charles Street and the courtyard leading to the Colonial Office where he was scheduled to appear at eleven o'clock. When he entered the office building from the courtyard, the porter would have directed him through the spacious, grand entry hall and up the imposing stairs circling around the octagonal stairwell, perhaps that day flooded with natural light from the leaded panes four storeys above, to the room of Frederick Graham, one of the Assistant Secretaries of State, who had been designated by Omman-ney to receive him and to give him his assignment.

At the time Keith started, the Colonial Office was housed in the 'new' building completed in 1895 which had been specifically designed to suit its functions and purposes by Sir George Gilbert Scott, the noted architect who gained commissions for several of the major buildings in Whitehall. It com-pleted the northeast corner of the quadrangle which, on the western side, included the Foreign Office and the India Office, both of which had many windows with views over St James's park. The Home Office, the other depart-ment within that quadrangle, shared its façade facing Whitehall with the Colonial Office. That façade presented, and still does, the solid, studied, serious aspect of the palace of a Renaissance prince or banker rather than the Gothic fancies and traceries found in several buildings erected at about the same time in other parts of Westminster. The Colonial Office had some exterior offices with windows providing views on to Whitehall or Downing Street. The rooms for the principal officials were particularly well-designed in terms of size, shape, arrangement, and location in relation to secretarial and staff support, with that of the Secretary of State being the most spacious. 'Simply vast', according to one of its occupants, his room was large enough to contain with ease an enormous globe, a handsome map case for storing twenty-two maps of the world and of the colonies, a massive desk, a generous writing table, a large conference table, and numerous side chairs. A great chandelier added to the sense of height and graciousness while the mantelpiece, removed from the waiting room of the old office in Downing Street, added to the sense of continuity and power because Nelson and Wellington had had their only meeting when they stood before it as they waited to see the official then titled Secretary of State for War and the Colonies. A bust of Sir James Stephen, the greatest and most influential of the Victorian Under-Secretaries of State, was prominently displayed.[7]

As the newest member of the staff, Keith went, however, to one of the lesser rooms of which there were a great number grouped in a sort of labyrinth around a small, rather dark courtyard. These rooms were oddly shaped, ill-related to each other, poorly ventilated, marginally lighted even as electricity was being added to replace gas, and, in several instances, inappropriately situated and shaped in terms of changed functions. The entire building from the basement to the top was five storeys but with two mezzanines tucked in between the first, second, and third floors. In addition to space for the usual offices, it included a well-planned library; bedrooms, sitting rooms, kitchens, and dining rooms for clerks who had to spend nights in the office; and, on the very top floor, in a carefully isolated section, rooms for the copying branch including the lady typists. Lifts for passengers and for materials went to all floors. Space existed for the varied functions of the Colonial Office even though, and especially with the enlargement of responsibility that came during the South African War, there was always pressure for additional space. For instance, the heads of the Colonial Office were eager to gain the space that could come from relocating the offices of the Crown Agents for the Colonies which occupied twenty-four rooms in the basement and ground floors; that only happened in 1903 when the Crown Agents finally moved across to Whitehall Gardens. Keith, except for brief service with the Crown Agents, found his professional home in this building during the years he worked in London. His assignment to various sections of the Colonial Office meant that, over time, he worked in rooms in different places, from the rather confined space of his first assignment in a geographical department to the more generous space provided by his last as Private Secretary to the Permanent Under-Secretary of State.[8]

Functions and Organisation of the Colonial Office

In order to understand Keith's actual work at the Colonial Office, it is necessary to describe the functions and organisation of that office during his time. It was one of the two principal offices responsible for administration and supervision of the British Empire. It carried responsibility for all the territories of the empire including most protectorates except for the vast and populous subcontinent of India to which Burma had been added after its conquest and annexation in the nineteenth century.[9]

Jurisdiction over India was never part of the Colonial Office. Rather that area was under the India Office which had been established as a result of the Sepoy Mutiny in 1857 when Parliament took the last step in the process of removing control of British interests in India from the hands of a trading firm, the East India Company, chartered in the last years of Elizabeth's reign. It placed that control directly in the hands of the head of a government department who normally was in the Cabinet and who, in any event, was always in the ministry; thus, he was answerable and accountable to Parliament. The Secretary of State for India carried responsibility for the operation of governments covering the single largest concentration of population within the Empire, both those portions directly under British rule, that is, British India under the Government of India, and those portions indirectly under British rule, that is, the states with their native rulers, joined to and allied with the Crown by treaty. The Viceroy of India represented the Crown for both categories of government in India, but he functioned under the direction of the Secretary of State, although there were some Viceroys prepared to dispute that control. With its mandated custody for the 'jewel of empire', the India Office, obviously, had greater prestige than the Colonial Office.[10]

Whether by accident, by design, or by decision to ignore such prestige, Keith elected to join the staff of the Colonial Office which carried responsibility for all other parts of the British Empire. Created in 1854, shortly before the India Office, as an entity separate from the War Office, it was headed by the Secretary of State for the Colonies. Part of the political majority of the day, the holder of that office was always included in the Cabinet because of the significance of the Empire. For all parts of the Empire under its jurisdiction, the Colonial Office was the formal link between the colonies and the government of the United Kingdom, and thus, the Crown. The other political leader in the Office was the Parliamentary Under-Secretary of State, selected from the chamber different from the Secretary to ensure a spokesman on imperial issues and a guide for legislation about imperial matters in each house of Parliament. These two political leaders were responsible for setting colonial policy, for seeing that it was co-ordinated with other aspects of strategy developed by the Cabinet, and for pointing general directions for the staff.

Under their leadership came the establishment of the Colonial Office which, in 1901, consisted of 109 positions.[11] The Office was organised in what had become the normal pattern for a department of state: it was a bureaucratic pyramid staffed by persons in various levels of the Civil Service. The Permanent Under-Secretary of State, a non-political civil servant, was responsible for the entire operation of the Office. Under him were four Assistant Under-Secretaries of State who supervised specific sectors. Seven Principal Clerks, seven First Class Clerks, and nineteen Second Class Clerks comprised the upper division or 'the intellectual' level. In all, then, thirty-eight professional staff conducted the business of the Office with some of them assigned as private secretaries to the three primary officials, the Secretary of State, the Parliamentary Under-Secretary of State, and the Permanent Under-Secretary of State. The rest of the staff, the 'mechanical' lower division, drawn mainly from Second Division Clerks, directed the supporting functions of library, accounting, legal drafting, registry, printing, copying, control of access to the Office, and carrying messages. A group of 'lady typewriters' was attached to the copying department.[12]

What was the nature of responsibility that the staff carried? Perhaps they had the development of an understanding of the British Empire as their fundamental task, essential to all else they did. To say that they were responsible for the administration of all the Empire except India and Burma does not begin to indicate the great diversity encompassed in territories under the jurisdiction of that Office. To sketch some of the diversity with respect to area, history, level of political development, population, resources, strategic location, and cultural differences may provide a basis for realising the range of knowledge that staff members in the Colonial Office, including Keith, of course, had to acquire in order to carry out their work.[13] As one of the consistent operating principles for colonial administration, the Colonial Office maintained that colonies should be governed, insofar as possible, in a manner appropriate to their history and to existing traditions; that principle resulted, obviously, in lack of uniformity throughout the Empire.

It is possible to illustrate diversity in an area by indicating that the Colonial Office oversaw relationships, for example, with governments spread over two of the greatest land masses in the world, and, at the same time, with two of the very tiniest. It dealt with Canada, covering nearly four million square miles and even then the world's second largest country, and the continent of Australia, nearly three million square miles. Near the other end of the scale, the Office dealt with Malta, an island in the Mediterranean, with slightly under one hundred square miles on the main island, and with St Lucia in the Caribbean with a little more than two hundred square miles.

In addition to size, it is possible to illustrate diversity further by contrasting how each of these four areas varied in historical development and in the level of internal political control achieved by 1901. Canada, originally founded along the St Lawrence River and the Great Lakes within the French Empire, had been acquired by Britain at the end of the Seven Years War in 1763, with specific guarantees to the conquered French population with regard to the continuation of French language, Roman Catholicism, and French civil law. Loyal British colonists after the American Revolution joined that French core and, also, the many British who were already in that area by leaving the new United States to go by land across the Niagara bridge into Upper Canada or by the lake and river system up the Richelieu valley into the eastern townships or by sea into the maritimes largely populated by Britons; in each case, they brought with them experience of participation in assemblies and councils as a normal part of British colonial government. Canada also confronted, and solved, the task of stretching from the Atlantic to the Pacific, in the course of which some of the indigenous population was displaced. By 1901, its political institutions were well-developed and stable at both federal and provincial levels including integration of the French population into the political process. Canada which achieved responsible government in the 1840s as a result of Lord Durham's Report was the premier and model dominion with virtually full control of its affairs. By contrast, Australia, originally established as a British penal colony, was dominantly British in tone and population as the various sections had been established by successive waves of British emigrants including those who participated in settling South Australia as part of Edward Gibbon Wakefield's scheme of 'systematic colonisation'. As the colonists spread across the whole continent to link east and west, indigenous peoples were pushed far into the interior. The Australian colonies moved quickly through governmental stages to responsible government and to the point where each state had a well-developed, mature political system. In 1901, the new feature was the federal union through which, and with the states, Australians controlled their own destiny.

The two islands had very different experiences. Malta, located so as to divide the Mediterranean into two basins, had been ruled over the centuries by, perhaps, Phoenicians and, certainly, by Romans, Carthagenians, Vandals, Goths, Arabs, Normans, the Knights of Malta, Sicily, France, and, finally, Britain after the Napoleonic Wars. Each group left some trace in the population. Most of the people spoke Italian and were Roman Catholics; the designation of English as the official language simply alienated many persons. Essentially, Malta was a key naval base along the British route through the Mediterranean and Suez Canal to India and the East, and, therefore, both the Admiralty and the Foreign Office had interests in it, as well, of course, as the Colonial Office. Malta was a crown colony in which British subjects there had virtually no control over their political affairs in 1901. Very different from Malta was St Lucia, located in the Windward Islands. Originally colonised by the French in the sixteenth century, it was one of the areas in the West Indies to be traded back and forth between France and Britain during the numerous wars of the eighteenth century, ultimately coming under continuing British control during the Napoleonic Wars. As with other islands in that region, its indigenous population had been replaced with black slaves imported from

West Africa to work in sugar plantations. The abolition of slavery throughout the British Empire in 1833 adversely affected its economy. By 1901, its inhabitants, primarily descendants of former slaves, had only limited and indirect participation in the government of the colony which was also a crown colony.

It is possible to illustrate diversity in several other ways, as well: for example, to consider population. The Colonial Office was responsible for British interests in Nigeria, both the colony and the protectorate and, indeed, the expansion of control into the north. This entire area contained, perhaps, twenty to thirty million people or more than half that of the United Kingdom or more than three times that of Canada. That enormous population was divided among several tribes. At the other end of the population scale, the Colonial Office supervised the Falkland Islands, a group in the south Atlantic, where, perhaps, some fifteen hundred persons lived, almost entirely emigrants from Britain. Staff in the Colonial Office had to understand the implications of the density and dissimilarity of the population in Nigeria and, at the same time, of the sparseness of population in the Falklands. Consider the range in resources which spanned the areas in southern Africa with enormous and almost incalculable wealth in the gold mines and diamond fields as compared to the barrenness of colonies like Pitcairn or Nauru in the Pacific or even several of the islands in the Caribbean. Consider the different value placed on the strategic importance of territories from those of great significance such as Gibraltar, Malta, Aden, or the Straits Settlements as contrasted with those of little significance such as New Zealand or the Bahamas. Consider the diversity in cultural patterns which ranged from the virtual dominance and homogeneity of Britons in New Zealand to the great differences among groups in southern Africa where Afrikaners and Britons, descendants of European emigrants, were in virtual control and, yet, were an infinitesimal minority, even if one included Coloured and Asiatics in their number, in comparison to the large variety of Bantu-speaking persons divided among many tribal groups which comprised the overwhelming majority. Within the Empire, all religious groups could be found: the established Church of England in every territory; concentrations of Methodists, especially in the West Indies; the Church of Scotland where Scots had emigrated; other forms of Calvinism in South Africa and Ceylon; Roman Catholics in many different places, particularly where Irish emigrants settled; Muslims in various African countries and the East; Buddhists and Hindus in Ceylon and elsewhere; and animists, as well. What different sets of religious values!

It is evident, therefore, from these illustrations that that portion of the British Empire under the jurisdiction of the Colonial Office reflected astonishing diversity. Keith, along with others on the staff, had to comprehend the details of that diversity in order to make reasonable decisions as issues emerged.

Beyond developing an understanding of the diverse nature of the British Empire as essential to the conduct of their work, the staff of the Colonial Office had to know, as well, the stage and form of government in operation in each colony. On this aspect, Keith soon became a specialist. The basic model used for government in royal colonies from the seventeenth century onward had that government headed by a governor, appointed by the Crown, and assisted by an appointed executive council dealing primarily with law, defence, lands, and finance. That form of crown colony still existed in the early twentieth century although, where appropriate, in terms of the level of economic development and population, an elected legislative assembly was usually added to provide representative government. The crises and deadlocks in the colonies of Upper Canada and of Lower Canada in the late 1830s demonstrated the weaknesses of that form of representative government and led to the recommendations of Lord Durham that, when colonies reached a certain level of political development, in fact, they should be granted full responsible government so that a ministry would arise from, and be responsible to, the majority in an elected assembly of the colony and that, therefore, the governor of the colony would stand in a constitutional relationship to such a ministry in a manner approximately analogous to that of the monarch to the Cabinet in the United Kingdom. Durham made the point clearly:

> When a ministry ceases to command a majority in Parliament on great questions of policy, its doom is immediately sealed; and it would appear to us as strange to attempt, for any time, to carry on a Government by means of ministers perpetually in a minority, as it would be to pass laws with a majority of votes against them.[14]

By contrast, in protectorates, the inhabitants had almost no role for participation in government since the area was either attached to the administrative responsibilities of the governor of an adjacent colony or was directly administered by a governor, often a military officer; frequently, both the Foreign Office and the Admiralty had concerns over protectorates. Obviously, the staff of the Colonial Office functioned quite differently in relation to these various forms of government, from exercising direct control and supervision of officers in a crown colony or a protectorate to virtually no control in colonies with responsible government. In the latter case, even the four restrictions of imperial interest enunciated by Lord Durham had been eroded by the logic of responsible government:

> The matters, which so concern us, are very few. The constitution of the form of government,—the regulation of foreign relations, and of trade with the mother country, the other British Colonies, and foreign nations,—and the disposal of the public lands, are the only points on which the mother country requires a control.[15]

In fact, by Chamberlain's time, only the matter of foreign relations was clearly in the hands of the imperial government; Canada had led the way in securing control over the other areas, and would lead, as well, in gaining greater direction over her foreign affairs. Although formal control of constitutional changes remained in the imperial Parliament, it was unthinkable that the government in the United Kingdom would undertake, for example, such a major constitutional change as the federal union of Australia unilaterally; it could only proceed according to the proposals, negotiations, and wishes of representatives from the six states who had been appointed by, and were accountable to, ministries holding majorities in the assemblies.

The staff of the Colonial Office had to understand both diversity in the Empire and the different forms of government in the colonies. They had to acquire such understanding as a prerequisite to carrying out a wide range of functions and tasks.

Among those functions, a principal one concerned the appointment of governors and, in the case of the great federal unions, of governors-general. For this, the staff handled all details in the process by which men were appointed to those posts. Every colony, regardless of its stage of governmental development, was involved in this process and affected by it. While all appointments were made by the Crown, that is, under a Royal Commission issued by the monarch on the advice of a minister, in this instance the Secretary of State for the Colonies, the actual selection of persons for such offices came in the first instance under the patronage of the Secretary of State. The procedure may have been as casual as that described by Edward H Marsh, one of the private secretaries to Chamberlain, who recalled that he kept four registers in a back room at the Colonial Office, that he added names of likely persons to the appropriate register from time to time and that, when a vacancy occurred, he played the primary role in suggesting names to his chief.[16] Persons who undertook careers as governors tended to remain in that role for many years and, thus, to serve in several different colonies. For each move, naturally, they looked to positions of greater authority, prestige, and income. Persons selected for such offices usually possessed three common characteristics: they were either members of the peerage or, if not, likely aspirants for inclusion, or were members of the chivalric order of St Michael and St George which was administered under the Colonial Office; they were favoured by, or closely allied to, the political party in power at the time; and they certainly had to be acceptable personally to the monarch. By the time Keith joined the staff, a fourth element entered in, as well, if a colony had responsible government; in that case, the ministry of the day in that colony had to be consulted and to indicate its concurrence. When all these matters had been arranged and the designee had accepted the appointment, the staff of the Colonial Office then attended to all details preparatory to the person actually assuming office. This included correspondence with the colony, both written and telegraphic, over such matters as salary, housing, and staff, since another fundamental principle for operating the Empire was that colonies were to pay their own way and not to reflect a direct claim on the British Treasury. Sometimes the staff of the Colonial Office had to engage in substantive negotiations with the ministry of the colony in order to secure terms which would be favourable to the designee. Further, the staff conducted conferences with the newly appointed governor to inform him about the regulations of the Colonial Office, some 403 specific ones, and the expectations of the Secretary of State with regard to reports and to the exercise of authority. They made certain that he understood the difference in despatches: numbered, which had to be laid before responsible advisers and could be printed; formal, which included schedules and records of telegrams; confidential, which could not be made public without permission from the Secretary of State, but could be shared with advisers; and secret, which could not be communicated to anyone without approval from the Secretary of State.[17] The staff also discussed the range of issues before the colony. Since all governors were servants of the Crown, the staff prepared the appropriate and necessary prerogative instruments: the Letters Patent which specified the ways in which the office of governor was related to Crown authority in its creation and was to be administered; the Royal Instructions which dealt with such matters as oaths, commissions, assent and reservation in regard to legislation, and the power of pardon; and the Royal Commission which actually appointed the person to the particular office. The staff worked out plans for travel and the dates for transfer of authority from incumbent to successor. Often, the staff had to co-ordinate arrangements for the newly appointed governor to be presented to the King formally at a levee and to meet representatives of the colony in London.[18]

In addition to the appointment of governors, the staff of the Colonial Office had to oversee the appointment of numerous other officials, the extent and level depending upon the nature of government in the colony. Marsh's description of the four registers provides a convenient summary of the various categories and functions within which appointments fell: 'Administrative, Legal, Medical, and TAC (Treasury, Audit, Customs).'[19] In several areas, military persons had to be appointed which required liaison with the Admiralty or the War Office. In each instance, whatever the particular appointment, the staff of the Colonial Office carried out all the detailed work related to it: settling salary and other terms of service with the colony; receiving medical clearances; preparing documents authorising the designee to hold office; making travel and other arrangements; interpreting policies and procedures of the Colonial Office; and providing suitable background and technical information.

Another function performed by the staff was that of dealing with all communications between the governor and the Colonial Office. These communications included an enormous body of written materials: despatches, fiscal and economic reports, medical data especially as the Colonial Office and other departments developed increased interest in tropical diseases, and legal queries. Copies of legislation, court decisions, colonial newspapers, gazettes, journals of debates, and the like all were transmitted to the Colonial Office. In addition, the staff handled the tasks of encoding and decoding messages sent by telegraph and cable.[20] The volume of work was substantial. When Keith entered, the Colonial Office handled about 85,000 despatches and letters annually, almost equally divided between receiving and sending, and about 10,000 telegrams or cables; by the time he left the Office in 1914, the number of despatches and letters had grown significantly to about 190,000.[21] The process for handling each item was clearly delineated. When an item, in whatever form, entered the Office, it went first to the appropriate registry where a staff member created a file with cover sheet on which he assigned a number, simply following an arithmetical sequence from the beginning of each calendar year, gave labels related to colony, geographic area, and content, provided a summary of contents, identified the other files to which it had reference or was related, and then, with those related files, routed it to the appropriate section of the Office. There, a Second Class Clerk would write the first minute on it in which he reviewed the significance of the content, recommended appropriate actions, and prepared necessary drafts to go with those recommendations. The file then moved to the First Class Clerk or Principal Clerk in the particular section who reviewed the first minute; he might concur or dissent or make modifications. In any event, he wrote a further minute and sent the file on to an Assistant Under-Secretary. That officer might make the final decision on action, depending on the nature of the material, or he might judge that file needed to go forward to the Permanent Under-Secretary for review or that it might involve another department of government. After review, he would write a minute reflecting his decision. Usually, it was only if the file contained material of very considerable significance that it would get to either of the political leaders in the Office although they had, obviously, the right and responsibility to review and act on any file in the Office. Once an official in the bureaucratic chain had made the decision specifying the desired action, the file was returned to a Second Class Clerk, usually the one who had handled it in the first instance, who prepared the draft of a response. At that point, the file might go forward to his immediate superior for approval or go directly to the copying department to prepare the letter or despatch or telegram for final review and signature. When that document finally left the Colonial Office, the registry received the file again to indicate and date the disposition of the matter, to enter it in the index or register, and, then, to deposit the file for future reference. (See copy of file p 52.) This procedure might take considerable time, or if the issue involved was of great importance, it could occur very quickly.[22] It is this elaborate procedure that Hartmann Just, in Keith's time a Principal Clerk and later an Under-Secretary of State, memorialised in his poem, 'Ballade of Red Tape', one verse of which is especially appropriate for the tasks facing a Second Class Clerk:

> He sits with his quill of grey goose feather
>   By an ink pot; to trim his thoughts to flow
> His inborn soul to a desk they tether
>   Whilst messengers entering in dumb show
>   Deposit the bundles row on row
> For this dull-eyed hermit in his retreat
>   Away from the fields and flowers that blow
>   It is all red tape in Downing Street.[23]

Because the Colonial Office held the red tape and was, as well, the central point of liaison between the colonies and all other parts of the government of the United Kingdom, the staff of the Office had to know about the work of all departments of state. They were involved by correspondence, telephone,

AUSTRALIA

14685

C.O
14685

REC. 1 MAY 13

Bd. of Trade

1913

30 apl.

Last previous Paper.

F.O. 13617

Immigration Restriction Act.

Concurs in action proposed.

Mr Davis.

    See with this the telegram from the Governor
General in 14745. It seems to me unfortunate for
the Secretary of State that no Governor General of the
Commonwealth appears to realise the limits precisely
of his duties and his powers. Lord Hopetoun was guilty
of a grave indiscretion early in his term of office
by assuming responsibility which he need not have
assumed; Lord Northcote made an unfortunate mistake
with regard to the question of the reservation of the
Judiciary Bill, and now Lord Denman sends in a telegram
which shows that he is at the mercy of any advice which
his Ministers may give.

    Mr Hughes the Attorney General is an acute and
clever man, but he admittedly knows no law, and certainly no constitutional law. The Minister for
External Affairs has no pretentions to know any law,
and Mr Fisher is singularly ignorant of Constitutional
law

Next subsequent Paper.

14745

6   Colonial Office File, Cover Page. Crown Copyright. Courtesy of Controller of
HM Stationery Office.

or personal conference with their opposite numbers in different departments, most frequently in the Foreign Office, the Admiralty, the War Office, the Board of Trade, the Law Officers, and, as with every department, the Treasury. In these relationships, the staff performed various functions for a colony: they might provide information, seek co-operation in a particular enterprise, ask for action, or request clarification. In each exchange, the staff attempted to make certain that, as appropriate, the government of the colony was informed about how its interests were being handled.

Another important function that rested usually with the Permanent Under-Secretary was supervision of preparation of draft responses for the Secretary of State or the Parliamentary Under-Secretary to give to written and oral questions in the House of Commons. Typically, under direction from one of the professional staff, someone in the appropriate registry would search out and assemble related files. These, then, moved through channels to the particular members of staff designated to prepare the initial draft. Often, in these instances, the minister would indicate the lines upon which he wished the answer prepared.

Yet another set of relationships that the staff had to handle concerned the way in which colonies purchased supplies in the United Kingdom. Depending upon the form of government, this involved reference either to the Crown Agents for the Colonies for those organised as crown colonies or to the office of the Agent-General for those possessing responsible government. The Crown Agents had existed in some form or other from the eighteenth century but, by mid nineteenth century, had had their role clarified and more formally defined, and their activities restricted to crown colonies; they were to act as the 'commercial and financial agents' in Britain for all such parts of the Empire.[24] The office of the Crown Agents, although an independent, self-supporting, and profitable agency specifically designed to serve the colonies, came under the direct supervision of the Secretary of State for the Colonies, but not under the Colonial Office. The Secretary of State had the power to appoint the three men who were the Crown Agents. His responsibilities were defined as exercising 'a general supervision and control over their compliance with the directions of the Colonial Governments'.[25] These directions could involve orders to purchase anything in the wide range, for example, from postage stamps, specifically designed and manufactured for the colony, all the way to railroad tracks complete with engines and rolling stock to run on them. The staff of the Colonial Office in their role of representing the interests of a colony had to be certain that the Crown Agents carried out such orders accurately and in a timely fashion. Relations were different when a colony had responsible government. Under those circumstances, it conducted its commercial and financial affairs in the United Kingdom through the office of an Agent-General. Those persons, with their staff, were appointed and paid by the colonial government to perform such functions; as well, they represented, to some extent, the colony's interests in the political sphere, on an informal basis to be sure. They dealt directly with British suppliers and made contracts on behalf of their home government. Yet, for all relationships to the various offices of the British government, they were required and expected to go through the Colonial Office. In short, the staff of the Colonial Office possessed detailed information about economic, commercial, and financial aspects of every colony through supervising its dealings with the Crown Agents or with the Agents-General as well as through the governor's regular reports on such matters.

It was on the political side that the functions of the Colonial Office expanded most rapidly as the nature of the Colonial Conference shifted from an inclusive gathering related to a royal occasion such as those of 1887 and 1897 to mark the Jubilee years of Queen Victoria or in 1902 in conjunction with the coronation of King Edward VII to a gathering more exclusive as it involved only those colonies with responsible government, coming with a planned cycle of meetings of premiers at least every five years.[26] For the earlier gatherings, the role of the staff was simply to assist generally in arrangements when the meetings were being held. As the shift occurred, the staff played an increasingly important role in helping to give shape to the meetings: developing the design and working out the calendar; eliciting subjects for discussion from the various colonies; drafting papers and memoranda setting out possible positions to be taken by HM Government in relation to issues and concerns raised by the colonies, with those papers studied by the leadership of the Colonial Office and, frequently, the Cabinet, as well; preparing the actual agenda; making arrangements for the housing and entertainment of participants; and providing secretarial and other staff support during the sessions. In time, these expanding functions required some form of continuing, regular support. That came, ultimately, from the Colonial Office and led to the creation of a secretariat for the Conference which, in addition, carried responsibility for monitoring the steps necessary to put into effect the decisions made during the Conference. That involved the staff in working with various departments in the British government and, as well, in a somewhat different way with the governments of those colonies possessing responsible government.

Beyond the major functions already discussed (that is, appointment of governors, selection and appointment of staff for the colonies, handling of all correspondence and communications with the colonies, provision of liaison for the colonies with the entire apparatus of the British government, preparation of answers to parliamentary questions, supervision of colonial commercial and financial relations with the Crown Agents or the Agents-General, and support for the evolving institutions of the Colonial Conference), the staff had numerous responsibilities that can be more briefly described. They wrote many papers for departmental use that went into the Confidential Print series.[27] Often, these papers covered specific points which required clarification and explanation as a basis for understanding the issue, for discussion, and for developing policy. The staff of the Office provided co-ordination and, often, the secretarial support for certain enterprises run on behalf of the whole government such as the Emigrants' Information Office and for certain interdepartmental committees such as the one dealing with tropical diseases. Persons from the staff participated in certain of the discussions on defence as regular members of the Inter-Departmental Committee on Military Honours, the Committee on Imperial Defence, and the committees dealing with the

West African Frontier Force and the King's African Rifles.[28] Beyond all that, the staff was involved in numerous social functions as, for example, when the premier of a colony, or some other noteworthy public figure from a colony, took the trip 'home'. In that circumstance, the staff was helpful in arranging suitable interviews, appointments, receptions, presentations, or whatever was desired and possible.

The precise form of organisation which the Office took varied in relation to the shifting roles which were assigned to it; its organisation was never static. Ommanney, in 1903, seeking an expansion of staff to support expanded responsibilities, indicated the work of the Office:

> The business of the Colonial Office is probably more varied than that of any other Department. It includes political questions, domestic, international, and fiscal; legal and constitutional questions; questions of great public works; financial questions; military, postal, and telegraph questions; questions of administration, frequently of an extremely delicate and difficult character; and, in addition, the control of a very large public service, carrying on its duties under every possible variety of climate and circumstances. ... The charge for salaries in 1873 was 29,601 1., and in 1902 it was 45,895 1., and, as already stated, the work increased in this period fourfold. In other words, an increase of 300 per cent. in the work has been attended by an increase of only 56 per cent. in the charge for salaries.[29]

To be sure, the Colonial Office had other functions, but this analysis may provide a convenient summary of the range of essential responsibilities. It was this particular milieu into which Keith entered in the autumn of 1901.

West African Department: Nigeria

When he was interviewed by Graham on that Monday morning in October, Keith learned that he was to be assigned to the West African Department. He was to fill one of the three new Second Class Clerkships which had been granted to the establishment of the Colonial Office; the other two went to the South African Department.[30] At the time Keith joined the Office, it was organised into five geographic departments: the two for parts of Africa, the North American and Australasian, the West Indian, and Eastern. These departments included all the colonies within the geographical region indicated without any differentiation of the form or level of government existing there. Most of the areas with responsible government, however, were within the North American and Australasian department. The administrative structure for each department was similar along the bureaucratic lines already indicated: one of the Assistant Under-Secretaries of State provided general supervision; one or more Principal Clerks or First Class Clerks gave more immediate direction to two to four Second Class Clerks. The actual size of the department, naturally, reflected the volume of business. In addition to the geographical departments, the Office organisation included the General Department which handled general and miscellaneous correspondence, relationships to the

Crown Agents, and the like, and the office of the Chief Clerk which, among others, handled certain military matters.[31]

When Keith was assigned there, the West African Department had become sufficiently large that, in fact, it had been subdivided into two departments: one dealt with Nigeria which consisted of three related segments, the protectorates in Northern and Southern Nigeria and the colony of Lagos; the other dealt with the rest of the region, the colonies in Gold Coast, Sierra Leone, and Gambia and, curiously enough, Malta. All these West African areas were under the direct supervision of Reginald L Antrobus, an Assistant Under-Secretary of State. One of the first men to join the staff through the new Civil Service examination route in 1877 after he completed classical studies at Oxford, he was named to his post in 1898 after service in several capacities in the Office, including a brief tour as Governor of St Helena. Clearly, he was a mature member of the staff, experienced in procedures, knowledgeable about persons, and informed on issues of policy. Keith was one of the three Second Class Clerks in the Nigerian Department, the other two being F G A Butler with four years of service and Percy H Ezechiel with three years of service. By the early part of 1902, F W Brett, a supplementary clerk transferred from the service of the Royal Niger Company, was added. Their immediate supervisors were the Chief Clerk, Sir William A Baillie-Hamilton, a Scot and a senior member of the staff, and a First Class Clerk, Charles Strachey, also an experienced officer.[32]

Work in the Nigerian Department had grown substantially in the six or seven years prior to Keith's entrance. The basin of the Niger River was one of several regions in Africa where British claims were being staked out in contest with French and German. In 1894, Frederick J D Lugard, direct from successful experience in extending British influence in East Africa and then writing a book interpreting it, undertook work on behalf of the Royal Niger Company. By 1897, Lugard's work had been sufficiently effective that Chamberlain named him HM Commissioner for the Nigerian Hinterland in which capacity, with Chamberlain's concurrence, he raised the West African Frontier Force in August 'in consequence of the political implications on the Niger'.[33] That force included about 4,500 to 5,000 men. Lugard, and subsequently a specially selected British commander, led it. Its officers were British officers seconded to that assignment. Its troops were partly British but with about three-quarters of the approved strength recruited from indigenous tribes, especially the Yorubas in the south and the Fulani from the Hausa states in the north. Initially supported by the Imperial Treasury, the force, by 1901, was supported partially by local funds out of Lagos and the Southern Protectorate. Lugard conceived that the force would provide the military means to extend and defend British claims and policy in that region; eventually, that conception led to the amalgamation of all defence forces throughout West Africa. The West African Frontier Force came under the purview of the Colonial Office as part of its responsibilities for the colonies and protectorates in West Africa. By 1900, Lugard's work led to a shift in authority when the Royal Niger Company was dissolved and the areas and functions formerly under its control were assigned to the colony and the protectorates under the

Colonial Office. These additional responsibilities supported the claim of the Colonial Office for an expansion of staff in the West African Department. Under Lugard's leadership, Nigeria, with its large population, was one area where British control was dramatically, and perhaps fatefully, extended in the closing years of Victoria's reign.[34]

Keith entered the Department when the staff were still in the process of trying to understand the implications of all these changes in Nigeria. That task was substantial. Nigeria included several forms of government both native and British, a geographical region of $\frac{1}{2}$ million square miles with widely differing landscape from humid, wet lowlands in the south to the drier uplands in the north, a large population organised into various tribal and religious groupings, and both a known and an unknown amount of natural and mineral wealth.[35] Keith's initial experience and training as a Second Class Clerk came, therefore, in a Department which handled a very wide range of materials. Nothing of significance, no important issue of policy in the complex operations in Nigeria escaped his attention since he handled half to three-quarters, or more at times, of all the files which came through that Department in the nine months that he served there.[36] Because of the recency, intricacy, and, to an extent, delicacy of the British position in Nigeria, he received thorough exposure to every aspect in the operations of the Colonial Office. In fact, the existence of the West African Frontier Force and the military operations that took place mainly in the Northern Protectorate and the Southern Protectorate provided him with experiences that he could not have gained in any other department of the Office, except the South African Department which was concerned with the conduct of the South African War.

Through his work, he learned about the ways in which the Foreign Office was related to British interests in Nigeria since every despatch that was concerned with borders in the north and west involved some relationship with the French government while those dealing with borders in the east described German activity in the Cameroons; all such reports had to be transmitted to the Foreign Office for response and direction. He acquired knowledge of Lugard's approach to the chiefs and, especially, to the Emirs of the north where, in fact, principles of British colonial rule were applied under a new name, 'indirect rule', that is, the High Commissioner supported and encouraged existing religions, laws, languages, and customs in the British protectorate so long as they did not conflict seriously with British concepts of justice and essential points of policy as, for example, British determination to stamp out the last vestiges of slave trade and to control the traffic in liquor. Thus, the High Commissioner, or a Resident, worked indirectly through existing leaders to control and govern the territory. Keith wrote the first minutes on many of the files that dealt with aspects of administration under 'indirect rule'.[37]

As well, he read despatches from Sir Ralph Moor, High Commissioner of the Southern Protectorate, and from Sir William MacGregor, Governor of Lagos. MacGregor was a Scot trained in medicine whose career in the colonial service evolved from an initial appointment as a medical officer in Fiji to successive appointments as a governor. MacGregor was naturally interested in local health issues wherever he was serving and so Keith, through reading the despatches and reports from Lagos, learned about various tropical diseases. MacGregor also believed in education and, to the extent he was able, created schools and institutes. In the fall of 1901, MacGregor opened the Lagos Institute, its purposes being 'chiefly literary, scientific, and intellectual', with an extended address from which Keith realised what Macgregor felt were advantages gained from the form of government as a crown colony and what he saw as the ultimate aim of British policy in Nigeria. Within that address, MacGregor said:

> Our form of government is that of a Crown Colony. That means that all matters of serious importance are submitted to the consideration of His Majesty's Secretary of State for Colonies, who is a member of the Imperial Cabinet. We have the advantage of having our affairs closely examined by the trained staff in the Colonies Office. ...
>
> My own personal views are that the Government of the hereditary chiefs of the country should not only be retained, but be steadily and consistently strengthened and developed. ...
>
> It is made perfectly clear by climatic and political reasons that the future development of this country must be by its own people, through its own people, and for its own people.[38]

Through reading this address and the wide range of despatches, Keith learned about the ways in which laws were made and enforced and how that process differed among the two protectorates and the crown colony to reflect the particular legal basis upon which each rested.

In addition, Keith came to understand the numerous roles that the Crown Agents played. He handled many references to their office with regard to matters such as personnel needs and payments, roofing tiles, uniforms, stamps, steamers, launches and other boats, railroad equipment and supplies, wharfs, pensions, accounts, and money order exchanges. He became thoroughly familiar with the nature of military activity, and this concerned the Crown Agents directly, for which he minuted on files that involved initial appointment of personnel, or their subsequent discharge, their payment, leaves, and pensions, the matter of discipline and the use of court martial, the assignment of temporary rank for officers serving in that area, and the actual approval of plans for expeditions and operations with great detail covering objectives, routes, transport, strength of troops, strategy, and calendar. He learned how the military operations of the West African Frontier Force were related to the War Office and drafted some of the memoranda that went there.[39]

Quite early in his work, Keith distinguished himself for the sort of thorough, detailed, informed, logical analysis he could bring to specific issues. For instance, on 28 December 1901, within his first months of work, he received a file which dealt with the suspension of officers by Moor in Southern Nigeria. The file had already been handled by others on the staff and, indeed, a return despatch had been sent to Moor on 12 December. Keith, when he reviewed the file, was not satisfied with the position taken and, in a minute addressed to Antrobus and to H Bertram Cox, Assistant Under-Secretary of State, who carried particular responsibilities for legal affairs, pointed out the inconsistencies and suggested a solution. He minuted:

> The difficulty raised by Mr Probyn having occurred to me, I consulted Mr Cox and was referred to these papers. I think I have found the reason why the OAG [Officer Administering the Government] of No Nig had dismissed or proposed to dismiss several officers rather informally. The No Nig O in C para V provides that the H Cr may subject to confirmation by the S of S, *remove* any officer appointed by him (Deputy Commissioners, Residents, Judges, & etc) & para X provides for the suspension of any officer however appointed. The *Instructions* para IX limit suspension to officers appointed under the King's authority or in his name. Therefore legally the H Cr has (a) power to remove any officer appointed by him—subject to the S of S's confirmation—and (b) power to suspend until the decision of the S of S is made known any person not so appointed. Only in case (b) is a formal procedure laid down, and so after all the H Cr was within his legal powers in dismissing officials without any proceedings. We desire, I understand, that the suspension proceedings should take place in every case. To effect this ? we might (as empowered by O in C para IV) send instructions to the H Cr that in every case when he desires to remove an official the forms prescribed in *Instructions* para IX are to be followed.
>
> At the same time, I think it should be settled whether the suspension proceedings are to apply to officers receiving less than 100£ a year (who are, I presume, all formally appointed by the H Cr). I think Mr Probyn is right in saying that P 83 of the Rules and Regulations must still legally govern this case. The P is 'The following rules, *unless* the mode of suspension is otherwise provided for by some local law, must be strictly observed in proceeding to suspend from the exercise of his office any public officer who has been appointed by virtue of a Commission or warrant from the Crown or whose emoluments exceed 100£ a year.' i.e. certain rules apply to all officers except those who have less than 100£ a year. The *Instructions* surely must be regarded as repealing any rules on this pt of the Niger Coast Protectorate.
>
> The *Instructions* para IX substitute other rules but these rules cannot apply to officers with less than 100£ a year. Our general remark in P 4 of our letter to S Nig on this paper seems to me too wide. In any case the suspension proceeding is rather too elaborate for such a case.
>
> ?Inform H Cr as above re the general application of the suspension rules, pointing out this exceptional case, & give a general authority as to S Nig to provide passages home for suspended officers, but to grant no leave (I would not send the correspondence with Mr Probyn as it is rather confusing.)
>
> ABK   28 Dec[40]

The interesting result of Keith's analysis is that both Cox and Antrobus concurred with his position. They recommended that, in order to get the same rules in Northern and Southern Nigeria, there should be legislation either by Proclamation or by instructions to the appropriate High Commissioner. In fact, that was done in the summer of 1902.

In addition to such careful analysis, Keith was early identified with another area. His concern with the practice of flogging, as it turned out, was one that he pursued throughout his time at the Colonial Office. Flogging was a form of punishment given primarily to indigenous persons in a colony or protectorate. While he would have preferred to have the practice abolished as inhumane, he regularly took a forceful position among the staff that if flogging had to exist as an approved form of punishment, then its administration absolutely must conform to the rules and regulations stipulated by the Secretary of State. In Keith's view, any administrator who allowed sentences to exceed those rules should be censured promptly and soundly. Each colony without responsible government where flogging was a permitted punishment had to send an annual return summarising the sorts of offences for which that sentence had been levied together with details of each sentence, that is, the actual number of lashes ordered. Keith's earliest minute on flogging is written with a sense of outrage and makes his position clear. It was written on the file containing the flogging return for 1901 from Southern Nigeria. On 30 June 1902, he wrote:

> I confess I am unfavourably impressed with the magnitude of some of these sentences.
> The 30 lashes must be called attention to again. S Nig. seems very slow to learn the rule.[41]

Even though he had left the Nigerian Department, he handled this same file again early the following year; he still was incensed:

> Mr Butler in his minute has overlooked our despatch No. 14 of 18 January 1901 (HC 27043/01) which I now annex. You will see that 24 & 12 for prison offences are quite clearly laid down. This despatch must have been two months and a half in the H Cr's hands before the flogging I referred to took place. Further on *8 March* the H Cr did make an Order (which would be in the hands of all officials in Old Calabar at once) prohibiting the infliction of more than 24 & 12 strokes, so that the flogging I referred to was absolutely illegal. My minute could therefore have been carried out without unfairness to Sir R Moor.
> I think it is too late to do anything now, but if any cases occur in next year's report we may remind him?[42]

Certainly, it was in this first assignment that Keith learned other aspects of the work. He mastered the various codes that were used for telegraphic communication; he was able both to encode and decode. Also, he must have had in mind the differences in time zones around the world in relation to receiving and sending of telegrams or cables since the Colonial Office functioned around the clock on a daily basis. He knew that most of the area under the jurisdiction of the Office was accessible by cable. In addition, he learned the style for formal drafting of correspondence. Much of it was essentially standard and merely involved filling in blanks on lithographed forms. But the formal style involved such elements as: the use of indirection in phrasing, for example, 'I am directed by Mr Secy Chamberlain to request you to lay before the Lords Commissioners of the Treasury'[43] or 'I have the honour to inform you that';[44] the form of numbering each paragraph after the second with a sequential arabic number; the structure in which the first paragraph essentially recapitulated the issue, document, or inquiry, for example, 'I have the honour to transmit to you for your information, with reference to your despatch No. 267';[45] the ways in which enclosures were to be identified and attached; the steps necessary for approval; and the system used by the registry to be certain that every piece of correspondence had a number which connected it to the related file, subject, and content. Keith mastered the tedious bureaucratic style expected and accepted in the Colonial Office; he used it for the rest of his life.

Unfortunately, no letter or note of Keith's survives in which he indicates how he felt about those first months of work at the Colonial Office. Likely, he was particularly interested in the issues of policy relating to Nigerian affairs especially as these provided him with the opportunity, indeed required him, to learn how the major offices of the British government functioned. He must have been intrigued with the variety, range, and significance of the material he minuted. To judge by his handling of files in the Nigerian Department, he learned his role quickly, competently, and thoroughly. Quite soon, his superiors recognised his particular value as a member of the staff and that recognition took tangible form when he was invited to transfer to another department, the North American and Australasian.

CHAPTER 4

Two Transfers: North American Department, Crown Agents, 1902–1905

Following his work on Nigerian matters, Keith was invited to transfer to the North American and Australasian Department. He did that in 1902, but his time there was equally brief for he soon had an opportunity, which he took, to leave the Colonial Office and move across Whitehall to work for the Crown Agents for the Colonies. During these three years, he completed the first formal part of his preparation in law. In addition, he carried on study and scholarship in Sanskrit. Work, studies, research, and writing were normal dimensions in his life, all carried on concurrently.

Officials in the Colonial Office who had wondered whether he could attend to his work there and also keep terms at the Inner Temple did not apprehend Keith's abilities or anticipate the ease with which he could engage in unrelated activities. How could he do so much so well? Clearly, as already indicated, he possessed an unusual mind; few persons are given that rare intellect which permits them to carry on two different intellectual tasks, equally well and simultaneously.[1] Such capacity meant that whenever he was at work, he could accomplish a great deal both on the task immediately before him and, as well, on the next task, even if it were totally different. He combined that mental gift with incisiveness; he was able to read in a way that he perceived quickly the central issue or question or point. This was as true for his reading of scholarly articles as it was for handling despatches in the Colonial Office. Together with incisiveness, he possessed unusual retention and memory. All these qualities which he received as natural gifts were reinforced through the educational programmes he pursued which put a premium on effective performance on examinations. It is no wonder that he excelled! To these mental qualities, he added abundant energy; he soon became known as a prodigious worker. He went through sets of files in the Colonial Office quickly and precisely, while writing, in varying degrees of legibility, an appropriate and helpful minute on each file. He worked at great speed. His work was helped along when he learned to use the typewriter. That happened in the first years he was at the Colonial Office when he mastered the skill sufficiently to prepare drafts for secretaries and typists to put into polished form. And, of course, he was the centre of the household so that in his time away from work he could focus his attention upon the other interests in his life.

North American and Australasian Department

In June 1902, Sir John Anderson, the Principal Clerk who headed the North American and Australasian Department, under the general supervision of Cox, proposed to Keith that he apply for the vacancy which had come into existence in the Department when Charles T Davis, one of the Second Class Clerks, was named Private Secretary to Ommanney. Keith acted upon that proposal. On 26 June 1902, he wrote a note to Antrobus from the National Liberal Club in which he restated Anderson's suggestion that he seek transfer and, also, acknowledged his indebtedness to Antrobus for help in learning the work of a junior: 'As you know, I am very much interested in our work, and fully realise the amount of trouble not only the Department but you have taken in training me.'[2] On the same day, he talked with Davis and, on his advice, sent the formal application to Strachey to go forward through appropriate channels. The next day, he wrote notes to Anderson and Antrobus, again from the National Liberal Club; in these, he followed up the formal application with a personal request that each man use his influence to support the transfer: 'Will you be so good as to use your influence to get my application sanctioned? ... I shall be very much obliged to you if you would be so good as to help in my application.'[3] Higher authorities acted favourably on his request, and he commenced work in his new assignment on 14 July 1902.[4]

That assignment brought him into close contact with Anderson, a relationship, both professional and personal, that was to continue for many years. Anderson, a Scot who took his first degree at Aberdeen University and his legal training at Gray's Inn, 'was a lovable man ... and a most efficacious and encouraging trainer in the drafting of despatches and all the other chores of a budding clerk'.[5] He had been on the staff of the Office from 1879, rising through the ranks, with service as Private Secretary to the Permanent Under-Secretary, as a member of the delegation involved with the Bering Sea Arbitration in London and Paris in 1892–3, as Secretary to the Conference of Colonial Premiers in 1897, and, at the time Keith transferred, playing that same role for the Colonial Conference which had opened at the Colonial Office on 30 June 1902. Later, Anderson would leave the Office to become Governor of the Straits Settlements from 1904 to 1911 and, at the end of that time, return to become Permanent Under-Secretary of State.[6] While Anderson provided leadership to the Department, Keith was also supervised by a First Class Clerk, initially A E Collins until his transfer to the West Indian Department and then W D Ellis. Keith shared the daily work on files with H E Dale, another Second Class Clerk, appointed in 1898,[7] with whom he became a friend, perhaps helped in that relationship since both were Balliol men and since Dale, too, had headed the Civil Service list in the year when he took the examination.[8]

Under those two superiors and with that colleague, Keith had an extraordinary opportunity to build upon the knowledge and to utilise the skills he had acquired in his initial assignment in the Nigerian Department. By contrast to that Department, the North American and Australasian Department included much greater diversity in terms of geography, population, history, and forms of government. Here, Keith had his first experience in analysing, studying, and understanding in detail the differences in governmental forms and operations through comparing crown colonies to those colonies with representative or responsible government, the latter increasingly referred to as self-governing colonies or dominions. The following colonies and territories were under the supervision of the Department:

> Canada, Newfoundland, Bermuda, Bahamas, and British Honduras, New South Wales, Victoria, South Australia, Queensland, Western Australia, Tasmania, New Zealand, Fiji, British New Guinea, Western Pacific High Commission, Cyprus, Gibraltar, and Falklands.[9]

As well, it included the Commonwealth of Australia from its creation in 1901 although the *Colonial Office List* did not incorporate that specific entry until the edition of 1906.

In addition to having responsibility for handling files from all these areas, Keith was fortunate in his new assignment to learn about the nature of certain forms of co-operation within the British Empire. Through Anderson's involvement as Secretary, Keith had access to information about the work of the Colonial Conference which continued for about six weeks until 11 August 1902.[10] The Colonial Conference, of course, was still at a primitive level as compared to developments that would occur in the subsequent decade. Then, many of the issues considered were solely the concern of the British government and, thus, had little preliminary study by the premiers of the self-governing colonies even though they were the principal participants. The documents only became available at the time and site of the Conference. Keith's transfer came at precisely the time when premiers were in London participating in the festivities of the Coronation and also in the meetings of the Conference. Keith met some of the premiers, and governors, also, as they came to the Office; and, as part of his assignment, he played a major role in minuting their correspondence to the Secretary of State. By the time the Conference concluded, it had adopted a series of resolutions. From his particular vantage point, Keith had first-hand information which allowed him to understand not only the text of the resolutions but also their intent. Among the most important were these: a decision that the Conference meet regularly, at least every four years; a role for self-governing colonies in treaty-making, both the expectation that they would be consulted when their interests were involved and that they would be permitted to adhere to such treaties when they were finally negotiated; continued financial share in support of naval defence by Australia and New Zealand; an agreement to grant preferences, in so far as possible, to British goods with the hope that Britain would somehow or other reciprocate; an understanding that government contracts should go to firms within the Empire; an agreement that shipping should be in imperial ships; and agreements dealing with equitable handling of postage, cables, and patents.[11]

That group of resolutions, especially the inability of British leaders to increase colonial support for defence,[12] indicated that relationships were changing among Britain and the more important of the self-governing colonies. Indeed, the title that the King used at his coronation on 9 August 1902, was expanded by inserting the phrase, 'British Dominions beyond the Seas'.[13] Primarily, that reflected the maturity of political development in Canada and, as well, the recent creation of a new structure of government for all of Australia. Moreover, it reflected the support that Canada, New Zealand, and the states of Australia had given to Britain, to be sure, with varying degrees of enthusiasm, in the South African War by raising troops, equipment, and funds. That support certainly deserved recognition especially as it had been interpreted as a clear demonstration of the merits and wisdom of extending responsible government to those areas, now no longer to be referred to simply as colonies, but rather as dominions. That new term gradually acquired special meaning as applying to governments more mature, more fully self-governing, more nearly equal, and more important within the British Empire than other areas at lower levels of political development. Support for Britain in her colonial war earned those dominions the right to speak about their interests and needs in the Colonial Conference in a new, more vigorous way.

Keith had to understand these changes in relationships with the subtleties in status that resulted. In the work that went through the North American and Australasian Department, he had a fine chance to get a clear view of the gradations existing among the dominions. He handled files in all areas covered by the Department during the twelve months that he served there.[14] The only files on which he did very limited work were those of British Honduras where, because of interest and expertise in the region, Dale carried primary responsibilities.

Keith's work across the whole Department added enormously to his experience and to his fund of knowledge. For instance, he had to distinguish between the sort of federal system existing in Canada and that in Australia, and the ways in which the differences affected the role and responsibility that the Colonial Office played. In Canada, the Colonial Office dealt only through the Governor-General and, then, only with matters raised by the federal government. Since Canada had led the way in establishing precedents for expanding the domain over which a self-governing colony or dominion had effective control, there was little beyond the conduct of foreign relations where the staff needed to be involved in Canadian affairs. Even there, conditions were changing as, for instance, the Governor-General often sent a despatch directly to the British ambassador in Washington, DC[15] who cared for Canadian interests related to the United States, obviously the most important country to Canada, with a copy of such a despatch going to the Colonial Office. In Canada, the Lieutenant-Governors of the provinces were appointed by the federal government so there was no role for the Colonial Office below the federal level. Materials that came to the Colonial Office from the provinces, and these were transmitted by the Governor-General, included copies of statutes and of decisions by the law courts, primarily. Thus, while the Colonial Office received information from Canada regularly, little of it required decision or substantive response. The staff had great confidence in Canada, in part, because Sir Wilfred Laurier, the gifted Prime Minister at the time and the first French-speaking person to hold that office, had supported the imperial cause in the South African War and, in spite of serious internal dissension especially in Quebec, ultimately had seen Canadian troops involved. As the Prime Minister of the premier dominion, he was something of a 'hero' to the staff of the Colonial Office.

By contrast to Canada, Australia had a very different federal structure. In the constitutional conferences when the Commonwealth was being created between 1897 and 1900,[16] the six states were eager to be the locus of reserved powers and were especially anxious not to lose any of their prerogatives and powers other than those expressly granted to the federal system. Continuity with past practice in the states was ensured, in part, by each of them continuing to receive a governor appointed by the Crown without any part in that process being played by the new office of Governor-General. Moreover, each state retained direct and separate access to the Colonial Office through the Governor without any role for the Governor-General. This arrangement, so different from that in Canada, resulted in the staff of the Colonial Office having to deal, at least during Keith's year in the Department, virtually with seven Australias: each of the six states plus the Commonwealth.[17] And, of course, the experience of the staff in working with the states was of much longer standing than that of dealing with the Commonwealth. The staff faced some problems because successive governors-general, starting with the second, Lord Tennyson,[18] felt that they really should be in a position superior to that of the governors in the states in more than just the table of precedence for social, military, and public occasions; they wanted all communications to and from the Colonial Office to pass only through their hands and be subject to their review and judgement as well and also that of their ministers in the federal cabinet. Often, in this set of circumstances, the Colonial Office was forced to play an unwanted role as mediator and interpreter. The 'Vondel' case during 1902–3 is illustrative of such a role.[19] This case involved a Dutch ship that put into the waters of South Australia where authorities refused to arrest the crew on behalf of the owners who then appealed to the Colonial Office. The Secretary of State put the issue to the Governor-General who, through his ministers, required a report from South Australia which refused to give it on grounds that the federal government lacked jurisdiction. The staff of the Colonial Office, therefore, had to prepare a memorandum to South Australia setting out their interpretation of the intent of the Commonwealth constitution as giving the federal government jurisdiction in all matters of external policy over which there could be but one Department of External Affairs. The despatch prepared by Anderson and sent by Chamberlain under the date of 15 April 1903, stated, among other points, the way in which the Crown functioned in relation to each level of government:

> The Crown undoubtedly remains part of the constitution of the State of South Australia, and in matters affecting it in that capacity, the proper channel of communication is between the Secretary of State and the State Governor. But in matters affecting the Crown in its capacity as the central authority of the

Empire, the Secretary of State can, since the people of Australia have become one political community, look only to the Governor-General as the representative of the Crown in that community.[20]

For the states of Victoria and New South Wales, matters were equally complex since the government of Victoria had vacated its parliament buildings and its Governor's mansion in Melbourne to make them available to the Commonwealth and the Governor-General thus creating a situation where state and federal government were in the same city; the government of New South Wales had a claim that, for a certain portion of each year, the Governor-General would conduct his business from Sydney with the result that, again, head of a state and that of the Commonwealth functioned from the same city. Beyond these circumstances, it should be noted that the governments of the states and of the Commonwealth tended to be penurious in financial and other support for their governors, perhaps simply to keep such matters under regular negotiation or perhaps as a reflection of the existence of republican sentiments in certain sectors of the Australian political spectrum.[21]

In addition to learning the differences in federal structure between Canada and Australia, Keith expanded his knowledge through responsibility for the very special concerns of Cyprus. He wrote the initial minute and prepared the subsequent drafts on virtually every file related to that island.[22] To look at his work there in summary fashion may indicate the depth of materials he had to master.[23] British rule in Cyprus resulted from Anglo-Turkish relations in the third quarter of the nineteenth century where British policy was aimed at helping the Ottoman Turks resist Russian expansion through the Straits and into the Mediterranean. As part of the settlement following Turkish defeat by the Russians in 1877, the Sultan agreed, by the Convention of Constantinople of 1878, that Britain would hold and govern Cyprus under certain conditions: that Muslims, about one-fourth of the island's population, would have their rights protected, including law and schools; that Britain would pay Turkey the excess of revenue over expenditure which, in 1879, was fixed at £5,000 per annum with other revenues held to offset British claims against Turkey; and that, when Russia returned Batoum and Kars, Britain would leave Cyprus. Its government, created by an Order-in-Council of 14 September 1878 and subsequently modified, called for a legislative council of eighteen members, six non-elective or official and twelve elective, with these latter distributed so that Muslims would elect three and non-Muslims would elect nine. At the time Keith worked on these files, it was clear that British rule rested rather uneasily on the island which, even then, was torn by the tenuous relationships among Greeks, Turks, and Cypriots; whatever Britain did for one group was seen by the others disadvantageously. The Archbishop of Cyprus, by virtue of his office, had certain power but, when a vacancy occurred in 1903, the election had to be postponed several times, so it was claimed, in the interests of public order.[24] Specifically, Keith dealt with such issues as keeping the Foreign Office, the Crown Agents, the Treasury, and the Auditors fully informed about related matters; reviewing and judging the administrative adequacy, or inadequacy, of Haynes Smith, the

High Commissioner, who headed the government of Cyprus; examining and interpreting economic reports and requests especially that arose out of a year of bad harvest and drought; and facilitating necessary public works projects on railroads, a general office, building, and harbour improvements at Famagusta. It is interesting to note that, in connection with this last project, Keith expressed great concern that care be taken to preserve any remains of ancient civilisations that might still exist or that might be found in the process of excavation: the classicist in a position to safeguard antiquities![25] In regard to one death sentence that had been referred to the Colonial Office by the High Commissioner, Keith showed the precision of his mind and the emerging use of his legal training. He was clear about what to him would be the injustice of following the High Commissioner's decision:

> I have carefully looked through the evidence submitted. It is entirely circumstantial and without the statement by the prisoners would be of little weight. But in connection with the statements, although the detail is not trustworthy, the evidence appears conclusive that these men murdered Achillea. That there was any difference in their degree of guilt I do not see and I do not agree with the HCr's views as to the advisability of commuting Kiamil's sentence if the other man is hanged.
>
> On the general ground of not trusting too much mere circumstantial evidence? advise the HCr to commute both sentences.[26]

For that particular line of argument, Keith had no support and his superiors directed him to draft a telegram that the Colonial Office saw 'no reason to interfere with the sentence of the court'.[27] Near the time that he was leaving the Department, in July 1903, Keith provided testimony for the Colonial Office in support of the Cyprus Vote in Aid in the Civil Service Appropriation Accounts.[28] In that, he answered questions about the revenue of Cyprus, the recent drought and its effect on revenue, and the nature of the Turkish Tribute. Clearly, in all ways, he was the Department's spokesman in matters related to Cyprus.

With that illustration of the sort of detail Keith had to master, it is possible simply to say that he mastered in similar depth the particulars of the affairs of Gibraltar, the Bahamas, Bermuda, the Falklands, New Zealand, and the islands of the Pacific. There is little doubt that Anderson was glad that he had initiated Keith's move to that Department.

Even as Keith was working full-time at his various assignments in the North American and Australasian Department, he brought to completion another catalogue of materials. Obviously, he continued his life as an active Sanskrit scholar. It is some indication of the way in which he used his time efficiently that he was able to journey to Oxford and undertake the task of going through materials in the Indian Institute Library. He must have taken some of his holidays to find the necessary time to go through that collection. Macdonell and others had been pleased with the work that Keith did on the manuscripts in the Bodleian library and so supported him in his analysis and listing of more manuscripts. Those who prepare catalogues undertake work essential for other scholars. In 1903, Clarendon Press published Keith's next significant contribution in Oriental studies: *Catalogue of Sanskrit and Prakrit MSS in the Indian Institute Library, Oxford.* That work was useful, and still is, for persons wishing to find their way into that specific collection of manuscripts.

To complete the picture of his year of work in that Department in relation to his growth in understanding the ways in which the constitution of the British Empire functioned, it is important to consider three additional aspects: his personal correspondence with colonial officials, his special interest in certain issues and themes that went beyond the concern of one colony, and his work in conjunction with the Alaska Boundary Commission.

It is likely that Keith corresponded unofficially with several officers and governors in the various colonies during that year. The only letters that are available to illustrate the nature of such correspondence during 1902–3 are those from Eyre Hutson, at that time in Bermuda as Colonial Secretary, the position immediately below the governor.[29] It is worthwhile noting their content and nature because they indicate the sort of letters Keith received and, obviously, sent not only in that particular year but also in his later assignments in the Office. Hutson's letters were usually marked 'Private'. Those which remain are the ones which Keith kept with his personal papers. What the letters represent is a route by which an officer or a governor could get his ideas and concerns before the person in the Office initially handling the files for the colony, could raise questions about points or decisions that either had occurred in the past or were likely to arise in the future, and could elicit a response from a person on the staff knowledgeable about the affairs of the colony, about the larger concerns of the Colonial Office, and about related policies of HM Government. The governor or officer would not need to share such an unofficial response with anyone but, rather, could simply make use of the information in an appropriate manner. Officials and governors saw this route of sharing and receiving information as advantageous. But this route was of assistance, as well, to a staff person like Keith. From such informal, unofficial, personal letters he could learn more, and in greater detail, about the problems in the operation of the particular government as well as about the concerns of the writer, information and views which would not properly belong in any formal despatches. A comment of Hutson makes clear the purpose of such correspondence:

> I am much obliged to you for your kind letters & I apologise for the trouble I have given you. At the same time, it is enormous assistance to me to be able to get information direct from the Col office in little matters which are hardly worthy of forming the subject matter of a despatch.[30]

In that same letter, Hutson reported that he had attended to another matter of concern to the Colonial Office, and especially to Keith, by sending copies of the Official Gazette. Hutson continued, as well, to provide explanatory comment on the last Confidential despatch from Bermuda: 'I trust that Sir John Anderson will not consider the Conf despatch by last mail on the subject of the Powder Fund too revolutionary! The policy advocated is not an original one, although so far as I know a new one here.'[31] In subsequent letters, Hutson and Keith exchanged ideas about the Powder Fund and its use. Hutson repeatedly thanked Keith for his letters, advice, and help. Such exchanges were a part of the way in which staff of the Colonial Office worked and, while they naturally did not share all these personal letters, Keith made no secret about the fact that he was writing to Hutson. For example, on 23 April 1903, Keith annexed to a numbered despatch in the Colonial Office files a copy of a private letter he sent to Hutson advising him to be certain that the government of Bermuda proceeded cautiously on the scheme for the improvement of St George's Channel[32] and, especially, to be careful to keep confidential the cost estimates made by engineers sent out by the Crown Agents, at least until tenders could be received. Quite obviously, Keith used the informal route to send supplementary advice to a key official in a colony.

Through such correspondence and, of course, through work on the wide range of files in the Department, Keith kept himself informed about certain general colonial issues, developments, and policies in which he was interested or for which he was assigned responsibility.[33] These included, for example, Keith's monitoring of the request made by the Colonial Office in a circular despatch of 21 August 1902 that all colonies establish a branch of the Society of Comparative Legislation.[34] That Society with its headquarters in London had been created to provide a forum for consideration of law on a comparative basis, primarily with regard to its origins and development. In addition, the Society was increasingly interested in the legal implications and comparisons in the situation which frequently arose at that time when one of the great powers transferred jurisdiction over a given territory to another power, or simply acquired jurisdiction by annexation, with the result that quite different legal systems came into conflict or, at least, into some form of concurrent standing. Since the British Empire represented the largest and most complex political structure in the world, it is not surprising that the Society had close links with the Colonial Office and looked to it for help in collecting materials that could be studied. The Society published a journal which started in 1896–7 and, after a brief hiatus, resumed continuously from 1899.[35] It is important to observe Keith in his regular role in the Department in 1902–3 urging colonies to find ways to create branches of the Society in accordance with the circular despatch because he soon became seriously interested in the legal problems involved in successive rule over territories. Further, starting in 1908, Keith contributed an article or briefer comment on some constitutional point to almost every subsequent issue of the *Journal of Comparative Legislation* until 1943.[36] This is but one illustration of the ways in which he was led through his professional responsibilities in the Office into more substantial scholarship.

Three additional subjects of general concern which Keith studied through his work in that Department were the Pacific Cable, imperial defence, and merchant shipping. The completion of the Pacific Cable in October 1902, represented the achievement of a goal which the colonies in the Pacific had identified and argued for as early as the Ottawa Conference of 1894. Several colonies sent messages of appreciation in 1902; one will illustrate the spirit: 'a new and important means of communication with all parts of the British Empire.'[37] Keith minuted these despatches and so knew how officials especially those in Canada, Australia, New Zealand, and Fiji felt about the importance of the cable. Practically, the cable meant that the Colonial Office, and other offices of the British government as well, now had several possible routes by which messages could be transmitted rapidly throughout the Empire. In a parallel development, a cable linking South Africa to Australia had been completed in 1901 across the Indian Ocean from Durban to Perth and, then, extended to Adelaide in 1902. Thus, messages from London could travel to Australia and other places in the East by way of cable through the Red Sea and India route laid earlier, or around the African coast and across the Indian Ocean as well as, now, by way of the Atlantic, Canada, and the Pacific. All these developments meant that the staff of the Colonial Office could receive and send messages to most of the major parts of the Empire in order to deal with issues that required immediate response. This made an enormous difference to New Zealand or Fiji, for example, where the usual route of a despatch going by ship could take six to eight weeks to move in one direction. By the time the staff of the Colonial Office, or the colony, reviewed the content, prepared a response, and sent it, three to four months could easily elapse. Cable meant the likelihood of a message being received in London within hours after the time it was sent and, depending on the time of day it arrived, the staff could return a response within twenty-four to forty-eight hours. Generally, cable, in part because of cost, was used only for those issues where a governor needed immediate response in relation to some urgent decision or problem. For any sort of detailed analysis or explanation about affairs in the colony, the governor still used despatches. The same principles guided the staff in London. Codes were developed and regularly changed to provide security in the content of messages. Keith saw these changes in communication and accepted them as providing new ties for Empire. He drafted a response to New Zealand on those lines: 'HM Govt deeply appreciate congratulations on completion of cable which forms new bond of union between England and dominions overseas.'[38]

At the same time, Keith was fully aware that the British government had hoped the colonies would be more interested in another form of bond, namely more extensive participation in imperial defence. That had been one of the subjects discussed at the Colonial Conference of 1902 but, in an unanticipated result, the colonies which supported the South African War gained some greater sense of independence even while serving that imperial cause. That view comes through most clearly in reports and despatches dealing with Canadian defence. Australia and New Zealand still looked to the imperial navy as their first line of defence and were willing to make modest contributions to support it. Yet, even there, Australian nationalism was beginning to emerge and to insist on greater Australian controls. Keith also learned about the strategic role of Gibraltar in defence schemes. He saw, as well, the immediate questions that resulted from the end of the South African War where Canada and Australia, especially, raised the matters of payments, property, medals, and the like and where, specifically, Bermuda sought direction about the disposition of prisoners of war located there. Together with the Pacific Cable, defence concerns provided some sort of bond for the Empire.

So also did the fact that British merchant shipping was dominant in the world. In 1902–3, British ships represented just over half of the world's total tonnage. Keith knew about discussions related to shipping at the Colonial Conference of 1902. Issues of merchant shipping involved the entire Empire and revolved around questions such as whether the British government should provide some subsidy for maintaining superiority, whether harbours needed to be deepened in various ports throughout the Empire to accommodate the larger ships then being constructed, whether colonial shipping should be related to domestic and, if so, on what basis, whether imperial statutes on merchant shipping were appropriately applicable to the self-governing dominions, and whether Britain and the Empire should apply restrictions to coasting trade conducted by vessels of non-British registry, and if so, what they should be. In the Department, Keith had his introduction to these complicated questions, related to a subject which only a few years later he would master and interpret through published articles.

One other issue about which Keith continued his interest was flogging. His initial concerns with flogging in the Nigerian Department have been discussed already.[39] In this new assignment, he had access to a wider range of reports on the subject because there were so many more governments under the North American and Australasian Department. In almost every instance, he minuted the file with the annual, or other, reports on flogging. He held staunchly to the views on the issue which he had developed through his earlier experience. Thus, he strongly supported the decision of the Department, the heads of the Office, and the Secretary of State to develop a model ordinance on the subject which would specify precise conditions, terms, restrictions, and procedures about the matter. Under Chamberlain's name, this model ordinance went out on 13 August 1902, in a circular despatch to every colony without responsible government with the Secretary's strong direction that, whatever the particular form of government, the governor seek its enactment in the colony.[40] It is worthwhile noting that this policy was one of the very few where the Colonial Office tried to establish uniformity of law and practice. Keith monitored the response of the colonies to that despatch and identified those circumstances where some adaptation of the model might be necessary and permissible. In minuting the file on the model ordinance, Chamberlain directed that materials on the general issue be prepared for him to use in debate, if necessary. What he wanted, he wrote, was 'a summary of my actions in regard to Flogging since I have been in office & the result'.[41] The assignment to prepare that report travelled down the bureaucratic pyramid and ended in Keith's hands. He undertook a careful study of all related files and papers from every section in the Office. He assembled and organised available data on the incidence of the penalty, on the degrees of severity permitted, and on the current legal status. He prepared these data and the report under four heads: 1   Whippings for prison offences; 2   Whippings for serious crimes by order of the Courts; 3   Whippings for praedial larceny under special laws; 4   Whippings of children. In the opening paragraph, he summarised Chamberlain's intent with regard to the issue: 'to give clear expression of his views on the subject, to endeavour to set limits to the practice, and to fix the responsibility in the event of these limits being transgressed.'[42] Further, he reviewed the positions Chamberlain took on the issue in his initial despatch of 1897, in subsequent correspondence, and in the circular despatch of 1902. Keith prepared all of this in a memorandum, the first of several he did on various subjects that became part of the series of papers in Confidential Print. He completed the report on 31 December 1902.[43] He knew there was no place in such a formal report for personal views but he did note, as an argument in one of the opening paragraphs, that Chamberlain had some 'common sense reasons' for permitting the practice to continue such as lack of adequate gaols, equipment, officers, and the like. Through preparation of this report, Keith not only knew precisely the situation with regard to flogging in every part of the Empire under the Colonial Office but also he learned about the ways in which the government functioned in each of those colonies without responsible government.

In the process of monitoring responses to the circular despatch, Keith, in July 1903, became involved in a substantive debate over the unwillingness of the Bahamas to enact the model ordinance. The Assembly there flatly rejected it. The problem was complicated by the facts that in the Bahamas no limits existed to flogging and, furthermore, that women could be subjected to the sentence. Keith argued that, in view of the recalcitrance of the Assembly, the governor ought to use his prerogative of mercy to see that each sentence given would be adjusted to conform to the conditions of the model ordinance; further, he argued that the governor ought to be instructed to direct the prison warden to observe applicable rules.[44] None of his superiors supported Keith's suggested solution to the problem. J S Risley, Legal Assistant in the Office, rejected it as being a form of de facto legislation. Chamberlain was disturbed about the issue. While he did not override others in the Office, he did, on 23 July, direct that a strong despatch be prepared exhorting the governor to press the Assembly to enact the model ordinance by 'giving general reasons against unlimited power of flogging—pointing out changes accepted by all other British colonies'.[45] Further, Chamberlain wanted the governor to know 'that flogging of women is repudiated by civilised nations'.[46] Not satisfied with that solution, Keith, some days later resumed his argument and restated his position succinctly in a minute. In that, he reasoned in a logical manner that the Secretary of State could instruct a governor to exercise prerogative of mercy and that it would be constitutional to do that:

> 2   Pardon *is* an executive act. H.M. has full power to remit any sentence or any part and he can & usually does delegate his powers to the Governor, and H.M. can issue any instructions to the Governor through the S. of S., who of course is H.M. for these purposes in the Colonies. I cannot therefore see anything constitutionally objectionable in the S. of S. determining that the Prerogative should be used in a certain way. He has full control over the executive acts of a Gov, & why not over this one?[47]

He ended his minute by pointing out the inconsistency of the position in the Colonial Office where instructions had gone to the governor of Barbados along those lines. Why not send, he pointed out, similar instructions to the Bahamas? But Keith did not prevail in the debate and none of his superiors accepted his points. He suggested several ways to get a bad situation under direct control. He felt deeply and passionately about the abuses of flogging.

In addition to work on the issue of flogging and to handling several matters that involved more than one colony, Keith became very knowledgeable about affairs in North America where both Canada and Newfoundland were concerned about relations with the United States. While the staff of the Colonial Office felt Canadian interests the more important, still those of Newfoundland had to be considered. Quite a separate colony, Newfoundland occupied a distinct place as the most significant base ideally situated for the North Atlantic fisheries and as the oldest territory within the British Empire, a claim based on John Cabot's expedition of 1497. In addition to the main island, it included the Labrador coast. Moving from government under a naval officer to the grant of responsible government in 1855, the colony became self-governing but always was handicapped in its development by its insular location, its lack of resources other than timber, its small, scattered population, and its dependence on fishing. In form, it certainly possessed full responsible self-government but, because of its particular circumstances, it always seemed somewhat anomalous and exceptional as a dominion in the councils of Empire. Keith handled files from Canada and Newfoundland and learned about a series of disputes over boundaries, fishing, and trade, disputes often with several sides as they arose from successive changes of rule in North America from the sixteenth century and, particularly, from treaties that Britain made in the eighteenth century after a series of wars. Keith saw the interplay of differing interests in those disputes whether between Canada and the United States or between Newfoundland and the United States or between Canada and Newfoundland. Since Britain still carried responsibility for the conduct of foreign relations, the Foreign Office and the British ambassador in Washington were the channels through which the staff of the Colonial Office had to route the concerns of Canada and Newfoundland. Yet, the proximity of those dominions to the United States often led to direct, informal relations. Since Canada and Newfoundland were themselves in conflict over many points, some of the disputes took on an intra-mural dimension, as well. Keith was in a position to experience the North Atlantic Triangle, the reality, later named and analysed by J B Brebner,[48] that the primary concerns in relations between two of the areas, such as Canada and the United States, could only be understood adequately by reference to the third, that is, to Britain. Any two points of the triangle inevitably involved the third. The emerging power of the United States in the first decade of the twentieth century led Britain to seek resolution of many differences that were long-standing, any one of which involved either Canada or Newfoundland, and sometimes both.

The dispute over the Alaska boundary was one of those old issues that Britain and the United States finally agreed to settle; clearly, the issue was more important to Canada than to Britain. Keith played a role as the clerk

who was assigned specific responsibility for following all related correspondence, for preparing drafts of materials to the Foreign Office and to
Canada, and for undertaking research on specific points that the British
commissioners in the matter needed to have clarified. The issue of the Alaska
boundary had been unresolved, at least, from the time of Canadian Con-
federation in 1867 and from the Russian transfer of Alaska to the United States
in that same year. By that purchase, the United States acquired possession of
Russian rights contained in the Treaty of 1825 where Britain and Russia
settled conflicting claims in the Pacific Northwest and agreed on a definition
of the boundary. While Britain and the United States agreed to resolve some
disputes through establishing an Anglo-American Joint Commission in 1898,
the Alaska boundary was not included in the list of items to be considered.[49]
Subsequent British efforts to add it were unsuccessful. The issue became more
important as the implications of the discovery of gold in the Klondike in 1896
became apparent; Canada wanted assured access to the goldfields from the
coast. Since the attempt to refer the matter to the existing bi-lateral commission failed, Britain, in the autumn of 1902, proposed reopening the matter
for arbitration. Between mid October and 25 January 1903, when a treaty
was signed between the two principal countries agreeing to a procedure to
resolve the matter, triangular negotiations occurred to define the terms of
reference for the issue and to settle the composition of the commission that
would deliberate.[50] The United States adamantly refused to accept arbitration
which would have involved impartial, international jurists. What Britain and
the United States finally agreed to was a commission to be comprised of 'six
impartial jurists of repute', three appointed by each of the principal parties to
the dispute. Further, they agreed upon the wording of seven questions as
constituting the terms of reference for the commission.

In the development of the treaty, Keith followed successive expressions of
concern from Canada that its interests were not getting sufficiently serious
attention at the Foreign Office. The actual negotiations, in this instance, took
place in Washington between the British ambassador, on behalf of the British
government and, of course, Canada, and representatives of the United States
government. The route for messages and concerns from Canada to be considered in those negotiations was, at best, indirect, if not simply cumbersome.
A minute or memorandum from Laurier or the Canadian Privy Council
travelled through the hands of the Governor-General, Lord Minto, to the
Colonial Office where either it or its substance was sent along to the Foreign
Office which, in turn, transmitted the information that was appropriate in
the view of that staff to the British ambassador who conveyed it to the
representatives of the United States; the same route, in both directions, was
followed as each step of negotiations took place in Washington. Regularly,
the Canadian government felt its views were not adequately represented and
were uncertain as to whether that was the fault of the Colonial Office, the
Foreign Office, or the ambassador in Washington. Almost to the end, Laurier
urged that there be independent jurists on the commission; however, the
position of the United States precluded that option.[51] Further, Laurier kept
suggesting ways to modify phrases in the proposed terms of reference to

ensure the best possible definition of the Canadian position. Reluctantly, however, Laurier accepted the lead of the British government in shaping the treaty, in part, because he did not have full support of his cabinet for the probable alternative, that is, breaking off negotiations. When Laurier learned of the men appointed by the United States, he was appalled: Elihu Root, Secretary of War; Henry Cabot Lodge, Senator from Massachusetts; and George Turner, Senator from Washington. None was a jurist, one was a member of the President's cabinet, and each, prior to his appointment, had stated positions in full support of the claims of the United States. There was no likelihood of impartial review. Laurier felt that Canadian good faith had been violated, but, that so long as the British government, after hearing of the appointees, did not break off the process, he had no alternative but to participate in it. Keith was sympathetic to Canadian views as were others in the Colonial Office. For example, Anderson minuted that the Foreign Office had not been sufficiently sensitive to Canada: 'The whole thing has been badly conducted all through. Too much haste and too little consideration for the feelings and wishes of Canada.'[52] After numerous exchanges between Canada and Britain, British members of the commission were appointed: Lord Alverstone, Lord Chief Justice of England; Sir Louis Jette, KC, Lieutenant-Governor of Quebec; and the Hon John Douglas Amour, a Judge on the Supreme Court of Canada, later replaced by A B Aylesworth, KC, of Toronto. In contrast to the members appointed by the United States, these commissioners were obviously legal experts.

The treaty provided for three segments to the work of the commission. In the initial stage, from 3 March to 2 May 1903, the case for the British-Canadian position would be prepared for presentation. The next two months were allocated for the statement of the counter-case by the United States while a further two months after that were to be given to arguments so that, presumably, a decision could be reached in September. The final stage would be held in London. The British-Canadian case was presented within that time schedule with appropriate support from the Colonial Office. Keith assisted as necessary in all stages.[53] He undertook research on four essential points: a map of 1827 that gave details of the boundary under the Treaty of 1825, certain Russian documents related to that Treaty, reports of the governor of Alaska during the nineteenth century, and specifics about the canal at St Clair Flats. For this research, he went to the various departments of the British Museum. He found the appropriate documents, including a copy of that early map. He studied materials carefully and, for each topic, prepared a report setting out details. He undertook translations of materials from Russian and French. His work was of importance and use to the commission. He received several notes of thanks and congratulations for his assistance:

Before leaving for Canada, the Honourable Clifford Sifton, British Agent for the Alaska Boundary Commission, asked me to convey to you his sincere thanks for the excellent and efficient service you rendered to the British side of the boundary dispute, in your examination of the reports of successive Governors of Alaska, and in many other matters. Since Mr Sifton's departure, I have been so busily engaged that I have not been able to communicate with you. I only hope you will overlook this, and that you will allow me the liberty of adding my thanks to those of Mr Sifton.[54]

I am most awfully obliged to you for all the trouble you have taken on my behalf as regards the Russian translating work. I hope that your services to the Alaska Boundary Commission will receive a becoming recognition too![55]

I have been so pressed during the last few days that I have not had a moment in which to acknowledge receipt of your note *re* the St Clair Flats—Let me do so now, and thank you for the information contained therein.[56]

The last of these notes was from Joseph Pope who was to become the chief person in the evolution of the Canadian Department of External Affairs, initially within the office of the Prime Minister and eventually becoming a separate department of state. Keith knew Pope; they corresponded from time to time so that the contact which Keith made in the summer of 1903 provided him with a correspondent to keep him informed about developments in the Canadian government.

For Keith and his superiors, to say nothing of Laurier and the Canadian government, the decision given by the boundary commission on 20 October 1903, was a bitter disappointment. Lord Alverstone agreed with the commissioners of the United States in support of their claims for the boundary; the two Canadian commissioners were so angered that they refused to sign the decision. Laurier, and others as well, felt that Canadian interests had been sacrificed in a political decision where the Foreign Office was more anxious to placate the United States than to defend Canada's interests. Laurier demanded publication of all related correspondence to show that Canada had protested the qualifications of those commissioners named by the United States while Britain had not lodged any formal protest. In an impassioned speech in the Canadian House of Commons, Laurier expressed his irritation at the way Canadian foreign relations had to be conducted:

> I have often regretted that we have not in our own hands the treaty-making power, which would enable us to dispose of our own affairs. But in this matter we are dealing with a position that was forced upon us—we have not the treaty-making power ... we have no such power, our hands are tied to a large extent owing to the fact of our connection—which has its benefits, but which has also its disadvantages—the fact of our connection with the Mother Country making us not free agents, and obliging us to deal with questions affecting ourselves through the instrumentality of the British Ambassador.[58]

Lord Alverstone's letter to Laurier, and the later publication of a formal statement reviewing the legal points in his decision to support the position of the United States, provided some help in assuaging Laurier's feelings. In addition, the calm, good sense of Aylesworth in accepting the decision for what it was worth helped ease the tension in Canada. Keith's direct connection with the entire process, even though he transferred to the Crown Agents in mid July, led him to anticipate that Canada would be seeking more direct, definitive, and effective control over its relations with the United States, in short, that Canada would be seeking a further extension of the meaning of responsible government to include control over external affairs.

Secretary to the Crown Agents for the Colonies

While his interest in the growth of responsible government continued, Keith, in fact, made a move that took him away from the direct work of the Colonial Office. In an unusual action, he broke his time for building seniority there and, as well, his appointment under the provisions of the Civil Service Commission in order to take up a newly created post, Secretary to the Crown Agents for the Colonies. He held that for nearly two years, from 20 July 1903 until 30 April 1905.

In the spring of 1903, the Crown Agents concluded that, since the pressure of their business had grown to such an extent, they had to create a new position which would have considerable responsibility and which would come immediately under the Crown Agents themselves. Sir Ernest E Blake, the senior Crown Agent, explained in a letter to Chamberlain on 9 May; his memorandum also provides a clear picture of the existing mode of operation and of the ways in which that would be changed with the addition of a Secretary.

> I have the honour to state that owing to the very great increase in our work we find it necessary to apply for the Secretary of State's authority for making a change in the organisation of this office.
>
> 2   Up to the present time all correspondence and tenders have been opened in the room of one or other of the Crown Agents and have not been passed out to the Office until they have been seen by a Crown Agent and have had his initial placed upon them and we consider it essential that this or some similar system should be maintained with the view of securing that all complaints or representations as to the conduct of our business reach us and that there shall be no possibility of tenders being tampered with. Similarly all letters and orders and cheques emanating from the office have been signed by one or other of the Crown Agents.
>
> 3   The result of this system has been to keep a very thorough control by the Crown Agents over their business but it has imposed upon us personally an enormous amount of detail labour and the business of the agency has now reached such dimensions that we find it difficult to give to the larger and more important questions with which we have to deal the time and attention which they require.
>
> 4   In the circumstances it has become absolutely necessary that some change should be made in the existing business and we have considered whether we could safely delegate any of our duties to any of the members of our staff. The only suitable officer is our Chief Clerk and Accountant, but he is already so fully engaged with his own proper duties that such an arrangement is out of the question.
>
> 5   We have therefore arrived at the conclusion that the best way of meeting

our present difficulties would be by the appointment of a Secretary to the Crown Agents to whom we could delegate the supervision of the opening of letters and tenders and their distribution to the office, the conduct of the minor routine correspondence of the office, and the signing of cheques up to a specified amount and any other suitable duties which we find that we can entrust to him.[59]

F R Round, Principal Clerk in the General Department, minuted this letter and noted that there had been no increase in the establishment of the Crown Agents since 1898, that their work had indeed increased, and that the position should be authorised.[60] Ommanney supported that minute and went on to point out that the Crown Agents should appoint the person who, in their judgement, would best serve their needs since their Secretary:

> must occupy a most confidential position, will write in their name and sign for them and will have the power of signing cheques up to a certain amount. These powers have never been delegated by the C.A. to anyone and I think it is the last appointment in regard to which their power of nomination should be controlled.[61]

When Blake wrote his proposal, the Crown Agents had already talked with Butler about leaving the Nigerian Department to assume the position. At the last minute, however, Butler changed his mind and rejected the offer. Apparently, after he weighed his options and prospects for advancement from his present post and noted that he was high in seniority among Second Class Clerks, he concluded that he would do better to remain where he was. The Crown Agents then turned to Keith, quite junior to Butler, and talked with him. Blake made Keith the same offer as the one proposed to Butler: important, non-trivial duties in the position of Secretary, advantageous financial terms with a starting salary of £500 rising to a maximum of £1,000 in due course, and approximately the same terms of vacation, sick leave, and pension as those provided under the Civil Service Commission.[62] At that time, the other Crown Agents were Major Maurice Cameron, an engineer appointed in 1895, and William H Mercer, formerly on the staff of the Colonial Office who, in 1900, replaced Ommanney when he left to become Permanent Under-Secretary of State.[63] Keith considered that offer carefully and reflected on the time it might take for him to secure any significant advancement in the Colonial Office. He talked with Mercer about the offer at some length. Clearly, Mercer was anxious for him to make the move and even corresponded with Keith's mother about the potential advantages. In a letter to MSK, Mercer acknowledged that the work might not be as interesting for a young man as that in the Colonial Office but that the advantages 'are very solid and increase as time goes on'.[64] He urged that she encourage Keith to make the move especially with the prospect of great advancement in the long run: 'As his friend, I shall advise you and him to take this view.'[65]

Keith did take that view and made the move. What were the reasons for his decision? He left no memorandum summing up his reasons but these seem likely, on the basis of what evidence exists. The position offered a substantial

Sir Ernest Blake. Courtesy of the
Crown Agents.

Major Maurice Cameron, by Walter
Stoneman. Courtesy of the National
Portrait Gallery.

Sir William H Mercer, by Walter Stoneman.
Courtesy of the National Portrait Gallery.

7   The Crown Agents, 1903–5.

increase in salary. Keith started as Secretary at the rate of £500, more than twice what he was then earning as a Second Class Clerk where his salary in two years had risen only slightly above the starting amount of £200. For a twenty-four-year-old man with a household to support, that move accomplished in a week what it might have taken him a decade to achieve in his former post. But it was not salary alone that attracted him. As Blake described the position in writing and talked about it and as Mercer discussed what the Crown Agents hoped the Secretary might do, Keith came to understand and to believe that he would have the opportunity to hold a post of primary importance and power. He expected that he would be but one step below the Crown Agents themselves in the hierarchy of that office, in effect, a *de facto* junior Crown Agent. He felt the position would give him a fine opportunity to apply his demonstrated abilities for efficient, effective work to a post where he would be able to exercise a wide degree of independent judgement through authority delegated directly to him from only one echelon higher. In view of his brief experience near the bottom of the bureaucratic pyramid in the Colonial Office, he must have found the chance to move almost to the top in a related office very attractive. Still quite young, he was ambitious and eager to use his many talents in a position that appeared to offer greater scope than where he was. As well, he was attracted to the expectation that Mercer held out for the future; Keith understood that to mean the virtual certainty that he would be appointed a Crown Agent. He would be in line for such a vacancy which might occur in either of two ways. A fourth position of Crown Agent might be created, a not unlikely possibility in terms of the very considerable increase in business handled, to give but one illustration, out of Lugard's work alone through extension of British control into northern Nigeria and creation of the West African Frontier Force. Or, if a new position were not created, Blake might retire in the near future since he had already served over twenty years and was seventy-five years old. The likelihood of being appointed to such a profitable position at an early age was the lure that finally caught Keith. In 1903, each Crown Agent received a salary of £2,500, at that time a princely sum. Keith anticipated that such an appointment would provide him with financial security and free him to carry on studies in his other areas of interest. For these reasons—immediate doubling of salary, a higher position with greater independence, and the possibility of becoming a Crown Agent—Keith left his work in the North American and Australasian Department and went across Whitehall.

Earlier in 1903, the Crown Agents finally vacated space they had occupied for many years in the lower levels of the Colonial Office and moved diagonally opposite to Nos 3 and 4 Whitehall Gardens. In one of its prior uses, No. 4 had been important as the home of Sir Robert Peel.[66] Located where the great Whitehall Palace once stood and set in a lovely row of terraces with gardens stretching to the Thames, the house provided, in Peel's time, a gracious residence for a man of prominence. But its ownership and use had shifted subsequently so that Peel's dining room, with signs of its former grandeur still evident, instead of providing the setting for fine meals now served the purposes of the payroll office for the Crown Agents. No. 4 was joined to No.

8   Crown Agents, Payroll Office, Whitehall Gardens. Courtesy of Crown Agents.

3 and both were remodelled to create office space. While they retained some of the architectural elegance and pleasing features from their former functions, actually they did not provide very adequate or efficient working space. If the rooms in the lower reaches of the Colonial Office came in odd sizes and shapes through fairly recent design, the new offices in converted buildings presented even greater oddities. Limitations imposed by inappropriate space created issues in terms, for example, of the location of the room for the new office of Secretary in relation to those of the Crown Agents themselves. Keith may not have gained much in working space, yet, he felt the position itself was a great improvement.

With the encouragement of Mercer and the support of MSK, Keith joined the staff. Colleagues and friends in the Colonial Office wished him well. For instance, Dale wrote:

> Most hearty congratulations on your appointment to the CA: though it will mean a heavy loss to me personally (not to mention such an insignificant institution as the CO), you know how I rejoice in the recognition which your innumerable merits have obtained. What a plutocrat you will be—always provided you don't celebrate your exaltation by a debauch of milk and curds which will assign you to an early grave (of unusual size).

> I think on the whole you are right to accept: very probably you will like the work—& of course the pay & prospects are infinitely better than the CO at any rate, & I for one would certainly never say that you are wrong to accept ... I hope you won't desert the CO altogether: how the tea-party will get along without your cheery presence ... I trouble to contemplate![67]

Almost as soon as Keith took up his new work, he was granted the financial responsibility designed into the position of Secretary. On 21 July 1903, Blake wrote to the principal banks used by the Crown Agents, the Bank of England, the London and Westminster Bank, Ltd, and the Standard Bank of South Africa, Ltd, to inform them of Keith's appointment and his authorisation 'to sign cheques and to endorse and accept bills on our behalf, for amounts not exceeding £1,000'.[68] Blake sent along a specimen of Keith's signature with a request that each bank honour it just as if it were a signature of one of the Crown Agents. All responded accepting these instructions except for the Bank of England which insisted that Cameron sign documents to indicate his personal approval. Within a matter of weeks, Keith was exercising the financial aspects of his post.

However, his ability to conduct some of the other aspects included in the position was constrained and limited, in part, by the existing operation of the office and, as well, by the unease that often occurs in an organisation when a new position is created with a definition putting it high on the bureaucratic scale which, in effect, reduces staff who have been serving for some time to a considerably lower level. The position of Secretary, as Blake and his colleagues defined it, required everyone in the office from the Crown Agents themselves downward to function differently since all business was to go through the new officer who was specifically intended to relieve the Crown Agents from most of the daily responsibility with correspondence, tenders, payments, and routing of business, and to ensure effective co-ordination of the entire operation. But existing ways of conducting business do not change necessarily or easily into new, smooth procedures. Such change may be even more difficult to accomplish especially when the initial person in that new position of authority is a man like Keith: brilliant, confident, and competent, but very young compared to the rest of the staff and, as well, an outsider totally without direct experience in the work of the Crown Agents. Would he be successful in directing and co-ordinating the work of staff, older in age, much longer in service, and more knowledgeable about the work?

When Keith started his new work, he had to learn about the complexity and extensiveness of the operations of the Crown Agents. With the three men on the top, the whole operation was 'a highly stratified and organised bureaucracy'.[69] Stratification certainly was essential. Most of the operation had departments housed directly at the central office in London. As well, some staff spent much time in other parts of the city to supervise procurement of supplies, packing of orders, and actual shipping of goods; many of these functions were carried out through firms contracted to handle them. Moreover, the operation included overseas staff to supervise deliveries and installations in the colonies and territories served. At the centre, the organisation was divided on functional lines into eight departments: Chief Clerk and Accountant, Registry of Inscribed Stocks, Cashier, Engineering and Works, General Stores, Shipping, Correspondence, and Appointments. Below the head of each department were assistant heads while the departments themselves, as appropriate, were subdivided into sections. In addition to the heads and assistant heads of departments, the rest of the establishment included sixty-six staff members, three City Office clerks, sixteen Lady Clerks, Office Keeper, Housekeeper, and six Office Messengers. In all, the central staff, now including Keith, numbered well over one hundred persons, comparable in size to that of the Colonial Office.[70] Of necessity, the central office had on-going relations and contracts with consulting engineers for six specific areas: railways, harbour works, water and sanitary works, telegraph and electric lighting, military stores, and ship design. Further, it retained engineers to supervise various technical aspects of the work in Britain and employed inspectors to check on specific parts of the operation. Among others, the Crown Agents performed one very important function: the design and printing of currency and postage stamps. That involved designers, engravers, and printers, and, to be sure, inspectors to certify that every item was precisely and accurately produced. At the time Keith entered service, the Crown Agents served forty-four colonies and protectorates as well as the West African Frontier Force, the King's African Rifles, the South African Constabulary, and the Uganda and Central African Railways. Growth in the work of the Crown Agents resulted in considerable increases in their revenues. As an independent, self-supporting organisation, it had only an indirect line of accountability to Parliament through its supervision by the Secretary of State. Increasingly, its accountability was understood as being to the governments which it served. From time to time, there were calls in Parliament for information and reports about the operation of the Crown Agents. Chamberlain in 1901 asked the colonies served by the Crown Agents to indicate whether they were satisfied with the service they were getting and, if not, to suggest specific instances of problems.[71] After he studied the results, Chamberlain concluded, in 1903, that there were very few complaints of any substance, that the system appeared to be working very well at reasonable cost to the colonies and no cost to the British taxpayer, and 'that the Crown Agents had deserved the confidence alike of the Governments of the Crown Colonies and of successive Secretaries of State'.[72] It was not until 1908 that a Parliamentary investigation into the work of the Crown Agents was voted by the House of Commons which created a Committee of Enquiry headed by the then Parliamentary Under-Secretary of State, Colonel J E B Seely.[73] That Committee did recommend certain changes in the operation, mostly in the status of staff. In the course of its work, the Committee enquired into the origin of the post of Secretary and raised questions about Keith's work in it, about the terms of his initial appointment in relation to the Civil Service Commission, and, particularly, about the conditions of his retransfer. Nothing negative to Keith was found.

It is clear that Keith, in taking up the new appointment, faced a substantial task in coming to know members of the staff and to learn the various parts of this complex operation. He had to master those things in order to make the office of Secretary fulfil the functions specified by Blake and his colleagues. Quite soon, Keith found his actual role and his range of authority very different from what he expected when he accepted the post. As early as the fall of 1903, he started keeping notes on the various problems he encountered. He continued that practice through the series of episodes which led to his request for retransfer to the Colonial Office in the spring of 1905. Therefore, Keith's side of the experience with his disappointment, dismay, disillusionment, and difficulty can be described and discussed from his own notes. It is not possible to examine his work directly from the perspective of the Crown Agents, individually or collectively, since no files exist in the Archives of the Crown Agents to shed any light on their views of Keith's work.[74]

Obviously, Keith's move did not turn out satisfactorily for him, except for the financial rewards. The reasons why can be deduced from his notes and such correspondence as he retained with Blake and Mercer. The biggest single problem he encountered was Blake. Many years Keith's senior, old enough almost to be his great-grandfather, Blake apparently had considerable difficulty in permitting himself to be freed from routine responsibilities. Although he carried the argument to create the post of Secretary, Blake seemed unwilling to delegate the authority explicit in its definition. Regularly, Blake intervened in the flow of papers through the Secretary: he would ask some staff person well down in the bureaucracy to bring papers directly to him rather than permit them to come through Keith.[75] Keith, of course, was sensitive to every such move that weakened or ignored his position, in part, because he understood it to be his responsibility to establish the new office so that it would function in accordance with its description. Perhaps it is harder for those with power at the top of the bureaucratic pyramid to learn new ways of conducting business than for those nearer the bottom. Naturally, any uncertainty about new ways demonstrated by the head of an organisation will be reflected by the staff. In addition to Blake's unwillingness to use the new structure fully, he had an abrasive personality which, to put it mildly, made him difficult to get along with. There is no question about his being knowledgeable and efficient. Arthur Abbott, the historian of the Crown Agents, recalled that, when he joined the staff in 1912, Blake, who had finally left only three years earlier in the wake of Seely's Commission, was still remembered as a 'born autocrat' and a 'tyrant'.[76] Those qualities would have made it difficult for Keith to work with him since Keith was never bashful about asserting what he understood to be correct. Keith's ability to be forthright and tenacious on an issue where he felt in the right had been demonstrated in his early years at the Colonial Office. How much more he would display those qualities in defence of his new position near the apex of authority! Perhaps, given the differences in age, experience, and personality, clashes were inevitable between Blake and Keith; whether inevitable or not, clashes certainly occurred. In those instances, Keith turned to Mercer for help in countering Blake's actions but, in fact, the junior Crown Agent could scarcely cross his chief too many times. Mercer's usual counsel, as from a confessional, was for Keith to accept the situation, to be patient in dealing with it, and to hope for the future. Keith was neither accepting or conformable nor was he patient in his relations with Blake; he still had hope but even that waned in time. At the very end, they sparred vigorously in the letters they exchanged.

A logical outcome of Keith's difficulties with Blake was that the position of Secretary lacked the full range of authority that Keith had anticipated. It was not long before he found that heads of departments were questioning his role and were unwilling to accept his directions. His first note on such an issue, at least the first one remaining, was on 26 November 1903:

> Went to see Mr Heath [Engineering Assistant and Head of Works Branch] to borrow E/228/1. He said he could not obey instructions from me—re lv. Jamaica tel. & commenced to discuss my position. I replied I was instructed by Maj Cameron to do what I did in re Jamaica and declined to discuss the position.[78]

In his forthright way, Keith, on the next day, carried the incident directly to Blake for clarification. On this particular occasion, Blake supported Keith who then added to his notes:

> Sir E Blake came to me (2.10 PM) and spoke very nicely and promised me in a few years the position of a Crown Agent. He asked me not to be discouraged but to go on & that all would be right soon. He promised me no repetition of Heath incident in future.[79]

If he had difficulty with Heath, it is likely that he had problems elsewhere as well. Prior to the creation of the Secretary's position, the post nearest to the Crown Agents themselves was that of the Chief Clerk and Accountant. That post was held by E G Antrobus, a brother of Keith's former superior in the Colonial Office. Keith's papers contain no note about any difficulties with Antrobus, yet there may well have been tensions since any full assignment of authority to the Secretary would have had the clearest effect on the work of the Chief Clerk.

Keith's problems continued. In January 1904, he wrote to Blake and Mercer indicating procedural difficulties in working with J G Leslie, Head of the General Stores Branch.[80] The specific issue was the way to handle tenders received in the office after the closing date. Keith understood that 'Received Late' was the correct stamp and that such tenders could not be considered without the concurrence of one of the Crown Agents. However, Leslie indicated that often the General Stores Branch considered late tenders without reference to a Crown Agent. With such a situation, how could Keith function effectively to co-ordinate the work of the office? The only thing he could do, and he did that forcefully, was to press his superiors for clarification of procedures.

As the months went by, Keith could detect no signs that Blake was about to retire or that anyone was about to initiate the creation of a position for a fourth Crown Agent. What was he to infer from Blake's and, especially,

Mercer's repeated assurances that he would be appointed to such a post? Increasingly, he saw that prospect receding since nothing in the activities of either man suggested any concrete action in the near future. Keith had been led to believe, or had wanted to believe, that his future for such an appoint- ment was not off in the far distance but rather was on the near horizon. Certainly, he was discouraged by all the encouraging words uttered without any evidence of action. By 23 February 1904, seven months after he joined the Crown Agents, he wrote to Mercer making his first request for assistance in arranging for reinstatement in the Colonial Office 'in such a way that I would retain my seniority'.[81] Keith had concluded, finally, that he never would secure the range of authority and independence of action he had anticipated would be his in the position. In that letter, he reviewed his unhappiness:

> I must admit that I think that, perhaps owing to the inherent difficulties of the situation, the Crown Agents have not given me the position which I understood was to be mine, and I cannot help thinking that I have not received the support to which I was entitled, nor have the Crown Agents shown such confidence in me as I might reasonably have expected. ...
>
> It is naturally disappointing to me to have thrown away so much time and work but I took the post because I understood that it was one of dignity and authority and I confess that I do not consider that the failure of the experience can fairly be attributed to me.[82]

A characteristic Keith statement: he made his position clear and he implied the source of his difficulty. Mercer again gave assurances about the future and about immediate improvement in the situation. Keith remained, although he was unhappy and dissatisfied.

In addition to these various difficulties, Keith may have found that the work itself was not very satisfying, although he referred to this only obliquely. In the Colonial Office, he had been involved with a wide range of issues and concerns which he found to be of intrinsic interest especially in conjunction with his continuing legal studies. He had become particularly interested in the legal consequences of a succession of governments over certain territories, in certain penal regulations such as flogging, in legal codes themselves, and in a range of constitutional problems. Nothing of that nature was available in his post with the Crown Agents. Bills, tenders, specifications, cheques, orders, and so on which came across his desk presented many problems in operations and in engineering but no constitutional or, even, theoretical ones. The Crown Agents ran a business and he was simply Secretary to the heads of that business. While he had excelled in mathematics, he had not gone into engineering or accounting or any other applied area. Yet, the bulk of the work of the Crown Agents dealt with engineering and other technical matters. Certainly he learned much about the operation of the Crown Agents: the way in which they served the crown colonies, the manner in which the Secretary of State exercised general supervision, and the role that the staff of the Colonial Office played in protecting the interests of the crown colonies in their dealings with the Crown Agents. But he already knew all those things, in principle, from his work in two departments of the Colonial Office. Perhaps Abbott's comment about Keith was right, 'too academic for us'.[83]

The final difficulty that led him back to the Colonial Office was one in which he felt he had been badly used. The record that remains supports his view. Early in 1904, the Crown Agents decided to bring in a Royal Engineer to head the Works Department in order to give that section professional leadership. Mercer explained his thinking and that of his colleagues to Keith; he indicated that such a move might make it possible to manage with only two Crown Agents. In Mercer's view that would serve to improve Keith's chances of appointment since, as Keith noted, 'it would avoid a senior man getting in above me'.[84] Captain J F Carmichael was the person named to fill the appointment as head of the Engineering and Works Branch, as it was renamed. Keith perceived Carmichael as the person who would, in fact, advance in position and power at his expense.[85] Carmichael and Keith had their differences but apparently concurred on one point: Blake was impossible to get along with.[86] Keith expressed his uncertainties and fears about Carmichael's position to Mercer.[87] At the same time, Blake responded to criticism from the staff and, with his colleagues, set up an internal enquiry into the operation of the office during 1904–5.[88] Keith knew about the enquiry as well as the desire of heads of departments to have the office restructured so that they would have greater independence of action. The enquiry was bound virtually to have some suggestions for realignment of functions which would change Keith's position. All of his experience and his dissatisfaction led him to fear the worst. By late February or early March 1905, and before the enquiry had concluded its work, Keith found out from G Hodgson, Head of Correspondence Branch, and H Martin, Head of Appointments Branch, that some decisions about change had already been taken of which he had no direct knowledge and about which he had not been consulted. What he learned indirectly was that Blake had decided that Keith was to be removed from his present room and relocated on the second floor to share a room with the Appointments Department. Ever sensitive, Keith interpreted the move to imply a shift in the position of Secretary towards being redefined as head of a department. Keith was incensed about not being consulted. His anger erupted when Carmichael appeared in his room indicating that he had authorisation to start moving his instruments in. In raging fury, Keith wrote to Mercer on 28 March 1905:

> At the time [when Hodgson and Martin told him] I did not take much notice of this announcement as I did not conceive that it could be seriously intended to decide a matter of this sort without reference to me ... and this evening Carmichael told me that he had received instructions to start moving his instruments prior to a change of habitation and was going to do so at once.
>
> I need hardly point out that to make such an appointment without a hint to me shows clearly that I do not possess in the slightest degree the confidence of the Crown Agents. As Carmichael said to me, it appeared a device to prevent me protesting until too late. I cannot think that there has been any justification for such a mode of procedure. ...

> Not only does this action show how little the Crown Agents trust me, but also it points to a tendency, which I have always perceived to reduce me to the level of a Head of a Dept. ... I need hardly point out that it is only proper that the Secretary should be on the same floor as the C Agents, and should have a room to himself. Both those points were so arranged when my appointment was under consideration and to alter them now, without any consideration or even consulting me, seems to point clearly to a fundamental difference in the view which the CA and I take of my position.[89]

He went on to recount his attempts to get along and follow Mercer's advice. He expressed regret that things had not worked out because Mercer had been so encouraging and helpful. Mercer talked with him again, but Keith was not to be appeased this time. Indeed, Mercer, in his kindly way, simply confirmed all of Keith's worst fears about Blake's intentions. On 29 March, Keith again wrote to Mercer, recapitulating his anger and hurt at the way a decision involving him had been taken with no attempt to discuss it with him.[90] He ended his letter with a strong appeal to Mercer to talk with officials at the Colonial Office and to arrange for Keith's transfer. By this time, Keith felt so angered and so badly treated that he was prepared to transfer without any consideration of salary or seniority. In the next weeks, Keith spent time talking with people at the Colonial Office,[91] and so did Mercer. There were some problems to be worked out in the transfer, for example, the question of whether Keith needed another Civil Service Certificate. Finally, terms were agreed upon and Keith was named to a vacancy for a Second Class Clerk in the Colonial Office: at the bottom of seniority but at the same level of salary as when he left. He did need a new Civil Service Certificate but the fee was waived. His pension rights for the nearly two years of service with the Crown Agents were, according to the Treasury, to be the responsibility of the Crown Agents, not the Colonial Office.[92] His post as Secretary was taken by a colleague, Ezechiel, who transferred from the Nigerian Department of the Colonial Office. Keith finished his service as Secretary on 29 April.[93] He was two years older and, without any doubt, he was much wiser about the ways in which persons and bureaucratic systems function.

Legal Preparation

It was during the time that Keith spent working for the Crown Agents that he brought to completion the first step in his legal studies. On 17 November 1904, he was called to the Bar as a consequence of his fulfilling the requirements of the Inner Temple and of the Council of Legal Education. Five years earlier while he was still at Oxford, he had applied for permission from the authorities there to commence legal studies[94] and, at the same time, for entrance to the Inner Temple. Both requests were granted. It was not, however, until Keith actually moved to London in 1901 that he was able to take up, on a continuing basis, attendance at the Inner Temple. Clearly, he had decided to seek a calling at the Bar as part of his intellectual and professional competence; but whether or not he intended to follow that with any actual practice is unclear.

The requirements set by the Inner Temple were quite straightforward in those days. A candidate had to be admitted as a student member, had to be twenty-one years of age, had to have eaten the requisite number of dinners over a period of three years to be certain of association with men having exceptional knowledge of the law, and had to sit the examination designed by the Council of Legal Education.[95] For Keith, of course, proximity to the Inner Temple was essential. He took advantage of that and did fulfil all the necessary requirements. There were no set lectures which he was required to attend, but it is likely, given his keen interest in legal matters, that he took advantage of his schedule of work at the Colonial Office to hear some lectures in order to expand his knowledge.

By his time, a degree of rigour had been introduced into the call to the Bar. As a result of enquiries into the nature of legal education in the middle of the nineteenth century, the Council of Legal Education had been created. It was intended to introduce some degree of order into the preparation of men for the profession in a manner related to other educational reforms of the times. For some time, standards, both for admission to an Inn and for being called, had become rather lax and while the Inns still existed, they provided little in the way of systematic legal training. While England had in the Inns of Court the continuation of old, historic foundations for bringing together men of the law, the days when the Inns symbolised rigour had long since disappeared. A note in a bulletin of the Council indicates that 'Dining in Hall was the only survival and it was virtually true to say that a man ate his way to the Bar'.[96] The Council of Legal Education, once established by the Inns, was given authority to control the design and administration of the examinations to be given to men who sought admission to the Bar. Through that mechanism and through the Consolidated Regulations, the Council introduced a degree of order into legal training, designed a programme of studies, and soon established effective standards. When Keith sat the examinations in the fall of 1904, he was the recipient of several decades of reform and he could be assured that he had undertaken the best programme of legal studies then available. He passed the examination with his usual distinction.

In the years from 1902 to 1905, Keith expanded his knowledge in many ways. He continued his scholarship in Sanskrit. He learned a great deal about imperial matters through the range of assignments he fulfilled in the North American and Australasian Department. He also learned in detail about international law as he worked on the various matters related to the Alaska Boundary Commission. And, he added further to his formal preparation by being called to the Bar.

CHAPTER 5

Conflict in the South African Department, 1905–1906

On 1 May 1905, Keith resumed work on the other side of Whitehall as a clerk in the South African Department of the Colonial Office. The two years had increased his value since he brought with him full understanding of the office of the Crown Agents. As well, he had completed the first step in his legal preparation, having been called to the English bar in the fall of 1904 on finishing terms at the Inner Temple. His work in the South African Department provided him with extensive insight into the problems Britain faced in the process of reconstructing South Africa, into the ways in which the apparatus of the British government responded to a shift in party control, and into the issues related to the extension of responsible government to the former Boer states. All this, Keith would have found of great interest and value. Yet, in part because of the intensity of his interest and of his convictions, he found himself in conflict with his political superiors over their response to the actions and policies of the government of Natal towards natives. Thus, his actual time in that Department lasted exactly one year, to 7 May 1906. This is a critical year in Keith's development, especially in his acquisition of additional knowledge about principles and practices of the constitution of the British Empire which he would use for subsequent articles and for his first major book in that area.

Continued Studies

During his initial year back at the Colonial Office, he continued his studies in two important ways. He took his BCL at Oxford and he saw into print the catalogue of Sanskrit materials in the Bodleian. Both added to his intellectual equipment and to his stature in the Office and outside it, as well.

His taking the examinations at Oxford for a law degree was, in effect, an extension of the earlier decision he had made to equip himself as a lawyer and as a legal scholar. He took an alternate route to prepare himself for the degree at Oxford since he pursued studies at the Inner Temple. By this time, many men seeking a degree took their studies right at Oxford under the direction of one of the tutors associated with the Law School. It was logical for Keith, in view of his work in London, to follow an accepted alternative.[1]

The Oxford Law School had had a varied history, somewhat similar to that of the Inns of Court in London, with a period of laxness in the eighteenth and early nineteenth centuries leading to a period of reform. Legal studies, like those in other fields at Oxford, had never been a matter of set classes or lectures. Rather such studies involved working with some person in preparation for examinations. Even after the Law School was established in 1850, the men who held positions in legal study tended to function in a quite independent fashion and only gradually did they come together to develop examinations which reflected satisfactory rigour. F H Lawson in his history of the Oxford Law School pointed out that after that finally happened 'the examinations have been exceptionally corporate, reflecting as little as possible the idiosyncrasies of individual teachers; and they have perforce been employed to test capacity rather than knowledge'.[2] Keith easily met the basic requirements for candidacy which were few: a candidate had to hold a BA degree, had to have his name on the books of some College or Hall, and had to have twenty-six terms elapse from initial matriculation. He then had to pass the examinations which were held once a year and which were conducted by the Regius Professor of Civil Law or his deputy together with the three or four other examiners whom he appointed. The examination covered four areas summarised in the *Oxford University Calendar*: '(1) Jurisprudence, general or comparative, (2) Roman Law, (3) English Law, (4) International Law: it is partly in writing, partly *viva voce*.'[3] The thrust of the examinations was to focus upon historical and literary elements of law. Questions in jurisprudence dealt with general principles of law and made particular reference to Bentham's work on morals and legislation. Candidates were expected to have facility in Latin as a result of holding the BA and so they could translate and comment upon materials from Justinian or Gaius. Candidates needed thorough knowledge of English constitutional history, of the practical working of the constitution, and of certain important statutes. For international law, they needed to know about general principles, about the law of the seas, shipping, and navigation; one suggested work was Wheaton's, *Elements of International Law*, a work which, interestingly enough, Keith, in his later years, would carry through two revisions.[4] It is clear that much of the work Keith had actually handled in his assignments at the Colonial Office assisted him in preparation for these examinations. Keith passed them with distinction. He took the degree in Michaelmas Term, the autumn of 1905. A V Dicey, one of the most distinguished legal authorities at Oxford, commented about the value of that degree:

> Not a few have perceived that to go through the examination necessary for the attainment of the BCL degree well repays the work needed for going through it with success. It gives one of the best law degrees to be acquired in the United Kingdom. ... A man who reads for the BCL degree is, moreover, provided with as good, as sensible, and as thorough-going a scheme of legal study as any person can desire ...[5]

If Dicey's evaluation was correct, then Keith, with the combination of legal work at the Inner Temple and at Oxford, was as well-equipped as a lawyer as he possibly could be.

Yet, even as he completed his legal studies, he continued his role as a Sanskrit scholar. He had undertaken the complex task of cataloguing Sanskrit manuscripts while he was still up at Oxford.[6] Earlier, he had completed the task for those manuscripts in the Indian Institute Library. In 1905, he completed the second volume of a catalogue which had been started by M Winternitz. He saw that work through the process of publication: *Catalogue of Sanskrit Manuscripts in the Bodleian Library*.[7] That, as with all catalogues, proved an indispensable aid for scholars who wanted to use those materials; the catalogue remains useful.

Work of the Department

When Keith entered, the South African Department had only recently been divided into two separate departments because of the great increase in work stemming from the results of the South African War.[8] One department dealt with the Rhodesias, Central Africa, Bechuanaland, and, curiously, St Helena. Keith joined the other Department that worked with Cape Colony and Natal, British colonies from the early part of the nineteenth century, and Transvaal and Orange River Colony, formerly the South African Republic and the Orange Free State, which had been annexed to the Empire at the end of the War. Basutoland was included in this Department, as well. All South African work came under the general supervision of Graham, Assistant Under-Secretary of State, with legal matters still going to Cox or Risley. Because of the significance of the issues handled by the Department that Keith joined, Graham was in frequent contact both through minutes, which he usually wrote in bright blue ink, and conversations with Ommanney and the political leaders of the Office. Keith's immediate superiors were Henry C M Lambert, a First Class Clerk, and Just, a Principal Clerk, both of whom had been involved with South African affairs for many years, before, during, and, now, after the War. Both men were competent senior officers and thoroughly knowledgeable about the complexity and sensitivity of the issues, tasks, and decisions facing that Department. They were not unhappy to have Keith join them for they knew about his prodigious ability to handle large amounts of work with accuracy, insight, and speed. The volume of work required just such skills. Shortly after Keith joined that Department, the Colonial Office was restructured in order to create an East African Department when control of territories in that region was shifted from the Foreign Office to the Colonial Office.[9] This led to a series of changes in the assignment of staff. One primary result from those shifts was that Keith became the sole clerk in the South African Department handling communication with the four colonies. Under earlier organisation, two Second Class Clerks had been assigned there; now Keith served the entire Department by himself. Thus, Keith minuted virtually every paper from those areas from late summer of 1905 until his reassignment in spring 1906.[10] Occasionally he handled papers from the other South African Department, but his principal responsibility was with the four colonies.

Nothing that happened in those colonies during that time escaped his attention, review, and judgement.

Issues before the Department

During the time that Keith was in that assignment, at least two changes occurred which had significant consequences for the design and conduct of British policy in South Africa: the appointment of the Earl of Selborne as High Commissioner for South Africa in April 1905 to replace Viscount Milner who had become discouraged about his work and had resigned; and the collapse of Balfour and the Conservative-Unionist government in December 1905, to be replaced by Campbell-Bannerman heading a Liberal government which brought the Earl of Elgin and Winston Churchill to the Colonial Office as Secretary of State and Parliamentary Under-Secretary of State respectively.[11]

The first change came while the Conservatives were still in power. Milner was one of those Liberals who followed Chamberlain into the Unionist camp in the split with Gladstone over Irish Home Rule. Chamberlain named Milner as High Commissioner in 1897 subsequent to the various inquiries into the Jameson Raid. Milner was a dedicated, skilled administrator, determined to use his powerful office to advance what he understood to be British interests. The office of High Commissioner had been created some years earlier, in 1847. It was designed to ensure that one person on the scene in South Africa would be superior to the Governor or Lieutenant-Governor in each of the colonies and so be able to co-ordinate all aspects of British policy since, in addition, that office would be the channel for advancing British affairs and relations in the Rhodesias, in the protectorates of Bechuanaland and Basutoland, over native policy generally, with Cecil Rhodes and the British South Africa Company, and with indigenous tribes such as the Matabele, Zulus, and Swazis. Milner gave that office its distinctive shape, especially as he assembled his 'Kindergarten' class, men who would learn about colonial administration on the spot under a master teacher. Milner's understanding of British interests led him to support the series of steps against the South African Republic which eventually led to war. His role in bringing about that war certainly raised questions among the Boers and, as well, in some quarters at home about his fitness to fill the post during the years when Britain had to design policy to deal with the former Boer states. Milner strongly supported the policy of importation of Chinese labour to work in the gold mines of the Rand as the only feasible way to secure workers to develop South African wealth: that was the single policy that brought greatest opprobrium on Balfour's government and hastened its end. Selborne, appointed by Alfred Lyttelton who became Secretary of State after Chamberlain left the Cabinet to argue for the introduction of protection and imperial preferences as a way to imperial unity in September 1903, was also a Liberal Unionist. He had been Parliamentary Under-Secretary of State for Colonies from 1895 to 1900 under Chamberlain and had gone on to become a member of the Cabinet as First Lord of the Admiralty where he provided outstanding leadership. With his skills in leadership and administration clearly demonstrated and with his experience at the Colonial Office, he seemed the right person to go to South Africa: conscious of its complicated problems, aware of the strategic importance of South African harbours, recognising that the existing scheme of things required changes, and possessing a very different temperament from his predecessor. He continued to serve under the Liberal regime since, after he had made an analysis of the situation, he found that his ideas actually fell into line with their goals. He remained in this influential position for five years, a period of swift change during which time all necessary steps occurred to lead to unification of the four colonies as the Union of South Africa.[12]

The other major change that occurred during Keith's year in that Department was the shift in ministry. For the first time in a decade the Liberal party was in power. Balfour failed in the gamble he took in resigning office in December and in hoping that the Liberals would be unable to form a government. Perhaps he might have been able to survive if the only issue had been to patch over the differences within his party between the free trade and the protectionist wings. But other elements entered in. In part, the failure came because the Tories still had about them the aura of having caused the War but, primarily, it came because Balfour had not anticipated the indignant hue and cry that would be raised from many sectors of public opinion over the decision to introduce indentured Chinese coolie labour on the Rand. By the end of 1904, six months after the first Chinese arrived, some 20,000 were at work, with the number growing each month. That policy was criticised by humanitarian and nonconformist spokesmen as the virtual equivalent of slavery, a practice which Britain long ago had determined to stamp out, by emerging trade union and Labour leaders as a total violation of proper labour standards since human labour could not any longer be considered a mere commodity, and by nearly all parts of the Liberal party as inhumane and antithetical to British ideas of expanding liberty and humanity. The Liberals certainly had greater unanimity about the unacceptability of that policy than they had ever had about the War itself. The Liberals followed their assumption of power with a dissolution and general election. In the election of 12 January 1906, the result exceeded their expectations for the Liberals won a resounding victory, a clear majority over all other parties of more than eighty seats. Campbell-Bannerman was in a strong position to pursue his policies for South Africa: to end coolie labour as quickly as possible; and to take the 'grave risk', that is, to extend responsible government immediately to the Transvaal and the Orange River Colony in trust that former enemies would perceive the virtue of British magnanimity and the value of British forms of government to become loyal partners in the British Empire. Elgin, Churchill, and the staff of the South African Department in the Colonial Office were responsible for seeing that those policies were carried out.[13]

The new political leaders at the Colonial Office came with widely differing experience and temperament. Neither had been in the Cabinet; neither had led a major and complex department of state. Elgin did have prior experience in public service in two areas. In 1886, he served as First Commissioner of Works in Gladstone's brief, third ministry. More importantly, he held high office for five years in India, that great part of the Empire not under the Colonial Office. As Viceroy of India from 1893 to 1898, he found his tenure troubled by numerous difficulties, yet his achievements were solid and substantial. While competent, he brought no particular lustre to the viceregal office, his time seeming especially dull, in part, by contrast to the swirl and sparkle generated by his successor, Lord Curzon. Elgin returned to Britain as a quiet elder statesman among Liberals. From a family with a long record of distinguished, dedicated, faithful service to the Crown, Elgin came into Campbell-Bannerman's Cabinet as part of the balance needed between members in Lords and Commons, between age and youth, and between dutiful dullness and brash brilliance. Elgin helped to provide what R C K Ensor characterised as giving 'the combination a sufficiently Gladstonian air'.[14]

The Parliamentary Under-Secretary of State provided a sharp contrast to Elgin. To his first ministerial post, Churchill brought the reputation of an *enfant terrible*, a young man only thirty-one years old who had already fought in several wars, pursued an enviable career as journalist and author, and published a biography of his father. Further, he, himself, had become the subject of the first of many biographical studies. Tory turned Liberal over the issue of free trade and a relative newcomer in parliament, he took the post in the Colonial Office, in part, because it gave him an opportunity to speak on colonial policy in the House of Commons. Even in this initial ministerial post, Churchill lost no time or opportunity to use his extraordinary gifts for rhetoric. His very brilliance must have posed a challenge to the stolidity of Elgin. 'Unabashed confidence, unsquashable resilience, push, dash, flair, contempt for humdrum conformity—so Baroness Asquith summed him up.'[15] The two men could scarcely have differed more widely, yet, both worked in remarkable harmony to carry out the major policies of the Government. Indeed, together, they led the Colonial Office, and Britain, through what Ronald Hyam calls 'the watershed between the nineteenth century empire and the twentieth century commonwealth'.[16] Whether the term 'watershed' is best applied to their time at the Colonial office or to the time of the Great War of 1914 may be argued, but there is no argument about the importance of the changes they initiated in structure and policy which were essential to the evolving process of altering the nature of the Empire in the direction of the Commonwealth. For the day-to-day detailed work required to carry out their policies for South Africa, both political leaders, in the final analysis, were dependent upon Keith, the civil servant, as the sole clerk in the South African Department.

From his post low in the bureaucracy, Keith was directly involved in putting British policies into effect in South Africa, for the initial six months under Lyttelton's leadership and for the last six months under Elgin's. An examination of the numerous files that Keith minuted indicates not only the enormous volume of precise work he performed in that year of shift in policy but also the areas which he seemed to mark out for his particular concern. He continued to express dismay over flogging, especially where he identified abuses; when he could, he argued for its abolition or restriction and, in the absence of seeing that achieved, at least for ensuring that the regulations were followed scrupulously.[17] In addition to that continuing concern, he confronted the issue of native rights in one of the most complex settings in the entire Empire.[18] In South Africa, persons of European descent comprised only a small minority and controlled all political and economic institutions, yet were divided by language and tradition into two primary groups, Boer, or Afrikaner, and Briton. British victory in the recent war scarcely eliminated Boer suspicion of the British. Segments of Boer population still held aspirations of restoring the republics and of gaining total control at the expense of Britons. It is clear in retrospect from the vantage point of the latter part of the twentieth century that it was actualy this hard core view held intransigently by some leaders that provided the political dynamic for developments in South Africa throughout this century. Native policy was a term that applied to rules and regulations applicable to all persons who were not of European descent. A special problem existed for those who made such rules and regulations since a substantial group of Indians lived in South Africa, Indians who, by virtue of the role of the Crown in ruling India, were British subjects. How could British subjects be treated at greater disadvantage in southern Africa than in India? Should not British subjects be treated similarly wherever they lived under the authority of the Crown? It was in leading Indians to seek clarification of these questions and to establish their rights that Mohandas K Gandhi, a young Indian lawyer, first came to prominence. But the larger non-European population consisted of the various Bantu-speaking tribal groups. It was particularly for those groups that Keith felt regret that the terms of the Peace of Vereeniging, in effect, precluded the imperial government, and the Colonial Office, from being able to exercise vigorous leadership in the direction of seeking justice for natives since that treaty provided that the matter of native franchise would not be addressed until the successor colonies received responsible government. That meant the certainty of Boer majorities in the Transvaal and the Orange River Colony and, equally certain, the unlikelihood of them making any effective or substantial movement toward justice for natives. Keith chafed at such restriction on the authority of the British government and saw that the Colonial Office would have great difficulty in protecting and extending rights for natives in addition to the franchise in such vital areas as landholding, ability to move throughout the country, and employment.[19] One society in Britain that was in regular correspondence with the Colonial Office over issues related to native rights was the Aborigines Protection Society. Keith handled correspondence with that group sympathetically but always, of course, under the direction of his superiors.[20] He handled petitions, as well, from Cape Coloureds who felt that the direction of policy in the former Boer republics would put them at a disadvantage with the loss of rights they presently enjoyed. Moreover, he was eager to see the Liberal government take steps to end the further importation of Chinese coolie labour. He read reports from inspectors of the mines and in his minutes expressed great concern about ill-treatment of the Chinese. He noted Lord Selborne's repeated concern that, in the absence of any white men supervising the Chinese who spoke their language, disturbances seemed likely to continue.[21] He recognised again the ways in which the imperial government was constrained by the various governments in South Africa, especially the Transvaal, and was anxious that the whole practice of using Chinese be stopped. He wrote some of the papers in the Confidential Print series on the matter.[22] In one other area, Keith expressed his concern. In every place where it was appropriate, he argued for the Colonial Office to ensure that due legal processes were followed as providing the most equitable way to handle the wide range of problems in South Africa.[23] To promulgate or to enact fair and effective legal codes and then to follow them faithfully in subsequent administrative orders and in court proceedings seemed to him the best way to proceed.

During this time, two different approaches were taken to bring Boers into government in the former republics: Lyttelton proposed to do that through extending representative government; Elgin, as has been noted, was committed to responsible government.[24] When Keith joined the staff, Lyttelton's proposals were still under consideration. Keith provided numerous minutes setting out constitutional and procedural points. He felt that due deliberateness should be taken in the steps towards any extension of participation, especially in the hope that some role might be found for the Colonial Office to intervene with respect to native policy.[25] He felt Lyttelton's proposed constitution might be a reasonable first step. Even in that step, Keith was concerned that accurate and sound constitutional precedents be followed; he had no hesitation in pointing them out in his minutes. When the shift in parties came with the resulting decision of the Liberals to move immediately to responsible government, Keith was just as assiduous in identifying and discussing significant constitutional points.[26] He assisted in the preparation of papers in the Confidential Print series and wrote one dealing with the nature of second chambers in the colonies.[27] Clearly, the expertise he had acquired with regard to constitutional matters was of very substantial use to the South African Department in the development of constitutional instruments for the former Boer Republics. Clearly, he made important contributions to the discussion. Yet, he ran into difficulty.

Crisis in Natal

Given the nature of Keith's experiences, concerns, interests, contributions, and temperament; given the complex set of interlocking problems—political, economic, institutional, racial, strategic, moral, and ethical—posed for the British government in the continuing process of developing policy for the reconstruction of South Africa; and given the substantial pressure of work on the South African Department in terms of its crucial importance and its increase in sheer volume, it is perhaps not surprising that Keith found himself in contention with his political superiors and, at the same time, with certain of his immediate superiors in the bureaucracy. With the numerous and varied matters to be solved especially in the Transvaal and the Orange River Colony, it might be anticipated that Keith would become involved in controversy over issues rising in those colonies. But, instead, it was in Natal where the issue rose.[28]

There, Col Sir Henry McCallum, RE, had been Governor from 1901; there, responsible government had been extended eight years earlier, in 1893. The issue was complicated and came out of a particular set of circumstances starting early in February and continuing through April 1906: the racial and economic policies of the government of Natal; the assassination of two white policemen; a Zulu rebellion, or what was perceived and handled as a rebellion; the request by that government for the deployment of imperial troops and their dispatch; and the trial of a group of natives under court-martial leading to the conviction, sentencing, and, ultimately, execution of half the group. The sequence of events from those circumstances forced questions in Natal and London about the role and responsibility of McCallum as Governor as well as about the role and responsibility of the Colonial Office. What prerogative was inherent in the office of Governor? How was this related to royal prerogative? To what extent, and under what circumstances, was the Governor amenable to instructions from the Secretary of State for Colonies? Could the Secretary of State, in fact, issue such instructions and expect them to be followed? Must the Governor act only upon the advice of ministers in Natal? How did the imperial government fulfil the goal often-stated for the Crown to protect natives and to ensure fair treatment for them? How did the Crown's responsibility in that regard differ in a colony with responsible government? What difference did it make that the Royal Instructions for the Governor of Natal varied in certain details from those for other governors? It is obvious that, from many points of view, Keith would be concerned with these issues as the staff of the Colonial Office struggled to find appropriate responses to Natal. Keith was inevitably involved, in the first instance, because he was the clerk who handled, almost without exception, every single file from Natal during those crucial months. Further, he saw in the particular configuration many matters about which he had special concerns: the role of the Crown in the protection of native rights; legal and constitutional points about the office of Governor, about royal prerogative, and about the very nature of responsible government. He wrote his minutes in detail, with precision, and, at certain points, with passion.[29]

The story of events in Natal must be recounted in order to understand Keith's role and the positions he took. Natal, as well as the rest of South Africa, ended the War with substantial economic problems. In the depression which followed, various schemes were proposed for increasing the revenue of the colony. In 1905, the parliament of Natal, following the precedent of similar legislation in Transvaal, decided to require natives to participate in solving these economic problems by passing a poll tax of £1 per head on every man in the colony with certain exceptions such as indentured Indians and Africans already paying 14s. hut tax. It was in the process of collecting that poll tax early in 1906 that magistrates ran into open resistance.[30] While the amount was obviously small to those persons of European descent, it represented a cash sum to natives, many of whom still functioned under a barter economy. In addition to the poll tax, other reasons existed for unrest:

the 'Ethopian' church movement was alleged to pursue a goal of fostering rebellion, and Dinizulu, the great Zulu leader, was reported to be seeking elimination of all Europeans. But the poll tax was the trigger. On 7 February, magistrates at Umgeni ran into serious native opposition when they attempted to collect the tax. They called for assistance from the government. The next day, 8 February, the government sent a small force of mounted police to support the magistrates and to assist in enforcing compliance with the law. About twenty miles southwest of Pietermaritzburg, that troop was attacked by Zulus. Two of the white policemen were killed. Response by the government of Natal was rapid and extensive: martial law was proclaimed by McCallum on the advice of his ministers on 9 February, the militia was mobilised on 10 February, censorship was imposed throughout the colony although it was soon lifted because of protests from Churchill and Elgin, and patrols of troops quickly swept through native areas.[31] Still, the government felt insecure and anticipated a substantial uprising among Zulus. McCallum cabled to Elgin on 10 February seeking the assistance of British troops in Pretoria.[32] The Colonial Office, after consulting with the War Office, responded by directing him to the High Commissioner:

> The SAC has full discretion to act in any emergency on your representations and to override his discretion here might give to the trouble in Natal an exaggerated gravity which might produce an undesirable effect both locally and to the larger area of European politics at the moment.[33]

By 12 February, a battalion of the Queen's Own Cameron Highlanders under Col D Mackenzie was dispatched to Natal under orders from Selborne. Within days after the assassination of the policemen, twenty-six natives were apprehended and charged with guilt for that crime. Two of them were summarily tried by 'drumhead court-martial' and shot on 15 February.[34] The other twenty-four were held and tried by regular court-martial; twelve were sentenced to death, while an additional seven had the sentence of death commuted. McCallum and the Executive Council reviewed these sentences and sustained the decision of the court-martial that the twelve should be executed. On 27 March, McCallum telegraphed to the Colonial Office reporting briefly on the procedure and on the sentences.[35] The next day, Elgin responded with a telegram asking for delay in carrying out the sentences and for further information.[36] When Elgin's telegram was known in Durban on the 29th, McCallum's ministers resigned en bloc in protest at what they alleged was imperial interference in the internal affairs of a self-governing colony. After further exchanges and with McCallum's assurance that he had considered the evidence and the sentence for each of the twelve men individually, Elgin, on 30 March, indicated that the Colonial Office never intended to interfere with actions of the government of Natal.[37] An appeal was attempted on behalf of the convicted men to the Judicial Committee of the Privy Council which, on 2 April, found no basis for allowing the appeal. The twelve were shot at noon on 2 April.[38]

The telegrams of 27, 28, 29, and 30 March are central to the difficulty

Keith had with Elgin. The text of each needs to be stated together with certain of the minutes.

27 March, TELEGRAM No 2, McCallum to Elgin
[Received in Colonial office at 9.45 a.m. 28 March]

Court Martial which tried murderers of police officers have sentenced twelve prisoners to be shot out of twenty four tried for offence. Proceedings of Court Martial have been carefully reviewed by Governor in Council. Proceedings being in order and no injustice committed I have accepted unanimous advice of my Ministers that sentence shall be carried into effect. ...

[28 March, Minutes on Telegram No 2]

Mr Just
Surely this is very serious. These sentences cannot be justified by the Common Law and as we must assent to an act of indemnity we must be able to do so with a clear conscience. We cannot do so unless these executions are checked. We are morally responsible for the executions as it is the presence of our forces and reliance on our aid alone which renders possible these occurrences.
?Tel a warning to the Gov

ABK [Keith] 28.3

I entirely agree with what Mr Keith says. The justification for keeping the whole of Natal under martial law is not apparent. At the same time it is difficult to interfere with the government of a self-governing colony. But I think a carefully worded telegram should be sent, based upon the position of HMG as being involved by the presence of this battalion of regular troops.

HWJ [Just] 28/3

Note that the offence charged is murder and therefore, so far as my recollection goes, the case is not on a par with that which got Governor Eyre into difficulties.
All the same, if the object is to make an example by the infliction of the death penalty, there is the less reason for acting under martial law, for if the evidence is clear, the civil court would pronounce the same sentence. I would ask the Govr to suspend execution till he knows further.

FG [Graham] 29-3-6[39]

28 March, TELEGRAM, Elgin to McCallum
[Sent 7.40 p.m. 28 March; drafted by Ommanney]

Your telegram 27 March No 2 continued executions under Martial Law certain to excite strong criticism here & as HMG are retaining troops in Colony and will be asked to assent to the Act of Indemnity, necessary to regularise the action taken, trial of these murder cases by Civil Court greatly to be preferred. I must impress upon you necessity of utmost caution in this matter & you should suspend executions until I have had opportunity of considering your further observations.

E [Elgin] 28.3[40]

29 March, TELEGRAM No 1, Elgin to McCallum
[Sent 7.10 p.m. 29 March with minor modifications; this text is as originally drafted under Ommanney's direction, together with notes by Churchill]

Agent General informs me that your Government has resigned in consequence of my telegram of 28th March. It appears to me that this action must be based on a complete misapprehension of the meaning I intended to convey.

The object of my telegram was to press upon you and your Executive Council through you the desirability of taking further time for consideration before the irrevocable step of execution was taken.

HMG recognise that in a matter which affects the peace & security of the colony they have no right to overrule the deliberate judgment of those on the spot who are responsible but they do not consider themselves debarred from tendering friendly advice and from asking for information.

I feel confident that these explanations will remove any feeling which has led your Government to tender their resignation at a critical moment in the affairs of your Colony.

Please telegraph fully as to situation and in reply to my telegram of 28th March. Cabinet meets tomorrow morning.

[Two notes by Churchill]

> I should not send this telegram. Let us first await the arrival of the Governor's message.

> [Alongside mark in third paragraph]
> But this is a complete surrender. The lives of these men have become a matter of vy serious public importance.[41]

29 March, TELEGRAM No 2, McCallum to Elgin
[Received in Colonial Office, 8.45 p.m. 29 March]

Referring to my telegram No 1 March 29th if suspension be not cancelled I shall be face to face with serious constitutional problem. I am doubtful whether I can secure any alternative administration who would be willing to be responsible for the action which I have taken under your instruction.[42]

[30 March, Minutes on Telegram No 1, 29 March]

Mr Just
On this it may be sufficient to say that when a Gov acts against advice of Ministers on Imperial instructions, it is the constitutional duty of Ministers to carry on and not to resign, so long as they wish the Colony to remain part of the Empire. Otherwise the Imperial Govt would be unable to control any legislation of a Colony by the veto. If a Bill is vetoed, it is not constitutional for ministers to resign, not if a Gov on imperial grounds exercises the discretion as to pardon or respite entrusted to him. This might be made clear to the Colony, which has a short experience of self-government.

ABK [Keith] 30.3

It appears to me to be somewhat of a paradox to argue that it was unconstitutional to resign. Ministers declared the country was in danger and that the Execution of the offenders was necessary. To find the policy which they declare to be essential frustrated by the S of S what obligation can there be upon them to retain office and carry out a policy which is ruinous?

Whether their contention as to the danger was really justified by the facts, and whether they may not have been anxious to put HMG into a difficulty are other questions but I do not see how it can be contended that a Ministry deprived of the power of executing a vital policy is under any obligation to retain office. On the contrary resignation was not only their natural protest but was likely to be and was in fact an efficient means of carrying their point. It is possible to be unpatriotic, even factious, and yet to remain within the limits of constitutional action.

HL [Lambert] 4/4[43]

30 March, TELEGRAM, Elgin to McCallum
[Sent 4.20 p.m. drafted by Churchill; coded by Keith]

Your telegram 29th March, No 1 giving full information as to the procedure and circumstances of trial and the opinion of the Attorney-General thereupon, and your own careful examination of the whole case and of the evidence against each individual prisoner, and the conclusive manner in which the indicated guilt of each prisoner was established ... has received careful consideration of HMG.

HMG have at no time had the intention to interfere with action of Responsible Government of Natal, or to control Governor in exercise of prerogative. But your Ministers will, I feel sure, recognise that in all the circumstances now existing, and in view of the presence of British troops in the Colony, HMG are entitled, and were duty bound, to obtain full and precise information in reference to these martial law cases in regard to which an Act of indemnity has ultimately to be assented to by the Crown. In the light of the information now furnished HMG recognise that the decision of this grave matter rests in the hands of your Ministry & yourself.

The manner in which you have placed the various aspects of this question before your Ministers from 16th March onward has my approval; but I regret that you did not keep me informed by telegraph of the steps you were taking, or that the telegram announcing the imminent execution of these twelve men did not contain the detailed information which has now been given in reply to my telegram of the 28th. It was this lack of information which necessitated my telegram.[44]

Although he clearly carried out all work assigned to him during this time, Keith was unhappy about the entire sequence of events in Natal, especially since he felt that the British government had lost an opportunity to influence policy in Natal, an opportunity which, in his view, HM Government was clearly entitled to seize on legal and constitutional, as well as moral, grounds. He set his position out in minutes, those cited above and others, and in several lengthy memoranda.[45] On many points, he was not alone initially. He felt that McCallum had given insufficient attention to the clause in his Royal Instructions which directed and empowered him to act independently of his ministerial advisers in native affairs. Keith believed that the Secretary of State would have been within his authority to have taken a strong line with McCallum by sending out specific instructions under that clause to ensure just and fair treatment for the accused natives, a prospect which he rightly saw as being unlikely in the state of fear existing in Natal. Keith argued that McCallum, acting either independently under the Royal Instructions or responsively under instruction from Elgin should have rejected, at the very least, any judgement from the court-martial and, rather, insisted that the men be bound over for trial in the regular courts which were then sitting.[46] If the evidence against them was so overwhelming, Keith reasoned, the regular courts would most certainly come to the same conclusion but, and this was the critical point for him, the sentences would have been unquestionably legal. Further, Keith contended that the imposition of martial law was not an appropriate response to the situation which he perceived met neither of the requirements for ordering it: there was no threat of invasion; there was no serious domestic rebellion. On the latter point, Keith had difficulty in seeing the assassination of two policemen on patrol as sufficient or as substantial evidence of internal rebellion. In a tart comment, he noted, 'Natal desires with the aid of British troops to terrify by executions the native population.'[47] Keith also maintained that the imperial government had a direct interest and responsibility for natives in Natal which rested fundamentally on the inherent prerogative of the Crown. In addition, he pointed out that, in the specific set of circumstances in the spring of 1906, the imperial government had an explicit right to act, in addition to other legal, constitutional, or moral rights, for two particular reasons: imperial troops were directly involved in maintaining public order, and the Secretary of State would have to respond eventually to an act of indemnity by advising assent or disallowance, the act, of course, would have to be passed by the parliament of Natal when martial law was eventually lifted in order to validate actions taken by the Governor, his ministers, and others under their authority during the period of martial law. He went so far as to argue that, even in a colony with responsible government, the imperial government had the legal and constitutional right to intervene on issues such as those which arose in Natal. He summed up this position in a memorandum of 8 April where he wrote:

> the doctrine of non-interference appears at least as dangerous as the doctrine of constant supervision and like the latter to point logically to the disappearance of self-governing colonies, non-intervention leading as assuredly to the break-up of the Empire as constant supervision to the withdrawal of responsibility.[48]

In Keith's view, the resignation by the ministers of Natal en bloc was unconstitutional. Did that mean, he queried, that any time imperial interests were in conflict with local interests, a ministry could simply resign and, so, force the imperial government to give way? That could hardly be constitutional in his view because of the superior authority of the Crown, the imperial parliament, and, thus, the imperial government. Ministers in any colony would have to accept that in certain areas, such as native policy or the conduct of foreign affairs or defence, imperial interests could be, and should be, maintained and defended. Responsible government did not, in his considered judgement, equal action independent from ultimate imperial review.

That summarises Keith's views and outlines the positions he held during the weeks when affairs in Natal consumed a great deal of his energy, and, of course, that of other persons in the Colonial Office. How and why did he get into difficulty? It is clear that Keith did not hold his views unilaterally. On martial law, others in the Colonial Office and outside it, as well, felt that its imposition was an overreaction to the assassination of two policemen. Churchill, initially, was equally strong in his disapproval of that action. On 12 February, he minuted:

> The action of Governor and Ministers is preposterous. The proclamation of martial law *over the whole colony*, causing dislocation and infinite annoyance to every one, because two white men have been killed, is in itself an act wh appears to be pervaded by an exaggerated excitability. The censorship exploit descends to the category of pure folly.[49]

Elgin joined Churchill in denouncing censorship and insisting on its removal. On the justice of executing natives under sentences passed by court-martial, Just, Graham, Ommanney, Churchill, and Elgin all shared Keith's view that it would be far better to have those men brought to trial under civil court to obviate any question of the legality of the sentences. On the issue of whether HM Government had legal and constitutional power to intervene, Keith was not alone.[50] Elgin later argued that the crucial telegram of 28 March did not represent intervention but simply was a call for delay pending the receipt of information; that construction scarcely agrees with the text and with the fact that it was a form of intervention since the sentences were not carried out until four days had elapsed, following further exchanges of telegrams. Even Churchill was troubled by the text of Elgin's telegram of 29 March and indicated that it represented 'a complete surrender'.[51] In this connection, it should be noted that Elgin later in 1906 had no hesitation about applying very strong substantive pressure to keep the government of Newfoundland in line with the position desired by HM Government in regard to North Atlantic fisheries and to avoid a rupture in British relations with the United States. On the constitutionality of the resignation of the ministry in Natal, Keith found no support from the legal experts in the Colonial Office but, even on that point, his immediate superior, Lambert, was near to the mark when he suggested that the resignation may have been to force the hand of HM Government which, indeed, was the very outcome.[52] In the subsequent case of Newfoundland, MacGregor, then the Governor, was obviously more skilled in keeping Sir Robert Bond, the Premier, in line and preventing him from using the precedent of resignation, than McCallum had been in Natal. But fish and natives represent vastly different categories for imperial policy.[53] Keith retained his views about the legal and constitutional aspects of the situation in Natal that he worked out in the context of those events even as he later wrote about the role of governors in successive editions of *Responsible Government in the Dominions*.[54] He never doubted that he was correct, and that McCallum and Elgin were in error.

The explanation of Keith's difficulties with Elgin, then, cannot be found solely in the positions that Keith held and argued. Rather, the explanation is to be found in two other aspects. In the first instance, Keith was utterly impolitic in his minutes. One sign of bureaucratic wisdom is to know enough to retreat gracefully before pursuing a position too far, especially a position which, however logical and sound, is known to be unacceptable to superiors. That was Keith's problem. He persisted in pressing his views when even those who supported him, at least in certain aspects, knew that the political leaders were going to take quite different positions. Keith and Elgin could never concur on the intent and meaning of the telegram of 28 March. 'But Mr Keith is certainly wrong in his interpretation of the telegram of 28th March,' wrote Elgin on 26 April as he read Keith's memorandum which turned out to be the last straw.[55] There is nothing wrong with politicians trimming opinions to prevailing winds, but Keith was not a trimmer while Elgin had learned to be one. Impolitic importuning may be the best way to characterise Keith's behaviour. And, moreover, it is true that some of his minutes drove Elgin and Churchill to distraction not just for their tone but because they were almost illegibly written.[56] Small wonder that Elgin became impatient and directed Keith's transfer from the politically sensitive South African Department.

There is another aspect to consider as well: it is in the arena of politics that the larger explanation of Keith's difficulties must lie. It is obvious that the turn of events in Natal put HM Government in a very awkward position. When the affair started on 8 February, the Liberals had been in office just two months and their energy in that interval had had to be focused upon the general election and almost simultaneously upon the overriding and complicated problems of extending responsible government to the Transvaal and Orange River Colony and of finding the way, legally and quickly, to end importation and use of Chinese coolie labour on the Rand. Natal became a serious irritant to the Cabinet. Elgin's initial response to the sentences under martial law had to be tempered in terms of larger goals for the Liberal government. Keith's importuning for intervention on behalf of natives found no favour with a Liberal Government already committed to extending responsible self-government to former enemies. If HM Government intervened extensively in Natal over a relatively minor matter of the death of two white policemen and of the proposed execution of twelve natives, how could former Boer leaders in the Transvaal and Orange River Colony accept Selborne's assurances on behalf of the Government that, in fact, Boers were really going to be in charge of their own affairs, including native policy? Could HM Government intervene in an old British colony and not be suspected of finding ways to intervene or to keep control in the former Boer states? Keith, of course, would have been perfectly satisfied to have such intervention in those colonies on behalf of native policy and would have hastened to build legal and constitutional arguments to support that position, but intervention in a self-governing colony anywhere in South Africa could not be acceptable policy to the Liberal government. In effect, the Liberals inherited the Tory settlement at Vereeniging and could not intervene in any colony in South Africa in native affairs. Liberals, perhaps not unhappily, were caught in a *de facto* self-denying ordinance. Trust in the future wisdom to be gained by former Boer enemies under responsible self-government was the theme of the larger policy to which they were committed.[57] Keith's insistence on intervention and his continued reference to the telegram of 28 March as evidence that Elgin had intervened and so ought to continue to intervene was an irksome irritant. Elgin could not accept that construction since he knew that in terms of the larger, more important goals the Liberals had set for South Africa the issue of handling the relatively trivial matter in Natal had to be left to its governor and his ministers.

In a clash between political leaders and civil servants, it is the political leaders who, properly, carry final responsibility and authority. Elgin made the decision to move Keith late in April. It is important to be precise on Elgin's reason for that decision. It did not rest on the lengthy memorandum that Keith wrote on 8 April entitled 'The Right of His Majesty's Government to Intervene in the Executive Government of a Self-Governing Colony' since that paper was a contribution to the discussion within the staff of the Colonial Office about the nature of a despatch that should be written to Natal setting out legal and constitutional aspects in the relations of the Secretary of State and the Governor. Others joined in this discussion, including Chuchill who directed the drafting of an interesting paper along lines he set out. In fact, no such despatch was ever sent. Elgin's decision on Keith came after he read the supplemental memorandum that Keith wrote on 17 April in which Keith restated his analysis, argumentation, and views, including his interpretation of the telegram of 28 March. He ended with a pseudo-apology that, in Keith's typical manner, aggravated:

> I much regret that the S. of S. should have cause to find fault with the tone of my minutes. May I however venture to point out that the outrage on the population conveyed in my minute was based upon the Col. Sec. of Natal's (Mr Smythe's) remark that if there was to be blood shed it should be done at once? And also that my minute was written in support of the action of the Govt in sending the tel of 28 March 1906 (for which I was of course in no way responsible) which action was hardly consistent with a belief in the man on the spot such as is held by Mr Cox.[58]

The acerbity of Keith's minute left Elgin with no alternative but to get Keith out of the South African Department and replace him with a Second Class Clerk who would know his place better. Later, Elgin wrote to Churchill:

> As to Keith, I may just say that I should never have wanted him moved if he could have restrained his propensity for smart sayings and attended a little more to the correctness of his law: but the position was getting awkward.
> [Keith] with all his ability is not, in my judgement, a very safe guide.[59]

Ommanney summoned Keith on Friday afternoon, 4 May, to tell him of Elgin's decision. Keith was incensed, in part because he felt his views on the Natal affair were correct and, also because it was just a year earlier that he had been in conflict with Blake at the Crown Agents. Keith went directly from his interview with Ommanney and wrote himself a memorandum on the matter. His feelings are quite clear:

MEMORANDUM OF AN INTERVIEW BETWEEN SIR MONTAGU OMMANNEY, KCB, GCMG, PERMANENT UNDER SECRETARY OF STATE FOR THE COLONIES AND ARTHUR BERRIEDALE KEITH MA (EDIN), BA (OXON), BCL (OXON), MRAS, ETC. ETC. ETC. BARRISTER AT LAW OF THE INNER TEMPLE

Sir Montagu Ommanney sent for me on the afternoon of the 4th May 1906 and said that it had been determined to make a change in the office arrangements and that I was to go to the West Indian Department in place of Vernon transferred to the South African Department. He explained that Lord Elgin had spoken to him and had said to him that while he wished him to tell me that he fully appreciated the great ability, knowledge and care which I showed in dealing with South African questions, yet he did not think that the tone which I adopted showed a sufficient recognition of the position which should be taken up by a junior in the office and he considered it desirable that I should be employed in another department for some time. Sir Montagu said that Lord Elgin made these observations after he had seen my supplementary minute on the subject of martial law in Natal. He said that he regretted to have to convey to me the decision of the Secretary of State and that it would have gratified him much if he could have transferred me at once to the Australian Department, but that could not be arranged at present. He would however if he were still in the office when a vacancy occurred in the Australian Department secure my transfer thither. I expressly asked for an assurance on this point and received it. He said that he was aware that Vernon desired a transfer to the Australian Department but that he did not consider that if he were transferred to the South African Department he had any claim to a transfer to the Australian Department and he considered that I had a very strong claim to seek a transfer. I thanked him and withdrew.

(NB Had it not been for the meanness of my eldest brother I would have informed him that I would prefer to leave the office.)

[NB No 2 It may be noted that his eldest brother against whose meanness AB inveighs expressly told him that he was quite prepared to keep him till he tried the Bar.[60]]

Interestingly enough, Keith worked in the South African Department on the following day, Saturday, before taking up his new assignment at the start of the next week.

His immediate superiors, Just and Lambert, expressed their sympathy for his plight. Just, in typical manner, did this in a sonnet:

> For just one year as a South African
> > Keith laboured, with his desperate flowing hand
> Inditing minutes seduously scanned
> > By statesmen's eyes, albeit none fully can
> > The script decipher. Life's too short a span!
> Behold his ardent backer, Churchill, stand
> Applauding David slinging at the Rand
> > And crying 'Youth, Truth, Courage, Mark my man!'
>
> > Ah, but our fold was built for meek eyed sheep
> Led by their shepherd and a docile ram!

His faithful flock we know that Elgin's grace
From noxious lion's whelp will safely keep—
(Within his fold none save the sheep or lamb)—
Casting the lion forth with frowning face.[61]

Lambert turned to the form which various members of the staff had used as an exercise. He wrote a parody of a Latin epitaph, starting properly with the words, 'Memoriae sacrum', and ending with a variation on the usual phrase, 'tibi terra sit levis', by writing, 'SIT TIBI JAMAICA LEVIS'. The sense of the epitaph indicates the affection and regard that Lambert held for Keith:

Sacred to the memory
of a most illustrious man
skilled in all branches of knowledge
but especially in jurisprudence
wherein he very often destroyed
all official counsellors of the law
with a most savage attack:

A B Keith

He spent his most innocent childhood
among the Americans.
As a youth he went to the Crown Agents,
a separate group,
whence he escaped, barely unscathed,
the most vicious harrassment
from a certain Gorgon.
Afterwards, assigned to the Africans, ...
a friend of the Blacks,
a bold assailant of authority,
he so raged
that tyrants trembled.
Alas, he died unexpectedly.
His body, cast out on the shores of the West Indies,
was buried in a distant and foreign land.
MAY JAMAICA REST LIGHTLY UPON YOU[62]

And so Keith was transferred to the West Indian Department. Hurt and unhappy by his second dismissal within a year's span, he directed his energies to drawing from his experiences to begin assembling materials for his book on responsible government. He made his arguments on policy in Natal as long as he could within the South African Department. But, he did not forget those arguments when he came to write about the role of governors and the constitutional position of responsible government.

CHAPTER 6

Changing Assignments, 1906–1908

Keith's reassignment brought him into a position to work with some of the oldest colonies in the British Empire. The West Indian Department, at that time, lacked any of the high drama or any of the significant problems which faced the South African Department. Elgin, obviously, felt that it would be a relatively safe assignment for Keith. Yet, this new assignment provided Keith with more exposure to the varied ways in which the constitution worked in the Empire and gave him further illustrations for his writing. In addition, this assignment into which he plunged with his usual vigour and thoroughness, even though his enthusiasm was rather dampened, turned out to be but temporary since, by March of 1907, he commenced work on Canadian and Australian files[1] again in accordance with the assurances Ommanney had given which were honoured by Sir Francis J S Hopwood, his successor as Permanent Under-Secretary. Further, in the summer of 1907, Keith became one of the original members of the staff selected for the newly created Dominions Department. While Keith was a valued, trusted, and effective member of the Colonial Office and, increasingly, was given more direct responsibility, he never was promoted beyond the level of Second Class Clerk, primarily because of the two years of seniority he lost through his time with the Crown Agents.

West Indian Department

In the West Indian Department, he worked under the general supervision of Lucas, an Assistant Under-Secretary, and under the immediate supervision initially of A A Pearson, a Principal Clerk and the most senior member of the staff in the Colonial Office; late in 1906 Pearson retired to be succeeded by Sydney Olivier who held the post until he went to be Governor of Jamaica in May 1907. His other immediate supervisor was T C Macnaughten, a First Class Clerk. His colleague as a Second Class Clerk was H R Cowell who had entered the Office in 1902 and so was junior to Keith in actual service but senior in terms of the reckoning of seniority.[2] The Department, at that time, included, 'Jamaica, Turks Islands, British Honduras, British Guiana, Bahamas, Trinidad, Barbados, Windward Islands, and Leeward Islands.'[3] By 1907, Bermuda and the Falkland Islands were transferred to this Department from the North American and Australasian Department. The islands in the West

Indies contained several forms of government: a federal scheme existed in the Leeward Islands while variations of crown colony government could be found in Jamaica, Trinidad, Tobago, St Lucia, and elsewhere; some colonies such as Bahamas and Barbados possessed full representative government. Further, the West Indies provided several illustrations of colonies which, at one point, had virtually achieved responsible government or extensive local participation and control through representative government and subsequently were obliged to give up these gains in the face of economic difficulties.[4] The economy of the West Indies, primarily dependent upon a single crop, sugar, suffered because the market for West Indian sugar tended to be depressed as new areas emerged for growing sugar and, especially, as competition from sugar beets, often raised with state subsidies and behind protective tariffs, lessened demand for cane sugar in the world market. Alternatives to an economy based on sugar were not readily available although a Royal Commission on the West Indies reporting in 1898 had urged diversification of crops into citrus, tropical fruits, and the like together with expansion of steamer services equipped with refrigeration.[5] Eventually, by the outbreak of war in 1914, some modest improvement took place as a result of these recommendations. Yet, in Keith's time, these colonies were poor. British Guiana could scarcely profit from the rich deposits of bauxite which were still to be discovered. Serious rebellions had occurred earlier in Jamaica and more recently in Trinidad. Sharp stratification in society left blacks, former slaves, in the numerical majority but without effective political power or social status in the face of the white, British minority which, by contrast, had high status and political control. Many of the planters and land owners came from families that had lived in the West Indies for many generations. In short, the area held none of the economic promise of South Africa or many other places in the Empire. Its time of economic promise had occurred in the seventeenth and eighteenth centuries.

In the West Indian Department, both Second Class Clerks worked, at some point or other, on files of all the colonies. Yet, there was a division of work on a day-to-day basis where Keith carried primary responsibility for materials related to Bahamas, British Honduras, Trinidad, the Leeward Islands, and the Windward Islands.[6] In his time in the Department, Keith learned about boundary issues both in British Guiana, in relation to Brazil and Venezuela, and in British Honduras, in relation to Mexico. He gained insight into the serious economic problems throughout the entire region. He saw how the Brussels Sugar Convention of 1902 which increased bounties paid for sugar beets by continental countries, mainly Germany, had, in fact, simply worsened the situation of the West Indies especially with reference to the market in the United States. He came to understand the degree to which all of the islands were dependent on shipping to provide links for trade among themselves, to Britain, and to world markets and, as well, for communications and information. The islands were isolated and only the arrival of a ship connected them with the rest of the Empire and the world. He handled some of the files dealing with the effects of the earthquake that created extensive damage in Jamaica on 14 January 1907.[7] In that connection, he worked with files from which he learned about the interests of the United States in the Caribbean.[8] He knew better about the ways in which assemblies and executive councils did, and did not, work effectively. The period of his most intensive work in the Department ended in the early months of 1907.[9]

Secretary to the Navigation Conference of 1907

By February 1907, although he was still assigned to the West Indies, Keith moved into one of the special roles which he would play during the rest of his years at the Colonial Office: secretary to conferences and committees. Here, his superiors recognised and put high value on his prodigious memory and his extraordinary capacity for speedy, accurate work.

Because of the numerous problems involved with colonial shipping, the leaders of the Colonial Office decided to call a conference on shipping law as a preliminary to the Colonial Conference scheduled to open in mid April. As the person in the Colonial Office with an extensive, detailed knowledge of the issues related to merchant shipping, Keith was assigned as the staff member to serve as Secretary to the Navigation Conference held in March and April.[10] This occurred within the period when relations of Britain and the dominions were undergoing significant redefinition. The Navigation Conference included Britain, Australia, and New Zealand. Complex issues involving the jurisdiction of merchant shipping legislation within the British Empire formed the substance of the Conference about which the two dominions furthest from Britain had very particular concerns. Indeed, it was recent legislation in those dominions which required review of the basic imperial statute, the Merchant Shipping Act of 1894. Keith, through his correspondence with A V Dicey, late Vinerian Professor of Law at Oxford, and, at that time the pre-eminent legal authority in Britain, had become interested in the legal intricacies that rose out of the conflict of laws, especially in the international sphere.[11] Dicey had made the conflict of laws a subject for legal study when he gave it definition in his book, *A Digest of the Law of England with Reference to the Conflict of Laws*, which appeared in its first edition in 1896. Dicey wrote to Keith regularly to secure information and examples about various precise points of conflict in law and, especially, about navigation laws.[12] Keith's responses to Dicey, together with the minutes he wrote on the matter in the files of the Colonial Office provided Keith with knowledge that made him of substantial assistance to the Navigation Conference. It was particularly in merchant shipping legislation where the conflict of laws was most likely to arise. In a subsequent article, published in 1908, Keith set out the matter:

> Every merchant vessel which does not confine its operations to coasting round the coasts of the country in which it is registered must necessarily fall under at least two jurisdictions, and in many cases under more. Over-seas vessels find themselves often within the limits of several foreign jurisdictions in addition to the jurisdiction of the country in which they are registered. From this fact there inevitably arises a conflict of laws, and if each country which at any one time

could *de facto* exercise jurisdiction over merchant vessels were to do so, it would clearly be impossible for any vessel to be constructed or manned which could comply with all the regulations to which it might be made subject.[13]

In the Navigation Conference of 1907, Keith was able to cite cases and statutes, both imperial and colonial, and, of course, to keep track of the various arguments advanced in the discussions. His contributions assisted in the development of some operating rules for the parliaments of Australia and New Zealand in relation to imperial legislation on shipping. He restated the basic operating principle in one of his later books:

> that the vessels to which Australian and New Zealand conditions should be applied were vessels which were registered in those Dominions while trading therein, and all vessels while engaged in the coasting trade, including vessels from overseas which took up passengers or cargo at one port of a Dominion for delivery in another, with a saving for the case where passengers or cargo were landed at one port to be taken to their destination by another steamer.[14]

Keith fulfilled his special role as Secretary admirably and would soon be assigned to similar tasks.

Search for an Academic Post

Yet, it was during 1906 and 1907 that Keith made attempts to leave the Colonial Office for the academic world. No letters or notes remain in which he spoke specifically as to his reasons, so that it is difficult to know for certain whether his desire to move represented dissatisfaction with the work at the Colonial Office or simply the desire to find greater opportunities, and perhaps salary, to support his research work and scholarly interests. The fact that he sought these positions indicates his desire to move even if his motives cannot be adequately assessed. In the event, he was unsuccessful in securing either of the appointments in Sanskrit; however, he was successful in securing a position at Edinburgh, but withdrew after a contretemps.

In April 1906, he submitted his application for the chair of Professor of Sanskrit at Cambridge.[15] He was twenty-eight years old, still a very young person even to be considered for such an appointment. His application was impressive. In it, he recounted the preparation and honours he received at Edinburgh under Eggeling and at Oxford under Macdonell. He reviewed the numerous, substantial works he had written or edited and seen into publication; he cited catalogues, translations, books, and articles. Yet, he was not elected to that chair. Rather E J Rapson of London was chosen by the electors.

Keith was not daunted by that outcome. He went right on in June 1906, to apply for the now vacated chair at University College, London. Since this application followed so closely on his quest for the chair at Cambridge, he used the same application materials including an array of letters attesting to his substantive achievements.[16] In addition, he included a more current testimonial from Macdonell who extolled Keith's superior qualities:

> I am convinced that of all available Sanskrit scholars in this country who might be candidates for the post no one equals him in general ability and power of work on the one hand and in knowledge and achievement in Sanskrit on the other. Nor does any young Sanskritist hold out promise of such distinguished performance in the future. ... Mr Keith has not only made himself familiar with the various branches of Classical Sanskrit Literature; he also knows the Vedic language better than any other young scholar in this country. ... As Mr Keith has handled hundreds of Sanskrit MSS. his paleographical knowledge of Sanskrit is more extensive than that of any other young British scholar.[17]

It is significant to note that Keith, in the fourth paragraph of his letter transmitting the application, suggested that he would be able to take up the post at University College and still retain his position in the Colonial Office: 'My official duties occupy my time between 11 a.m. and 6 p.m.; I could therefore lecture either at 9 a.m. or 10 a.m. or at any hour after 6 p.m.'[18] In spite of the strong support from Macdonell, Keith was not selected for the position at University College. However, he still was interested in leaving the Colonial Office or, at least, in staying there and extending his activities into the academic sphere.

Some months later, he applied for the Lectureship in Ancient History at Edinburgh University. He sent his application forward on 2 January 1907.[19] By that time, he had already been named as Deputy to the Boden Professor of Sanskrit at Oxford for the period from October 1907 to March 1908 while Macdonell was to be away conducting research in India. In the application, in addition to summarising his work and accomplishments in Sanskrit, Keith, naturally, emphasised those various aspects of his preparation and career which centred on Classics. He placed particular emphasis on the ways in which he had made choices systematically in his studies and examinations to be able to build a basis for the comparative analysis both of legal systems and of religions in the classical era. In connection with the latter, particularly, he had become seriously interested in the relationships of ancient Indian religions to those of classical Greece and Rome. The testimonials he included in his application were the same ones he used when seeking the Sanskrit chairs at Cambridge and London.[20] An additional one came on 4 January 1907, from Ingram Bywater, Regius Professor of Greek at Oxford, who characterised Keith as 'a man of unusual power and promise of distinction'.[21]

This time his application was successful. Because the contretemps in connection with this lectureship has been unclear, it is necessary to deal with it in some detail. Acting upon the recommendation of the appropriate committee, the Edinburgh University Court appointed him to the Lectureship in Ancient History on 18 February 1907.[22] However, he was uncertain about whether he should accept. Having found, finally, an alternative to the Colonial Office, he was undecided about leaving. The reason for his indecision, apparently, lay in his desire to continue to combine various aspects of his life and work simultaneously, a goal which the location of Edinburgh, distant from manuscripts and from documents on constitutional matters, seemed to make difficult to attain. On 21 February 1907, when he wrote to the Secretary of the University Court to acknowledge his appointment, he restated his desire to hold the position of Deputy to the Boden Professor at Oxford concurrently with the Lectureship at Edinburgh. He proposed, thus, to extend the course of lectures on Roman History in the fall 'over both parts of the session instead of being confined to the first half only'.[23] The Court received a report from the Board of Studies for Languages on this latter point; such a proposal was not acceptable, but the Board would accept two lectures a week instead of three so long as the lectures were separated by 'an interval of a day or days' with the course ending in January or early February.[24] Keith never received any formal answer to his letter of 21 February on the questions of holding the Boden post and, at the same time, the Lectureship and of spacing the lectures. Therefore, during late February or early March when his energies were involved with the Conference on Merchant Shipping, he continued to have doubts about whether he could properly take up the appointment. In the absence of any response from Edinburgh, he finally decided early in April to decline the appointment; on 17 April, he wrote a letter to the Secretary of the University Court to that effect, a letter which University authorities did not receive until two weeks later because Keith became ill.[25] Also, on the 17th, his mother wrote him a lengthy letter from Dunbar in which she gave her advice on the matter. He could not have received MSK's letter prior to making his decision. Her letter is worth citing in full both as an illustration of the way in which her mind worked in relation to Keith and also as a summary of her views of Keith's accomplishments and potential.

17 April 1907
Dunbar

My dear wee Berr-boy—

I am such an ignorant old woman, that it seems presumptuous on my part to give *you* advice: yet I am going to say what I think about Edinburgh, trusting to your own good clear idea of how things stand *re the C.O.* for guiding you to a decision.

In *accepting* the Lectureship, you have it in your power to bring your name into prominence, as a man of unusual ability, and abundance of leisure would fall to your lot; enabling you to donate time and brains to legal, classical, and other studies. You would be your own master, and what you did certainly would redound to *your* credit and not to that of the Senior Clerks (or Upper Officials) of the Colonial Office. If by *any* chance the Legal Appointment becomes yours at Oxford, you could—if at Edinburgh?—at once accept *it* and resign your Lectureship, and at any rate Berr, if Prof Eggeling retires, by your presence in Edinr the Sanskrit chair *wld* almost certainly become yours. In the C.O. you have interesting work often; but what *you* do often goes unrewarded, and your name is unknown outside of the office and a few Government Servants. I am certain that your work at Edinburgh, as a lecturer, your legal studies, your

Sanskrit work, would become more and more fascinating, and you would look back on your C.O. life, as a rather narrowed limited one: lacking in opportunities of distinctions and individual assertion.

Of course I know that it would be a wrench to quit the known for the—so to speak—unknown; especially as of-late, interesting side-issues such as being Sec to the Med Tropical Diseases Inquiry and Deputy to the Shipping Affair, have fallen to your portion: yet, on the other hand, *this* may be the opportunity given to you to traverse a more distinguished career, and also a more encouraging one. Whatever is your decision my dearest Berr, rest assured that I shall be satisfied. *I have not the slightest* doubt of your ultimate success at the Bar and *as a Scholar*, but I do not want you to delay—too long, lest I should not live to triumph in your greatness: God has not bestowed such gifts upon you without designing that they—should shine forth for the benefit of your fellow creatures. Berrie, you do not know how grateful I am to Him, for having sent you into my life, and somehow I resent the knowledge that His gifts to you are hidden 'under a bushel', otherwise go only to increase the reputation for brilliancy *in others* at the C.O.

I am writing just what I feel; but again I implore you to remember *that your* decision will meet with my approval; for *you* know, as *I* do not know, whether the C.O. holds out any inducements or prospects in the future, which would render your leaving it an error.

> With my dearest love, and true sympathy,
> Believe me,
> (now, and as long as my soul lives)
> Your most loving mother,
> Margaret S Keith[26]

While MSK in her letter urged him to take the appointment, Keith had already made up his mind to refuse it. In the weeks following his decision, a series of unhappy events took place. On the day Keith wrote his letter to Edinburgh University, he broke out with German measles, an illness of considerable concern at his age. He was quite ill and was forced to take leave from his work at the Colonial Office for twenty-two days.[27] When, in about a week, he was sufficiently able, he travelled to Dunbar to join his mother and to recuperate. It was there that his sister, Nan, found that his letter of the 17th had never been posted. She promptly sent it along to the University on 25 April with a brief note of explanation and apology: 'My brother suddenly became ill after writing the enclosed letter, & is still confined to bed. I regret that thro' inadvertance on my part, the letter has not been posted until now.'[28] But the machinery of the University did not move quickly enough to avoid embarrassment all the way around. The *Evening News* of 3 May 1907 in an article with the headline, 'A Missing Edinburgh Lecturer', reported on a curious event of 1 May:

> The opening lecture was fixed for Wednesday, and the Senatus Academicus in their robes, with the bedellus and the mace were in attendance to give eclat to the occasion. The students were also there, but the lecturer came not.[29]

In fact, Keith was in bed at Dunbar still recovering from measles. He assumed that the authorities had already received his resignation at least by 30 April. Naturally, Keith was distressed when he read the report in the *Evening News*. He promptly wrote two letters on 5 May to the Secretary of the Senatus.[30] In the one, he apologised for any inconvenience and then stated his understanding of the facts of the matter: he had received no response to his queries of 21 February; he had erred in not getting the letter of 17 April posted, but he had been ill; he knew, however, that the Secretary had his letter 'on the 30th of April in ample time to allow notice to be given to the Senatus and to any students'; and he had never received word from the University to specify the opening date for the lectures. In the other, he addressed his reasons for resigning and made it clear that 'the ground on which I decided to resign was the fact that I could not obtain any answer from the Court that I could hold simultaneously the Boden Deputyship at Oxford and the Lectureship at Edinburgh'.[31] In due course, he received a letter of apology from the Secretary of the Court and the matter was closed. Keith certainly felt that he had been in the right and the University in the wrong; the records of the University support that conclusion.

By the time that Keith recovered from his illness and returned to London and to work at the Colonial Office, the Colonial Conference of 1907 had occurred between 15 April and 14 May. In the months following, Elgin directed a reorganisation of internal operations of the Colonial Office. Keith was transferred from the West Indian Department to take up a substantially more interesting assignment in the Dominions Department.

St Margaret's, Dunbar

The year of 1907 saw one other significant development in Keith's life. Whether this occurred during the time that he was in Dunbar recovering from German measles or shortly thereafter is not certain, but, at about that time it seems likely that MSK persuaded her sons to purchase land on which they would build a family home to her specifications. She had long been attached to Dunbar. Keith, too, knew the community well both through relatives and through the fact that he had regularly joined his mother there during his holidays from the Colonial Office.

The Keith brothers purchased $2\frac{1}{2}$ acres of land at the end of North Road on a rocky spit reaching out into the North Sea.[32] During the next two years, St Margaret's was built, the name coming from the house where MSK had grown up in Dunfermline. In those years of construction, this became MSK's major project and Keith, naturally as the son in regular residence, was involved.

While the house was not completed until 1909, this may be a good place to describe the house and its setting.[33] Using local sandstone, the builders and architect created an imposing, spacious, and extensive house for MSK. In its time, it had a spectacular and dramatic quality. As Keith approached it by carriage or motor from the centre of town, after the train journey up from London, he would catch glimpses of a large, reddish-orange house, in an

9   St Margaret's, Dunbar. Photograph by Jacki Morton.

isolated setting, appearing to rise from the water. In the distance, towards the northwest, he would see come into view those well-known peaks that mark the area of North Berwick and the eastern side of Portobello Bay. As he came closer and turned at right angles from North Road, he would enter a long, tree-lined drive to arrive at the portico framing the entrance to the house. Entering through the tall door, he would arrive in the great hall which, surrounded by an open gallery, rose the full height of the house to a skylight, surrounded by elaborate and delicate plaster filigree. He would have come 'home', or, at least, to the place where MSK would await him.

Clearly built on a baronial scale, St Margaret's contained four, well-appointed public rooms on the ground floor. A gracious, broad staircase rose upwards opposite the main door and, at the landing, a bay window provided sweeping views of the ocean scape in several directions. In addition, the house had 'eight bedrooms, cloak room, ... three maid's bedrooms, ... kitchen, scullery, double larder, wine cellar, coal cellar, wash house and ample press accommodation'.[34] It had full central heating. Space existed for at least four additional rooms to be completed in the attic. The grounds eventually included flower gardens, a tennis court, a putting green, croquet lawns, and a kitchen garden. Because of its location on a promontory, every room at St Margaret's offered extraordinary views of the ocean, the bays, and the rocky coast, set off by the manicured greens and fairways of the neighbouring golf course. For MSK and her third son, it provided a total contrast to life in the area around Battersea Park in London. All her sons and daughters, of course, stayed at St Margaret's at various times since it had been designed on a scale to make prolonged visits possible.

No letters or plans or notes remain to indicate which of the many bedrooms or other rooms Keith actually used when he spent his holidays there. One room on the ocean side of the house might well have been his. Rather small and somewhat isolated from the rest of the house, it contained a pleasing fireplace and built-in bookshelves. It offered views of the ocean and shore similar to those from the other principal rooms of the house. Whether that small room was his cannot be determined but what is clear is that he carried typewriter, books, and papers with him to St Margaret's, or, before that house was built, to whatever accommodation MSK arranged for in Dunbar. His scholarly work and his work for the Colonial Office never ceased simply because he was on holiday in Dunbar.

Theory of State Succession

In a continuation of combining scholarly work in several areas with staff work, he took another step, during these years, in his pursuit of legal prep-aration and, at the same time, made a significant contribution to scholarship in the field of international law. Following achievement of the BCL at Oxford, he proceeded to the preparation of a dissertation which might be offered there for the DCL. He wrote most of this work, *The Theory of State Succession with Special Reference to English and Colonial Law,* in the fall and winter of 1905–6 and presented it to the Faculty of Law in June with the approval of the Regius Professor of Civil Law, Henry Goudy. In the introduction to the book which was published by Waterlow in 1907, Keith acknowledged the helpful criti-cisms offered by T E Holland, Chichele Professor of International Law and Diplomacy.[35] Statutes governing the awarding of the doctorate required a space of five years from the time of admission to the bachelor's degree so that Keith could not complete the degree until that time had elapsed.

In this work, he undertook the study of state succession, that is, to inves-tigate what the actual legal status was when territory moved from the juris-diction of one country to that of another. His work in the Colonial Office had provided him with numerous illustrations of the sorts of questions that arose when such shifts took place. Canada clearly posed numerous, continuing examples because of the particular legal basis for the province of Quebec.[36] Many of the islands in the West Indies, particularly those which had been French or Spanish at some point in their history, offered other examples.[37] The thorniest illustrations of the time, clearly, arose in South Africa where forcible annexation of two republics after the War raised countless questions. The particular theory that Keith challenged was the one which argued for continuity, that is, that when a successor power took over a territory it gained not only control of the territory but assumed responsibility for all of the existing obligations, internal and external, involving that territory. In twelve carefully reasoned and tightly written chapters, Keith set out his theory which

he argued gave a better basis for addressing the series of related questions.
Early in the work, he stated his principle:

> It is submitted that the true doctrine of International Law with regard to the
> annexation of states is that the annexing power seizes all the rights in the
> country which can be obtained by possession of the territory of the country
> and its material resources, but it does not succeed to the obligations of the
> conquered Government nor to such rights as were personal to that Govern-
> ment.[38]

He assembled evidence to sustain that principle through the rest of the work.
The range and depth of his learning was clear throughout the book as he
drew examples from the history of the United States, including the very recent
cases of the annexation of Cuba, Puerto Rico, and the Philippines, from
the situation in South Africa, and, as well, from the history of European
international relations. Technical in detail, clear in analysis, and logical in
argumentation, the work was Keith's first formal essay in international law.
He was to continue his interest in such matters.

Colonial Conference, 1907

In August 1907, the Colonial Office was restructured by Elgin along lines
which participants in the sessions of the Colonial Conference, the last to be
called by that name, had agreed upon a few months earlier. Two major
changes affected Keith: creation of the separate Dominions Department and
formation of the secretariat to support the work of the Imperial Conference,
the new name for periodic meetings of Britain and the dominions. Keith
was assigned to the new Department and, as well, named Junior Assistant
Secretary to the Imperial Conference. These changes are important ones for
Keith's continued development as a specialist in the constitution of the British
Empire. Both changes put him in an unusual position to follow changing
relationships.
    The Colonial Conference of 1907 was significant in recognising the trans-
formation which had occurred in the actual status of the self-governing
colonies, clearly now, all to be referred to as dominions. The Conference met
in accord with the decision made in 1902 for regular meetings; that it was a
five year interval rather than four had to do with the change in political
power in Britain and, as well, internal political problems in both Australia
and New Zealand.[39] Keith knew about the agenda for the Conference and
about the issues that would arise, in part, because he was directly involved
with Australia and New Zealand in the specific problems of merchant shipping
legislation. Moreover, he maintained a friendly relationship with Just and
Cox, even after his abrupt transfer from the South African Department to the
West Indian Department. He was consulted by them as the time of the
Conference approached. Of course, during most of the weeks when the Conference was actually in session, Keith was out of the Office on sick leave. But,

when he returned to the Office in mid May, he had access to reports of the Conference and to members of the staff who had served it. He had good information about its accomplishments and the ways in which various issues had been resolved.[40]

One of the issues to be addressed concerned the ways in which closer union might be created among Britain and the self-governing colonies. This took its source from the despatch which Lyttelton had sent out in April 1905 suggesting the creation of an Imperial Council and the establishment of a permanent Commission.[41] Keith was not in the least surprised to find that members of the Conference ignored or defeated or simply put to one side schemes and proposals for closer political union of the Empire whether along the lines of federation or of creating a Council in favour of more general discussion about the Empire and the Conference structure itself resting upon the 'freedom and independence' of its members, words that were used by Campbell-Bannerman in his speech opening the proceedings. Keith had already concluded from his work, especially with Canadian correspondence and other materials, that proposals for union put forward by the Round Table group[42] or even by Lyttelton were not likely to be acceptable because they ignored the reality and logic of responsible government. When responsible government was granted, Keith reasoned, ministers had no alternative but to act in relation to the views held by the majority in the elected assembly or chamber to which they must be accountable. Thus, it was only logical that such ministers must give primary emphasis to pursuing the interests of their government and could not be expected politically to see those interests subsumed, and perhaps lost, within some larger imperial federation. That view had much evidence to support it: Canada, after receiving responsible government, levied tariffs as early as 1847 in her own interests in spite of Britain's conversion at the very same time to the principles of free trade as the new economic orthodoxy.[43] The Conference of 1907 implicitly rejected the goal of any organised form of imperial unity beyond what already existed. As Hyam comments, 'In the view of their opponents, the Liberals opted for autonomy and disintegration, rather than centralisation and integration'.[44] Keith understood that the lack of movement toward unification or centralisation was consistent with the principles of responsible government in the dominions. It is interesting to note that in his views against federationist ideas, Keith held the same position as Elgin.[45]

Keith was well aware that while the dominions were disinterested in closer political union, they were not averse to co-operation in the realm of defence. The reality of self-interest supported such a position. They were willing to organise and equip their military forces in ways compatible with those of Britain. Indeed, the Committee for Imperial Defence, created in 1902, which, from time-to-time included representatives of the dominions, became the body to design and advocate ways to achieve greater integration of defence forces throughout the Empire in the years preceding the First World War. Australia and New Zealand because of distance, small populations, and presumed vulnerability were especially co-operative in this regard while the other dominions were somewhat more hesitant.

One other major decision was taken by the Colonial Conference of 1907. Participants agreed on the nature of the Conference itself: it was clearly a conference of governments to be chaired in the future by the Prime Minister of the United Kingdom rather than the Secretary of State for the Colonies who would serve only as deputy. It was to meet every four years in sessions 'at which questions of common interests may be discussed and considered as between His Majesty's Government and his Governments of the self-governing Dominions beyond the seas'.[46] Keith saw this as further indication of the consequence of responsible government.

The decision of the Conference which had the most direct effect on Keith was the one to reorganise the Colonial Office itself. During the summer of 1907, Keith's superiors examined various ways to respond to that determination; they concluded that the best way was to create a separate section of the Office to be concerned principally with the self-governing dominions. On 15 August 1907, Hopwood, on Elgin's behalf, sent a lengthy memorandum to the Treasury in which the full details of restructuring the Office were outlined, together with an estimate of the net savings that would occur with the realignment of staff. Treasury approval was requested for the 'financial proposals contained in it'.[47]

The scheme may be summarised briefly. Elgin, with advice from the staff, found it best to restructure the work of the entire Colonial Office into three departments, each headed by an Assistant Under-Secretary of State: a Dominions Department under Lucas and Just to handle work with all colonies possessing responsible government together with adjacent dependencies; a Crown Colonies Department under Antrobus to deal with all other parts of the Empire, not necessarily to function internally any longer along geographical lines; and a General Department under Cox to incorporate all the responsibilities of the Chief Clerk plus work with regard to appointments, transfers, and other personnel matters. Hopwood also indicated that Elgin proposed the creation of four standing committees because of 'the want of co-ordination and concerted investigation in dealing with certain very important questions which at present arise in various Departments of the Office':[48] Patronage and Promotion, Railway and Financial, Concessions, and Pensions. He wanted authorisation to pay additional stipends to certain staff who would be assigned to ensure that those committees would function effectively. The Treasury eventually approved all these proposals and, by the end of August, the Colonial Office was reorganised.[49]

The Dominions Department incorporated all the work formerly performed by the North American and Australasian Department and the South African Department. In addition, it included responsibility for Fiji and the Western Pacific along with all other territories in South Africa: Rhodesia, Bechuanaland Protectorate, Swaziland, and Basutoland. For Keith, the new organisation and assignment meant very little actual change since he continued work on files from Canada, Australia, and New Zealand, work he had commenced in the spring, and simply added the files from Newfoundland and the Pacific. He was joined in this Department by R H Griffin and H F Batterbee as Second Class Clerks. Again, Keith was longer in actual service in the Office although Griffin, appointed in 1903, had seniority. Between the Second Class Clerks and the Assistant Under-Secretaries who headed the Department came two Principal Clerks and two First Class Clerks: G W Johnson (Principal), H C M Lambert (Principal), C T Davis (First Class), and W A Robinson (First Class). Keith had earlier worked under Lambert and he knew all the other men quite well. The staff of the Department valued Keith's work and contributions.

It is important to note that Keith did not handle any substantial South African work during his time in the Department; he occasionally wrote minutes on an odd file but that was all.[50] No note of Keith remains nor is there anything in the existing files of the Colonial Office to indicate that Elgin gave a directive to Lucas or Just to keep Keith away from South African materials. Such a restriction would have been logical since Keith, after his transfer to the West Indian Department, was back so soon, slightly over a year, in a section where South African materials were of major importance. Elgin and Churchill were still very much in control. The only significant change in leadership had been the retirement of Ommanney. Of course, Keith had developed considerable substantive knowledge about North American and Australasian matters especially with regard to complex issues of shipping, fishing, and international relations. Perhaps his superiors judged that those areas, together with his committee work, gave sufficient scope for his knowledge and energy without involving him in volatile South African issues. In any event, while Keith certainly had inside information, and must have had great curiosity as well, about the stages leading to the amalgamation of Cape Colony, Natal, Orange River Colony, and the Transvaal into the Union of South Africa, he did not play any direct part in departmental staff work to accomplish that result. It is highly likely that Just talked with Keith and consulted him on an informal basis, but no record exists to document such contacts. While Keith wrote extensively, both at the time and subsequently, about the nature of that Union[51] as it joined Canada and Australia to provide another illustration of a federation within the British Empire, he depended upon public documents, published debates, and personal knowledge for information, but he did not acquire his personal knowledge from a position of actually handling and minuting related files or from giving extensive, formal advice on constitutional points during the time when the Union of South Africa was being created.

Responsible Government in the Dominions

Late in the summer of 1907 as the Dominions Department was being created and Keith was assuming responsibilities there, his special knowledge was recognised in a public sense. He had become the member of staff particularly knowledgeable about the nature and limits of responsible government. When the Royal Society of Arts invited him to prepare an address analysing the development of self-government in the colonies during the nineteenth century, Keith was singularly well-qualified for the task and more than willing to undertake it. He received the invitation in late August and accepted it after securing approval from Hopwood early in September. Thus, during the fall of 1907, in addition to carrying on all his other work which included deputising during terms for Macdonell at Oxford, Keith prepared the lecture, 'The Development of Colonial Self-government in the Nineteenth Century', which he gave on 28 January 1908 before the Society with Sir Charles Dilke, MP, author of *Problems of Greater Britain*, in the chair.[52] Dilke introduced him as 'a great official'. That lecture was a success and, as Keith acknowledged, the genesis for the first edition of *Responsible Government in the Dominions*. For that book, which he completed by the end of 1908, Keith clearly drew on his lecture and on his knowledge of the deliberations and decisions of the Colonial Conference of 1907. Further, he took advantage of the brief experience he gained through serving in the Dominions Department as well as earlier experience in other sections of the Office. As a matter of fact, he had become a specialist in the affairs of the dominions, in a very real sense prior to the creation of the Department through his work earlier on the files of Canada and Australia and at the Navigation Conference.

The first edition of *Responsible Government in the Dominions* which Keith wrote subsequent to that lecture and which was published by Stevens and Sons in 1909 was an extremely important work. At the time, it provided the clearest, current description of the nature, status, and practice of responsible government and, because of Keith's particular role in the Colonial Office, it carried a ring of authenticity about it.[53] The reviewer in *The Athenaenum* recognised that: 'No one can be more competent to write on *Responsible Government in the Dominions* that Mr Keith of the Colonial Office'.[54] He summarised his comments on the value of the book by writing: 'Whatever view may be taken, his volume may be commended as an example of how to expand the Imperial Constitution.'[55]

The particular importance of this book lay in the fact that it followed in a great tradition of works which sought to interpret the constitution. The basic principle of that constitution has been, and remains, that whatever the King-in-Parliament approve is statute and, thereby, the law of the realm, including the Empire. Neither a single document nor any particular collection of documents exists to give full details on what constitutional usage was at any particular time. Rather, constitutional usage had to be deduced from, and described in terms of, the laws and customs of the constitution, a concept which required knowledge of statute law, of court decisions based upon common law, and of the whole range of customary understandings, principles, precedents, and practices enforced by the law courts, carried out by Parliament, and exercised by officers of the Crown in a given period. In the absence of any single document comprising the principles, boundaries, and rules of the constitution, treatises explaining and interpreting the laws and customs of the constitution take on singular significance and importance. Judges, lawyers, civil servants, and other servants of the Crown must turn to the treatises to find out about the constitution. This has been the case in the long history of persons who have prepared such treatises from the earliest attempt by Henry Bracton in the mid nineteenth centiry in *De Legibus et Consuetudinibus Angliae*, through the work of Sir Thomas Smith in *De Repub-*

licae Anglorum where he provided analysis of changes that had taken place in Elizabethan times,[56] on to the classic, influential formulation by Sir William Blackstone at the end of the eighteenth century in his *Commentaries on the Laws of England* which evoked sharp dissent from Jeremy Bentham who, in *Fragment on Government*, argued for utilitarian rather than historical principles as the basis for law. The nineteenth century was especially rich in the number of treatises to be produced. It was a time of great interest in constitutional matters, in part, because that was the period when the British were evolving principles for parliamentary reform and the related expansion of suffrage towards democracy and, at the same time, for the redefinition of the role of the state in an emerging industrial society. Three particularly influential books were those written by Walter Bagehot, *The English Constitution* (1867), A V Dicey, *Introduction to the Study of the Law of the Constitution* (1885), and Sir William R Anson, *The Law and Custom of the Constitution* (Part I, 1886, Part II, 1892). These writers explained and interpreted the ways in which the constitution had grown and changed over the centuries and in which it actually worked in Victorian times. They identified and described several of the most important continuing principles and customs of the constitution. They saw particular virtue in the constitution which, by contrast to political systems in Europe many of which rested on written constitutions, reflected continuity over a long period of time, yet which contained inherent flexibility and resilience so it could be adapted to new and different circumstances. That century also saw the start of the great projects to compile and edit constitutional documents by such persons as Bishop William Stubbs in *Select Charters and other Illustrations of English Constitutional History from the Earliest Times to the Reign of Edward I* (1870). In addition, the process of calendaring state papers and of publishing the Rolls series started.

Keith's role as an interpreter of changes in the twentieth century, thus, can be seen from the long view as one of those persons who undertook the task of analysing and explaining the nature of the constitution, especially as it operated in the Empire. In some senses, the constitution with respect to the British Empire was even more complex to understand and interpret than that within Britain itself, although one needed a thorough mastery of the law and custom of the constitution in Britain in order to approach its application to Empire. In part, this reflected the decentralisation inherent in the way in which the Empire was acquired and governed. But, as well, it reflected the fact that, in virtually every circumstance, the mode by which Britain governed a colony resulted in the creation of a body of written constitutional documents which could be assembled, studied, and analysed. These written constitutional documents included charters to trading companies, corporations, or proprietors giving authorisation to establish and govern a particular colony; in addition, they included Letters Patent and Royal Instructions given to governors setting out the position and power of the governor in relation to other governing elements in the colony.

Prior to Keith's work, the standard authority on government in the colonies was that of Alpheus Todd, *Parliamentary Government in the British Colonies* (1880; 2nd edn, 1894). Keith's position in the Colonial Office at the time of substantive changes in the relationships among the dominions and Britain provided him with an unusual opportunity to see directly what was happening. Then, in the tradition of earlier commentators, he wrote the first edition of that treatise on responsible government to explain the constitutional principles and practices in relation to the Empire; subsequently, he carried it through two further editions.

CHAPTER 7

Dominions Department, 1908–1912

In the spring of 1908, Keith, and others on the staff, experienced change in leadership at the Colonial Office. With deteriorating health, the Liberal Prime Minister, Campbell-Bannerman, was forced to resign in early April and turn over his role to H H Asquith who proceeded to reorganise the Cabinet.[1] Elgin was promptly dropped from the Colonial Office and, as well, from the Cabinet to be replaced by the Earl of Crewe as Secretary of State for the Colonies. Churchill, who remained in the Ministry, was replaced by Lieut-Col J E B Seely as Parliamentary Under-Secretary of State. These changes occurred by 16 April. It is interesting to note that Keith, in spite of the summary treatment he had received in 1906, wrote to Elgin's family to express appreciation for his time and leadership at the Colonial Office.[2] In the rest of the time that Keith was in the Colonial Office, one other significant change in leadership took place. In the autumn of 1910, Lewis Harcourt replaced Lord Crewe in order to have leadership of the Colonial Office in the House of Commons, especially with the prospect of an Imperial Conference on the horizon. Harcourt brought considerable experience with him.[3] So far as Keith was concerned, both Crewe and Harcourt, together with the various Parliamentary Under-Secretaries, appreciated Keith's work even if they, like their predecessors, occasionally complained about the obscurity of his arguments and his handwriting.

Range of Keith's Work in the Department

There was, however, a continuous sense of disappointment on Keith's part that his situation never seemed to improve. He hoped for some sort of promotion, but that had to be related to seniority which he, of course, never regained following his retransfer from the Crown Agents. He hoped that all of his industriousness would receive some sort of financial recognition. In September 1910, he wrote to Lucas about 'the possibility of improving in some measure my position in the Office'.[4] He argued that he wanted no special gratuity for a specific piece of work, but that he wanted an improved situation. He continued:

> I deal with far more papers than any other junior in the Dominions Department and by my legal attainments which are admittedly superior to those of any

other junior clerk in the department. ... But my position in the office generally is absolutely hopeless and I feel certain that my services in my present capacity are much more valuable than they would be in any other.[5]

The rules and regulations for staff permitted no variation in the principle of seniority and, thus, Keith remained where he was, for the time being.

What was the work that he was doing that led him to feel inadequately rewarded? A review of the work he handled in the time before he finally received a transfer as Private Secretary in December 1912, gives some justification for his feelings. Each of these areas requires further analysis. But it is possible, here, to indicate the categories to be considered: he continued his work at minuting despatches and other papers; he wrote two of the major studies for the Confidential Print series and several lengthy memoranda on various constitutional points; he served as Secretary to, and member of a variety of committees, especially interdepartmental ones; he played an unusual role in liaison with new governors and with political leaders in the dominions; he received considerable external recognition as the authority on dominion matters; he was the member of staff designated to be the liaison member of the International Colonial Institute, in Brussels, eventually becoming a corresponding member of the Executive of that organisation; and he was in the secretariat of the Imperial Conference. Simply to summarise the categories related to the Colonial Office, without mention of his external work, is to suggest that Keith's activities went substantially beyond the bounds normal for a Second Class Clerk.

To turn for analysis to the first of these areas, minuting of papers, it is clear that Keith continued with the files he had started working on in the spring of 1907, North American and Australasian, plus some work on matters from islands in the Pacific.[6] Correspondence from Canada, of course, involved only the office of the Governor-General. Newfoundland continued its life as a distinctly separate colony and so its governor and Premier dealt directly with the Colonial Office. In contrast to Canada, the files from Australia were quite extensive since each of the states maintained its direct link to the Colonial Office, and so did the Commonwealth through the Governor-General's Office. In addition to expanding his knowledge about the two different federal unions, Keith knew about the small-scale, isolated nature of New Zealand and, in his view, its legitimate desire for status similar to the other dominions.

From time to time, questions were raised in the House of Commons about certain colonial matters. Keith was one of the staff to whom leaders of the Office turned for information. For example, he prepared materials for Seely on land taxation in the self-governing colonies, on the nature of second chambers throughout the self-governing colonies, and on the ways in which the referendum worked in the Australian constitution.[7] He prepared lengthy minutes on such matters as the crisis in Queensland in 1908 where, in fact, a stalemate occurred as a result of the elections.[8] Crewe needed a summary so that he could understand the despatches and files; Keith provided it. Similarly, Keith was the person to write memoranda to interpret the constitutional issues involved in the crisis in Newfoundland in 1909.[9] He knew the constitutional laws and principles as well as the political scene stemming from the election in 1908 which, analagous to Queensland, resulted in virtual deadlock.

In one interesting minute dealing with a request from the Imperial Federation League of Australia for Lord Crewe to go out and visit, Keith wrote:

> There is no doubt a great deal of feeling in the Doms because our leading men will not trouble to visit them, tho they can visit the Continent or the USA. People have often talked to me of it.
> On the other hand all the talk of closer union is vague, useless, and misleading. Closer union is a very long way off, if practicable at all in our time.[10]

His views, thus, about the nature of imperial federation or some sort of union were reflected in the comments he prepared.

In late 1910, Harcourt, in his initial month at the post, needed to be clear about the nature of amendments to the Australian constitution; Lucas drafted a memorandum on the subject but handed it to Keith for checking and additions. Keith noted:

> I agree, therefore, with the 'Times' correspondent that federation has not had a fair trial, but I think the cause really is the attitude of the High Court and the attempt *in originally forming the constitution of the Commonwealth* [Lucas' insertion] to introduce into a British colony the principles of the interpretation of the United States Constitution. It may be doubted if these principles are legitimately consistent with responsible party Government as practiced in this country.[11]

Constitutional principles, the nature of responsible government, political practice, all came within Keith's purview and he wrote on these, and numerous other subjects, in the minutes.

Yet, it was not only on minutes that Keith expressed his knowledge and ideas; it was also in papers specifically prepared at the request of his superiors. Two papers that went into the Confidential Print series are indicative of this: *Memorandum on the Reservation of Bills of the Commonwealth Parliament* (June 1908)[12] and *Memorandum on the Question of Treaties as Affecting Dominions* (September 1908; reprinted in October 1910).[13]

The first of these papers was prepared expressly at the direction of Lucas in order to give information to the then Governor-General of the Commonwealth of Australia, Lord Dudley, who was having difficulty in being clear on how he should handle the matter of reservation of bills. Keith wrote the memorandum as an internal document to be shared with Lord Dudley for his information. Lucas directed that it be printed because of its usefulness. Lord Crewe minuted, 'I am very glad this has been done.'[14] What was the issue? It rose out of Dudley's predicament in trying to follow imperial policy with regard to merchant shipping and, at the same time, to follow constitutional practice by acting only on the advice of his ministers, at that time, led by Alfred Deakin who took a rather dim view about any imperial interests as over and against Australian ones. The precedent in the matter of reservation had occurred in the preceding administration of Lord Northcote with respect to the Judiciary Bill passed by the Australian Parliament in 1907. In that situation, the Colonial Office had recommended reservation to permit time for the Lord Chancellor's Office to make some suggestions. Deakin did not accept that reservation was appropriate, given the nature of responsible government. Deakin's biographer cites from the Deakin Papers about this as 'the foolish intervention' and 'another reminder of what ineptitudes the "rearguard" Colonial Office is capable of perpetrating'.[15] In the paper, Keith started out by restating Section 58 of the Constitution of the Commonwealth and then pointed out the dilemma which rose from the wording:

> when a proposed law passed by both Houses of the Parliament is presented to the Governor General for the Queen's assent, he shall declare, according to his discretion, but subject to this Constitution that he assents in the Queen's name, or that he withholds assent, or that he reserves the Law for the Queen's pleasure.[16]

The problem of acting consistently under that phrasing was the sort of legal problem that Keith liked to untangle. How could one exercise 'discretion' and still be 'subject to the Constitution' which required consultation with Ministers? The thrust of his analysis was that the Governor-General ought to 'communicate with the Secretary of State so as to secure that he shall not place himself in conflict with his Ministers unless it is clear that the Imperial Government desires the reservation of the Bill'.[17] That conclusion could scarcely have been satisfying to Deakin but, in the event, did apparently help Dudley.

The other paper that went into Confidential Print had to do with the complexity of treaties and dominions.[18] This theme and issue emerged as of very great significance in these years. The premise was that the British Empire was an entity, a unity based upon the existence of a single monarch and a single Crown; thus, relations between the British Empire and other states were to be conducted between the Foreign Office in Britain and all foreign powers. But, that premise was already breaking down in the area of commercial treaties. Interests of a particular Dominion were not necessarily congruent with interests of Britain itself. How to reconcile these conflicting demands? Again, this was the sort of intricate problem that appealed to Keith. From the paper he prepared in 1908, which was reprinted in 1910, he continued to be the person in the Colonial Office to whom questions about treaties and related matters were put. In the paper, he restated the premise for foreign relations and treaty-making. He then acknowledged that there was the possibility of separate adherence to, and withdrawal from, treaties by the Dominions. Further, it was possible for Britain to negotiate treaties that involved the interests of only one Dominion, as well. Yet, ratification and implementation of treaties involved the Crown. It is interesting to note that in this paper Keith began what was going to become a long-standing practice, the practice of quoting from himself. Several references occur to his book on *State Succession* as well as to a recent article published in the *Journal of*

Comparative Legislation. It was Keith who provided guidance within the Office when it became clear that Canada was going to create a Department of External Affairs within the Prime Minister's Office. Keith felt that Canada might do whatever it wished with regard to such a Department. In other words, Keith did not oppose the creation of a Department of External Affairs, perhaps because of his earlier knowledge of Joseph Pope who would head it, but on principle he saw no reason to oppose it even as he insisted on the existence of a single route for information, instructions, and inquiries between the Governor-General and the Secretary of State for Colonies.[19]

In addition to the two papers published in the Confidential Print series, Keith wrote many other substantive memoranda. It may be sufficient here simply to indicate the subject and times. In the autumn of 1908, he developed a thorough discussion of colonial naturalised British subjects.[20] In March 1910, he oversaw the collection and compilation of data about the functioning of second chambers in the dominions and then wrote the memorandum to interpret and explain the data.[21] In the fall of 1910, he prepared many papers for use by the staff of the Colonial Office as they engaged in preparation for the Imperial Conference in the late spring of 1911. Among those were papers on divorce and marriage laws (November),[22] exclusion of aliens, that is, immigration control (November),[23] interchange of officials between the Colonial Office and the dominions (November),[24] appeals to the Judicial Committee of the Privy Council (December),[25] and navigation laws and related matters (December).[26] In May 1911, he prepared another lengthy memorandum this time dealing with the position of state governors in Australia, especially in relation to the position of the Governor-General and the Crown.[27] In all, these papers, and others he prepared, represent a very substantial body of work providing staff of the Colonial Office with information, data, and interpretation upon which decisions might be based. On these various papers, other members of the staff commented and, frequently, disagreed. Yet, Keith's work was the basis for valuable discussion.

In addition to the papers he prepared and the minutes he wrote, he served in yet another important capacity, that is, as secretary to or member of a variety of committees. Here, his known diligence, his memory, and his reputation for speedy production of minutes, drafts, and reports were all brought into play.

For several years, he was Secretary to the Advisory Board for Tropical Disease Research Fund. This was a body which included representatives from other departments of government and, as well, from the medical profession. It had an important role to play in determining the allocation of funds to the various schools specialising in the study of tropical medicine. The Committee usually met in the late afternoon once a month, except during the summer. Agenda, minutes, correspondence, and follow-up activities were part of the Secretary's task.[28] Established in 1904, the advisory committee oversaw, as well, the creation in 1908 and subsequent operation of the Sleeping Sickness Bureau to which Keith also served as Secretary.[29] It had a steering committee which was a subgroup of the larger Tropical Disease Advisory Committee. The bureau was essentially devoted to the collection and publication of data

10   Arthur Berriedale Keith *c.* 1910. Photograph courtesy of Mrs J Walcot Burton.

about the incidence of that disease. Keith served both of these bodies dealing with tropical disease until the time he left the Office. Numerous expressions of appreciation were extended to him during that time for the excellence of his work.[30]

In the autumn of 1911, Keith received another assignment to an inter-departmental committee, this time, as member rather than as secretary. When Lucas retired from the staff of the Colonial Office, Keith was named in his place to represent the interests of the Office on the Visual Instruction Committee.[31] This is a body that was created in 1902. It included a dozen persons: representatives from the Board of Education, the Scottish Education Department, the India Office, the Crown Agents Office, the National Gallery, the Victoria League, the Colonial Office, and elsewhere. Its purpose was to prepare a series of lectures about the nature and variety of the British Empire to be illustrated with lantern slides. An extensive syllabus was developed to incorporate the lectures. Essentially designed for schools, the slides and lectures could be used, as well, by various groups interested in imperial concerns or adult education. Here Keith's role was slightly different. Yet, again, he worked diligently for the committee, attended the monthly meetings, and saw that the staff of the Colonial Office was kept informed about its work. He reviewed the text of the syllabus as it was developed and made various suggestions, but was not a principal author.[32] This committee, moreover, brought him into working relationship with another important group of persons.

Minutes, special reports, committee assignments all were part of Keith's work. In addition, in carrying out his assignment at the Dominions Department, he became involved with numerous colonial governors and with political figures in the dominions. This relationship was at two different levels. At the formal level, Keith was responsible for writing minutes on the despatches from the various governors. That required him to develop knowledge of the issues which the governor raised. Often, too, he commented on materials which had been transmitted by the governor from one of the political leaders in the dominion, usually the Premier. Also, at the formal level, Keith was responsible for the necessary paper work and arrangements that were the essential result after a person had been named by the Crown as governor. To give but two examples, Keith was the staff person designated to work with Sir Thomas David Gibson-Carmichael after he had been named Governor of Victoria in 1907. This required Keith to draft the Letters Patent and the Royal Instructions for the new governor. He then corresponded with Carmichael and answered the numerous questions he raised about the post in Victoria. He corresponded, as well, with persons in Victoria to apprise them of the requirements of the new governor. And, finally, he carried on necessary liaison to be certain that Carmichael had arrived safely and assumed his post.[33] Similarly, in 1911, Keith was the staff person who carried out the various details involved in the appointment of the Duke of Connaught as Governor-General of Canada to succeed Earl Grey.[34]

However, it was on the informal level, that Keith displayed unusual energy and maintained an extensive network of relationships through correspondence. He had started this in his early years on the staff and simply expanded the practice.[35] Because of this correspondence which his superiors at the Colonial Office knew about in a general sense, Keith was often better informed about political developments in the dominions than anyone else on the staff because the letters that governors wrote were fuller, more detailed, and more freely expressed than the formal despatches. Thus, Keith worked through formal channels as well as through informal ones. One of the constant requests he saw placed into formal despatches was that governors should transmit on a timely basis copies of parliamentary debates, of statutes passed in the dominion, and of reports on court decisions that had been rendered. These went into the Library of the Colonial Office; of course, Keith, with his interests, was desirous of having this sort of information readily available to him. Often, he would reinforce the formal request with a personal letter to the Governor or to the Colonial Secretary in the dominion or someone on the Governor's staff.

It may be sufficient here to give a few illustrations of the range of materials covered in this extensive informal correspondence. In October 1908, Sir Gerald Strickland, one of Keith's most frequent and continuous correspondents, wrote from Tasmania to indicate that 'to save public money, the official recording of debates in the Tasmanian Parliament has been discontinued for years past'.[36] The only thing he could send would be newspaper cuttings! In December 1908, Sir Eyre Hutson, by that time Governor of Fiji, wrote to acknowledge the receipt of the Parliamentary Paper of the House of Lords dealing with the Fiji land question. He then continued at considerable length about the need for land development in Fiji, the possibility of sugar refineries, and the interests of an Australian company.[37] Strickland in December 1908, indicated that he was glad to know from Keith 'that my quarterly reports appear interesting', and, in his usual petulant tone, commented that 'the Tasmanians are getting the best part of my life and of my wife's at half the market value of twenty years' experience at this business'.[38] In February 1909, Hutson wrote asking for 'some information as to the constitution of the Lands Board in British East Africa Protectorate, and a copy of any Regulations under which the Board acts'.[39] In April 1909, Sir William MacGregor, by that time Governor of Newfoundland and on his way to assume that same post in Queensland and whose work as Governor of Lagos Keith had known in the West African Department, acknowledged Keith's letter: 'Thanks for your kind congratulations on the Queensland appointment, which, as you know, is the most acceptable I could have had.'[40] He then continued with an extensive review of the political situation in Newfoundland, just the sort of inside report which Keith was delighted to receive. In July 1909, Sir Ralph Williams, newly appointed to Newfoundland, but still in London wrote to Keith to ask that a telegram be sent indicating his arrival time. He continued on with complaints about the pay he would receive. 'I confess I fail to see why I, who wanted to start earlier shd go without pay & two other Governors who did not shd receive the pay. However let it wait till I see you.'[41] In August 1909, Edward P Morris, the Premier in Newfoundland, wrote from London, 'Thanks very much for your kind note of the 17th. Please do not take this as the ordinary backhand expression. I mean it in its fulness.'[42] He continued with further complimentary words for Keith's kindness to him. But then, of course, he had business to transact: he asked Keith to look 'into the cable dispatch question ... let me know *privately* what you think of the matter'. He ended the letter with cordial greetings that suggested this informal correspondence should continue: 'Hoping you have had a pleasant holiday & that sometimes you will not mind my troubling you with an occasional line on Nfld matters.'[43] In yet another in the long series, Sir Gerald Strickland, now in Western Australia, wrote at length 'Private and Confidential' in September 1909:

> I am glad to send the photograph you desire under separate cover. ... I am very sorry to hear that MacGregor is suffering from an operation ... a long interregnum is very bad ... Neither MacGregor nor his wife have the slightest chance of upholding the highest average social status of the King's Representative in this part of His Dominions, and Queensland is the last place to which you should have sent a man who is so old that he is not working for promotion. ... In fact, it is the bane of the service here that so few of the Australian State Governors have been in a position to work for promotion. The life of a Governor is not conducive to strenuous effort. He is told by the Colonial Office that the first requirement is to avoid trouble, by the Press that he has to reign without governing, by Ministers that he is to do what he is asked, and by his family and staff that he is to amuse himself and them ... I am doing my best here in the hope of getting New Zealand.[44]

Also in September 1909, in one of many letters, Carmichael asked Keith for his opinion on two matters: 'Can an executive councillor chuck his position by resigning the council, with the full intention of going on to it again whenever he gets a chance'[45] and the matter of support for the Imperial Institute. Further, he asked for Keith's views on the South African Constitution. In January 1910, Keith wrote a lengthy memorandum to Walter Callan, secretary to Lord Dudley, Governor-General of Australia, in which he responded, as requested, to queries about the prerogative of mercy:

> I have read the correspondence with much interest and I will now give my views on the matters involved.
>   You will please understand that my opinion is quite unofficial as was desired by His Excellency and that if it appears dogmatic, it is merely for the sake of brevity. I know perfectly well how difficult the questions involved are and that what I write is open to serious criticism, though I think it is on the whole a correct view.[46]

He then continued with an explication of legal cases, of points in the Constitution of the Commonwealth, and of related precedents. In May 1910, Keith wrote to MacGregor reminding him of the need to send forward to the Colonial Office copies of the Law Reports. 'I am adopting the same procedure as I have been doing in other cases, and asking you as Governor if you would mention the matter informally to the Prime Minister ...'[47] Keith continued,

'We can hardly realise yet the death of the King. It is most remarkable that he should as late as Thursday morning have received your Agent General and accepted the souvenir from Queensland ...'[48] Numerous other examples of this sort of informal correspondence exist but this brief sample is sufficient to indicate the diversity and range of topics that were referred to Keith for his opinion or about which he had particular knowledge because a correspondent provided information to him.

Indeed, Keith was significantly different from other Second Class Clerks not only in matters relating to his assignments in the Office but also in the ways in which he became involved with various persons and activities beyond his immediate work. In order to understand his development, it is necessary to examine external recognition of his special talents, abilities, and knowledge.

Again, numerous illustrations exist. For example, it was Keith to whom fell the responsibility of responding to a request from *Webster's Dictionaries* of Springfield, Massachusetts for guidance on the definition and meaning of the term 'dominion'. He wrote the first suggestion for a response:

> The title 'Dominion' is now applied to the larger and more important of the self-governing Colonies of the British Empire in order to indicate their status being higher and their position of greater standing than that of an ordinary colony.
>
> 2   In the plural the term 'Dominions' denotes two or more of the self-governing Colonies, even if those are not all styled 'Dominion'.[49]

Keith's proposed definition generated discussion and disagreement among his colleagues, especially as he suggested providing a list to go with the definition. Several of his ideas, however, were incorporated in the response that was sent based upon a draft by Vernon.

In a different arena, Keith had correspondence with Lowell Oppenheim, Whewell Professor of International Law at Cambridge, and with D W Reeves, Director of the London School of Economics in late 1908 and early 1909.[50] Oppenheim enlisted Keith to put together a selection of cases dealing with the succession of states that could be published in *Zeitschrift für Volkerrecht and Bundesstaatsrecht* and also suggested to Keith that Reeves was interested in having him give a series of lectures on colonial self-government at the London School of Economics. Keith responded promptly with the cases; Oppenheim thanked Keith for them in cordial terms and continued: 'When I told her [Mrs Oppenheim] what an enjoyable evening I had spent with you she was quite satisfied.'[51] In the event, Keith did not give the lectures at the LSE because of other commitments on his time.

Another form of external recognition came through the various societies to which Keith belonged. He was active in the Royal Asiatic Society and in the African Society. He was a regular contributor to the *Journal* of the former while he held office and attended meetings of the latter.[52] He gave papers, joined in discussions, and came to know many of the members of the societies. He also participated in the Society for Comparative Legislation and by 1908 became one of the most constant contributors to that *Journal*.

Keith's knowledge about the development of self-government was tapped in other ways. It was Keith to whom Hugh Egerton, Beit Professor of Colonial History at Oxford University and then one of the most distinguished historians of the British Empire, turned when he wanted to have his new book on federations and unions checked for accuracy. Egerton initiated correspondence in 1910 and 1911; Keith read the book and provided analytical and editorial comments. Egerton expressed his appreciation to Keith in the letters and in print. 'By the bye should you object to my saying in the Preface that you had kindly read my text & helped me? I might possibly thusly help bring to the knowledge of a few readers your admirable book on "responsible government".'[53]

Another person who reached out to Keith for assistance was James Bryce, then the British Ambassador to the United States. Bryce desired accurate data for his book on *Modern Democracies* especially with regard to experience in Australia. It is worth quoting from Keith's letter to the state governors in Australia to illustrate the way in which he used his informal network to assist Bryce:

> There is a matter, quite unofficial, on which I should be very glad if you could help me.
> Mr James Bryce, the Ambassador at Washington, mentioned to me the other day when he was calling here that he was writing a new book on Democracy, and he was anxious to have a considered opinion by a good judge as to the influence of Civil and Railway servants in the Australian states on political questions ... he thinks that one of the chief dangers of democracy is the growing power of State employees and the difficulty of resisting their demands.[54]

After Keith collected responses from Australia, he sent them along to Bryce who, in due course, expressed appreciation.[55]

Numerous other persons contacted Keith and asked for his assistance and participation. Here it may be useful to mention three others. In August 1911, Keith received a letter from Booker T Washington, President of Tuskegee Institute in Alabama, seeking his participation at an International Conference on the Negro in the spring of 1912.[56] Keith was invited to be present and take part in the deliberations. A second person who reached out to Keith was C P Lucas who, after his retirement from the Colonial Office, went to Oxford as a Fellow at All Souls. There Lucas engaged in writing a number of works. He regularly called on Keith for assistance in such books as his edition of Lord Durham's Report as well as in the preparation of articles for the *Dictionary of National Biography*, and his editions of the historical geography of the British Empire.[57] A third person who should be mentioned is A V Dicey. The correspondence that he and Keith started much earlier continued throughout the time that Keith was at the Colonial Office, and beyond. Dicey regularly sent questions to Keith. He also sent proofs of books for Keith to review and check. One set of queries may suffice to illustrate the relationship. In 1909, Dicey wrote:

I am delivering a set of lectures of rather a miscellaneous kind on the things which ought to be known to persons who begin reading English Law. I shall come, inter alia, to the different division of the King's dominions, and shall probably attempt to point out under what bodies of law they are, speaking very generally, governed. These questions occur to me ... Will you when you can do it without too much trouble, give me your opinion on ...

1st   Can the colonies be divided exhaustively into Crown Colonies & self-governing colonies? ...
2nd   How, if at all, can one define a Crown Colony? ...
3rd   Am I right in thinking that the Government of British India must be treated as quite a separate thing from our ordinary system of colonial government? ...
4th   Am I right in thinking that the native states of India are not part of the British dominions so as to make a person born there a natural born British subject? ...[58]

Within two days after receiving these queries, Keith had a response to Dicey in which he provided clear-cut answers to each one: affirmative, with some qualifications, to the first, third, and fourth questions; a clear definition for the second:

... the most satisfactory definition would appear to be that it is a Colony in which the control of the Executive, including the appointment and dismissal of the Officers, rests with the Secretary of State. In this sense of the word, which is, I believe, the most proper sense at the present day, the term covers all Colonies except those which have Responsible Government.[59]

This is but one illustration from a lengthy correspondence between the two men.

Still another way in which Keith's role in the Office differed from that of his colleagues had to do with his responsibilities for liaison with the International Colonial Institute. This was an international organisation established in 1894 under the initiative of King Leopold II of Belgium.[60] It was a body that had its headquarters in Brussels, and had support from the Kingdom of Belgium. Its stated purpose indicated that it was an 'association exclusively scientific and without official character'.[61] In part, it appears to have been created to give some degree of objectivity to the collection of information about various colonial systems; in part, it may well have been some sort of public effort on the part of Leopold to put a rational front on colonialism especially as he practised it in the Congo Free State. In any event, Belgian support and interest was very clear especially as Camille Janssen, its Secretary General, was a former governor of the Congo. Membership specified in the initial statutes for the Institute included sixty persons distributed among the various colonial powers: Germany (5), Britain (11), Belgium (3), Denmark (2), the United States of America (3), France (7), Italy (3), the Netherlands (6), Spain (3), Portugal (3), Russia (5), Latin America (3), and others (6).[62] Many of the persons involved had had direct experience in colonial service or as governors of various colonies.

The Institute held sessions on an irregular basis. For example, the first sessions were organisational ones in Brussels in 1894–5. There was then a

hiatus before the next session in Paris in 1900. Subsequent sessions were in
The Hague (1901), London (1903), Berlin (special sessions in 1903 and
1904), Wiesbaden (1904), Rome (1905), Brussels (special sessions in 1906,
1907 both April and May, with a full session in June), Paris (1908), The
Hague (1909), Brunswick (1911), Brussels (1912), and London (1913).[63]
The session for 1914 had to be postponed because of the outbreak of war.
What sorts of activities took place at these sessions? Papers were presented
and information was exchanged about various colonial matters ranging from
fairly technical aspects such as those related to mining or agriculture or
irrigation or transport or tropical diseases to more administrative aspects
such as those dealing with the applicability of laws, the extension of education
to natives, the forms of justice, and the like. Following each session, a complete
report was published together with the papers which had been prepared for
consideration and discussion.[64]

In addition to its meetings, the Institute compiled and published an extensive collection of materials about colonial affairs. In effect, it was an organisation specifically designed to deal with certain aspects of comparative colonial policy and practice. The publication programme involved ten classes of
work with materials edited and produced regularly under each of the classes:
manual labour, colonial civil servants, financial operations, administration
of protectorates, railroads in the colonies and adjacent territories, mining,
systems of irrigation, fundamental legal systems, education for natives, and
hunting rights and conservation.[65]

Further, the Institute compiled a library of materials at its offices in Brussels.
This library consisted primarily of copies of official publications from the
various governments involved. A catalogue published in 1908 indicated that
the largest single collection of materials, appropriately enough, came from
the British colonies and British India.[66]

British participation in the work of the Institute was essential and significant from the beginning. Lord Reay, for example, was present at the
organising meetings and continued to be an active participant for many
years.[67] Other persons from Britain who were regular participants included
Sir Hubert Jerningham, former Governor of Trinidad, and Sir Alfred Lyall,
former Governor of the Northwest Provinces and a current member of the
Council of India. Keith first became formally involved with the Institute in
1908 when he was named the member of staff in the Colonial Office to be in
liaison with the Institute and to provide information for the publication
programmes from materials collected by the Office.[68] By February 1909, he
was seen as an important asset by the Secretary General of the Institute and
others and, so, was elected as a 'membre effectif' of the organisation.[69] This
meant that not only did he continue to provide information from the Colonial
Office for the various programmes of the Institute, but also he was expected
to become involved in policy matters and the operation of the Institute itself.
In fact, Keith never attended a meeting of the Institute other than the one
held in London in 1913. Regularly as a member of the organisation, he was
invited and expected to attend but in each instance he found reasons for
seeking an excuse for not attending. He did, however, meet the other British

members as they assembled in London. Thus, from 1908 through to 1914, his relationship to the Institute depended primarily upon correspondence.[70] He also carried on correspondence with various members of the Institute as they would seek his counsel and advice on various matters of colonial policy, especially about the succession of laws. Keith worked with British members of the Institute and assisted in the arrangements for the meeting in London in 1913. His work for the Institute was useful to him as he was the person in the Colonial Office to collect information and see that it was transmitted to Brussels. Clearly, he was interested in the sorts of information that the Institute assembled since it helped him in his understanding of comparative legislation and, indeed, gave illustrations for the ways in which responsible government in the British territories was significantly different from what was happening in any of the other colonial empires.

Staff of the Imperial Conference

The last of the special assignments which Keith carried out was related to an important development in relationships between Britain and the self-governing dominions, that is, the emergence of the Imperial Conference as an organisation with its own secretariat. Keith was Junior Assistant Secretary to the Imperial Conference and, thus, a member of that secretariat from its creation in 1907.

It is quite clear that at least one of the self-governing dominions would have preferred the creation of a secretariat for the Imperial Conference which would have been detached from the Colonial Office.[71] If, as the Conference of 1907 had determined, subsequent conferences were meetings between heads of governments with the Prime Minister of the United Kingdom as Chairman, would it not seem to continue the predominance of the Colonial Office if the secretariat were housed there rather than in, for example, the Prime Minister's office? As Elgin and his staff considered the matter, they concluded that it would be more efficient to have the staff for the Imperial Conference closely linked to the staff for the new Dominions Department. Thus, as the Office was reorganised in the summer of 1907, a parallel structure to support the Imperial Conference was created within the new Dominions section and, in fact, used personnel from that group. Just, Assistant Under-Secretary of State, and one of two persons sharing direction of the Dominions Department, had his range of responsibilities expanded to become Secretary to the Imperial Conference. Two persons assisted him in carrying out those responsibilities: Robinson, First Class Clerk in the Dominions Department, became Assistant Secretary to the Imperial Conference while Keith was named Junior Assistant Secretary. What was this secretariat to do? It was to become specifically responsible for the affairs of the Imperial Conference, as such. In other words, three staff persons would carry the task of seeing that materials for the next sessions of the Imperial Conference were assembled, that concerns of the dominions were properly related to the agenda, and that details of arrange-ments for the meetings of the body were attended to. In addition, the secretariat was, from time to time, to collect information and data from the dominions and then to produce papers analysing and summarising[72] that material. In short, the secretariat, although intimately interlocked organisationally and personally with the Dominions Department, was designed to serve the new purpose and structure of the Imperial Conference. Keith was involved in the work of the secretariat from the outset.

During Keith's time, several different meetings occurred which involved the United Kingdom and the dominions. Whatever the meeting and whatever his actual relationship to it, Keith, because the staff of the secretariat was within the Dominions Department, had full access to information about all such meetings.

In the summer of 1909, the Imperial Conference on the Defence of Empire met from 28 July through to 19 August. Six sessions took place during those weeks. It had one focus: imperial defence and the role of the self-governing dominions in this. Meetings were held principally at the Foreign Office with one session at the War Office where the Subcommittee on Military Defence also met; the Subcommittee on Naval Defence met at the Admiralty.[73] In all these meetings and discussions, it was clear that the representatives from the dominions wanted an imperial defence scheme to continue to exist and were prepared to have the United Kingdom continue to carry the principal financial and strategic responsibility for that even as they emphasised that the extent of dominion participation would be determined locally in relation to each of the parliaments involved.

Keith was not present at the sessions of this conference on defence. Earlier, he had had his summer holiday approved and, so, went off to Dunbar by 19 July. Of course, he did know about the preparations for the conference including the desire of the British government to secure stronger commitments from the dominions about funding and support of an imperial defence strategy. Likely, he read accounts of the outcomes of the conference with interest.

The summer of 1909, however, took an unanticipated turn for Keith. He contracted a serious case of scarlet fever and that illness was followed by 'scarlatinal rheumatism'.[74] He had to remain in Dunbar for many months. In all, he was absent from the Colonial Office for seventy-nine days, not returning to work until 20 November. He received letters of concern from colleagues in the Office as well as from his various correspondents throughout the dominions.[75]

By the time of the next imperial gathering, Keith had recuperated and was able to play his role as Secretary. In May 1910, the Imperial Copyright Conference took place. Joining Keith in his role at the meetings was T W Phillips of the Board of Trade. In preparation for the sessions, Keith wrote two memoranda: 'The Legal Position of Copyright with Special Regard to Canada' (sixteen pages) and 'On the History of the Question of Copyright' (forty pages).[76] In the latter, he summarised the various problems involved with the present status. The basic issue was whether or not legislation enacted in the United Kingdom with regard to copyright had overriding applicability to the self-governing dominions or whether they could, in fact, develop other requirements for copyright. Keith wrote many drafts of material for this conference and also carried on principal liaison for the Colonial Office with the Board of Trade.[77] The result of all this work was to accept as a matter of principle that the parliament of the United Kingdom, the imperial parliament, could legislate on the matter for the entire empire with the understanding that the applicability of such legislation to a self-governing dominion would require an action by that dominion either through its parliament or some other legal instrument; and that dominions could legislate on copyright themselves. Keith then, with others, drafted a model bill for copyright based on those principles.[78] Keith participated in subsequent discussions involved with enactment of the legislation in the spring of 1911.

Copyright matters involved not only relationships among the United Kingdom, the self-governing dominions, and the British Empire but, as well, with all signatories of the Berne Convention which included the principal countries in the world. Copyright was simply one of the issues on the international scene which brought the staff of the Colonial Office into an unusual role as being, for all practical purposes, the representative of the self-governing dominions to the Foreign Office. This role requires interpretation.

It was clear, and Keith understood this well on the basis of direct experience and personal liaison, that the Colonial Office was the principal route through which the governments of the self-governing dominions related to the branches of the British government. The Colonial Office was the clearing-house or nerve centre for all communications. Moreover, it really served as the foreign office for the dominions since, in these years under consideration, there was no shift in the fundamental position about the unity in foreign relations that Keith had outlined in the paper on treaty-making in 1908: the Foreign Office headed by a cabinet minister of the British government was the sole foreign office for the entire British Empire. But there were serious problems with that principle and each of the dominions sought somewhat different interpretations of it. New Zealand was most ready to accept it in its entirety, especially if practice coupled with the principle guaranteed naval defence. Both Canada and Australia increasingly had serious problems with the principle, Canada because of her need to deal with the overpowering presence of the United States and Australia because of distance, of tension between the states and the Commonwealth, and of political differences between Deakin and Fisher. Newfoundland frequently felt that her interests were totally forgotten by everyone, but accepted the principle if her ministers could have some opportunity to influence the Foreign Office. The creation of the Union of South Africa brought into the arena a new entity, eager to set a mark of independent action. As the years moved along towards 1914, it was clear that the unitary principle was subject to considerable modification both in formal documents and agreements and, also, in actual practice.

One major series of international negotiations in this period involved the United Kingdom, Canada, and Newfoundland in addressing several issues involving the United States.[79] These issues consumed a considerable amount of energy on the part of Keith and others on the staff of the Dominions Department, precisely because of the role that the Colonial Office had to play with relationships to the Foreign Office. It is obvious from the vantage point of the latter part of the twentieth century that Britain was determined to find solutions to many of the issues which had plagued British-American relationships from the time of the settlement after the War of the American Revolution. In retrospect, it seems as if the extensive trade and financial networks that had evolved during the nineteenth century needed to be paralleled with solutions to problems of borders, fishing rights, sealing agreements, and the like especially as Britain began to feel threatened on the international stage. The tasks facing Keith and others were enormous, in part, because the Canadians were increasingly resistant, especially after, from their view, the ill-fated award on the Alaskan boundary, of trusting their relations with the United States solely to the Foreign Office. And, Newfoundland found herself in conflict not only with the United States over fishing matters but also with Canada, a sister dominion. Negotiations were complex, in part because Bryce would sometimes go from Washington to Ottawa to talk directly with the Governor-General and with Laurier, then report the results of his visit to the Foreign Office which, in turn, would send a copy along to the Colonial Office which, then, would have to repeat instructions to the Governor-General about the proper route for relationships between the United States and Canada, that is, via the Colonial Office to the Foreign Office to Washington back to London, interdepartmental memoranda, and then to Ottawa. Cumbersome, to say the least, is the way in which the Canadian government viewed the matter. It is some measure of the patient skill of the staff of the Colonial Office that so many matters were settled, in one way or another, in the relationships among the principal members of the North Atlantic Triangle, the United Kingdom, Canada, and the United States, or quadrangle, if Newfoundland is included. The list is impressive: Pecuniary Claims Convention, International Waterways Commission, Boundary Treaty (northern United States, southern Canada boundary), a General Arbitration Treaty to put many issues before the court at The Hague, Conveyance of Prisoners Treaty, Wreckage and Salvage Treaty, Fisheries (Inland) Treaty, and Pelagic Sealing in the Bering Sea.[80] The matter of the North Atlantic fisheries was incorporated into the items to go to arbitration. In virtually every one of these matters, Keith was involved at some stage or other, writing minutes, clarifying legal points, searching out documents, and preparing position papers. It is interesting that some of the Canadians anticipated that Keith would, in fact, be part of the British group at The Hague to handle some of the argumentation before the International Court of Arbitration in the summer of 1910. He, indeed, had proposed to Hopwood earlier that, instead of the Office retaining some barrister to do some of the work, he be assigned the task:

> As you know, I have had N Amer work in the main for the last two years ... and I have I suppose read nearly everything on it at some time or another. And so far as legal qualifications go for the sort of work, I can confidently refer to Prof Dicey who knows my books and other work.[81]

He certainly had full knowledge and carried on considerable correspondence with officials in Canada and Newfoundland about the various issues, but, as it turned out, he was not part of the British delegation.[82]

While some of these matters were under consideration, the next formal Imperial Conference occurred in 1911. Here, Keith did play a direct role and participate, as secretary, in the various sessions. The sessions, following the precedent of 1901, were planned to coincide with the Coronation of King George V. They were designed to last for approximately a month, some measure of the more leisurely pace afforded to statesmen in those days. They started on 23 May and concluded on 20 June.[83] Long before the Conference itself, Keith and other members of the secretariat were busy eliciting ideas from the dominions about items which should be considered for the agenda. Proposed matters were carefully reviewed by the secretariat and appropriate departments of the British government in order to be certain that suitable positions had been prepared.[84] In time, the proposed agenda was distributed to the dominions.[85]

When the sessions of the prime ministers, that is, the principal participants, took place in the Foreign Office rooms, Keith was present each time.[86] Various subcommittees met, especially the one dealing with imperial defence, a continuation of the discussions and concerns raised in 1909. In addition to following the work for meetings, Keith had an additional worry for it was during the time of the Conference that his mother's health was worsening. He attempted to keep in touch with her and to write in a way to cheer her up. An excerpt from his letter of 28 May is illustrative as he tells about one of the many receptions planned for participants at the Imperial Conference:

> The reception was huge & brilliant! There were any amount of Ministers, officials, soldiers, sailors, MP's & peers and pre-eminent among them for beauty and grace your son. ... The Duke of Connaught was there, and when the Duchess & he left the Ladies in Waiting also curtsied: I nearly laughed right out, so funny were they, but luckily didn't, for the Duke stopped to talk to Morris [Premier of Newfoundland] who was talking to me & who had just said in a loud voice how funny it all was. I saw Watson [Colonial Secretary, Newfoundland] & went off at 12.15. So far as I know, I alone of all the guests went on foot! ... I do hope you are a little better each day.[87]

The work of the Conference was significant. In the first resolution adopted, the principle of consultation of dominions on international agreements was approved, not, to be sure, in as definitive language as Canada would have desired, but still the point was made. In all, twenty-eight resolutions were approved covering a wide range of matters, such as: imperial defence; merchant shipping; copyright, patents, and the like; international exhibits; emigration and naturalisation; provision for deserted wives and children; court of appeal; support for cable, telegraph, post; commercial treaties and provisions for the dominions to withdraw; creation of a Royal Commission to study the resources of the dominions and the Empire; and the desirability of exchange of civil servants and of visits by ministers to enhance personal connections.[88] A review of the discussions of the Conference indicates that,

11   Imperial Conference, 1911. ABK top row, on the right. Courtesy of Peter Burron, Foreign and Commonwealth Office Library.

in spite of a generally harmonious tone to the meetings, and good support, though not unanimous, for the final resolutions, the principle of unity was seriously breached. It is clear that the dominion prime ministers understood that they had to live with the results of the Conference not in London but in their own parliaments when they returned home. Asquith's somewhat optimistic welcoming remarks were, in reality, not feasible in terms of responsible government:

> There are sitting at this table to-day six Prime Ministers, all holding their commission from the same King, and all deriving their title to its exercise from the voice and vote of a free democracy. We are all of us, I suppose, in our own Parliaments party leaders, holding and using power by virtue of the confidence of a party majority. But each of us when he entered this room left his party prepossessions outside the door.[89]

No one of the Prime Ministers could, in fact, forget the reality of party politics, especially since several of them had confronted change themselves in recent years.[90] Keith, on the basis of his direct experience with the discussions, debates, and decisions of the Imperial Conference of 1911, was extremely well informed about the positions held by each of the dominions. He had a unique basis for unusual insight into the workings of responsible government.

Keith's contributions to the work of the Imperial Conference received special recognition for he was awarded a Coronation Medal. He expressed his thanks to Harcourt in a note: 'I have the honour to acknowledge the receipt of your letter of the 13th of July forwarding the Coronation Medal which His Majesty has been pleased to award me. I desire to express my sincere thanks for your kindness in procuring for me the Medal.'[91]

Clearly, Keith's work in the Colonial Office, and beyond, exceeded that which would usually be expected of a Second Class Clerk. He carried out the range of tasks with speed, knowledge, and confidence. Yet, he felt, with some justification, that somehow the financial and other rewards he received failed to be commensurate with the work he was producing.

Changes in Domestic Life

Earlier, in her letter of 1907 in connection with the Lectureship in Ancient History at Edinburgh, his mother took the view that he received insufficient recognition and inadequate rewards for his work.[92] She hoped that, at some point, he would receive adequate recognition both in terms of status or position and in salary. MSK continued to be a dominating force in Keith's life, arranging the household to her desires, to be sure, but always with a view to seeing that he was well cared for. In these years, she saw St Margaret's completed at Dunbar and she organised her life around her house. Keith regularly took his annual holidays there.

Yet, with Keith busy in London, MSK had to find principal support from someone who would be close by when she was in Dunbar. She found that in a young woman, Margaret Allan, of an age to be a daughter. Margaret joined the family as her companion, eventually as virtual nurse, and as supervisor of the household. Unfortunately, no letter or note remains to document the precise time when Margaret entered into MSK's service. It seems likely that she had been with the family for, perhaps, five or six years by 1911, moving with them between London and Dunbar. From a respectable family in Bathgate, where her father was Town Clerk, Margaret came to know MSK, Keith, and other members of the family very well. She must have understood the mutual dependence that Keith and MSK shared.

Unfortunately for MSK, she was not to live to enjoy St Margaret's for very many years. While her health had always been precarious, she commenced, by 1909, or 1910, a series of debilitating illnesses which meant that, from 1910 onwards, she remained in Dunbar, still, as best she could, giving direction to the household in London. Keith went up as often as he could get away from London and wrote quite regularly. Two of his letters which remain indicate his affection for, and attachment to, his mother. Both are from the spring of 1911 when her condition was getting worse:

> 4 May 1911
> Park House
> 75, Albert Bridge Rd.
> London SW

My own revered Mother,

Just and Lambert (very reluctantly) have now consented to my departure, and your precious little boy will come (D.V.) to you on Friday with the milk-man.[93]...

> 18 May 1911
> Park House
> 75, Albert Bridge Road
> London SW

My own darling,

I hate having to put you off with such hurried notes as I have been sending you, and I am glad to sit down now and sent you less of a scrawl. ... I was so worried regarding you all yesterday. She [Margaret Allan] gave me a triple batch of news of you in her letter of the 17th which came as usual at 10.50 and so I felt more cheerful today regarding you. ... How good you are to me to take all the trouble you do for me. But you know how deeply I appreciate it.

> Ever most devotedly your son,
> A Berriedale Keith[94]

Her illness progressed and she died at St Margaret's on 31 July 1911 with the death certificate identifying Hodgkin's disease as the cause.[95] As it happened, three sons and her older daughter were in Britain at the time and so were present at her death.[96] They all participated in her funeral and burial in the cemetery at the Parish Church, Dunbar. The verse of scripture chosen for the stone marking her grave refers to but one aspect of her character, her piety: 'Blessed are the pure in heart for they shall see God.' She left a small personal estate of £125 and, by her will drawn up in July 1897, left everything, including personal and real estate, to her eldest son, Will, which meant that he inherited St Margaret's. Jean, her older daughter, was named to be executrix of the estate.[97]

For Keith, the death of his mother represented a major loss since she had guided and directed him, as well as run the household for so many years. How could he cope with such a change in his life? Clearly, he was devastated. In a letter of 8 August 1911, to Margaret Allan who had been closest to MSK in her final days, he expressed that devastation:

> When you go back, you will tell them what MSK wished about her things (do not forget the skirt for your sister) and then you will have done all you can for MSK. It is incredible to me that I have lost her for ever: it is utterly unfair that she should never have known happiness and that I of all people should have needlessly vexed her. Yet had I the faintest idea that she was in danger in 1910 nothing would have induced me to give her a moment's worry. Her death has deprived me of every incentive to action, for her pleasure was the only reward for which I really cared at all. I am satisfied with my own performance, and it was for her that I troubled to obtain marks of approval from others and whatever I do it is now useless.
>
> Do not think that I undervalue your interest or your kindness; you will realise (for you knew her) that there is nothing that can make up to me for her. I wonder if she realised that.[98]

Beyond the emotional loss, and the wrench must have been considerable after thirty-two years of attachment to and dependence on his mother, Keith had, as well, to confront the practical issue of how his day-to-day life would be supervised and managed. Who would purchase his clothing and see to it? Who would plan meals, see to the necessary shopping, and oversee preparations? Who would attend to travel arrangements? Servants in London would be able to keep things going for a short period of time but they would require supervision, management, and direction, matters about which he had never been concerned. Here again, unfortunately, there is no documentation to the sequence of events.[99] Apparently, in the months soon after MSK's death, he asked Margaret Allan simply to continue on in the household in her role as housekeeper. Merely a year younger than Keith, she rejected that offer on the grounds of propriety. Perhaps Keith even considered sending for the Australian cousin whom, some years earlier, he had found attractive only to have his mother prevent him from taking any steps towards pursuing that interest.[100] Both of his sisters were married and in the East. Presumably, he spent the winter of 1911–12 coping as best he could until he put a different sort of suggestion to Margaret Allan, this time proposing marriage. She accepted. Their wedding took place at Azledale, Bathgate on 1 June 1912 with the ceremony performed by the Reverend W L Webster of the parish church.[101] Certainly, this was a marriage of convenience. For Keith, it meant the continuing presence of someone who knew his routine, his work, his needs, and his dependency; for Margaret, or Betty as she was called, it meant the security and respectability of marriage, the opportunity to continue in the service and support of a great man, at least so his mother had thought of him, and the continuation of her life in a household she had come to know. For both, it brought companionship and support and, in time, affection.

Regrettably, no letters, diaries, notes, or pictures of Margaret remain.[102] Whatever one can conclude about her is totally inferential and speculative from other materials. Apparently, she was poised and attractive. Likely, she was quite a contrast to MSK in that she was able to give Keith support in positive, selfless, and understanding ways. She had been with the family long enough to know him and his needs quite thoroughly. It seems unlikely that she made the move from housekeeper to wife in any aggressive manner but rather gradually shifted from the role of subservience to that of authority. Soon, she became a gracious companion to Keith. Many references are made to her as a pleasing and delightful hostess in the few years they lived in London after their marriage.[103] Keith, in the preface to his books, acknowledged her crucial role in assisting him in his writing both through sharing ideas and doing some of the secretarial work.[104] She must have accepted his genius and the responsibility of nurturing it further. Immediately, Keith was dependent upon her; eventually, he became devoted to her as well.[105]

Growth as a Scholar

Whatever else may be said of the arrangements for his domestic life, it is clear that his mother, and then his wife, so ordered the household that he was freed from the necessity of giving any of his attention to daily concerns, at least once he got through the winter of 1911–12, so that his entire mind and energy could go not only into the work at the Colonial Office but, as well, into the burgeoning scholarly work. While Keith worked in the Dominions Department and carried out, in his energetic way, the range of activities already discussed, he continued, at the same time, his growth as a scholar, an aspect of his life that was essential if ever he were to leave the Colonial Office for the academic world. In these years, he published several significant works in Sanskrit, completed his final law degree at Oxford, continued his essays on points of law, and undertook a major revision of his work dealing with responsible government.

In Sanskrit, his principal field of specialisation, he gained stature as a scholar. He was already known and respected among the small universe of Sanskritists, of course, for his numerous articles and for the production of the splendid catalogues. He had deputised at Oxford while Macdonell was away in India. In spite of the contretemps over the Lectureship in Ancient History, the Edinburgh University Court appointed him in 1908 as Examiner in Sanskrit, a position he held until eventually he became a member of the faculty.[106]

He maintained his association with the Royal Asiatic Society and contributed to the *Journal*. Simply to count his contributions gives some indication of his participation: thirteen articles, notes, in 1908; twelve, including the text of a major lecture which he gave before the Society, in 1909; ten in

1910; eight in 1911; and eight in 1912.[107] What is particularly impressive about the reviews is Keith's mastery of the literature of the field. He was readily able to cite the principal works to which the book under review related as well as to summarise theories which had some bearing upon it. His erudition came through in the reviews as he referred to works in various languages. The articles or notes frequently had a contentious tone to them; he never doubted the accuracy of his assessments and interpretations, even when he debated with leading scholars in the field.

On 9 February 1909, he gave a lecture before the Society, 'Pythagoras and the Doctrine of Transmigration', published in the July issue of the *Journal*. Interestingly enough, it was at that meeting when his younger brother, Alan, was elected into membership in the Society. With Lord Reay in the Chair, Keith made his presentation. In good style, he discussed the present status of the argument as to whether or not Pythagoras drew upon Indian religious and philosophic materials to develop his doctrine of transmigration, his approach to vegetarianism, and his great theorem in geometry. He indicated that there was general acceptance among scholars that Pythagoras did probably draw upon Indian sources. From that point, Keith launched into a detailed, thorough analysis of all the evidence he could assemble, moving easily through the literature of Greek philosophy as well as through that of classical India. He then concluded that the evidence simply could not support the proposition that Pythagoras had access to or drew upon Indian sources. He put his conclusions into six statements, the first three of which summed up his case:

(1) there is no historic evidence or antecedent probability that Pythagoras ever visited India or Persia, or came into contact with persons cognisant of and competent to explain Indian philosophy to him; (2) that the doctrine of transmigration as held by him can be most easily explained from the religious history of Greece, and in particular from the tenets held by the Orphic societies; (3) that the mathematical doctrines of Pythagoras were a direct outcome of his arithmetic studies and of his practical knowledge of the Egyptian methods of measurement.[108]

He produced two important works, published in 1908 and 1909, one by the Royal Asiatic Society and the other by Oxford: *The Śāṅkhāyana Āraṇyaka with an Appendix on the Mahāvrata* and *Aitareya Āraṇyaka*. In these, he worked his way through existing manuscripts to provide a complete edition of materials which had formerly been unavailable. Then, he provided all the critical apparatus to interpret and explain the works. Rapson reviewed them in the *Journal of the Royal Asiatic Society* indicating that Keith dealt 'comprehensively and exhaustively' with the Āraṇyakas, that he 'edited with great skill and judgment', and that he 'fully translated and most carefully elucidated both of these obscure and difficult treatises'.[109] He praised Keith for the work and commented that the task 'demanded a combination of profound learning with critical ability and also ... an unusual degree of patience'.[110] While he had some differences over points of interpretation, he acknowledged that

Keith in recent years had done much to remove the obscurity surrounding these works.

In addition to these works, Keith completed and saw into print two more catalogues, the first completing the task he had undertaken years earlier: *Catalogue of Sanskrit Manuscripts in the Bodleian Library. Appendix to Volume I, Theodore Aufrecht's Catalogue*, published in 1909; *Catalogue of Prākrit Manuscripts in the Bodleian Library* published in 1911. Keith's contributions were obviously extensive.

It was in recognition of such work that, in April 1910, Charles R Lanman, Professor of Sanskrit at Harvard University wrote to Keith. In that initial letter, Lanman as Editor of the Harvard Oriental Series asked whether Keith might not have something that he would consider publishing in that series. 'The Series bids fair to maintain for itself a respectable place in several branches of Indic philology ... I wish you'd consider the matter carefully and let me know speedily.'[111] And Keith did. He responded positively and began preparation for a work to be published in that series.

In addition to continuing his work in Sanskrit, Keith completed his preparation in law. His taking the DCL at Oxford was the culmination of the process he had initiated in his earlier days by starting law studies at the Inner Temple, continuing them at Oxford, and then preparing and publishing a dissertation which could be offered for the doctorate.[112] He completed that process in the spring of 1911 while his mother was ailing at Dunbar and while the Imperial Conference was in session. In another paragraph in his letter to MSK of 18 May 1911, he indicated that Margaret Allan had sent along his 'pretty' cap, part of his academic regalia for the ceremony, and that he was to be recognised at Balliol:

> A L Smith, now Dean of Balliol, asked me to lunch with overseas visitors on May 27 at 1 PM, promising to look after me and my DCL if I accepted which I have accordingly done.[113]

A note in the *Haddingtonshire Courier* of 2 June 1911[114] reported on his receiving the degree and printed, as well, a summary of his various achievements. He had, in fact, completed the programme of legal studies which he set out for himself, and had done that with his usual distinction.

Sanskrit, law, and, in addition, essays on points of comparative law were all part of his production in these years. He published these essays in the *Journal of Comparative Legislation*. In many issues, Keith had some note or article. These dealt with matters of current interest, particularly items about which Keith had knowledge from his work in the Dominions Department. Seven articles between 1908 and 1912 covered a range of topics: merchant shipping legislation, the union in South Africa, judicial appeals in Australia, matters of referendum in Australia, and the like.[115] Each provided detailed reference to documents available in the public realm if any reader wished to pursue the matter.

Following the conclusion of the Imperial Conference of 1911, in spite of all the domestic changes that he was dealing with, Keith undertook a major revision of his work on responsible government. He approached Oxford University Press to see whether they might be interested in publishing such a revision. R W Chapman, with whom Keith had already had correspondence on earlier publications, responded with enthusiasm. In part, he was urged to do so by Lucas who was anxious to see the project move forward.[116] In 1912, he completed the new edition of *Responsible Government in the Dominions.*

CHAPTER 8

Private Secretary, 1912–1914

In his final period of time at the Colonial Office, Keith received recognition, at last, by being appointed as Private Secretary to Sir John Anderson, by then the Permanent Under-Secretary of State. Keith had long felt that, in view of his extraordinary work in the Dominions Department, to say nothing of the range of external scholarly and professional activities in which he was involved, he should receive some position of greater status.[1] Certainly, the preparation of a new edition of his book on responsible government was yet another way in which Keith distinguished himself from his colleagues as Second Class Clerks: no one else was writing that sort of material for the public. No one else of his contemporaries had completed a DCL at Oxford, either. No one else was producing catalogues of Sanskrit manuscripts or writing books and articles in that field. Keith's work inside and outside the Dominions Department was simply prodigious. While his time as Private Secretary turned out to be quite brief, not quite two full years, he carried on his many-faceted life, now with the assured support of his wife. It is interesting to note that he and his wife did considerable entertaining. While earlier, during his mother's life, there had been occasions when people had been in their home, it appears that his new domestic arrangements permitted him to expand social life. Just one note from Archibald Fleming in June 1913 may be sufficient to indicate the tone:

> Dear Dr and Mrs Keith,
> I wish to send you and Dr Keith a line of my hearty thanks for the most interesting evening you gave us last week. It was a special joy to have the opportunity of knowing you both better.[2]

Scholar, clerk, and, fairly recently, husband, Keith took on new responsibilities at the Office.

Role as Private Secretary

Anderson, himself, had returned to the Colonial Office to replace Hopwood in July 1911 after the Imperial Conference had concluded. An old boy known to the staff, he had been in charge of the North American and Australasian Department when Keith transferred there in 1902. Subsequently, after receiving a knighthood, he went out to the Straits as Governor between 1904 and 1910. During those years he and Keith kept in touch through correspondence.[3] Each man had respect for the other; each had actual working knowledge of how the other thought and functioned. It had been Anderson who, in a rather paternal way, had urged Keith to transfer to the Crown Agents and seek his fortune there;[4] on occasion, Keith blamed Anderson for giving him what turned out to be such poor advice. When the opportunity arose to name someone responsible, efficient, and industrious to the post of Private Secretary, Anderson did not hesitate to make the offer to Keith; Keith had no hesitation about taking it, as indicating, at least, some improvement in status if not in rank.

Keith assumed his new assignment in the Colonial Office on 1 December 1912. A notice in The Times for that date let the public know about his new assignment. Persons wrote from many different quarters to offer him congratulations and best wishes in the post. Fitzgibbon Young expressed the sentiments of several: 'It is a wholly inadequate recognition of your great merits, but I hope it will only be the beginning of a distinguished "cursus honorum".'[5]

The position of Private Secretary was a position of considerable responsibility. Keith's diligence, integrity, and acuity were just the qualities needed for the post. Confidential matters needed to be handled and, in addition, the Private Secretary needed to see that materials were well prepared for the Permanent Under-Secretary whose office was succinctly described in the Colonial Office List as encompassing: 'Political, Constitutional and Military Questions, General Supervision, Papers on all Subjects before submission to the Secretary of State.'[6] At the apex of the bureaucracy of the Colonial Office,[7] the office of Permanent Under-Secretary was crucial to the effective functioning of the whole and, particularly, to the work of the Secretary of State. Obviously, a competent Private Secretary was essential; Anderson felt that he had that in naming Keith. The assignment clearly brought Keith into the full centre of the work of the Office since all matters passed through his hands en route to the Permanent Under-Secretary. In addition, it brought him into a choice physical location with a private office adjacent to the rooms of his chief.[8] In his final years, Keith had the sort of physical setting which he had long desired, space for books, journals, and papers to be stored for his use and space, as well, for him to work with efficiency!

What were some of the responsibilities which Keith carried in this new assignment? It may be useful, initially, to point out some of the special tasks and, then, to indicate the many ways in which he continued with previous activities.

There were numerous new tasks with which Keith had to become familiar. On behalf of his chief, he had to see that the Office ran according to desired patterns. This involved him, for example, in circulating memoranda from Anderson on the need for greater care in drafting letters and in answering questions about how the new telephone system worked.[9] When Anderson was ill in the spring of 1913, he simply sent his instructions in to Keith who carried them out and covered as best he could.[10] Problems with the actual tying of bundles of papers in the West Indian and General Department came to Anderson's attention; Keith sent off the memorandum to straighten the matter out.[11] He intervened by indicating to the Chief Registrar that two newspapers dealing with woman suffrage should not be carried in official mail bags to governors of the dominions.[12] He wrote the initial minute on a matter involving the Foreign Office and their view of how the Colonial Office should be responsible for direct representation of dominion interests. Keith was very clear:

> In my own opinion the more and more frankly the self-governing dominions are treated as equal partners in the Empire, the more likely is a satisfactory result to be obtained. It is, I think, increasingly clear that we must advance in the matter and it is probably better to do so willingly than to wait to be shoved on.[13]

His draft response to the Foreign Office was, in fact, the one sent which made the point that the dominions were to have as much direct representation in diplomatic matters as they wished to have, especially in view of the assurances given by Sir Edward Grey at the Imperial Conference of 1911.[14]

In addition to these matters, Keith attended to others. He had the task of co-ordinating materials for the Dominions Department Report both in 1913 and in 1914. He actually wrote a great deal of it even though he had reservations about the usefulness of such a publication.[15] He also learned about patronage from several directions. For instance, he dealt with a request from Victor Hood, Secretary to the Governor of Victoria and a long-time correspondent, who was eager for Keith's help as he attempted to become Private Secretary to the Governor-General of Australia.[16] Or again, he dealt with a query from Herbert Thiskelwhite about securing a place in the West African Frontier Force for a young protégé.[17] In both instances, he was candid about the reasons why he could do nothing.

It is important to note that, from his new position, Keith was finally able to secure approval for one concern in which he had been interested for several years, namely the proper title of address for the Governor of New Zealand. He had raised the matter from time to time, especially after it was clear by 1907, that New Zealand had the same status in the Empire as Australia and Canada. He raised it again after the creation of the Union of South Africa. At last, in 1913, he was able to get the concurrence of his superiors to use the form, 'Your Excellency', for the Governor of New Zealand and of 'Her Excellency' for his wife.[18]

He also learned that there were times when the Private Secretary had to produce materials under great pressure of time. For example, he received a note from Butler on 11 March 1913, marked 6.30 p.m. in which, with a sense of panic, Butler indicated that Mr Scaddan of Western Australia was to see the King at 11.30 a.m. the next day: 'It is necessary that Lord Stamfordham [the King's Secretary] should have beforehand a brief note of Mr Scaddan's career and record, in order that HM may know what to say to him.

Can you possibly manage to let me have something here soon after 10 tomorrow morning?'[19] And, apparently he did.

Further, he learned that a Private Secretary has some responsiblity for the social side of his chief's official work. In one remaining set of notes, Keith and the manager of the Carlton Hotel, J Kraemer, arranged a luncheon party of fourteen persons for Anderson with the price of 21s. a head to include everything, 'wines, floral decorations, cafe, liqueurs, cigars and cigarettes'.[20] Keith approved the menu; he provided information so that place cards could be properly prepared. 'I shall turn up shortly after 1 o'clock to arrange the cards in the places'.[21]

Various matters were referred to Keith as, for example, the request that came from South Australia to have the newly created degrees of Adelaide University recognised as the earlier ones had been. He hunted up the precedents and wrote a minute for Anderson and Harcourt about the matter, concluding that it would be appropriate for Letters Patent to be granted to cover the new degrees developed by the University.[22]

With the outbreak of war in the summer of 1914, Keith was responsible for seeing that several details were attended to. On behalf of Anderson, he saw that a memorandum was circulated which ensured that every department of the Office would be covered by 10 a.m.[23] He handled a request to Anderson from Lord Gladstone, formerly Governor-General of the Union of South Africa, about the question of South Africans who were of German nationality.[24] These then, with the other examples given, indicate some of the special tasks which Keith carried out in his post as Private Secretary.

In addition, however, he continued on with many of the same activities for which he had been responsible earlier. He still minuted papers in the Dominions Department.[25] As he wrote to Lord Liverpool, Governor of New Zealand, 'Fortunately I still continue to do my Dominions work and so will have the opportunity of following your progress in New Zealand'.[26] He prepared memoranda on topics where his particular expert knowledge could be used, for example, on the nature of the Judicial Committee of the Privy Council.[27] He continued to serve on the Tropical Diseases Committee and the Visual Instruction Committee.[28] He maintained membership in the various societies related to the work of the Colonial Office. For the Society of Comparative Legislation, he took a hand in persuading several dominions to subscribe to the organisation.[29] For the African Society, he corresponded with Lord Lugard and was successful in enlisting him as a member of the society.[30] In spite of his attempts to resign because he felt it would be better for the International Colonial Institute to have direct access to the Secretary of State for Colonies, he remained a member of that body and joined the other British members in carrying out the work of that organisation, especially its conference which took place in London in 1913.[31] There was no slackening in his informal correspondence with governors and governors-general. There is a lengthy list of persons with whom he maintained regular contact, who provided him with information, and who sought his help and advice.[32] That correspondence was an important aspect to his functioning effectively in his new post since he often had information that could be helpful to his chief. He became involved in the orientation and preparation of several of the new governors and their staff, for example: H A Galway (South Australia, 1913),[33] A L Stanley (Victoria, 1913),[34] Ronald Munro-Ferguson (Commonwealth of Australia, 1914),[35] and Sydney Buxton (Union of South Africa, 1914).[36] In several instances, he met these men on an informal basis as well as responding to their formal queries about the assignment and work, including suggestions for books they might read to gain understanding of the region.[37] In his new post, as well, he carried some responsibility for certain aspects of work which flowed from the arbitration decision in 1910 and from the Imperial Conference in 1911, especially those dealing with treaties, navigation legislation, copyright, immigration policy, domicile, and, particularly, relations between Canada and the United States.[38] These, then, were some of the ways in which, as part of his responsibilities in the new post, he merely continued work that he had handled in his former assignment.

Dicey and the Third Home Rule Bill

Another form of continuity is the correspondence he maintained with A V Dicey, 'the greatest living constitutional authority'.[39] While Dicey had, for many years, regularly sought Keith's opinions and advice on various points as he was working on his books,[40] he became particularly eager to understand the status which the dominions had acquired by the Imperial Conference of 1911. He had a specific reason for wanting to know. The question of Irish Home Rule in which Dicey had long been interested had returned to the British political agenda with some urgency after being absent following the defeat of the Second Home Rule Bill in 1893 which effectively ended Gladstone's career. The inconclusive elections of 1910 left the balance of power in the hands of John Redmond and the Irish Nationalist Party.[41] The price that Liberals had to pay for Irish support was legislation for home rule.

Dicey, a determined Unionist, had been deeply suspicious of the Liberal regime of Campbell-Bannerman and was even more so when Asquith, whom he viewed as an unscrupulous party politician, became Prime Minister.[42] The People's Budget of 1909 which led to the Parliament Act of 1911 did nothing to allay his suspicions. Perhaps more impassioned about the dangers of home rule than many of his contemporaries, including some members of the Conservative party, Dicey was deeply disturbed that the issue of union seemed to be so much less significant in 1911 and 1912 than when he had first addressed it in the 1880s. His most recent biographer, Richard Cosgrove in *The Rule of Law: Albert Venn Dicey, Victorian Jurist* devotes a lengthy chapter to this period. He describes the extent of Dicey's frustration which pushed him beyond logical legal reasoning almost to the point of condoning civil violence.[43] But Dicey understood the implications of the election of 1910 and the great danger that confronted Britain when Asquith continued in power with the support of the Irish Nationalists. Dicey invested considerable energy in urging true Unionists to take up the cause, a posture which he felt the overwhelming majority of the British public held.[44]

As part of his campaign, he planned to bring out a new edition of *England's Case Against Home Rule* which he had originally written as a tract at the time of the First Home Rule Bill in 1886. Earlier, he had rejected any federal solution to the Irish question feeling that total separation would be a preferable alternative. After the Imperial Conference of 1911, he was struggling to understand the meaning of Dominion status and to see whether it might, or might not, have any applicability as an alternative to home rule. In December 1911, he put questions to Keith about treaty making and the Dominions, about Keith's analysis in *Responsible Government in the Dominions*, and then continued:

> You will of course conjecture, which is true, that I am preparing myself with a view to the discussions on the expected Home Rule Bill. I want with a view to these debates, to get my head clear as to the real relation between the Crown, or in other words the Government of the Ud Kingdom & the Dominions. My expectation is that the next H Rule Bill will be a step towards the federalising of the Ud Kingdom on the plea that this is a step towards federalising the Empire.[45]

He continued by pointing out that he was opposed to both, indeed was as strongly opposed to the idea of imperial federation as he was to breaking up the union. The correspondence continued through the winter with Dicey on 1 January 1912, exhorting Keith to hasten on with a new edition of *Responsible Government*: 'Within three months we shall be in the midst of the HR controversy. Your book will be certainly needed'.[46] Keith's forthright and prompt answers are an important statement of how he understood responsible government to have been modified and what that might mean for the Irish question. In a letter of 20 March 1912, Keith wrote:

> My chief criticism [to Dicey's earlier letter] as you will remember was, and is, that Colonial self-government would now in all probability be fully satisfactory to Ireland, as it means a great deal more in 1912 than it did in 1886 or even in 1893 when the Colonies were certainly in a much inferior position to that which they now occupy.
> The disadvantages of a Colonial position have now practically disappeared for though the control exercised by the Imperial Government has by no means finally vanished it has been greatly diminished and it is now exercised in a manner which minimises the objections which can possibly be felt to it. On the other hand the very completeness of emancipation of Colonies from minute control results in a certain danger which now renders it a very serious question to consider the grant to Ireland of complete Colonial independence.[47]

Both Dicey and Keith followed the progress of the home rule question after Asquith's government on 11 April 1912 introduced legislation to that end. Dicey asked Keith's interpretation of certain clauses in the legislation and particularly whether an Irish parliament would be able to repeal imperial legislation which involved areas devolved to the new body. Keith concurred with Dicey's belief that such powers were intended to be conferred: 'Indeed this intention is an essential part of the proposals of the Government; otherwise the action of the Irish Parliament would be extremely limited in effect.'[48]

In 1913, Dicey brought out his final tract against home rule and for maintaining the union, *A Fool's Paradise: Being a Constitutionalist's Criticism on the Home Rule Bill of 1912*. For many points in his analysis, he depended upon Keith's interpretations.[49] Dicey recognised that the time had passed when his book would have much influence: 'I don't think my book likely to excite much attention, or to be a success, but I wish much to avoid clear errors.'[50] He was right in his assessment since few, even some dedicated Unionists, gave it much attention.[51] He sent a copy to Keith who put it on his shelves along with other works of Dicey. Dicey and Keith had different views about what should be done with Ireland. While Keith was not fully supportive of home rule and the dissolution of the union, he had a less dogmatic and more pragmatic view towards Irish matters than Dicey held, as he had towards the evolution of the Empire itself.[52] They did, however, continue to share ideas and to clarify the various options in relation to the principles of responsible government.

In the event, of course, nothing that Dicey could write was able to stop the progress of the Third Home Rule Bill which became law on 18 September 1914, only to be suspended for the duration of the war. Dicey and Keith maintained their correspondence on Irish and other matters for many years. Perhaps it was this extended correspondence on Irish Home Rule that provided Keith with the detailed basis of understanding on which he would draw later as the series of events unfolded in relations between Irish nationalism and British democracy[53] over the next years which led, eventually, to dominion status being granted to the Irish Free State.

Scholarly Work

In what had become his usual mode of work, Keith maintained his full range of scholarly activities. In these years, he produced a remarkable number of major works, significant, if for no other reason, in that he was able to develop them concurrently with his responsibilities at the Colonial Office.

While he prepared notes for the *Journal of Comparative Legislation*,[54] from his studies on the constitution of the British Empire, he produced his most important work, certainly, in the revision of *Responsible Government in the Dominions*, dedicated to his mother's memory, which he brought out in the late spring of 1912. He undertook this for Clarendon Press at Oxford with the intention of providing a current statement about the legal, constitutional, and operational position of the dominions, or self-governing colonies. He, and others, understood this to be particularly important in order to incorporate the decisions and understandings of the Imperial Conference of 1911 and to describe the constitutional apparatus that had been created through the Union of South Africa in 1910.[55] The work turned out to be less a revision of the first edition than a new work altogether since he expanded it to three volumes with 1,670 pages. It became, thereby, a comprehensive treatise which included extensive citation of statutes and law cases[56] and full description of the details of each dominion government. One reviewer called it the 'work of half a lifetime'.[57] Following the same general scheme used in the initial version of 1909, Keith blocked the book into eight major sections: a discussion of the history and legal basis of responsible government from Durham's time forward; the executive authority including consideration of the Governor, of imperial dimensions of the Governor's role, of the cabinet, and of the civil service; the parliaments of the dominions with particular attention to dominion law in relation to imperial law, to the issues of upper houses, and to relations between bicameral assemblies; the two federations (Canada and Australia) and the one union (South Africa); imperial control over dominion administration and legislation with consideration to treaty making, immigration policies, and a chapter to each of the matters for which Keith had carried specific responsibility: merchant shipping, copyright legislation, divorce, and defence; the judiciary with particular attention to appeals and to the prerogative of mercy; the church in the dominions; and, finally, three chapters examining aspects of imperial unity and co-operation. Keith intended the book to be comprehensive and it certainly was. Beyond that, he wrote the book to describe and analyse what was in existence not to theorise about what might be or might have been. The greatest strengths of the book are its inclusiveness, its analysis, and its precision. For a jurist or political leader or journalist or, indeed, anyone who wanted to know what responsible government or, as it later would be called, dominion status actually was in 1911, there was, and still is, no better place to turn than to this monumental work.

The work was reviewed in several different places. J A Marriott wrote in *The Fortnightly Review* and gave the book very favourable notice as 'a monument of industry and erudition; at once meticulous and comprehensive; irreproachable in accuracy of detail; balanced in judgment, and sound in perspective'.[58] He saw the work as describing the story of the genius of the British Empire: 'It is the story—absolutely unique in the annals of recorded history—of the evolution of Colonial self-government under the aegis of a constitutional monarchy.'[59] Reviewers in *The Nation* and the *Glasgow Herald* found the work of enormous value, yet almost overwhelming in its wealth of detail. They recognised Keith's great industry and talent in writing such an extended study and acknowledged his powers of synthesis, his extensive knowledge, and his meticulous scholarship. However, they regretted that he had not put off publication for another year in order to devote his energies to polishing the prose and to clarifying certain of the constitutional principles. 'There is a lack of grip, definition, polish, which is all the more disappointing in that Mr Keith has the makings of a great constitutional writer.'[60] The reviewer in *The Morning Post* identified the work as of great significance, particularly because of the particular vantage point from which Keith was able to write. He saw the book, in spite of Keith's disclaimers in the preface, as a quasi-official work. He acknowledged that the merits of the book 'are not easily exaggerated' but went on to criticise Keith for 'keeping his gaze concentrated on legal points' to the extent that he sometimes did not give adequate treatment to the principal tendencies in development which, in the view of that writer, often came 'illogically, and, as it were, illegally'.[61] He concurred with the other reviewers in commending the book as the best, comprehensive statement about the subject that was available.

In the following year, Keith used his knowledge of African matters to bring out a new edition of two of the volumes that C P Lucas had written in the 1890s detailing the historical geography of the colonies. He undertook that revision at Lucas's request. Clarendon Press at Oxford published them: *Historical Geography of the British Colonies: Volume III, West Africa* and *Volume IV, South Africa*. Both works represented substantial effort in updating data and materials related to those parts of the Empire. The volume on South Africa included substantial new material and recent data. Keith, of course, was in a prime position to assemble information from the various reports to which he had access in his post in the Office. Both books were seen as 'valuable' and useful compilations.[62]

In addition to his works on imperial subjects, he brought several Sanskrit projects to completion. Macdonell, as well as involving Keith with the analysis of manuscripts in various collections at Oxford, invited him to co-operate in the production of a Vedic index.[63] That was a detailed, exhaustive project which Macdonell hoped would provide a complete listing and analysis of Vedic materials. Part of the reason that Macdonell went to India in 1907–8 was to assemble materials. Macdonell outlined the structure of the work and the approach to be taken to the complex subject; Keith, following that design, provided the major work of collecting materials for the project which, then, Macdonell edited.[64] The book, *Vedic Index of Names and Subjects*, was published by John Murray in the Indian Texts Series under the sponsorship of the India Office in two volumes in 1912. It, too, was a major undertaking since Keith attempted to assemble all the information he could find about Vedic matters including documentation of manuscript sources and of scholarly articles related to the subject. Arranged in alphabetical order, according to the Sanskrit alphabet, it provided, for each entry, a clear statement of interpretation and meaning, then listed the supporting evidence. At the time of its publication, it was acknowledged as a significant contribution to the field, 'an encyclopedia of Vedic, i.e., approximately of pre-Buddhist India ... It would be difficult to find two scholars as competent as Professor Macdonell and his most capable and energetic pupil for such work.'[65] While some reviewers found fault with the approach taken in the work and found some omissions, almost inevitable in a work which attempted to be so comprehensive, all acknowledged its usefulness and value.[66]

In addition, Keith kept right on with his contributions, both notes and articles as well as reviews in the *Journal of the Royal Asiatic Society*. The year 1914 found him heavily engaged in writing reviews.[67] In the notes, articles, and reviews, Keith continued to display the qualities which have already been noted:[68] he was thorough, he wrote concisely, he frequently engaged in arguments and debates in which he seldom doubted the accuracy of his position, and he was knowledgeable about the literature of the field.

During this time, he continued in correspondence with Lanman at Harvard University about the proposal which he had accepted to prepare a work for the Harvard Oriental Series.[69] He selected for that the task of translating and editing the Veda of the Black Yajus school, *Taittirīya Samhitā*, a major undertaking. Such a task involved, initially, the process of determining which, among the various versions of the work existing in manuscript form, would be the most likely one to use as the basis of preparing a translation. Further, he had to study all existing manuscripts to be certain that he understood clearly the nuances of difference among the various versions. He had, then, to set the work into English and prepare notes which would reflect his interpretations, would indicate other literature related to that work, and would explain certain passages. He completed the major portion of the work in 1912 and reviewed it with him when Lanman was in Britain during 1913. He and Lanman exchanged numerous letters about it.[70] In an introductory essay of some 175 pages, Keith discussed the approach he took to the prep-aration of the translation, aspects of the ceremonial and ritual which is at the heart of that Veda, and the specific problems involved in transcription and transliteration. It was published in two volumes in 1914 following some delays because of the outbreak of war—*The Veda of the Black Yajus School: entitled Taittirīya Samhitā.* Keith dedicated it to Lanman. It was then, and remains, an important work.[71] In a lengthy review in the *Journal of the Royal Asiatic Society*,[72] Macdonell praised the work and Keith: 'No scholar in this country is so well qualified as he for the present task.' He pointed out that the introductory essay was 'full of sound and acute discussions on all matters', that Keith provided an interesting discussion of religion and of various forms of sacrifice, that the book was extremely well edited and printed, and that 'it would not be easy to detect any point on which adequate information is not supplied'. Perhaps it was not surprising that the teacher should give the pupil such a strong review, but Macdonell also pointed out places where he differed from Keith and where he wished that some other interpretation had been considered.[73]

In his last years at the Colonial Office, Keith's stature as a Sanskrit scholar was recognised in many ways. He continued as an examiner in Sanskrit for Edinburgh.[74] Through Macdonell's influence, he was added in that same role for the Honours Oriental School at Oxford.[75] In response to Eggeling's suggestion, Keith initiated the process in late 1913 to secure a DLitt from Edinburgh for which he offered his editing and publishing of the *Aitareya Āraṇyaka*, and of the *Śāṅkhāyana Āraṇyaka*.[76] To secure that degree, he needed to have the works reviewed and approved by appropriate external authorities, to have the report of such review accepted by the University committee charged with supervision of DLitt degrees, to pay the stated fees to the University, and to be present at the degree-awarding ceremony. Stages of this process moved reasonably well until the final one, attendance at the ceremony.[77] Keith wrote to Eggeling in March 1914, irritated that, in contrast to his experience with Oxford in the preceding sixteen years, he found that Edinburgh, and he made reference to his earlier experience with the Lec-tureship as well, had handled the process badly. 'I begin to suspect that the theory of Scottish efficiency is a myth.'[78] He continued his letter by setting out the reasons why he could not take the degree in March:

> On the other hand the reason which prevents me from taking the degree in March will probably be equally in force in July. As Private Secretary to the Under Secretary of State, I really should not leave town while he is here and this March the absence of Sir Hartmann Just on his tour to Australia has precluded the Under Secretary from leaving London, as I had hoped he would do. Whether he can spare me on July 3rd, the next degree day is wholly problematical.[79]

As it turned out, Keith was able to make the July ceremony and, thus, received the degree on the basis of the two works which he had offered.

Regius Chair of Sanskrit at Edinburgh

The summer of 1914 was marked by considerably greater events than Keith's receiving another degree from Edinburgh. War broke out and *The Guns of August*, to use the title of Barbara Tuchman's book detailing those events, became the sounds for Europe for the next four years. The First World War changed many lives, and in a very real sense, it changed Keith's. During that summer of 1914 when no one really expected difficulties in the Balkans to result in war, Eggeling returned to Germany, as was his custom, where, with the outbreak of war, he, along with other British subjects, was interned. Well along in years and having served Edinburgh University since 1875, he took the honourable route under the circumstances: he retired and vacated the chair in Sanskrit.[80] Since that was a Regius Professorship, filling of the vacancy involved actions not only by the University but also by the King under advice from the Cabinet. The Scottish Office provided liaison between the Government and the University.[81] Not unhappy with the work as Private Secretary, but still feeling that he was deserving of greater financial rewards and more appropriate recognition, Keith was clearly interested in the vacancy. Unfortunately, the papers which would detail the stages of filling the Chair appear not to exist.[82] Likely, Sanskrit scholars in the other universities were sought out both for their interest in the position and for their recommendations on persons who might be considered. The process of search and review, especially given the other more important matters facing the Government and the University with the outbreak of war, moved quite quickly.

That process was completed by early autumn. On 23 October, Mackinnon Wood, Secretary of State for Scotland, wrote to Sir William Turner, Principal of Edinburgh University, to indicate:

> that after very careful consideration of the claims of the various candidates for the vacant Chair of Sanskrit and Comparative Philology in the University of Edinburgh, I have submitted the name of Mr Arthur Berriedale Keith to His Majesty, who has been graciously pleased to approve of this recommendation.[83]

Further, he indicated that an announcement would be released to the press on the next day. It appeared in *The Times*, in *The Glasgow Herald*, and *The Scotsman*.[84] That announcement made clear that Edinburgh was receiving not only a Sanskrit scholar but a scholar of imperial matters. 'He is also the author of a work on *Responsible Government in the Dominions* (Oxford, 1912, three volumes), which has been made a text-book in the Australian universities, and has been cited in the Parliaments and Courts of Australia as authoritative.'[85]

Keith's appointment was logical from many points of view. He had kept in touch with Eggeling and so knew directly about the work in Sanskrit at Edinburgh and, as well, knew about it from his experience as examiner. He had continued an active career in the Royal Asiatic Society and regularly published in the *Journal*. He had established an outstanding record at Oxford in the field. He had published extensively and was known both in Britain and the United States as an important scholar in Sanskrit. He certainly would have had full support from Macdonell and, equally, from F W Thomas, a Sanskrit scholar who was Librarian at the India Office. Men in the Sanskrit chairs at Cambridge and London had been there only a few years and might, in any event, view a move to Edinburgh as removing them from ready access to the great store of manuscripts in those universities and nearby. If Keith felt himself ready for either of those Chairs when he was twenty-seven or twenty-eight, he felt himself no less ready for the Chair at Edinburgh when he was thirty-five. Further, the fact that Keith was well thought of by Harcourt and, through Harcourt, by Asquith was all in his favour. A Regius appointment required not only competence in the field of the chair but also support by the government of the day; Keith possessed both.

From the time of his appointment and in the month following, Keith's energies were devoted to making the transition to Edinburgh. This involved the completion of work in the Colonial Office both as Private Secretary and as Secretary of various committees. He resigned effectively on 5 November, the day on which he presented his Commission from the King to the Senatus Academicus of the University of Edinburgh and was formally inducted as a member of that body.[86] Further, he and his wife—and she most certainly carried that responsibility—had to search for suitable housing in Edinburgh and close down the house in London. While he handled an odd file thereafter, he was finished with work at the Colonial Office on the day his resignation took effect.

Various forms of congratulations flowed in to him. Harcourt, through Anderson, expressed 'warm appreciation of the valuable service which you have rendered during the thirteen years ... He wishes you every success in the new and important duties which you are now undertaking at Edinburgh.'[87] Lanman wrote a long, warm letter from Harvard just as soon as he received the news; in part, he said:

> Mrs Keith and you may be sure that I was much more delighted than surprised to get your card yesterday morning announcing your appointment ... Full well I know the career of brilliant achievement that lay before you at the Colonial

Office ... I have had the clear impression that you were burning the candle at both ends and that you could not keep on that way indefinitely without most untoward consequences. There is no danger of *your* lapsing from the strenuous life. ... [He went on to express the hope that Keith's title from the Colonial Office could stay on the volumes in the Harvard Oriental Series] It is a particularly interesting and striking fact about you and your many sided powers and gifts. And the two volumes were *all on type* ere the appointment was made.[88]

Macdonell was equally warm in his congratulations and went on to express thanks to 'Mrs Keith ... for your joint hospitality when I visited you at the beginning of the month'.[89] He suggested that Keith immediately undertake the new edition of his text on the history of Sanskrit literature, as something for which Keith now had the position and the time. Just, one of his superiors in the Office and his colleague on the staff of the Imperial Conference, wrote as the new year started, offering his congratulations and, as well, his comments on the Office and Keith's talents:

> We pursue our existence here, forgetting and forgotten, as you know from your previous experience but, as occasion arises, we think with respectful memory of the great names which have been associated with us—yours among the number. Digby yesterday was asking me to suggest a subject for your lecture for his Society [of Arts], & I naturally replied—who am I to clip the wings of a Regius Professor, who will discourse upon anything between heaven & earth, & may decide to compose a Vedic hymn upon the war.[90]

With these congratulations and good wishes and with the support of his wife, Keith made the transition in December from his work in London at the Colonial Office to his new work as Regius Professor in Edinburgh, the post he held for the rest of his life. With his ability to recall materials he had handled, he was able to draw upon the thirteen years of experience he had in London in his later work at Edinburgh. And, indeed, he maintained relationships with men who worked in London at the Colonial Office for many years. Thus, after several previous attempts had failed, he was successful finally in leaving the Civil Service for another form of service.

Only one other note about his leaving London needs to be mentioned: he was eager to receive pension credits for the years he had worked under the Civil Service. After Anderson and others in the Colonial Office had carried on considerable correspondence with the Treasury and argued supportively, Keith learned that it was not possible for him to receive pension credit.[91] In a sense, then, he started his work at Edinburgh in a frame of mind similar to that which he had carried for some time. He probably was insufficiently rewarded for the work he had done and would do;[92] and, again, a move had lost him credits, this time not in seniority but in potential support for retirement.

PART THREE

Edinburgh University, 1914–1944

CHAPTER 9

Regius Professor at Edinburgh, 1914–1920

By December of 1914, in that first winter of the Great War, Keith and his wife had completed the process of moving to Edinburgh where, with the start of the new year and the new term, he would commence filling his position as Regius Professor of Sanskrit and Comparative Philology in the place of his mentor, Eggeling. In the initial years at Edinburgh University, he played a modest part in various matters facing the Senatus, the governing body which included all professors. Certainly appropriate and expected for his post, he continued writing and publishing in the field of Sanskrit and other languages. He maintained, as well, many of those relationships he had developed at the Colonial Office with correspondents in Australia and other parts of the Empire as well as with Dicey. Freed from the restraints of holding office under the Civil Service, he started what was to become one of his frequent activities: writing letters to newspapers, especially *The Times* and *The Scotsman*, relating, initially, to matters involving the dominions and imperial affairs and widening, eventually, to a large range of national and international issues. He was an acute observer of changes that came through the course of the war in the relationships of Britain and the dominions and, on the basis of his observations, put into print, in several different forms, the results of his reflections. It is no surprise to find that he continued simultaneously his studies, scholarship, publications, and correspondence in Sanskrit and related fields, in the constitutional law of the British dominions, and in English law. He had done that in London while he worked full time in a schedule more restrictive than the one which he would have as a faculty member. He simply added public affairs to his other areas of interest.

Most certainly, Keith and others in those years were almost forced to have their attention focused upon public affairs. For the first four years that he was in Edinburgh, Britain and the Empire, leaders of the Allies, were deeply involved in the conduct of the First World War which seemed to be more prolonged than any experts had anticipated.[1] Internal changes attracted his attention, as well. He understood, perhaps, out of his reflections on home rule, some of the depth of feeling and frustration behind the Rising of Irish nationalists who proclaimed independence for a republic in Dublin on Easter Monday 1916, even as he deplored it as unpatriotic.[2] He realised that the Irish question had taken a new and different dimension for which further discussion about home rule might just be no longer appropriate. He witnessed the shift in power, 'a revolution, British-style',[3] as, in December 1916, Lloyd

George seized control from Asquith thereby splitting the Liberal Party, dumped him as Prime Minister, restructured the cabinet to provide for more effective operation of the war, and became the principal source of power for the duration and in the immediate post-war years.[4] He appreciated the role that Smuts played both as general in the field in the South African theatre of war and as participant in the War Cabinet. Keith perceived that imperial relationships were being changed through the course of the war not only by Smuts playing his unique role but also as other leaders of Empire gathered in the Imperial Conference in 1917.[5] He followed those changes with particular interest. He saw the emergence of the United States on to the world stage when its president, Woodrow Wilson, led it to join the Allies in the war. As the course of war began to shift with the additional power of the United States, Keith was aware of the various schemes put forward for immediately after the war. As part of the Scottish Liberal Federation, he participated in the 'Khaki' election of November 1918, which, based upon expanded suffrage finally including some women, came immediately after the Armistice and the conclusion of conflict. Through that election, Keith thoroughly understood the divisions within the Liberal Party. A letter he received from Asquith's wife, Margot, left him in no doubt about their feelings: 'If Ll George gets in at this Gen Election the Liberal party is broken. ... Dear Professor *do* organise Yr young men to open the eyes of everyone to the corruption and chaos of this Gov.'[6] He gained direct experience in party politics.[7] And quite soon, Keith's attention was directed to the international scene where the victorious powers met at Versailles to design a peace settlement which would reshape the map of Europe, allocate German overseas territories to the victors, and create a League of Nations to make certain that wars would no longer occur.[8] Given Keith's interests, it is no surprise to find him following all these developments with keen observation.

Polwarth Terrace

In the transition to Edinburgh, he was, once again, well cared for in terms of domestic arrangements. His wife certainly tended to the tasks involved in locating a house, in making arrangements to rent it, and in organising its day-to-day operations. With his new responsibilities, where he lived and how he lived was of greater importance than it had been in London. Reasonably good access to the centre of Edinburgh and the University would have been one consideration. But the more important consideration would have been the internal arrangement of the house. It was essential that he had adequate space for study at home, since he no longer had a government office where he could assemble the books, documents, reference works, newspapers, journals, and the like that he needed for his studies. Over the years, and especially in his final ones at the Colonial Office, his room had become not simply the bureaucrat's office but the scholar's refuge as well. Then, the shelves in his room, together with the splendid library readily accessible, provided him with splendid resources. Now, he had to assemble all those materials for himself and have sufficient space to store them properly.

Initially, the Keiths lived at 122 Polwarth Terrace in the western section of Edinburgh, actually quite some distance from the University.[9] Located at the intersection of Polwarth Terrace and Colinton Road, the house was the western half of a semi-detached structure. Built near the end of the nineteenth century, it was constructed of the local stone widely used in Edinburgh. On the street side, it had a three-sided window that rose for two storeys to provide light and spaciousness to the front rooms. It had little or no garden on the front. From the entrance, the Keiths would have looked across stone walls to the playing fields of George Watson's College and up the hills to the outlines of the Royal Edinburgh Hospital in Morningside. Presumably the Keiths found that the house was satisfactorily arranged and that the actual amount of space was adequate for holding the materials he required for his studying and work. Also, it might have been that the rental was sufficiently low to off-set the possible inconvenience of location some distance from the city centre and the University. Although Edinburgh had a good tramway system at the time, Keith must have spent the better part of an hour going to his classes.

This, then, was the house where the Keiths lived from December 1914, until the spring of 1920. His correspondents soon became familiar with that address and some came to consult with him there, as well. In that setting, Keith carried on his work in his new role and in the various areas of his interests.

University Matters

With the start of the term, Keith became accustomed to making his way from his home to the city centre and on to the University. One of the younger men to hold a Regius chair and, thereby, one of the younger men in the Senatus Academicus, he entered the new life with his accustomed vigour and industriousness. He likely found the change of pace from daily responsibilities in the Colonial Office to the relatively freer schedule of professor, at least on a daily basis, to be agreeable, especially since that allowed increased time for his own work.

His actual assignment required him to give lectures and classes in Sanskrit at beginning and advanced levels as well as in Comparative Philology.[10] His classes were scheduled in the middle of the day and he took them in the Sanskrit room at the southwest corner of the quadrangle of the Old College where, not too many years earlier, he himself had been a student. The Sanskrit classes never had very many students. In his early years, there were students reading Sanskrit for a variety of purposes: some because of serious interest in learning it, especially as Sanskrit was thought to provide a possible bridge to other classical languages; others with a less scholarly motive because Sanskrit continued as one of the areas for Civil Service Examinations, especially for the Indian Civil Service; and, then, Indian students, often at an advanced level, who came to Edinburgh specifically for that field. While the classes were not large, Keith did have responsibility for a variety of students and he laid out the courses of study with care.[11] He quickly became known for his diligence and attentiveness to the accuracy of the work of his students. Students learned that he not only could take the class in Sanskrit but also, at the same time, pursue his own correspondence.[12] The class in Comparative Philology was given from time to time as the occasional student desired it. Keith never forgot that the chair he held covered both fields. On occasion, he was willing to remind some of his colleagues, specialists in the study of other languages, that he had responsibility for Comparative Philology.[13]

When he accepted appointment to the Chair, Keith worked out a specific arrangement for offering the courses. It may be recalled that, in an earlier instance when he negotiated with Edinburgh University over the Lectureship in Ancient History, he had desired an arrangement that would provide him with greater flexibility to organise his time. In the present instance, he was able to make it part of the condition of his appointment that, while examinations would be conducted at the usual time on the University calendar, he would consolidate the lectures and classes into two terms, fall and winter, rather than the customary three.[14] In years subsequent to the initial one, this meant that by mid March he usually completed his course obligations and had nothing left but examining. The result, of course, was that, while his salary would continue on an annual basis, he, in fact, had nearly six months in any year when he was free from direct class obligations to the University.

In addition to carrying out his responsibility for courses and for examining which continued to include other universities as well, he participated in some of the meetings and debates of the Senatus. That was, and still is, the central governing body of the University to which all professors belonged. In those days, it was a fairly small body so that men knew each other quite well. It set educational policy and standards; it acted on resolutions which could go to the Principal, the University Court, or General Council; it elected representatives to other University bodies, such as the University Court which dealt with financial affairs and passed Ordinances for the University.[15] In December 1915, with his somewhat impolitic tone, Keith introduced a resolution to the Senatus which would have restricted to eight years the length of time that anyone elected by the Senatus could sit on the University Court.[16] In addition to the tone of the resolution, Keith aimed at a precise target whom a more cautious man would have avoided: Sir Richard Lodge, one of the most distinguished members of the University, a very senior member of the History faculty, and a long-time—in Keith's view overly long-time—member of the Court. Keith argued for his resolution but, in the event, lacked support from his colleagues for it. It was scarcely the sort of episode for the younger Keith to earn favour with the older, senior members of the Senatus. He continued to have difficulty with Lodge.[17]

Shortly over a year later, Keith found it necessary to clarify his role in the war. Keith's position at the University meant that he did not need to become a direct participant. Younger members of the University faculty and staff and, of course, many students went. Two letters remain in which Keith made reference to the way in which he saw his responsibilities to the conflict. In

February 1917, in response to a verbal exchange with Thomas Jehu, Professor of Geology, he indicated that he would not be making an offer to participate in National Service. Rather, he wrote to his colleague, 'I have told my old office that by summons am at their disposal if they want to release one of their younger and physically fit men ... I shall remain here doing my work for the IO [that is, preparing men for the Indian Civil Service].'[18] Clearly, Keith was willing to return to government service if that was required in order to free others to leave the staff of the Colonial Office for military action. But it was not only in this way that Keith was prepared to serve his country. He was available and did, indeed, travel to London to consult with various governmental departments as they required. In a note of May 1917, he made reference to this: 'I have myself to go to town at the beginning of next week as the Admiralty War Staff wish to consult me as to certain colonial matters.'[19] He was ready to consult, to draw upon his extensive knowledge of colonial law and issues, and to write in whatever ways would be of assistance to the government. Those, he saw, as the best ways for him to serve his country.

It was also in 1917 that Keith introduced two resolutions into the Senatus and strongly seconded and supported a third. In February, he introduced a motion that dealt with a late entrance of students, leaving to 'the discretion of a Professor or Lecturer to decline to admit to a class conducted by him any non-graduation student who proposes to join the class more than two weeks after the advertised date of opening.'[20] Debate followed the introduction of the motion in the course of which someone pointed out that 'the University Court would be unlikely to sanction the power of refusal claimed in the resolution as a general principle'.[21] With no support for the motion, especially in the face of this argument, Keith withdrew it.

The second resolution which he sponsored that year was offered in July and dealt with a war-related issue, that is, the question of whether, specifically, a German subject could or should be appointed to a University office. Keith's resolution would have prohibited such an appointment:

> That in the opinion of the Senatus Academicus it is contrary to public policy that any person should be appointed to an office in the University, who, not being a natural-born British subject, is, or at any time has been, a subject of any sovereign between whom and His Majesty the King a state of war has existed at any period subsequent to 4th August 1914.[22]

Again, considerable debate ensued with Keith receiving some support for his position as a patriotic gesture. Yet, he and his colleagues were not successful in persuading a majority to favour the resolution. Keith called for a division list to be recorded: Six voted for the resolution, eighteen voted against it.[23] It clearly was defeated.

On the third resolution, not only did Keith support it but also a majority of the Senatus did as well. This was introduced by Professor Littlejohn and called for the Honorary LLD Committee to consider granting such a degree to 'General Smuts, Sir Robert Borden, and other Colonial Premiers who may be in the country in connection with the impending Imperial Conference'.[24] On the basis of that action, the University did grant that degree on 11 April 1917 to 'the Right Hon Sir R L Borden, Prime Minister of Canada, the Right Hon General J C Smuts, and Col H H the Maharaja of Bikaner'.[25] Keith supported this resolution because he knew rather directly about the role that Borden and Smuts had played in their own countries in support of the war. He would have had the opportunity, as well, of participating in the degree granting ceremony and, perhaps, of talking with them although no note remains that this did occur.

In his role as professor, Keith received, from time to time, requests for assisting persons. For example, in the late spring, 1917, R E Stubbs, who had been a Second Class Clerk in the Colonial Office with him and had later transferred to Ceylon, wrote about a man who needed a teaching position in Sanskrit and other oriental languages in Britain. Keith wrote a most generous letter back to Stubbs in which he made clear that he had reviewed the matter with the Director of the London School of Oriental Studies 'of the Governing body of which I am a member', but that there seemed no place there or at Oxford or at Cambridge where a man from Ceylon could seek appointment. Helpful and kindly in tone, Keith ended the letter with comments about the Colonial Office and with cordial greetings to Stubbs and his wife.[26]

In his initial years at Edinburgh and, indeed, throughout his career, Keith felt that he did not receive the financial rewards to which his numerous and extensive contributions should have entitled him. That had been his view from time to time in his years at the Colonial Office. He held the same view on the financial loss that he felt he had sustained in taking the Regius chair. Mention has already been made about his effort to seek approval from the Treasury to incorporate the years served under the Civil Service for pension credit and that that request, even though supported by the highest officials in the Colonial Office, had been denied.[27] In late May 1917, he had conversations and exchanges with his colleague, Baldwin Brown, Professor of Fine Art, about financial support for all professors and, specifically, about his own situation. He was explicit in detailing his feelings:

> I am very sorry that my devotion to art having caused me to take my wife to the Academy this afternoon I was unlucky enough to miss the pleasure of seeing you. ...
>
> My own position stands thus. When the chair of Sanskrit became vacant and when Macdonell urged me to stand for it, I had of course to ascertain whether Mr Harcourt would approve my leaving the Colonial Office. He was then good enough to press me to remain, giving me his personal promise to obtain for me the rank of a Principal Clerk with £850 a year rising by annual increments of £50 to £1000 a year. When I explained that I was very anxious to be free to devote my time to scholarship, he was good enough to approve my leaving the Colonial office.
>
> When I came here the late Principal ... asked me if I had lost pecuniarily as he understood was the case by taking the post, and on my explaining how matters stood he said that for the time being he was afraid there was nothing which could be done ... but expressed the hope that it might in due course be possible to make it sufficiently attractive to render it acceptable as a permanent settlement in life.

> Had therefore Sir William Turner still been alive, I should have anticipated that he would not overlook the claims of my chair for further consideration especially at a time when a new chair is being created in the Arts Faculty ... and having regard to the considerable sacrifice which I made to take the chair ...
>
> I shall therefore be very glad if you can see your way to bring the matter before the Principal.[28]

Unfortunately for him, nothing could be done at that particular time to improve the funds for that position. On this matter, as with others, Keith did not forget and, when the occasion was right subsequently, he felt free to raise the matter.

Sanskrit Scholar

His initial years, then, in Edinburgh saw him participating in various ways in the general affairs of the university. Of course, his principal role was not that of a member of the Senatus, although university policies continued to interest him, but rather that of a scholar actively at work in his field of Sanskrit and related matters. Here, he continued to be visible in print and in person in numerous ways.

During his first half dozen years in Edinburgh, he maintained the immensely active life of writing and publishing which he had carried on in his earlier career. In the area of his speciality, he saw three books move from concept to print: in 1916, *Indian Mythology*, as Volume VI in a series edited by Louis H Gray, *The Mythology of All Races*; in 1918, *The Sāṁkhya System: A History of Samkhya Philosophy*, in the series called *The Heritage of India*; and in 1920, *Rigveda Brāhmaṇas: the Aitareya and Kauṣītaki Brāhmaṇas of the Rigveda*, Volume 25 in the *Harvard Oriental Series*. In addition, he prepared an essay, 'Early-History of the Indo-Iranians', which was published in a *Festschrift* in 1917, *Bhandarkar Commemorative Volume*.

The first of these works was in a series designed for a general public interested in matters of mythology rather than for specialists. It provided Keith with the opportunity to draw from his extensive, detailed knowledge of Sanskrit religious works and then to interpret that material in concepts and language suited to the purpose of the series. The second of the works was more directed to specialists in the field. There Keith drew from his own preparation in and study of philosophy and made application and interpretation of that to a particular system. One reviewer commented that 'Dr Keith's small volume must be welcomed as a really useful publication calculated to aid and instruct modern students in understanding the nature of the Sāṁkhya system'.[29] The same reviewer found it of interest that Keith devoted a chapter to the exploration of possible relationships between the Sāṁkhya system and classical Greek philosophy, only to discount the likelihood of there being any significant connection. Although reprinted later, the work carried the cast of philosophic modes typical of the period when it was written. The third of the works was seen to be of considerable significance when it was published; as a reviewer indicated:

> Professor Keith's massive volume will enhance his reputation for recondite Indian learning. His name is a guarantee for the translation of the two Brahmanas from the original Sanskrit, and the translation is enriched throughout with scholarly footnotes. But, in addition, there is an Introduction of over 100 pages, dealing, in a masterly fashion, with the contents, relations, composition, and dates of the two Brahmanas. Questions of ritual, language, style, and metre are also discussed. The work is beyond praise, and rather calls for gratitude. The labour involved must have been prodigious.[30]

This translation was drawn from texts which Keith studied to determine which versions were most ancient, most nearly authentic, and most useful for scholarship. Keith's commentary clarified and interpreted the fine points from the texts. The work remains of value and has not been replaced.

His activities as a scholar in this field included not only these books but significant contributions, as well, to the *Journal of the Royal Asiatic Society*. He had, of course, been a long-time member of the Society by the time he moved to Edinburgh. He had served on the Council, and had regularly published in the *Journal*.[31] In effect, he simply continued his relationship to the purposes and work of the Society from his new position. The *Journal* continued to be the principal place for scholars to debate issues related to Sanskrit and other oriental languages; Keith never shied away from debate; often, in debate, he displayed his propensity for precision and petulance.

During these early years at Edinburgh, Keith had numerous and varied works in the *Journal*. He continued to produce in three categories: his own articles and notes; his reviews of books of other persons; and his notes and statements over points of conflict and debate. In each category, his writing was concise, informed, and focused. He wasted few words but came right to the core of whatever position he was elucidating. The ten articles and notes he published in those years covered many topics ranging, for example, from consideration of the number thirteen to the date of Ramayana to the possibility of a Zoroastrian period in Indian history. He provided evidence for each of the positions he took in these articles and notes, based on textual analysis, or on his studies into linguistic origins, or on his knowledge of historical sequence, or on his wide reading of the works of other people. There was a tartness to his comments as, for example, in his note on the number thirteen where he concluded, 'It may be hoped that this subject may receive further illustration and investigation, as Boklen's citations are wholly without importance in this regard.'[32]

He was asked to review nine books in those years. It is worth noting the range of materials that the editor considered that Keith could handle. Three books dealt with Indian thought and philosophy. Another, a first volume in a study of the history of religions covered China, Japan, Egypt, Babylonia, Assyria, India, Persia, Greece, Rome. Three were works by an Indian scholar, Jha, concerned with translations and commentaries. Another book was on comparative administrative law which covered not the ancient past but rather current aspects of the topic. In addition, a book on the religious literature of India was written by one of his Oxford mentors, J N Farquhar. Clearly, the editor thought that Keith had command of wide reading and information and, so, would be able to make appropriate comments in his reviews of such works. And, the editor was right. Keith did know about the works and he did bring his critical abilities to bear in the reviews which he prepared. Scarcely apologetic about his own work, he pointed out in his review of the book on administrative law that, 'Owing to his [the author's] unfortunate ignorance of the authoritative literature on responsible government in the British Dominions, he has failed to appreciate the precise distinction between the position of the Lord Lieutenant of Ireland and the Governor-General or Governor of a Dominion or Colony.'[33] Why this review in the *Journal*? The book under scrutiny was the published result of the Tagore Law Lectures for 1918 and, since the author was an Indian scholar, it was considered likely to be of interest to readers of the *Journal*. Who better than Keith to examine it from the viewpoint of its contributions to knowledge about present day India as well as to administrative law? He was generous in some of his reviews about the virtual impossibility of the task the author undertook, as, for example, in his words about the book on the history of religions: 'Despite these difficulties [range of material and space restrictions] Professor Moore's work achieves real and substantial success, and must be pronounced to be the best summary of the great religious systems which has yet been produced.'[34] Any scholar reading Keith's reviews knew what the books were about, what he considered to be of value, and where he felt there was need for greater precision or more information or more adequate interpretation.

In addition to writing reviews and to presenting articles and notes, Keith also engaged in sharp disputation and argument with other scholars. In this period, three persons came under his attack, and each replied in kind. With F E Pargiter, a retired member of the Indian Civil Service with long years in India and considerable knowledge of ancient languages, he continued an argument about the dating of dynasties of the Kali Age. He criticised Pargiter for referring to his theory of reading numerals as a 'wild conjecture;' Keith turned the phrase around by pointing out that Pargiter's views had 'no warrant in grammar or probability'.[35] With Sir William Ridgeway, Professor of Archaeology and Reader in Classics at Cambridge, he carried on a prolonged exchange about the origin of Indian drama.[36] Keith argued for drama in India, as in Greece, rising out of religious rites; Ridgeway argued for a popular basis rising out of rituals around the dead. The acrimonious debate went on in successive issues of the *Journal*: 'to trust Professor Ridgeway's statements of fact after this instance is impossible[37] ... his note is based in large measure on the assumption that I have misrepresented his views[38] ... Professor Keith's note ... may at once be described as a rearguard action of the cuttlefish type to cover the retreat of the Vegetationists. This he essays to accomplish by charging me with inaccuracy, want of scholarship, and by a series of mis-representations.[39] ... Professor Keith attempts to clear himself from my charge that he had repeatedly misrepresented both my statements and my doctrines but how vainly will be seen from the following';[40] and, finally, a note by the editor, 'This controversy must now cease.'[41] The third person with whom Keith differed was Dr J F Fleet, a long-time, prominent member, in fact, the Hon Secretary, of the Society. Here again, in issues of the *Journal* they aired their differences over the manner of reckoning day from night, an important point as to whether references in Vedic writings to the start of the day should be read as meaning sunset or sunrise.[42] Keith was certain that his analysis and interpretation was clearly right that night preceded day: 'The theory that night followed day in the conception of the Vedic Indian rests therefore upon the mistranslation of Vedic passages.'[43] Fleet disputed that and held to his understanding of the opposite as being the more accurate. At least, in that debate, the editor did not need to intervene to end it.

War and Empire

While Keith maintained his work in Sanskrit with vigour in those early years in Edinburgh, he used his new position to continue his interests in the relationships of Britain and the dominions especially as there were changes in constitutional law and constitutional practice. In that connection, he gave attention to the course and consequences of the war, the issue which, in reality, overshadowed all other issues until the end of 1918. In the two years immediately following the conclusion of hostilities, he examined the effects on imperial relationships of the twin tasks of domestic reconstruction and of making the treaties to set the terms for reorganisation of the international order. Mention has already been made of the various ways in which Keith felt that he could best contribute to the war effort, including his willingness to return on a formal basis to the Colonial Office should that become necessary.[44] He acted on his belief that his best contribution was through the preparation and publication of works to raise questions and elucidate specific points. In general, in those works, he examined issues of war and peace, of domestic and international policy, and of British and dominion relationships; he presented the results of his work in various forms. There are three books that belong to this period: 1916, *Imperial Unity and the Dominions*; 1918, *Select Speeches and Documents on British Colonial Policy, 1763–1917*; and 1919, *The Belgian Congo and the Berlin Act*. In addition, there are letters he wrote to *The Times* and *The Scotsman* plus the articles he continued to write for *The Journal of Comparative Legislation*. It is feasible, as well, to follow his interests and concerns by examining some of the correspondence from those years.

From a study of all these materials, it is possible, in addition to the general matters he addressed, to identify several specific themes and concerns. He continued to be interested in the conflict of laws and to correspond with Dicey on that subject. He maintained interests in selected issues that he followed in his time at the Colonial Office including attention to Australian and Canadian matters. On the basis of the first two editions of *Responsible Government in the Dominions*, he gave special attention to proposals aimed at imperial union and focused, as well, on the need to find some better solution for India in imperial councils. He looked at certain domestic issues, specifically the Irish question. And, as part of his direct contribution to the war effort and to the making of peace, he prepared his study on the Belgian Congo. Each of these themes requires analysis in order to understand his views and his concerns.

To turn to the first of these, the conflict of laws, Keith continued writing in response to Dicey's queries. Their exchanges on this issue had gone on for many years and, indeed, when, some years earlier, in 1908, Dicey brought out the second edition of *A Digest of the Law of England with Reference to the Conflict of Laws*, he acknowledged Keith's 'extensive knowledge of Colonial Law' and his assistance. While Dicey maintained his vigour and kept busily at work trying to understand the speed of change and the ways in which specific legislation modified his understandings, he felt that at his age—'I am now over 80'—[45] he needed to be certain that someone would carry formal responsibility for further editions of his classic work. On 25 March 1915, Dicey invited Keith to be that person since his publishers, Stevens and Sons, wanted a new edition shortly after the end of the war. Keith responded on 27 March and accepted the offer: 'I must admit that I am interested in the subject of the Conflict of Laws and have been so ever since I came upon your book. It would therefore be a great pleasure to me, if I could be of assistance to you ...'[46] Soon after, Dicey was struggling to understand the implications of the British Nationality Act, 1914, and how that would clarify or further complicate the conflict of laws. Keith provided his usual detailed analysis of the law, a summary of its applications for British subjects, especially on marriage and children in protectorates, and a comment on the adequacy of the law: 'The result seems to be brought about in an obscure and inconvenient way, but that is a matter of drafting.'[47] And so, Keith continued his work on conflict of laws but with a new focus since now he was to be collaborator and then solely responsible for undertaking further revisions of Dicey's work.

Other areas on which Keith focused, in these early years at Edinburgh, were those in which he had been particularly interested when he worked in the Colonial Office. He continued his concern with native races, with indentured labour, with immigration, with copyright, and with commercial treaties and navigation law. He brought his information on these up-to-date when he prepared *Imperial Unity and the Dominions* which was published in 1916 and dedicated to Harcourt, 'in recognition of his great services to the cause of imperial unity'.[48] He followed matters in Canada specifically with reference to Canadian development of a Department of External Affairs and to the nature of initiative and referendum in Canada. He had very close touch with developments in Australia since he regularly corresponded with A L Stanley about affairs in Victoria where he was Governor. Their correspondence ranged widely to consider the Commonwealth, Tasmania, and Australian matters, generally.[49] He also heard at great length and frequency from Strickland, by this time Governor of New South Wales, at least until he was involved in a crisis and had to withdraw in April 1917. Another regular correspondent was Ronald Munro-Ferguson, the Governor-General, who, it may be recalled, had been guided into that post by Keith in his last year at the Colonial Office.

Keith made use of all these connections to follow state–federal government relations, matters of initiative and referendum as different from Canadian practice, social legislation, and, especially, politicians and politics, the man-oeuvring of men for position and power. He was free in giving his opinions and impressions to his correspondents. To Stanley in May 1916:

> I am sorry for you in your visit to Sydney, but I expect that you will succeed with your usual tact in avoiding trouble with either the Governor-General or GS [Gerald Strickland] But I am really concerned at the strong antipathy of the GG to GS. I like both men, the GG because he is a very attractive specimen of the Scottish type of character which I appreciate because of my own nationality, and GS because he is interested in constitutional problems, because he is so amusingly conceited, and because I think people at home have often been unfair to him on the ground of his Maltese extraction, and his undeserved reputation for 'slimness'.[50]

He learned how Munro-Ferguson felt about Australia and his superiors in London: 'The great trouble with the CO ... is that it is too far removed from us—a disadvantage not to be remedied even by the study of Sanskrit!'[51] He had full information on elections, on the positions that W M Hughes, the federal Prime Minister, was taking in Australia and would likely take in imperial councils. In November 1917, Strickland spent an entire day at Polwarth Terrace in conversations with Keith to review, examine, and analyse the events which had led to his resignation as Governor of New South Wales. Keith later wrote to Stanley and recapitulated the substance of the day's discussion. Keith certainly had great sympathy for Strickland: 'I was very sorry indeed for him'; and he tried to be helpful in suggesting lines of discussion that Strickland might take with the Secretary of State for the Colonies in a subsequent meeting.[52] In this instance, at least, Keith was a shrewd judge of the man's character and failed to understand why Strickland was so deter-mined to secure a peerage.

In a very real sense, of course, these personal links provided Keith with information beyond that which he could secure in newspapers or in par-liamentary debates or in government documents. His special task, and gift, was to be able to interpret the various changes that occurred in the relation-ships between Britain and the dominions. Here, he had excellent information from Canada and Australia, the two great federal dominions, about the feelings of people and politicians.

One of the central issues that the war emphasised was the need for greater imperial unity. Since the troops were fighting in the name of a common sovereign, some reasoned, there needed to be a formal imperial structure resting on a common political and economic foundation. War, especially of such magnitude, required full co-ordination. In support of that view, it should be recalled that the entire Empire was at war after the declaration made by HM King George V. There was but one sovereign and, therefore, all areas under his rule were legally and simultaneously involved. The problem with that view, which Keith understood, was that the Empire had gone to war solely on advice of ministers in the United Kingdom. And the government of the United Kingdom had no practical way to require the governments of the dominions to lend support. Each dominion did give support but, and for Keith this was crucial, the nature of that support was determined by ministers responsible to their own parliaments. For one school of thought seeking closer union, primarily that of the *Round Table* group, Lionel Curtis was chief advocate and spokesman. Curtis argued that the existence of war created precisely the pressure necessary to recast the constitutional framework of the Empire into some form of imperial federation.[53] Federationist ideas were hardly new, since various persons had argued them since the latter part of the nineteenth century. But the war opened the discussion again. Keith, while he understood the desirable aspects of the goal of greater unity, had little sympathy with Curtis's position and felt—and here Keith was consistent with his analysis at the time of the Imperial Conference on 1911—that the existence of responsible government in the several dominions ultimately and logically was antithetical to any sort of formal union. Neither politicians nor people in the dominions, except perhaps for New Zealand, were prepared to have their destinies controlled by some imperial body which they could not control. Keith carried out his analysis and devoted the last hundred pages of *Imperial Unity and the Dominions* to the matter.[54] Canada, especially given its difficulties with Quebec over conscription and its experience of having been compromised by Britain on issues involving the United States, would scarcely wish to put its future in hands that Canadians could not control. Australia, with its sense of achievement and power, with its extraordinary contribution to the South African War and the present war, and with its particular state–federal problems, would not want to place its destiny anywhere but locally; indeed, many Australians felt that Crown-appointed governors could go in favour of locally appointed ones.[55] The Union of South Africa, barely achieving control of its affairs before the war, was not likely to hand over control to some composite imperial power, especially in view of native policy. So, reasoned Keith, who was prepared to join imperial federation? He developed these arguments in many places and, in fact, placed them before the University as one in a series of public lectures on 'The Future of Our Imperial Relations' in November 1916, where he traced the development of treaty-making power as illustrative of the fact that dominion interests were not necessarily congruent with each other or with those of Britain. At the final lecture in the series where he was in the audience, he restated his analysis and views and was forthright in his statement that no one of the Dominions was prepared to 'accept an Imperial Council which had the powers of a federal Parliament as regarded expenditure or control of foreign affairs'.[56]

If Keith opposed the moves towards imperial federation from his analysis of responsible government and of the situation in each dominion, yet approved the notion of closer union, how did he think that might come about? Interestingly enough, it was in correspondence with Dicey that Keith developed his thoughts. While they raised questions and shared ideas on the matter at various times, several letters in 1916 are given primarily to questions of imperial federation. It was in a letter of 30 November, just at the time of the lectures in the University, where Keith provided the clearest statement of his views:

> The proper solution in my opinion is (1) more frequent meetings of the Imperial Conference mainly for the discussion of foreign politics; (2) the development of the presence in London of ministers of Dominion governments in close and effective touch with the British Cabinet, keeping their governments au courant with foreign affairs of every kind; and (3) the according to the Dominions of a status in international law by extending to political Congresses the rule already established for commercial congresses under which the Dominions are represented by separate plenipotentiaries appointed by the crown. Unhappily, these simple suggestions will not even be seriously considered by admirers of federation, so that nothing effective will be done. ... Distance and many other considerations really forbid our being a federal empire.[57]

Keith studied documents from the various imperial conclaves that assembled during the war. He was not surprised that none of them resulted in the adoption of schemes of imperial federation. He felt that Smuts' role in the War Cabinet was significant but that, even there, that was a matter of the occasion of the war and did not provide a good formula for future constitutional relations.

While he observed these various matters and reflected on the effect of the war as more likely to strengthen the sense of dominion autonomy rather than any move towards union or federation, he prepared two volumes in the World's Classics series for Oxford University Press in which he assembled the principal documents to show the stages by which responsible government had occurred. He was able, as well, to include material from the Imperial War Conference in 1917. *Select Speeches and Documents on British Colonial Policy, 1763-1917* was recognised at the time as a very valuable contribution to the discussions about imperial matters, especially as Keith's introduction and notes provided such effective summaries and analyses of the materials. A reviewer characterised it as providing 'a service for which he ought to be thanked by collecting the leading cases, the final decisions, the most illuminating expositions of doctrine. More could not have been done in the two "pocket" volumes.'[58] That collection was the first of Keith's efforts in compiling and editing documents. Immensely useful, that book remains the best collection of such documents; indeed, it continued in print through several versions until the 1960s.[59]

In addition to concerns about imperial unity, Keith devoted some attention to an even more troublesome problem, that is, the proper place for India in the councils of empire. He knew the place of the India Office and of the structure of the Government of India.[60] He knew that the Indian Empire, both that controlled directly as British India and that controlled indirectly through treaties with the native states, was the largest single unit in the imperial realm. Yet, it had been, at least until the war, singularly outside any constitutional development moving towards responsible self government. How, then, could India play a part in the councils of empire and who would speak for India? Keith argued that, at the very least, it was important that an Indian from

India attend all future meetings of the Imperial Conference rather than have India represented by the Secretary of State for India who was, in fact, a member of the British government. Keith was pleased when the Imperial War Conference in 1917 adopted that position so that Indians were assured of a place in that council. Shadi Lal, one of Keith's Oxford contemporaries, and, by 1917, a district judge in India, wrote to commend Keith for his views and his influence in helping to shape discussion around the matter:

> I may tell you that the Indians are very grateful to you for the kind interest you have taken in Indian affairs and for your sympathetic and statesmanlike discussion of the Indian problems. India stands in need of help from impartial and broadminded men like you.[61]

Keith felt that, as a minimum, this first step in redefining the way in which India would be represented and would participate indicated a significant gain. That really modest gain, of course, has to be put over against Indian nationalist aspirations which were seeking some more forceful way in which Indians might secure in Lal's words, 'a larger share in the administration of their country'.[62]

Besides considering imperial unity and the place of India, Keith turned to examine certain domestic issues, chief of which was the Irish question. Earlier, he had corresponded with Dicey on the matter at the time of the Third Home Rule Bill.[63] But that act had become obsolete with the outbreak of war and even more so after the Rising. Keith's reflections on the matter of Ireland included some analysis of the possibility of a federal solution to the United Kingdom. He was dubious about the distribution of power that would have to occur in such a federal scheme. He could not see that Scotland would gain anything out of such a scheme. He was sceptical that it would satisfy Irish nationalists. Federalism, at least in its American, Australian, and Canadian versions, posed new problems even in those unions and it did not necessarily offer any easy solutions for the United Kingdom. Keith sympathised with Irish nationalist aspirations, yet could see no way in which home rule or dominion status or federalism would provide a solution. He believed that the Irish question was 'one which is strictly insoluble'.[64] He saw the strategic location and proximity of Ireland as a given handicap. Further, he saw, rightly, that 'the Dominions are on the highway to becoming mere allies of the United Kingdom though under the same crown'.[65] He simply could not see anything but danger for the United Kingdom in giving Ireland the status of a dominion: that 'would in all probability be a grave menace to the United Kingdom'.[66] Dicey supported Keith's analysis and felt that if Ireland were to have the status, for example, of New Zealand that 'would for all practical purposes soon make her independent. But no English Statesman living can deny that Ireland's independence might be fatal to Great Britain and the British Empire'.[67] Little did either man anticipate the outcome of the Anglo-Irish War in 1921 when precisely that imprecise status as a dominion was used to create the Irish Free State.[68]

One further area of Keith's work to consider in this period is that in which he gave attention to international problems and the making of peace. From 1917 in what turned out to be the last part of the war, he wrote letters to the press in which he raised questions about territorial changes that might be needed on the continent, on the future of German colonies, on how the peace aims of Wilson, especially, and of others would affect colonies, on what might be the proper role for the dominions in the peace conference and in the League of Nations as that body began to emerge as one of the central features of the peace settlement.[69] He continued to argue for his understanding of the ways in which dominions might be treated on the international stage as entities, separate from, although allied with, Britain.

The most significant work that he undertook in those years was the preparation of materials about Belgian, British, and French colonies, as part of a comprehensive series dealing with all colonies. G W Prothero, in 1917 attached to the Intelligence Division of the Admiralty and, later on, to the Historical Section of the Foreign Office, was the person who was responsible for co-ordinating an interdepartmental compilation of materials about colonial systems in anticipation that such information might be useful to the British Government in discussions at the end of the war.[70] Lucas from his location at All Souls, Oxford, was also involved in the project. But it was Keith to whom Prothero turned to prepare the materials dealing specifically with the British and French colonies and, also, with the Belgian Congo. The Peace Handbooks on colonies were, in effect, similar to compilations with which Keith was familiar through the International Colonial Institute, but this particular project was even more extensive. With a clear sense that this was an effective way in which he could contribute to his country during the war and, in all possibility to the making of peace afterwards, Keith tackled the work with his usual diligence, skill, and vigour.[71] He was responsible for twenty-one of the handbooks plus the material on the Belgian Congo. He had access to documents from the various departments of British government, from those supplied by the French, and such materials as could be obtained from the Belgians. From his work, he developed some specific notions about the necessary revisions in the Berlin Act and what needed to be done in order to bring the Belgian Congo under actual international supervision. He put his ideas into an article, 'The Revision of the Berlin Act', which he sent to the African Society, in May 1918, and which they accepted for publication in the *Journal of the African Society*. That paper attracted considerable attention, so much so, that it was put before the War Cabinet and was studied, as well, by key persons in the Foreign Office.[72] It was that paper which formed the nucleus of the book which Keith brought out through Clarendon Press early in 1919, *The Belgian Congo and the Berlin Act*. Publication of the book brought him into conflict with Prothero because, in the fall of that year, the Foreign Office decided to publish the entire series of Peace Handbooks, including Keith's contribution on the Congo. Keith reviewed Prothero's request and refused, in his usual tart manner, to permit publication of that portion of his work: 'As you know, I wrote what I did at your request as a confidential aid to His Majesty's Government in their negotiations and not for publication in any form'.[73] Moreover, he was concerned about apparent conflict with the financial and other interests of Clarendon Press. He rejected Prothero's suggestion that a reworked and abbreviated version might be included in the Foreign Office series. Keith prevailed and the series, for that reason, includes nothing about the Belgian Congo but does include Keith's works on African colonies held by Britain and France.

His study of the Berlin Act and the Congo was of significance. Reviewers noted that he was 'already well known for his kindly interest in the welfare of native races' and that the 'historical portion of the book is most thoroughly done'.[74] Another reviewer felt, however, that Keith had too optimistic a view about what had been accomplished in the Berlin Act and that, therefore, brought too hopeful an approach in his argumentation that, in the peace settlements following the war, it would be feasible to design some mode of effective international control. The book in its historical analysis, in its explanation of international law, and of its proposals for reform and change, remains, however, one of the important works on the subject, especially since Keith collected together into an appendix the principal documents. Anyone seeking an initial understanding of the tortuous history of the Congo will still find this work of immense value.

Scottish Liberal Federation

In yet another arena, Keith made contributions. When he moved to Edinburgh, his sympathies with the Liberal Party remained strong. He supported Asquith, Harcourt, and the rest of the Liberal government. With that interest, he became involved with the Scottish Liberal Federation in two significant ways: as a member of the Central Committee representing the universities of Scotland and as a member involved with developing the election manifesto for Liberals in Scotland. The split in the Liberal Party which came with Lloyd George's dumping of Asquith created problems for the party in Scotland, and elsewhere.[75] When it became apparent that Lloyd George would call for an election in 1918, Keith and other members of the party had to make decisions about where they would stand. Keith remained loyal to Asquith who held his seat from a Scottish constituency: Fife East.

One of the many tasks confronting the party as the election approached was to determine electoral strategy. Here, Keith along with the Duke of Atholl, Gideon Murray, and others played a part in designing certain aspects of a manifesto which would appeal to voters in Scotland and help, it was hoped, persuade them to return Liberals to power. Keith wrote a great deal of the draft. It is a surprising call for devolution to Scotland. In his draft much of which was accepted, Keith argued that there were differences in Scotland which 'render it desirable that matters predominantly of Scottish interest should be entrusted to a legislature and a government with headquarters in Scotland and in immediate touch with Scottish life and feeling'.[76] As one might expect, Lloyd George was depicted as the person who 'while recognising the strength and admitting the validity of Scottish feeling' would resist such a move 'as a grave obstacle' and, in effect, take shelter behind 'the reluctance of the English people to accept so far-reaching a change'.[77] What might be devolved to a Scottish legislature? Matters such as 'agriculture, forestry, fisheries, education, public health, local government in all its branches, public buildings, public records and printing, and the whole sphere of civil and criminal law'.[78] Keith who had earlier opposed any sort of federal solution for Ireland saw this proposal as non-federal; rather, he felt it feasible and consistent with his views: 'It could be adopted without prejudicing in any way the question of the government of Ireland or Imperial relations generally.'[79] In this Manifesto, Keith incorporated an idea that he was to pursue for many years, the notion of an appeal court representing the whole Empire; to such a court, appeals might go from the courts of Scotland under this proposed scheme of devolution.[80] In a letter to Murray about the matter, Keith voiced concern about the way this might affect Ireland:

> It is certain that we must concede to Ireland a measure of self-government which will go far beyond what I desire to see secured for Scotland, and when Ireland has that we shall be driven into demanding more than I personally desire to see given.[81]

As the election turned out, it was a sweeping victory for Lloyd George and the coalition; the independent Liberals who followed Asquith were virtually eliminated and Asquith, himself, lost his seat.[82] When it was all over, Margot wrote to Keith thanking him for sending her a copy of *Speeches and Documents*:

> I shall boldly thank you very much for the 2 little volumes without having read one word of them! Forgive me but I've had neither time nor spirits. This horrible Election & the wild wanton encouraging of every low Desire in the lowest of the low for the sake of votes by our great PM has made my heart ache. The speeches bribery, corruption, and camouflage of this election have made me unhappy.[83]

Yet, in his work to return a sound Liberal candidate for one of the Scottish universities seats, Keith was successful. He was able to assist in the entire process by which Dugald M Cowan of Glasgow was returned. In those days when plural voting still existed, university alumni had the opportunity, and responsibility, to cast a vote for university members of Parliament. Under provisions of the Representation of the People Act, 1918,[84] the four Scottish universities together comprised a single constituency to return three members. The task that faced Keith and his colleagues was to seek the election of a Liberal, if possible, to offset Unionist strength, especially as two members of that persuasion were already sitting from Scottish universities.[85] In the negotiations with Liberal colleagues at St Andrews, Aberdeen, and Glasgow, Keith played a significant role in supporting Cowan so that he was selected the candidate. Cowan, Headmaster of North Kelvinside Higher Grade School, had played an active role in educational matters in Scotland through his own writings and his work with the Education Institute for Scotland. With initial support from Liberals at Glasgow University, Cowan moved through the process to become one of five nominees for the Scottish universities seats.[86] At the meeting where Cowan was formally put forward, Keith spoke in support as he seconded that nomination. Keith also chaired the meeting in Edinburgh and introduced Cowan as he made a speech and responded to questions from those electors who attended.[87] In all ways, Keith invested energy in seeking Cowan's return and, when the ballots were all counted, that was the result.[88] Indeed, Cowan held that seat as a Liberal through subsequent elections and until his death in 1933.[89]

It is worth noting, as well, that the first hints of Keith's possible interest in seeking a seat came in these early years of his association with the Scottish Liberal Federation. After the election of 1918, he was waited on by two persons from Central Edinburgh constituency to consider being their candidate and, in December, received an invitation from James Black, Secretary of the Central Liberal Association, Glasgow, to talk with them, the initial contact in what would turn out later to be a serious offer for Keith to stand there.[90]

India Office Study

It is clear that, in his early years in Edinburgh, Keith led an immensely active life. He certainly fulfilled the responsibilities of his Chair both so far as university matters and so far as his scholarly works in Sanskrit went. Beyond that, he made significant contributions to the definition and understanding of a range of international issues and, more particularly, to changing relations in imperial affairs.

In addition, he was involved in another task for the government when, in the spring of 1919, he functioned as a member of a committee appointed to study the home administration of Indian affairs. This study resulted from the train of events set in motion by the Secretary of State for India, E S Montagu, who made his important announcement about the direction of British policy towards India in the House of Commons on 20 August 1917; the central feature was clear:

> The policy of His Majesty's Government, with which the Government of India are in complete accord, is that of increasing the association of Indians in every branch of the administration and the gradual development of self-governing institutions with a view to the progressive realization of responsible government in India as an integral part of the British Empire.[91]

Following that announcement, Montagu went to India to meet Lord Chelmsford, the Viceroy, to develop detailed plans by which such a principle could be translated into operation. The Montagu–Chelmsford Report on Indian Constitutional Reforms was issued in 1918.[92] Subsequent to that, several committees were created to examine particular aspects of the very lengthy, detailed proposals. While both the principle for change and the detailed proposals to achieve it were announced during the war in hope of encouraging Indian support for the conflict, the projected gradual changes and the proposed timing that called for study of them only after the end of the war were scarcely satisfactory to Indian nationalists, eager for immediate steps to occur to secure full Indian control. But even they welcomed the statement moving in the direction of greater Indian participation in the management of Indian affairs as a correct first step.[93]

While various groups examined aspects of the proposals, it was necessary under paragraph 293 of the Report to create a specific group to examine the operation of the India Office itself. It was logical to study the home administration of Indian matters in view of the detailed proposals because, depending on precisely which ones might be formed into a draft statute for the government of India, any change would require modifications in the way in which the India Office functioned. Montagu announced the creation of this committee of enquiry first, in parliament. Shortly thereafter, he wrote to Keith, and others, on 29 November 1918. Montagu specifically asked Keith to serve, 'in view of your experience at the Colonial Office and your great interest in constitutional questions'.[94] With his accustomed speed, Keith responded and accepted on 2 December. Keith's role was to bring his substantial knowledge of constitutional law of the self-governing dominions to bear on the discussions.

The work of the committee engaged Keith and other members during the spring of 1919. The committee was chaired by Lord Crewe whom Keith, of course, knew from the days when both were at the Colonial Office. In addition, there were nine men chosen because of their experience in India or their membership on the Council of India or their particular knowledge.[95] The India Office provided secretarial support for the committee. The terms of reference included five provisions of which the first two were most important:

1   To advise what changes should be made in:
    (a) the existing system of Home administration of Indian affairs; and in
    (b) the relations between the Secretary of State, or the Secretary of State in Council, and the Government of India, both generally and with reference to relaxation of the Secretary of State's powers of superintendence, direction, and control.

2   To examine in particular:
    (a) the constitutional powers of the Council in India, its relation to the Secretary of State as affecting his responsibility to Parliament, and otherwise, and the financial and administrative control exercised by the Council;
    (b) the composition of the Council, the qualifications, method of appointment and term of office of its members, and the number of Indian Members;
    (c) the workings of the Council in relation to Office procedure;
    (d) the general departmental procedure of the India Office;
    (e) the organisation of the India Office establishment, and the question of modifying the system of its recruitment so as to provide for:

(i)   the interchange of appointments with the Indian Services, and
(ii) the throwing open of a proportion of appointments to Indians;
and to make recommendations.[96]

Other points called, naturally, for the committee to look at fiscal matters, to suggest what legislation needed to be drafted, and then 'To enquire into and report upon any other matters cognate or relevant to the above, which it may consider expedient to take into consideration'.[97] The committee took its study from these terms of reference and, of course, from the principles which had been enunciated by Montagu in 1917 and from the proposals that he and Chelmsford made in 1918.

The committee held its initial meeting on Tuesday, 11 March 1919, and continued its meetings through June. In all, it met thirty-three times. It set out initially, under its terms of reference, to interview persons with particular knowledge about the operation of the India Office. In all, seventeen sessions were held where members of the committee had an opportunity to hear from and to examine twenty different witnesses. Those sessions continued until 21 May and were arranged so that members of the committee had the opportunity to meet privately to review and digest the evidence as it was presented. Of the sessions where evidence was taken, Keith attended all but the first three, presumably because they would have come right at the end of the winter term and he was obliged to remain in Edinburgh to complete it. Except for those initial meetings, however, Keith participated fully in the work of the committee and, in his forthright manner, engaged witnesses with questions and comments. His questioning was often sharply phrased and usually followed a legal mode where the response of a witness to one question led Keith to ask the next logical one which, perhaps, carried the witness in a direction he had not intended to take initially. At certain points, Crewe had to urge Keith to end his questioning.[98] It is also clear that he was vigorous in his discussions when the committee met in private to consider its findings and prepare its recommendations.

The work of the committee was complicated by the fact that the authorities in the India Office, while supporting the general principles stated by Montagu and Chelmsford, were quite resistant to any change in the role of the Secretary of State or the Council or, indeed, the operation of the Office itself. Yet, the terms of reference suggested that the study was quite open-ended about the home administration; in fact, in the view of the staff that was not what was desired at all.[99]

By June, the committee had completed its work, decided on its recommendations, and framed its report. In the final stages, Keith became unhappy about the direction the committee was moving and raised questions with Crewe and, through him, to Montagu himself about the meaning of the terms of reference.[100] Keith was eager not only to see some changes in the India Office, preferably the elimination of the Council of India and its supervisory control, but even more to see greater changes proposed for the Government of India. If, Keith argued, there was substance to the principle enunciated by Montagu, then certainly there would have to be dramatic reductions in the authority of the Secretary of State and, thereby, of the India Office. He was prepared to move more radically than other members of the committee who saw their work restricted directly to questions about the India Office. But, he did not prevail.

The Report of the committee was made on 21 June 1919. In six sections, it outlined its recommendations most of which represented minor modifications in the operations of the India Office except for the one which advocated abolition of the Council of India and replacing it with an Advisory Committee. One significant recommendation was that the cost of the India Office should become a claim upon the Estimates supported by the British government, rather than by the Government of India.[101] The Report also provided space for three members of the committee to register dissent: Sir James Brunyate, Mr B N Basu, and Keith. Brunyate argued, in effect, for retention of the Council of India with minor modifications, for 'conditional devolution' of power to India, and for retention of fiscal control in the India Office. Basu among other objections indicated support for the creation of a Select Committee of Parliament on Indian Affairs, a proposition which the committee had examined and rejected as superfluous.

The third to dissent was Keith who wrote a lengthy Minority Report, some twenty-two pages plus a copy of an earlier memorandum of three pages which he had submitted in April. His position covered a good many points but, fundamentally, he argued that nothing proposed moved substantially enough to achieve the principles which Montagu had announced and which Keith strongly supported. He argued that 'the reform scheme is a reality, and that it demands a definite decision of the Secretary of State to abandon the use of powers which he has long held'.[102] He strongly urged the creation of parliamentary structures in India within which Indian views would be effectively heard. He wanted reduction of control by the India Office: should the Government of India be subjected to greater control by the India Office than a crown colony by the Colonial Office? For each point in the terms of reference, he provided analysis and argumentation to support his views that what the committee proposed was not a radical enough shift to bring the India Office and the Government of India into accord with Montagu's principles. In effect, he argued that India should move speedily into dominion status both within the councils of the Empire and on the international stage through the League of Nations and elsewhere. His views, of course, were not supported by the committee.

With his work on the committee completed, Keith then felt it appropriate to enter into the public arena to discuss the various issues involved in Indian reform carrying some of the same arguments he had made in the Minority Report. He felt this especially important as the Government of India Act, 1919, made its way through the parliamentary process. Certain of the committee's recommendations were incorporated into that Act but, not surprisingly, none of Keith's primary concerns were.[103] Through serving on the committee, he had acquired a considerable body of information about Indian problems, concerns, and developments all of which he would be able to use in his later formal studies on Indian constitutional matters.

The India Office study was among the principal areas in which he invested time and energy in the early years when he was Regius Professor of Sanskrit and Comparative Philology at Edinburgh. As discussed earlier, he continued to make his mark in the field of his speciality and, as well, influenced the other fields in which he wrote and worked. In the years from 1920 to 1928, secure in his position at the University, he entered into a period of enormous productivity. It is that next stage of his life and work that must now be considered.

CHAPTER 10

Widening Interests and Expanding Scholarship, 1920–1928

In the spring of 1920, Keith had his forty-first birthday. Secure in his position as Regius Professor of Sanskrit and Comparative Philology and with good support for scholarship in his speciality, he entered, in the prime years of his life, into a period of substantial activity. The publication of the two-volume edition of *Responsible Government in the Dominions* in 1928 may be taken to mark the culmination of these eight years in which he wrote and published thirteen books: seven in Sanskrit and Oriental studies, five in the constitutional law of the British Empire, and one in law, his first.[1] His scholarship burst out in several directions and the range of his interests widened considerably, as reflected in the great increase in what he wrote in letters to newspapers, articles to journals, and correspondence with persons around the world. He found, in the events of the time, developments upon which he felt called to comment.

The decade of the 1920s in which he accomplished so much was itself a momentous one.[2] A period of considerable tension, unrest, and change, it started with the expectation and, indeed, with the hope that not only Britain but the world as well could return to normality after the end of the First World War and after the completion of the peace settlements at Versailles; it ended with the economic collapse of the world and with the emergence of totalitarian regimes. Newly defined issues, differently rooted crises, substantially changed shifts in the balance of power all led to an era which clearly marked a time of great transition. If the nineteenth century did not end with the war of 1914, it certainly was gone as a consequence of that war. Old solutions no longer applied. Whether on the domestic or the imperial or the international scene, the dynamics of change clearly moved Britain, the Empire, and the world in new and different directions.

Keith observed these changes. To understand some of his interests and concerns, it is necessary to make brief comment on some of the principal elements of change. This was the decade when economics became of central importance. Britain faced domestic economic difficulties which seemed unyielding and insoluble. Continuing industrial problems led by conflict in the coal pits led, eventually, to the General Strike in the spring of 1926. On the international front, economic matters were no better. There, Britain, now a debtor country, was tied into the complexities of war debt and, particularly, of reparations, a scheme which required Germany to 'pay' the costs of the war and which was a major element in the economic debacle of the decade. To compound economic problems, political parties in Britain lacked clear mandates, in spite of three general elections in less than twenty-four months from November 1922, and, rather, reflected the uncertainties of the electorate, expanded, at last, to include women fully on the same basis as men. The split in the Liberal Party between Asquith and Lloyd George continued, and, in effect, ended the long period of Liberal dominance. At the same time, Labour emerged as the new opposition and, although in an ambiguous parliamentary position, formed its first government in 1924 under Ramsay MacDonald. In the Conservative Party, power shifted, as well, after the death of Bonar Law into the hands of Stanley Baldwin as that party abandoned the economic orthodoxy of free trade and committed itself to protection. A general election in 1923, indecisive, was followed by another within the year, in 1924, decisively Conservative.[3] Yet, that majority government quickly appeared unable to cope with the problems it faced. On the imperial front, change, also significant and swift, saw Imperial Conferences in 1921, 1923, and 1926 resulting in a significant redefinition of the relationships between Britain and the dominions. The Irish Free State, a new creation in 1922, played, together with the Union of South Africa, decisive roles in bringing about such change.[4] Meanwhile, on the international scene, the brave new experiment of the League of Nations to bring rational discourse and patient diplomacy to bear on solving major world problems was launched, albeit without the participation of the United States, its chief architect. Almost immediately some of its long-term weaknesses emerged especially since it included neither the new Soviet regime in Russia nor the new great power on the world's stage, the United States.

Domestic change, imperial change, and international change: Keith's substantial entry into the public arena of discussion and debate in this period was, in part, a response to the numerous changes that were occurring, especially as he felt that he could make contributions to the discussion and debate of so many of the issues. In order to follow Keith's contributions during these eight years, it will be essential to examine five different aspects of his career: his shift in residence and its significance; his continuing role in Edinburgh University and his speciality of Sanskrit; his activity with the Scottish Liberal Federation; his further development in law and legal practice; and his works dealing with world issues and with changes in the nature of the British Empire. It should be remembered as each of these areas is examined that Keith, in fact, functioned in all of them simultaneously. The diverse body of work he published during these years is impressive through its sheer magnitude, even if it were not also of great significance.

Crawfurd Road

In May 1920, Keith shifted the actual setting where he carried on his studies and correspondence and produced his works.[5] While he had long lamented what he felt to be a meagre salary,[6] his financial condition, by that time, had improved sufficiently that he was able to buy the substantial house where he lived for nearly a quarter century, the longest of any place, and, as it turned out, for the rest of his life. Students, university colleagues, publishers, newspaper editors, politicians, and inquirers from all over the kingdom and the world became accustomed to addressing and receiving mail and telegrams from 4 Crawfurd Road, Craigmillar Park, Edinburgh. Persons who wished to consult or visit him made their way to that house on the south side of the city just a short way in from the main street, itself a continuation of South Bridge under one of the many names used.

The new location suited him admirably. A tram line ran due north on that main street from Crawfurd Road all the way to Princes Street. It went right past the University. A ride of perhaps ten minutes would put him in front of the Old College. If he was travelling to London, a few minutes more would put him within walking distance of Waverley Station. In addition, it was a short ride by cab in either direction.[7] He must have found proximity to the University and to the railroad station very convenient. Keith used the train to travel frequently to London and, on occasion, to other parts of the kingdom on business, research, and the usual holiday. No doubt he retained his youthful ability to absorb timetables and use that knowledge to good advantage.

While no note remains about the actual process of purchase, it is safe to assume that most of the search to find the house was carried on by Margaret Keith. It is also safe to assume that in organising the removal from Polwarth Terrace to Crawfurd Road, she carried the principal responsibility. And, of course, once the Keiths were situated in their new house, it is certain that she continued, as in several former locations, the task of supervising the household help and of establishing the procedures to support Keith's life and work.

Not only was the location more convenient and an improvement over Polwarth Terrace but also the house itself was better suited to his needs. Built about 1877 on nearly one-eighth of an acre of land as that section of Edinburgh was laid out and developed, it was a semi-detached house similar to others on the same street.[8] Constructed of the solid greyish Craigleith stone customarily used at the time and designed with a lovely bay window rising for two storeys, it comprised the easterly half of the structure. By the time the Keiths acquired it, the house was readily distinguished from its siamese twin: some previous owner had added a full second floor, best seen from the garden side rather than the street. That additional floor provided ample space for the Keiths.

The house, therefore, consisted of three full floors which were readily adapted to the primary purposes of supporting Keith's research, studies, and writing.[9] On the ground floor, a vestibule led through frosted glass doors to the hall with an open stairway to the right. A closet under the stairs hid the telephone, an instrument which Keith found intrusive. On the street side, the one large room with bay windows and fireplace was the dining room. The kitchen with pantry, a bedroom to be shared by the two maids, a bath for the maids, and a wash house completed that floor. On the first floor, the large

12a,b   4 Crawfurd Road. Two views of the entrance. Photograph by Ridgway F Shinn, Jr.

room over the dining room was the drawing room. In the area above the entry hall, Keith used a small room with fireplace as his lower study. His bedroom with adjacent dressing room, including a sink, and a bedrom for his wife were at the back overlooking the garden. The bath was situated off the hall near the stairway to the second floor. On that top floor, in the area which had been added to the original house, two large rooms faced the garden. Keith used one, with fireplace, as his upper study; the other was simply a spare bedroom. The rest of the floor, other than a toilet area, provided various forms of storage in a boxroom, closets, and cupboards.

All the rooms were pleasantly situated with views either of the walled garden in the rear or of the tree-lined street at the front. From the lower study and the drawing room, Keith could catch a glimpse of Arthur's Seat if he looked towards the east. The entry and the lower hall had colourful tiled floors. Dark woodwork, typical of the period, emphasised the spaciousness of the entrance to the house. The dining room and the drawing room, the two principal rooms, were large, gracious, and beautifully proportioned. In each, a fireplace with a handsomely designed mantelpiece was located in the centre of the long wall. High ceilings and airiness provided by the tall bay windows added to the sense of space. Filigreed plaster decorated the moulding at the top of the walls while an intricate plaster medallion was in the centre of the ceiling. This house, obviously, provided an efficient location and a comfortable setting for Keith.

Part of the explanation for his high productivity in these years is related to this house. Its two studies made it possible for him to separate his work and library. Detailed directions covering the placement of materials were prepared, in all likelihood, by his wife.[10] All books were catalogued and arranged according to a specific system which included, on the slip, the location of the book as being in the upper study, the lower study, the dining room, or the drawing room.[11] Further, the location for classes of books and periodicals in each room was specified. In general, the upper study was for Sanskrit, Oriental matters, and languages while the lower study was for constitutional and legal materials. But, according to the instructions, in fact, various classes of books and pamphlets were mixed throughout the principal rooms of the house. Further, the two studies made it possible to divide work another way: his secretary could be typing manuscripts in the one while he was working to prepare more material in the other, undisturbed by the clack of the typewriter. Further, the spaciousness of the house made it possible for Margaret Keith to arrange the routine of the household without any disruption to the rhythm of his work. In addition to directions about the organisation of books, pamphlets, and journals, she prepared instructions about such matters as stationery, typewriter, rugs, cakes, meat, flowers, clothes, and the daily routines of dusting, cleaning, and preparing Keith's clothing. Clearly, he was well-housed and well-supported in domestic arrangements for his work.

Professor in the University

It was from this comfortable house that Keith set out to conduct his affairs at the University as required. One of his students later described him as looking like something out of Mary Poppins: a rather rotund figure with commanding head, a quizzical and benign smile, bowler hat, stiff collar, filled case, and stick in hand appearing to 'fly' to town by tram to head to classes.[12] No fictional character but rather an actual professor in the University, he was, according to P P S Sastri writing in 1921 about the five principal specialists in Sanskrit in the United Kingdom, 'a storehouse of information on all conceivable subjects'. Sastri went on to describe Keith:

> A man of good physique, with a massive and commanding head, Dr Keith is always genial and pleasant to all who may have occasion to approach him. There is that atmosphere of scholarly brilliance about him, that attracts towards him many an ardent young inquirer, with confidence.[13]

Brilliant, industrious, and distinguished in several academic fields, Keith was, by this time, an impressive member of the University community.

During this period, he continued to attend meetings of the Senatus and the General Council and to be involved in University matters. For example, on 26 October 1923, he put before the General Council a motion calling for the establishment of a Royal Commission to examine the Constitution of the University:

> Considering that the constitution provided for the University of Edinburgh by the Universities (Scotland) Acts, 1858 and 1889 no longer provides adequately for the effective administration of the finances and exercise of the patronage of the University nor for the participation of the General Council in determining the educational policy of the University, it is desirable in the opinion of the General Council that a Royal Commission should be appointed to consider and to make recommendations as to the constitution of the University and matters arising therefrom.[14]

He spoke at length in support of that motion. In his arguments, indeed as the text of the motion makes clear, he addressed what for him was the principal weakness of the University, the inadequate administration of financial matters which rose from division of authority among the various constituted bodies, specifically that between the Senatus and the Court. Keith argued that while the Senatus had 'the general control of educational matters' its actions on those had to be taken without knowledge of the financial or other implications of the recommendations. The Court, on the other hand, had responsibility for financial matters but lacked anyone on it, in a structured sense, who had expert knowledge of finances; certainly those elected by the Senatus, and here he was back attacking Sir Richard Lodge who remained on the Court even after the affair of 1915, could scarcely be expected to have any qualifications to consider financial implications. He felt that the University's present crisis was directly related to the existing inadequacy of its constitutional structure.

He pointed out, as well, that the absence of what he considered to be sound approaches to filling vacant Chairs through the use of a body of external experts and electors, similar to practice at Oxford, Cambridge, and London, left too much to the discretion of the Curators of Patronage with potentially harmful results for the University. Although he argued effectively, the General Council failed to support the motion.[15] Because of his strong feeling about the inadequacy of the University's approach to financial policy, he refused, sometime later, in very tart, bitter language to have anything to do with a dinner that was being arranged to honour Lodge for his services to the University:

> I much regret that I could not with any regard to principle take part in a celebration intended to mark approval of Sir Richard's services, for while I cordially recognise his untiring energy I am satisfied that a serious portion of the responsibility for the present unsatisfactory position—financial and otherwise—of the University rests upon him, and his action in holding office on the Court for a longer period than eight years ... Nor of course on personal grounds does there exist any reason why I should depart from principle.[16]

There was a tenacity about Keith. Once he took a position, he held to it with vigour and with a sense of moral rectitude. On this matter, he felt very strongly that the University was not moving in the proper direction. Eventually, he responded as he did in other areas and simply withdrew from participation in University affairs.

He continued, of course, to meet his classes in Sanskrit[17] and, as the need arose, in Comparative Philology. Although he was a one-man department, he produced enough for several persons. From time to time, University authorities asked each department to make a return indicating the ways in which research funds had been expended or summarising the research which had been conducted by members of the department. Keith, naturally, responded to such requests for his area. In 1924, with characteristic forcefulness, he wrote to the Secretary of the University, in response to one of the requests for research information.[18] In that letter, Keith listed nine books that he had produced in Sanskrit in the time from 1917 and then listed, as well, nine books, essentially, in public and imperial affairs. For the latter, he noted, 'Apart from the work of my department I mention the following works as they are an addition to the output of staff of the University on which the public reputation of the University is in part founded'.[19] He concluded his letter with what was, for him, a continuing complaint about the inadequate funding of the Chair, especially in view of the rising costs of continuing research and publication in Sanskrit which, he felt, might hamper his scholarship.[20]

While he threatened to slow down production in Sanskrit after 1924, in fact, he kept right on with serious work. In the years from 1920 to 1928, the following works appeared: 1921, *Indian Logic and Atomism: An Exposition of the Nyāya and Vaiçeṣika Systems*; 1921, *The Karma-Mīmāṁsā* in *The Heritage of India* series; 1923, *Buddhist Philosophy in India and Ceylon*; 1923, *Classical*

Sanskrit Literature also in *The Heritage of India* series; 1924, *Sanskrit Drama in its Origin, Development, Theory and Practice*; 1925, *The Religion and Philosophy of the Veda and the Upanishads*, two volumes in the *Harvard Oriental Series*; and 1928, *A History of Sanskrit Literature*. Other than the works in a series, these were published by Clarendon Press at Oxford. In addition, he contributed two chapters to Volume I, *Ancient India* in the *Cambridge History of India*: Chapter IV, 'The Age of the Rigveda' and Chapter V, 'The Period of the Later Saṃhitās, the Brāhmaṇas, the Āraṇyakas, and the Upanishads'. Further, he wrote an essay, 'The Authenticity of the *Arthaçāstra*' for the *Sir Asutosh Memorial Volume*. Beyond this, he wrote for the *Bulletin of the School of Oriental Studies* and other journals. Significantly, he did not send anything to the *Journal of the Royal Asiatic Society* because he had become angered over the way in which his debate with Ridgeway had been cut off. All of these works represent a substantial body of production for those years.

What judgement can be made about these works? Contemporary reviewers generally praised them for the erudition and detailed knowledge that Keith brought to bear on them, for the fact that he tackled several of the subjects in new and original ways, for his 'critical instinct which never fails', for his 'fine expository power or faculty', and for the important contribution he made in extending knowledge about the field.[21] The compression of writing, especially for the two volumes in *The Heritage of India* series, posed some problems. One reviewer noted of the *Karma-Mīmāṃsā* that, 'The little volume constitutes the clearest and simplest exposition of the system we have in the English language, but one requiring the careful attention of the reader'.[22] One discordant note about *Classical Sanskrit Drama* was sounded by K Sisam as he and R W Chapman corresponded. Both at the Oxford University Press, though Chapman had more direct contact with Keith, Sisam, in reviewing the book for publication, wrote: 'his "Sanskrit Drama" is one of the most learned and one of the dullest books I ever tried to read. ... But a wonderful man.'[23] Yet the Press did publish the book! Some reviewers wished that he might have expanded or deleted at certain points but, in the main, they recognised these works as important contributions to the body of scholarship dealing with Sanskrit and Oriental matters.[24]

And, in the view of at least one of the more recent scholars, these works remain important to the body of Sanskrit studies.[25] While those that dealt primarily with philosophy tend to have become 'antiquated', to use one of Keith's terms, primarily because of the profound changes in twentieth-century philosophy itself, the works dealing with drama and literature as well as with the Veda and the Upanishads in the *Harvard Oriental Series* continue to be useful and of value to persons interested in the field.

Because of his prominence as a Sanskrit scholar, Keith had two opportunities to leave Edinburgh in 1926. In March of that year, A Lawrence Lowell, President of Harvard University, invited Keith to move to Cambridge, Massachusetts and to take up the professorship of Sanskrit together with the editorship of the Harvard Oriental Series. He pointed out that 'your friend Professor Lanman has been obliged to resign ... to take effect at the end of the current academic year' because of illness. Lowell indicated that the post had certain great attractions: 'there are not many students and that gives an unusual opportunity for research, writing, and publication'. And the financial offer was, for that time, the ducal sum of $8,000 per year.[26] Lowell, himself a scholar on the English constitution, knew the range of Keith's contributions and hoped that Harvard might be enticing:

> I do not know whether you would contemplate for a moment moving your home to this country; but your interests, from your experience in the Colonial office, have extended so completely over the whole modern world that perhaps this country would not seem strange to you.[27]

Keith considered the offer very quickly. Within a matter of days of receiving Lowell's letter, he wrote to Sir Alfred Ewing, Principal of Edinburgh, telling him about the offer and that he would remain especially in view of 'the recognition of my services conveyed in the recent decision of the University Court to fix the maximum salary of my chair at £1,000'.[28] Shortly thereafter, he wrote to Lowell expressing great appreciation for the offer, yet declining it. He pointed out that he was at work on a new edition of *Responsible Government in the Dominions* and of Dicey's *Laws* in light of which the arrangement he had at Edinburgh was particularly advantageous: 'the fact that the University here claims only my presence from the middle of October to the middle of March leaves me ample scope.'[29] Interestingly enough, Lowell in writing to express regrets at Keith's decision elicited his advice on two other men in Britain and, to the extent that he had knowledge of them, Keith gave his views.[30] Lowell tried once again, in 1927, to lure Keith to Harvard, this time for a series of eight lectures on the ancient civilisation of India and even suggested that he consider occupying a chair at Harvard for a year, 'but I suppose this is beyond hoping for'.[31] Once again, Keith was honoured to be invited, slightly tempted by the generous financial offer, but decided, instead, to remain immersed in his work in Edinburgh.[32]

The other opportunity, Keith must have found even more tempting. In the fall of 1926, he was asked whether he would take the Boden Chair at Oxford on the retirement of his mentor, friend, and colleague, Macdonell. The offer included a Fellowship at Balliol, his own college.[33] He knew himself to be the 'obvious successor'. Friends at Oxford expected that he would come to join them. Other Sanskritists in Britain fully anticipated that he would make the move, in part, because of his strong Oxford ties, and, as well, because it would provide greater proximity to manuscript collections than Edinburgh. Further, those who knew his range of interests expected that he would welcome the location of Oxford where he could more easily get to and from London to have access to persons and materials for his works on constitutional laws of the Empire. But, again, he made the decision to remain in Edinburgh; he was assured of his value because of the increase in salary for his chair; he acknowledged the real leisure which Edinburgh afforded which he knew could not be his as a Fellow of a college at Oxford. He summarised these reasons together with the fact that his pension scheme was tied to Scottish Universities in a letter to Lewis Farnell shortly after determining to stay in

Edinburgh.[34] Then, in a characteristically generous move, he wrote to the electors of the Boden Chair, after disqualifying himself from participating in the election process, and strongly urged the selection of his old friend, F W Thomas, then Librarian at the India Office.[35] In the event, Thomas, in spite of his age, was elected. His gratitude to Keith was enormous. He wrote saying, 'Nothing could be more effective or more characteristic of the extra-ordinary goodwill which I have always experienced from you.'[36]

Shortly after making the decision to remain in Edinburgh, Keith had an opportunity to make a further change in his position. In October 1926, he noted the resignation of the Lecturer in Indian and Colonial History at the end of the term and, in haste, wrote to Ewing urging that no steps be taken to fill that post 'without giving careful consideration to the possibility of utilising my services in this connection'.[37] He then sketched his qualifications to give lectures on colonial, Indian, and imperial history and suggested that the University might save the cost of a full Lectureship and, at the same time, add to Keith's salary which was 'still in purchasing power below that which I enjoyed on my appointment to the Chair in 1914'.[38] He also made it clear that, at the time he declined the Boden Chair at Oxford, he had no knowledge of a change in the situation for Indian and colonial history at Edinburgh. Considerable correspondence ensued since Keith's proposal scarcely fitted the normal pattern for such matters.[39] Eventually, it was agreed that he would give a course of lectures in the spring of 1927 and that the entire issue would be reviewed during that period. As things were finally worked out, the Court decided not to continue lectures in the previous form, covering Indian and colonial history, but rather to accept a recasting of the course to focus upon constitutional questions. The Senatus approved a report that called for a two-term—again Keith negotiated to protect his time—Honours Course to deal with 'the Constitution of the British Empire and with British relations to India'. Keith received £200 for the course, but not as part of his pensionable salary.[40] He prepared a syllabus for the course which was substantive and had readings in primary documents, many of which were already in *Select Speeches and Documents on British Colonial Policy, 1763–1917*. In addition, Keith's other books were included together with collections of documents covering Canadian, Australian, South African, and Indian constitutional developments. The recent report of the Imperial Conference, 1926, was listed, too.[41] Thus, by the end of the period under consideration here, Keith had added one more title which would continue as long as he lived, Lecturer in the Constitution of the British Empire.

Scottish Liberal Federation: Keith, MP?

It was not only in University matters that Keith was involved during these years. In fact, for the first half of the period, that is from 1920 to 1924, he continued his considerable activity in the public arena as a prominent, out-spoken member of the Scottish Liberal Federation. It will be recalled that he had played a part in securing the election of a Liberal to the Scottish Universities seat in the election of 1918 and that he had a strong commitment to Asquith and Independent Liberalism as over against those Liberals who followed Lloyd George and accepted coalition.[42] Keith was chairman of the Eastern Section of the Literature Committee of the Scottish Liberal Federation, a post which meant that he was responsible for the preparation of papers and manifestos stating the position of the party on various issues. Given the political uncertainty of the times, Keith was kept busy in that post. In addition, he continued to be an active member of the Edinburgh University Liberal Association, of the Scottish Universities Liberal Council, and of the Central Council of the Liberal Federation. He functioned in these various positions with his usual energy. He participated in discussions and decisions. He used his position, as well and as necessary, to write letters to newspapers with the virtual certainty that they would be printed. For example, it fell to him in the summer of 1922 to explain in letters to *The Glasgow Herald* and *The Scotsman* what the 'new rule' for the Federation meant: in effect, cleansing the Scottish Liberal Federation by restricting to Independent Liberal associations all elections to party units and, thereby, eliminating the National Liberals from participation.[43] He drew upon his knowledge of imperial policy to assist where that could be useful. For instance, Keith helped Asquith on a specific point in the fall of 1920 and the latter wrote acknowledging that help: 'I am greatly obliged to you for refreshing my memory as to the Naval agreement with the Dominions in 1911.'[44]

What is of particular interest in these years is the fact that Keith with support, as he expected, from Asquith seriously desired to stand for election to Parliament. He had been offered the opportunity to become involved in the selection process earlier shortly after the election of 1918 but turned it down, in part, because of timing. Glasgow Central opened discussions in 1919 about a possible candidacy but Keith rejected that overture.[45] Keith was, therefore, somewhat surprised to receive another letter from James Black of Glasgow Central in July 1922 raising the prospect again. If he were to stand, Keith knew that he would face a formidable challenge since the MP elected with an overwhelming majority in 1918 from Glasgow Central was Andrew Bonar Law, leader of the Conservative Party and, by 1922, the Prime Minister, although in somewhat precarious health. Black came to Crawfurd Road to discuss the possibility with Keith and to go into financial matters. On 28 July, Keith accepted the offer:

> I gather that you believe that my candidature would be a distinct help to the cause of Independent Liberalism in Glasgow, and if this is the case, I feel that I should not be justified in declining to avail myself of the opportunity thus afforded of assisting to the best of my ability the cause of which I am a convinced adherent. ... My reply therefore to your enquiry of the 10th of July is that if your Committee still desires it it would give me much pleasure to place myself at their disposal with a view to contesting the seat at the General Election, and to make as effective a fight as possible against Mr Bonar Law.[46]

But it did not work out as Keith had anticipated. During the month following his acceptance, Keith and his wife were in Oban on holiday. From there, he kept in touch with Black, continued to make himself available to the Glasgow Central Liberals, and prepared to make the stand.[47] By early September, Keith was concerned that there seemed to be some lack of response from the Central Liberal Office in London to provide the necessary endorsement and to commit funds to the contest. And, he was right. On 16 September, lacking such endorsement and guarantees on funding, Keith withdrew from any further consideration. He was annoyed and disappointed. He thought it was because 'Headquarters by their delay have shown dubiety as to the advantages of my candidature' yet, as reasons were set out subsequently, that was not the case at all.[48] Rather, Keith was caught in the midst of what had been a tentative agreement between Liberals and Conservatives: Law was to be unchallenged by Liberals, in effect, in Glasgow Central in return for which Asquith was to be unchallenged by Conservatives, in effect, in Paisley. Some of this, no doubt, was related to Law's health, but it was related, as well, to the split in the Liberal Party and concern that Asquith should be returned to lead it in Parliament.[49] Keith, even when the reasons had been explained to him, was still annoyed. He expressed that annoyance to Black, to William Webster who was General Secretary of the Scottish Liberal Federation, to Sir Donald McLean, Chairman of the Scottish Liberal Federation, and, eventually, directly to Asquith himself.[50] Asquith was reassuring; after indicating that he knew nothing of the affair, he said, 'Had I been consulted in the matter, I should have advised all concerned that you were an invaluable candidate.'[51] Before all this was over, however, Keith had a tiff with Webster who failed to sit down, to explain, and, especially, to soothe Keith's irritation. Keith's point was straightforward: he could accept that such an arrangement existed, but why was he not told about it earlier and well before he made, what was for him, the irrevocable decision to withdraw; had he had access to the information, he, then, could have made a more informed judgement about whether to let his candidacy go forward.[52] In the absence of information, he made incorrect assumptions about the matter and, thereby, ended his candidacy prematurely. Webster was not successful in calming Keith. On 17 October, Keith, in bitter pique and high dudgeon, wrote to Webster:

> Professor Berriedale Keith is in receipt of Mr Webster's letter of the 16th of October, but desire to remind Mr Webster that the time has not come when it can be expected that Regius Professor of the University of Edinburgh and a member of the English and Scottish bars will call upon a paid official of the Scottish Liberal Federation to receive an explanation of irregular proceeding of which that official has been a party, and that it was clearly Mr Webster's duty to have applied for an interview at which he could have offered the necessary explanations. As matters now stand the time is past when any explanations could properly be given by Mr Webster.[53]

Interestingly enough, a few weeks later, Keith was seeking from Webster an assurance of support for his candidature for the next election.[54] It is clear from all this that Keith was seriously interested in seeking a seat in Parliament.

What that would have meant for Keith, for the Liberal Party, and for the country is open only to speculation.

Keith's support for the Liberal Party remained constant. When the election of 1923 was in prospect, he indicated that he was willing to undertake whatever would be of help, 'especially as a very strong Freetrader'.[55] This time he was waited on by officers of the Liberal Asociation in the South Division of Edinburgh to be their candidate. He considered the matter carefully but stated that he felt his responsibilities at the University and elsewhere precluded him from making an active run. One wonders whether it was more that he wished to avoid the risk of being caught in larger political manipulations again. Thus, once more, he declined. It was not, however, until April 1924, that he finally withdrew from active association with the Scottish Liberal Federation. By that time, he felt that he could no longer be of direct assistance and that, although he believed in Liberal principles as firmly as ever, he should be free to address issues without any restraint that might come from being an officer of a political party.[56]

Development in Law and Legal Practice

In addition to his work at the University and his activities with the Scottish Liberal Federation, Keith, in these years, expanded his preparation and his direct work in law. This involved publications as well as actually being retained to consult in the case over Brisbane tramways. Once again, it must be remembered that he was involved in a range of activities, scholarly and otherwise, all at the same time.

In May 1920, just when the Keiths were moving to the house at Crawfurd Road, he was asked to be a consultant to the Brisbane Tramways Company, Ltd.[57] He put aside, for the moment, University responsibilities, minimal for him in any event at that time of year, and, as well, work on constitutional and Sanskrit studies, in order to devote the better part of a month to, what he found, an intriguing matter.

From his days at the Colonial Office, he had maintained correspondence with several of the persons who served as governors or as governors-general in Australia.[58] Through that route, as well, of course, as following materials in the press, in reports of law cases, and in summaries of parliamentary debates, he was quite aware of the details of politics and political developments in the various states of Australia. He had seen the emergence of the Labour Party in Queensland and watched, with interest, their various moves to translate socialist theory into practical terms. The specific case in which he became involved rose from the determination of both the state government and of the city of Brisbane to terminate private ownership and development of the tramway system in the capital city in favour of state ownership.[59] While Keith understood that the process of expropriation was a perfectly legal option for any government and that, indeed, there were times and occasions when that would be the best move in terms of public interest, what he found disturbing, troublesome, and important in the Brisbane matter was both the process used to achieve that end and the potential effect on investors.

Under the authorisation of legislation passed by the parliament of Queensland in 1882, 1890, and 1913, the Brisbane Tramways Company, Ltd had raised funds from investors in Britain to build, service, and run the city's transportation system; this included, as well, the building of a special power station.[60] This turned out to be financially a profitable venture. The initial act had provided for an equitable approach to expropriation in the event that that was desired at some subsequent time. The Labour government introduced legislation to put the tramway under state control but was unable to move it through the Legislative Council, that is, the upper house of the Queensland parliament. On two different occasions the bill met defeat in the upper house. Queensland law specified that, in the event of conflict between the Assembly and the Council, the matter must be put to referendum so that the electorate could decide.[61] Clearly, here was a case of conflict and the voters should have been given opportunity to express their views. But, a different sequence of events ensued. An Acting Governor was needed, in 1920, in the absence of the Governor. While the Acting Governor was in power, he was advised by his ministers to exercise his prerogative in accordance with Queensland law to enlarge the upper house.[62] This he did by appointing fourteen members, all Labour, enough to guarantee that the bill would be passed when next it appeared. The fragile Labour majority in the Assembly, thus, used its power to recommend one of its members as Acting Governor, then, to advise him to swamp the upper house to ensure passage of the legislation in order to avoid the risks of a referendum, and, finally, to give assent to the legislation. In addition to what appeared to be procedural irregularities, the effect of the legislation was equally irregular in that it did not follow the principles of earlier legislation on what should be done in the event of expropriation. In the legislation, as passed in 1920, present investors in the tramways company could be paid by Queensland Government Debentures over a twenty-one year period rather than in cash; if that route of compensation was to be used, it would have the effect of making it impossible for the Brisbane Electric Tramways Investment Company, Ltd, holder of all the shares, to repay a loan of £450,000 due on 1 January 1921.[63] Further, the legislation avoided the earlier principle of equitable payment. Should the British Government become directly involved in the case? Should Royal Prerogative be exercised to disallow the legislation or to guarantee some equitable resolution of the matter? These questions and, of course, the larger ones posed by the affair threaded into just the sort of constitutional and legal knot which Keith found intriguing and hoped he might help untie.

When H R Beeton of the Brisbane Tramways Company, Ltd wrote to ask for assistance on the constitutional and legal aspects of the case, Keith had no hesitation in accepting the invitation.[64] Beeton was clear that Keith was not to represent the Company if the issue went to the courts but rather to use his legal knowledge to clarify particular points in *The Times* and elsewhere. For this, Beeton asked Keith to come to London on 20 May and to remain for a week or so to be available to plan strategy since the Premier of Queensland,

E G Theodore, and his advisers were coming to London planning to arrive at about that time as were the leaders of the opposition, the Pastoralists. Clearly, the whole matter involved the Secretary of State for Colonies and the staff of the Colonial Office and here Keith was expected to bring his direct knowledge and his contacts into use.

For his expenses and a retainer of fifty guineas, Keith participated in various ways. He wrote three letters to *The Times*; he joined in a conference with the legal firm representing the interests of the Company; he participated in a meeting that heads of the Company had with Lord Milner at the Colonial Office; he helped phrase the petition from the Company to Milner and HM the King seeking disallowance of the legislation; and he wrote a lengthy memorandum setting out in a formal sense the various constitutional and legal points in the case, this memorandum to be used by the Company in various arenas of argumentation.[65] Further, he exchanged many letters with A L Stanley who, although not directly involved in this matter, was a person whom Keith thought most sensible in his understanding of Australian politics, who continued to be involved in various aspects of Australian affairs, and who, in this case, knew and talked with all the men comprising the intimate circle of power brokers. Through that correspondence, Keith was able both to send messages to and to receive them from various of the key persons involved.[66]

What did Keith actually accomplish for all his efforts in this case? Largely through his efforts and the publicity he gave to the matter, Theodore was persuaded of the legitimacy of the financial concerns of the Brisbane Tramways Company, Ltd and, so, offered a reasonable set of terms for settling the dispute. While it is possible that he may have done that in any event, it is equally likely that he recognised some of the force of the argument that Keith put forward. Perhaps he had some modest concern about the impropriety of the procedure he used to secure passages of the legislation and felt it best to placate those who held the stock especially since he was, at the same time, seeking to interest investors in the City to undergird Queensland's financial future, a venture for which he found few takers. Keith had made it clear that the faith and the fairness of a government had to be demonstrated, especially in financial matters.[67]

Keith was equally clear about the atrophy of disallowance. Although he helped draft the petition calling for the exercise of the Royal Prerogative through disallowance, he recognised that such an outcome was not likely and advised the Brisbane Tramways Company, Ltd to that effect.[68] What is significant is that Keith, in fact, accepted that disallowance on any matter coming from an area with responsible self-government was no longer feasible since the thrust of imperial constitutional developments moved in the direction of equality, not subordination, of legal positions.

The most interesting aspect of Keith's accomplishments on this case rose from his understanding of the implications of equality among various parts of the Empire and Britain. He used the Queensland case to give concreteness to the principle of arbitration as a way to adjudicate conflicts within the Empire. He made his argument on this quite public even as he reinforced it through correspondence with Stanley.[69] In a letter to *The Times* of 5 June 1920, he wrote:

> Mr Theodore is entirely in error in attributing my views to distrust of Labour whether in Queensland or elsewhere. The opinions which I have expressed in this case are merely an application of those set out in 1916 in my 'Imperial Unity', viz that (1) relations of equality should be substituted for relations of superiority and dependence between the United Kingdom and the self-governing portions of the Empire; and (2) simultaneously there should be adopted the system of inter-imperial arbitration for the settlement of divergences of view between different parts of the Empire, which otherwise might weaken the bonds of imperial unity. Such proposals, I conceive, are honourable to all parts of the Empire alike, and if the United Kingdom should propose arbitration, Queensland, I trust, would be slow to refuse it.[70]

Through this instance, he knew that his ideas of using the Judicial Committee of the Privy Council as the framework for arbitration would be considered by the Secretary of State for Colonies and others. It might have been used in the solution of the Queensland matter, and, indeed, Keith persuaded the Brisbane Tramways Company, Ltd to accept that means of resolution but, in any event, he knew the concept would receive a good hearing.

A year following the Queensland case, Keith took the step which Dicey had, as early as 1918, advised him to take: he became a member of the Faculty of Advocates in Scotland. When he first considered that step, Keith felt it pointless and explained:

> It is very good of you to suggest that I should consider being called to the bar here. There is of course nothing inconsistent with my Professorship of Sanskrit in the suggestion. But my experience of the English bar and what I observe of the Scottish bar satisfies me that any practice worth having can only be obtained through friendship with other members of the legal profession. In Edinburgh, as is natural, the legal firms have many relatives and close friends among the number of advocates, and there is therefore little or no opening for the entrance of one without any very close connection with legal firms. I must therefore, I think, rest content with my formal connection with the English bar.[71]

It may well be that changes in the policies of the Faculty of Advocates led Keith to reconsider the matter. That body undertook a revision of its regulations to make it possible to accept English barristers more easily. That change was made at a meeting of the Faculty in June 1921.[72] In effect, it called for a person who was a member 'of three years' standing' of the English Bar to be permitted to proceed to the 'customary Public Examination' without further studies. This was in recognition of the fact that the Inns of Court were revising the regulations for the English bar in a similar manner for persons already members of the Faculty of Advocates.

In any event, he decided in the autumn of 1921 to initiate the required steps. He had to meet four requirements: he had to take the Public Examination on Scots law; he had to pay the fees established; he had to take and pass the

'Private Examinations in Scots Law, Civil and Criminal, including Procedure, and in Conveyancing'; and he had to present a certificate from the Attorney General or Solicitor General of England about his fitness to be admitted.[73] He petitioned for admission on 6 October; he passed the Public Examination on 28 October and was 'found qualified and recommended'; he was admitted on 10 November. A notice to that effect appeared the next day in *The Scotsman*.[74] Through taking this step, Keith added to his qualifications in law and became one of a limited number of persons, in those days, who were members of both the English and the Scottish bars. Ten years later, that dual membership resulted in his being retained for two interesting legal cases involving marriage and divorce laws.[75]

In many ways, his membership of both legal bodies gave him further direct opportunities to examine conflicts between various bodies of law. He followed Dicey's advice on the matter of seeking membership of the bar in Scotland and, thereby, strengthened his fund of information when he continued work on his commitment to assist Dicey in the new edition of *A Digest of the Law of England with Reference to the Conflict of Laws* which he had agreed to undertake some years earlier.[76] Dicey was much relieved to know that his 'classic' work was in Keith's hands where he felt it would be appropriately updated and issued as necessary. He held a high opinion of Keith's legal acumen, of his almost incredible mastery of fine points of law, and of his ability to bring all that to bear on his writing and editing. Dicey expressed his pleasure over the arrangements for the new edition of *Conflict of Laws* in letters of 5 and 11 May 1921 to his old friend, James Bryce:

> My revision of Conflict visibly nears its close, but there may be a long bit of work before us though it will mainly fall upon Keith. I had always a high opinion of him, and our working together has greatly raised it as well as giving me the feeling that he is a most reasonable co-editor. ... I am getting cheered myself by the thought that the burden of the 'Conflict' will be soon wholly transferred from my shoulders to those of Keith, who is certainly one of the ablest coadjutors with whom I have ever met.[77]

The new edition was published in 1922. For the first time, Keith's name, and qualifications, moved from the acknowledgements paragraph in the preface right to the title page. From here on, Keith was responsible for this standard, classic work.

International and Imperial Issues

The final area of Keith's work to examine in the period between 1920 and 1928 deals with the writing, publications, and activities in which he engaged as he tried to understand, explain, and clarify issues and changes that emerged both on the international scene and on the imperial one. Here, again, he produced a significant body of work which included books, letters to news-papers, articles in journals, as well as private correspondence. Before considering the issues and themes which Keith found of interest and importance, it will be helpful to identify the materials that he published.

Early in the period, in 1921, Keith, 'a writer of high authority on Imperial questions',[78] brought out two books, a very brief one in *The World Today* series, *Dominion Home Rule in Practice*, and a much longer, detailed one, *War Government of the British Dominions*. This, he had been asked to write for the series the *Economic and Social History of the World War British Series* which James T Shotwell edited under the aegis of the Carnegie Endowment for International Peace. In 1922, he brought out a two volume collection doing for Indian history what he had done earlier for the history of the colonies: *Speeches and Documents on Indian Policy, 1750–1921*. In another series, *The British Empire: A Survey*, edited by Hugh Gunn, he prepared the volume dealing with constitutional aspects which came out in 1924 as *The Constitution, Administration, and Laws of the Empire*. At the end of the period under consideration, that is, in 1928, and after the Imperial Conference of 1926, he rewrote his now classic work and prepared a 'revised and rewritten' edition of *Responsible Government in the Dominions*, this time in two volumes, rather than three.

During this period, he made contributions in other ways. He wrote chapters in two books, one sketching the work of the dominions in a history of the Peace Conference edited by Harold Temperley[79] and the other, 'Makers of the Constitution', in a book, *Makers of the Empire*, edited by Hugh Gunn.[80] He continued to contribute to the *Journal of Comparative Legislation* where he wrote articles on some of the specific issues that arose and, in addition, had, in every issue, a 'Note on Imperial Constitutional Law'. Some of these notes were very brief while others were considerably more extensive.[81] In this journal, as well as in letters to the press, he commented upon and analysed the changes that occurred in imperial relations through the successive meetings of the Imperial Conference.

Perhaps the area where his work expanded most considerably in this period was that of letters to newspapers. While he had commenced speaking his mind and offering observations in that form almost as soon as he returned to Edinburgh, it was in the 1920s, in view of such substantial changes on all fronts, that he used his typewriter to write to the press. There is no way to know for certain how extensive this writing was since many of the newspapers lack indexes. But from what is known, it is safe to indicate that he sent letters to twenty different newspapers during these years, five in the United Kingdom, five in South Africa, four in Canada, four in Australia, and one in the United States.[82] He became, in effect, a commentator known in the principal parts of the British Empire for his observations on various events of both international and imperial significance. And it was often from his letters in the press that individuals wrote to him for clarification, for advice, and for further information.

Why did he become a commentator on international affairs? It is not unreasonable, in view of the works that he had written on imperial constitutional law and related matters since his initial work in 1907, to expect him to comment on imperial concerns, but, at first glance, that might not seem to be an appropriate basis for him to comment on international issues. Yet, it was precisely from his interest and concern about several imperial matters that he was drawn into the international arena. For example, one of his early concerns, even when he worked at the Colonial Office, was the role of the self-governing colonies, then, dominions, by this time, in making treaties.[83] He believed, quite consistently, that the United Kingdom had to find appropriate ways for the dominions to make treaties, especially in the commercial area, on a bilateral basis with the Foreign Office having simply a *pro forma* role. He rooted his view in the logic of responsible government and he saw his view practised, especially in relationships between Canada and the United States.[84] Furthermore, the way in which the dominions, and India as well, were involved as distinct signatories to the Treaty of Versailles and were seated in the League of Nations as separate entities, although within a British Empire category, provided clear-cut evidence in support of his view that the dominions ought to play and, indeed, were playing a role rising out of their own particular interests even as those were necessarily co-ordinated with common imperial concerns. He elaborated the details of this changed status in each of the books he published dealing with constitutional law of the Empire during these years.[85] When the Foreign Office continued to fuss about the separate role of the dominions and to act contrary to the new status which the dominions had achieved through the War, the peace settlements, and the League, Keith had no hesitation in setting out public criticism of such a position.[86] In this way, he was led to comment on the inadequate treatment given the dominions over the Anglo-Japanese Treaty, the Disarmament Conference of 1921, although he was in these instances equally critical of the United States, over the Chanak incident, the Lausanne Treaty, the Locarno Pact and the Kellogg–Briand Pact of 1928, all international issues, because he felt that the Foreign Office inadequately understood the new international status of the dominions and, thus, functioned in an inappropriate and insensitive manner.[87] How could the Foreign Office, Keith queried, merely notify the dominions of agreements which might involve them in international crisis and send such notification without full consultation and involvement?[88]

In short, Keith felt that dominion autonomy had been achieved quite fully in the domestic affairs of each dominion and, as well and by logical extension, was in the process of being achieved on the international scene. As conferences occurred and definitions emerged during the 1920s, he became even more convinced that the British Empire represented a new entity on the world's stage, especially as in those years the title, British Commonwealth of Nations, came into use in specific recognition of changed relationships among the United Kingdom and the dominions towards increasing equality and decreasing subordination.[89] He saw the dominions as sufficiently distinct in their own self-interests, which obviously varied considerably from dominion to dominion, to realise that new forms and procedures would have to be created for the Empire to endure within some common frame. It was from this perspective that Keith continued to argue for the introduction of the principle of arbitration, as has already been indicated in earlier discussion of *Imperial Unity and the Dominions* and of the Brisbane Tramways case,[90] as the method to resolve inter-imperial disputes and differences, a method which up to that time had been only used between independent international states. Keith felt that in the quasi-independent status of the dominions in relation to Britain such a procedure was quite correct. In these ways, then, Keith found that international and imperial issues were really intertwined.

Another issue which linked imperial and, indeed, international dimensions concerned the status of India and of Indians in the Empire. He followed this with great interest and concern through his works in this period. From his service on the India Office Committee, he had acquired detailed knowledge not only of the operation of that office but, as well, of the ways in which the British government committed itself to change in the constitutional status of India.[91] Keith's fundamental view remained unaltered: India should move to dominion status just as quickly as possible and the sooner the better. He was pleased that India received the same international recognition as the dominions through the treaties and the League of Nations and that India continued to be included as an entity in the Imperial Conference, to be represented there, not only by the Secretary of State for India, but also by persons from India appointed by the Government of India. In the introduction to his edition of *Speeches and Documents on Indian Policy*, Keith reported the existing status of India and expressed his hopes for her development:

> The elections to Indian legislative bodies at the end of 1920 mark a definite epoch in the history of the British Empire in India; they signify the close of the period of the preparation of the people of India to take a decisive part in the moulding of their own destinies, and herald the time when India will possess full autonomy and will rank as an equal with the Dominions and the United Kingdom itself as a member of the British Commonwealth. ...
>
> In internal matters the necessity of creating electorates and training ministers in administration has prevented the immediate grant of complete Dominion self-government; but, even if we may hold that a fuller measure of responsibility might have immediately been conferred on ministers, the fact remains that a sure path is now open by which the goal of complete autonomy within the Empire may be attained.[92]

It was not only upon matters related to constitutional developments in India that Keith commented; he was equally sensitive to the problems facing Indians throughout the Empire, and elsewhere in the world. He had had earlier experience, in his days at the Colonial Office, with the problems of immigration policy, especially in the states and the Commonwealth of Australia as well as with Canada and the United States.[93] What he attacked vigorously in the 1920s was the emerging racialism in other parts of the Empire. He had long lamented the fact that Britain had turned over control of native policy in South Africa to those who, in his judgement, would be least likely to protect native interests. When there was the likelihood of inequitable treatment for Indians in Kenya, Keith took to the newspapers to express his dismay. In August 1921, in a letter to *The Times*, for example, he wrote in response to the position taken by Sir William Joynson-Hicks when the Imperial Conference of 1921 had considered that matter. Then Keith pointed out:

> that the Secretary of State for the Colonies has already, and most properly, admitted that racial discrimination within territories over which the Imperial Government exercises control cannot be permitted.
>
> Nothing can be more unfortunate than the attempt to use the protection of the natives as a ground for refusing equal justice to Indians. The well-being of the native population assuredly demands that their fate should not be entrusted to the representatives of the British or the Indian settlers in the Colony, but it certainly does not require that Indians should be treated as an inferior race. No sane British statesman can desire to create in a territory under Imperial control the difficulties which exist in Natal or the Transvaal.[94]

Two years later he returned to the same issue in the same forum. Here, he argued clearly, but obviously not convincingly enough to persuade British public opinion or white settlers in Kenya or officials of the Colonial Office, that the franchise must not be denied to Indian settlers but must be granted on the same lines as to white settlers. To deny that, he reasoned, 'is definitely to deny racial equality even within that part of the Empire which is controlled by His Majesty's Government, and to undermine the foundation of equity on which alone the relations of India and the United Kingdom can be securely based'.[95] Equity, fairness, and racial equality were the principles which Keith advocated that the British Empire must embody and, especially, the ones which should be applied in relation to India and Indians.

If he felt these principles appropriate for Indian relationships, what, then, did Keith think about Ireland, where events from 1916 had created a crisis in the constitutional structure of the United Kingdom and where, after the settlement of 1921, the larger portion of it, at least, became a new entity, the Irish Free State, to be part of the British Commonwealth of Nations?[96] It is worth noting that, in many ways, Keith was pragmatic about the development of imperial constitutional law. Earlier, he had stated, especially in his correspondence with Dicey, his serious reservations about the extension of dominion status to Ireland as being unlikely to be workable given the proximity of Ireland to Britain and given, as well, the long history of relationships with Ireland.[97] Yet, in fact, when that was the solution that was arrived at in December 1921, between the Irish plenipotentiaries and the British Government to end the enervating and inconclusive Anglo-Irish War, Keith accepted that reality.[98] Without any clear definition of what that status meant, the Irish Free State was given the same status as Canada, Australia, New Zealand, and the Union of South Africa. Keith, naturally, moved into print and tried to point out the ways in which the Irish Free State would be similar to, and yet significantly different from, the other dominions.[99] It obviously had not gone through the stages leading to responsible self-government as had Canada or Australia, for instance, but rather had been plunged into a status which, although lacking precise definition, approached, by Keith's authoritative analyses, equality with Britain. Nothing in the new status modified the proximity of the Irish Free State to Britain or obviated the numerous problems that the two political units would have to solve in the dissolution of the United Kingdom of Great Britain and Ireland.

Keith certainly understood the republican cast of the Irish Free State. At times, he had mulled over the possibility that the British Commonwealth could be expanded to include a republic.[100] He followed most closely the creation of the constitution for the Irish Free State, especially as he was interested to see how the Irish could reconcile republican aspirations and forms with the stipulated requirements of oath to a monarch and of Crown authority through a Governor-General. As he pointed out some of his concerns in the press, he heard from Darrell Figgis, Vice Chairman and Secretary to the Constitution Committee for the Free State.[101] Several letters were exchanged and Keith, in typically generous manner, offered to be of whatever help he could. In each of his letters, Keith indicated that he understood the dilemma of the designers of the Constitution: to find formulas which would be as republican as possible, yet not offend the British Government or call the settlement into question.[102] Figgis sent a draft of one section dealing with extra-territoriality to Keith for specific improvement. Keith worked over the passage and sent the draft back:

> Something of the following kind would probably express your real intention:
>
> The laws of the Irish Free State shall, save where otherwise provided in any act, be in force throughout the territory and the territorial waters of the Free State and on all ships registered in the Free State; and, where expressly so provided in any act, they shall be binding on Irish citizens when beyond the limits of the Free State or on ships not registered in the Free State.[103]

He went on to explain the principles undergirding his proposed phrasing and pointed out that, in any event, there were many difficulties in whatever formulation was used, 'but that is inevitable in a case so novel as that of the Irish Free State'.[104]

Obviously, Keith continued a close interest in Irish matters as the decade went along and, especially after Eamon De Valera, a leader of the Rising, a committed republican, and an opponent of the settlement of 1921 and, indeed, of the Irish Free State itself, returned to legitimate political life in 1927 after W T Cosgrave, Figgis, and others had established the constitution, the operations, and the legitimacy of the Irish Free State.[105] Keith delighted in constitutional puzzles, and the Irish, repudiating, in so far as possible, monarchical forms in favour of republican ones, created a fair number for him.

The Irish Free State emerged as a member of the British Commonwealth of Nations and, thereby, of the Imperial Conference at a time of profound change in the relationships among the dominions and the United Kingdom. The Irish missed the Imperial Conference of 1921 because the Anglo-Irish War was still on, but they were present in 1923 for their initial exposure to the process and were, thereby, fully prepared for the crucial sessions in the fall of 1926. Not only did the Irish play a major role in seeking redefinition of relationships but the South Africans, as well, after the fall of Smuts' government and the emergence of J B M Hertzog as Prime Minister, were equally anxious and insistent on formal changes. The desires of the Irish and the South Africans combined in 1926 with the need of the Canadians to secure better definition.[106] With the premier dominion supporting, and with Irish and South African leadership and initiative, it is not surprising that the Imperial Conference of 1926 developed a constitutional formulation for the British Commonwealth of Nations. Keith, naturally, followed all these matters with interest both privately through correspondence and publicly in print.

Before looking at that critical formulation of 1926, it is important to understand why the Canadians were eager to secure some formal statement about constitutional relationships. W L Mackenzie King was Prime Minister, leader of the Liberal Party, and the principal Canadian politician in those days, and for long after.[107] In a manner somewhat similar to Britain, the Canadian electorate was rather inconclusive in the mid 1920s. King called a general election in the fall of 1925 from which no party won a clear majority. The Conservatives under Arthur Meighen, however, won fifteen more seats than the Liberals. With support from small third parties, King continued in power but in a precarious situation. In June 1926, following scandal in the administration of the revenue department, King was threatened with censure, and the precariousness of his situation meant he needed to find some way to avoid that.[108] Thus, he advised the Governor-General, Lord Byng, to dissolve parliament. At his interview with Byng, King, as he recorded in his diary, argued his case from Keith's authority:

> I had in my hand the two volumes of Berriedale Keith and Pickthorne and placed them on the table opposite me. ...
> I then said to him that it was for that reason particularly I have quoted to him the passage from Berriedale Keith, which said that it was not for the governor to decide as to the right or wrong of political parties or to concern his conscience with these matters; that in this regard his attitude must necessarily be an impersonal one; that it was the Governor-General, not the individual man, who was being asked to take a particular course.[109]

Byng exercised what he felt was the prerogative inherent in his office. He refused to grant the dissolution on the grounds that there had been a general election only a few months before and that Meighen should have an opportunity to form a government since his party had the largest bloc of seats. King was incensed. When, within days of forming a government, Meighen was promptly defeated in the House of Commons, Meighen then advised a dissolution. Byng granted it. King's fury increased. He made the action of the Governor-General a *cause célèbre* and effectively used that issue to screen the administrative fault and the potential of censure. King won a clear victory in the country and returned to power in triumph but determined to secure some clearer definition in the forthcoming Imperial Conference to limit the role of a Governor-General in relation to that of a Prime Minister.[110]

In all these developments in Canada, Keith, in addition to being cited to the Governor-General, played a supporting role for King. Not satisfied simply to be an observer, he wrote to King as soon as his government had fallen in June to express regret that it had occurred, especially, in view of the constitutional issue around dissolution.[111] Then, Keith lent his, by that time, considerable authority in support of King's contentions that Byng should not have refused him the dissolution and, then, within the week granted it to Meighen. He wrote words certain to cheer King:

> I confess it appears to me that it is incompatible with the principles of responsible government that a dissolution should be refused under the circumstances of the case, and that it ought to be one of the objects of the policy of the Dominion to secure the acceptance in these matters of the British principle under which the King would decline a dissolution only in cases where the Prime Minister was obviously and undeniably defying the principles of responsible government ...[112]

They continued their correspondence during the election. Keith was pleased that King won. King sent along some of the speeches he made on the issue. Keith thanked him by assuring him that the texts provided fresh material to use in his revision of *Responsible Government in the Dominions*, a task on which he was already at work.[113] From then on, and for many years, King and Keith corresponded, exchanged books, and sent yearly seasonal greetings.[114]

When King, weary from the political imbroglio of the summer, set off in the fall for London to represent Canada's interests at the Imperial Conference, he was clear about, at least, one matter that he felt required clarification; namely, that dominion autonomy should be understood to mean that the status of a dominion Prime Minister to the Governor-General should be as that of the Prime Minister of Britain to the King. King's interest in clarification and definitions, thus, joined with the interests of the Irish Free State and the Union of South Africa to bring about a major change in the formal statement of constitutional relationships among Britain and the dominions.[115]

While the Imperial Conference of 1926 dealt with a wide range of issues and developed a lengthy report detailing agreements on them,[116] the most critical work of the session, at least in Keith's view, was accomplished in meetings of the Inter-Imperial Relations Committee. This was a body consisting of the Prime Ministers of each of the dominions but with Lord Balfour, a former British Prime Minister and, by that time, an elder statesman in all senses of the term, in the chair rather than Baldwin. Through a procedure of discussion and debate, that Committee searched for ways to reconcile the divergent interests and objectives of Britain, the dominions, and India. It considered drafts of a constitutional statement prepared both by the Irish and the South Africans. Finally, it approved a statement, largely drafted by Lord Balfour who incorporated ideas from other drafts as well as from the various discussions.[117] That statement, at its core, defined dominion status in a passage which appeared in italics:

> *They are autonomous Communities within the British Empire, equal in status, in no*

*way subordinate one to another in any aspect of their domestic or external affairs,
though united by a common allegiance to the Crown, and freely associated as members
of the British Commonwealth of Nations.*[118]

On the basis of that principle, subsequent imperial conferences and drafting
sessions led to a formal statute of equality, the Statute of Westminster, 1931,
which ended control over the dominions by the British Parliament.[119]

Keith, naturally, followed all this with high interest. He recognised many
of the contradictions both in the constitutional statement about dominion
status and in the subsequent legislation. He followed the press reports about
the work of the Imperial Conference and studied the formal report as soon as
it was available. In addition, he had at least one first-hand account of the
working of Balfour's committee when King came to Edinburgh after the
conclusion of the sessions, went to Keith's home at Crawfurd Road, and dined
with him.[120] In that setting, Keith learned a great deal about the formal
report of the Imperial Conference and, as well, about the informal side of its
development. Indeed, Keith wrote to King in his Christmas greeting to offer
help:

> If in the working out of the issues referred to the Expert Committee there are
> any matters on which you wish to have my opinion, I trust that you will not
> hesitate to let me know. It will give me pleasure if I can be of any service in
> arriving at satisfactory solutions of problems which are never quite simple.[121]

In the years after the Imperial Conference, Keith had many opportunities
to explain the meaning of that constitutional principle. One particularly
significant public session took place in Edinburgh on 26 January 1927.
Balfour, as Chancellor of the University, was invited by the Principal, Ewing,
to speak about the work of the Imperial Conference. Ewing wrote to ask Keith
to be present and to join in the discussion after Balfour's speech.[122] Keith,
while being the acknowledged authority on responsible government and
on dominion status, was, by that time, seldom in attendance at University
functions. It will be recalled that it was precisely at that time that he was
involved in negotiations to add lectures in the constitution of the British
Empire to his responsibilities.[123] On this occasion, Keith wrote a lengthy letter
to Ewing in which he outlined all the questions he would wish to put to
Balfour and which, he felt certain, in view of a speech and response to
questions that Balfour had recently given in the House of Lords, that Balfour
would not wish to respond to in a public meeting. Thus, Keith declined
to attend.[124] Ewing, however, put Keith's concerns aside and 'earnestly'
encouraged him to attend: 'A meeting at the University on that subject
would be ridiculously incomplete without one who is so widely recognised an
authority upon it as you are!'[125] Keith did, in fact, attend the meeting,
had an exchange of questions and comments with Balfour, and made a
contribution to interpreting the work of the committee. Keith pressed Balfour
to explain about the italicised passage, but Balfour, and Keith had clearly
suspected as much, was reluctant to say much publicly. Instead, he wrote to

Keith the next day and offered to give him 'the *private* history of the italics' and assured Keith that it was 'not very interesting or exciting',[126] which turned out to be the case since it was an error of a typesetter who may simply have been more prescient than he knew.

It was in the next edition of *Responsible Government in the Dominions* that Keith had fuller opportunity to write and to reflect upon changes in imperial relationships than in his briefer letters to the press or in his notes to the *Journal of Comparative Legislation*. As early as 1924, he had raised the question of a new edition of his 'classic' work with R W Chapman of the Oxford University Press. Keith's last substantial work, *Imperial Unity and the Dominions*, describing shifting relationships had come out in 1916 during the war. His three volume edition of *Responsible Government* was sadly outdated since it had been published in 1912. While it reflected changes which had been set in motion by the Imperial Conference of 1911, it clearly needed large-scale revision in order to reflect the great changes that had occurred in the intervening years. In his letter to Chapman of 9 May 1924, Keith suggested that he would need to take account of Ireland, Malta, Rhodesia, and India as well as the other portions of the British Commonwealth of Nations which possessed responsible government.[127] Humphrey Milford to whom Chapman referred the matter supported the preparation of the new edition: 'What a man. Yes, tell him to get the new edition into two volumes.'[128] Chapman conveyed that news to Keith, urging him to condense the work as 'the best solution in this imperfect world' and going on to indicate that: 'The book will in that event exhibit a rare example of expansion followed by contraction, formula 1 : 3 : 2.'[129] Keith took that challenge and in the next years worked at the new edition.

When it appeared in 1928, it was favourably reviewed and received. More than 1,300 pages long, it was, for Keith, compressed and condensed. He left out many of the specific legal cases and dealt with shorter references. One reviewer talked about it as 'a classic' in its earlier versions to which the present edition was a worthy successor, especially as Keith elaborated material dealing with the dominions and treaty-making and with the dominions and foreign policy. The reviewer indicated that 'Dr Keith never leaves us in any doubt of his own views on controversial subjects' and valued the work the more because Keith did more than merely describe.[130] Another reviewer felt that the greater compactness had led to greater readability. Using the same structure and approach as in the earlier editions, Keith provided a clear description of changes that had occurred up to that time. Perhaps one of the most telling sections in the work was the preface where Keith identified eleven steps needed to achieve sovereignty for the dominions. He had identified many of these in *Imperial Unity and the Dominions*. For each of the steps, he indicated the status and made very clear the significance of the agreements reached at the Imperial Conference of 1926.[131] Each edition of *Responsible Government* at the time it came out was an important and significant statement about constitutional developments; each followed a conference, 1909, 1911, and 1926, where major decisions were reached by the participants to define relationships among Britain and the dominions.

These three editions remain among the best descriptions of the constitutional result of those conferences.

This edition, published in the same year as his *History of Sanskrit Literature*, marks the conclusion of this period of analysis. In these years between 1920 and 1928, Keith continued his career in the University, developed his work in Sanskrit, played an active part in the Scottish Liberal Federation, expanded his role and activities in law, commented on international affairs, and enhanced his standing as one of the authoritative interpreters of imperial constitutional law, especially as a consequence of the profound changes that came as a result of the Imperial Conference of 1926. In the next six years, that is, up to the spring of 1934, he continued work in several of these areas even as he became involved more extensively in cases and publications in law. It is to that period that analysis must turn.

CHAPTER 11

Scholar and Sage, 1928–1934

In the half dozen years between 1928 and 1934, Keith's life and career changed in several important ways. While he certainly was well established and well respected as a scholar in Sanskrit, it turned out that he had already completed his principal works in that field prior to this period during which he continued active scholarship, however, not through books but through writing articles and reviews, and contributing chapters to books. At the same time, he was recognised and consulted as one principal authority on imperial constitutional law and related matters by persons in the United Kingdom and throughout the British Commonwealth of Nations. In contrast to his publications in Sanskrit and Oriental fields, he continued his studies, comments, correspondence, and books on imperial affairs at an increased pace. Further, he observed and attempted to analyse the profound trans-formations occurring on the world scene especially as they had an impact on imperial relations. In these years, then, Keith shifted the focus of his work slightly, away from major studies in Sanskrit and towards studies in law, in general, and of its applicability, in particular, to imperial constitutional matters and to international relations. He wrote several works focused on legal questions and, in fact, became directly involved in giving advice with respect to the law in two cases involving Scottish marriages.

With high energy, with enormous productivity, and with continuing sup-port from the University and his household, Keith lived an active life in these years as a scholar who put his works before various publics and, increasingly, as a sage who was consulted for his knowledge, his opinion, his insight, and, some felt, his wisdom. Often in London for his own studies, he worked with various groups on issues in which he was interested or about which he was asked to consult. Never given to innocuous or vapid comments on controversial matters, Keith became increasingly sharp in some of his public and private debates. Never in doubt about the rectitude of his position, he frequently dismayed and exasperated colleagues, publicists, correspondents, and publishers.

His life of scholarship and of public commentary took his full attention. In that life, his wife assisted him in numerous ways. He was profoundly affected when she died in the spring of 1934, thus bringing to a close more than twenty years of marriage. Her death clearly marked for Keith the end of another significant phase of his life.

During those years which ended in such personal loss, Keith gave more and more of his attention to events on the international scene, and, especially, to the response of the British government to them. National political developments in Britain were, in part, related to international developments. Both on the national and the international stage, Keith became increasingly critical and despondent as he watched successive acts and actors reveal the drama. It will be helpful here to sketch some of the major elements and conflicts in those troubled times.[1]

On the international stage, four powers with differing and, often, conflicting interests and activities provided the principal dynamics: the United States of America, the Soviet Union, Italy, and Germany. America held the purse strings of the world, and the crash of the stock market in New York in October 1929 reverberated throughout the world. Cast, indeed destined, to play the leading and crucial role in the world of the twentieth century, America rejected the part, at that time, and, instead, remained in the wings screened behind George Washington's 'Farewell Address'. The Soviet Union, having settled, presumably, the issue of revolution in one country based upon the application of ruthless adherence to several *idées fixés*, even though the ideas themselves suffered from certain internal inconsistencies, began to seek some fresh part in the world in recognition of *A New Civilisation*,[2] and, in fact, was admitted in 1934 to the arena of the League of Nations where powers, greater and lesser, joined in disharmonious concert. Suspicion remained that the Soviets now were preparing to take up world revolution as their next act. Italy in 1932 would mark completion of the first decade of fascist rule under Mussolini's management with his position consolidated, with, at least, the trains running on time, and with, even, the Vatican reconciled to the new order. *Il Duce* was ready for a new part and searched for it by designing a new theatre especially in the Mediterranean. And Germany, the *enfant terrible* who had 'caused' the First World War, the presumed source of Europe's economic problems through her constant attempts to renegotiate her requirements for reparations and other indebtedness, and the incubator of the Nazi movement and of its messianic leader, Adolf Hitler, was poised to play out the entire new script of *Mein Kampf* which would end the Weimar Republic and bring in the revengeful world of the Third Reich. All these great powers, except for the United States, became members of the League of Nations and, thus, met each other, with some frequency during these years, at Geneva. Contrasting roles played by these four powers provided the dramatic events to which Britain had to respond.

It was not simply the sequence of international affairs which Keith found disturbing but it was, as well, the inadequacy, he felt, of leadership in Britain to respond effectively to those events. At least one recent writer, from the vantage point of later perspective, would concur about the inadequacy of British leadership: A J P Taylor in *English History, 1914–1945* characterises British statesmen in the years following Locarno as joining in the 'hey-day of conciliation in western Europe' where peace, on whatever terms, was the desired goal. There is little question but that this was a time of continuing uncertainty in domestic politics. From voting in a Conservative majority in the election of 1924, the electorate returned no majority in the spring of

1929 but, rather, divided their votes between Conservatives and Labour, and gave Liberals, still split between Lloyd George and Asquith, a weak third. No party had a mandate to do anything. With Labour holding the largest number of seats, MacDonald formed his second government putting Philip Snowden, a most traditional and conservative financier, at the Exchequer. This appointment ill-equipped that government to cope with the economic blizzard which swirled out of New York in the autumn. It was the falling pound which ended Labour's attempt to govern and led to the creation in 1931 of the first National Government, that is, a coalition essentially between Labour and Conservatives which included a mixed lot of Liberals initially more followers of Lloyd George rather than of Asquith. Regrettably, Snowden remained at the financial helm. National Governments, in these years led by MacDonald, in later years by Baldwin and Chamberlain, became normative for Britain as the way to cope with the depression and successive world crises. Weaknesses inhere in coalition governments; perhaps it was for that reason that Britain seemed unable to provide the vigorous, clear leadership which Keith would have wished. Or, perhaps it was the persons who led the Foreign Office: Austen Chamberlain, Conservative, committed to finding peaceful solutions in Europe, but, at that time, in his last years and with failing health; Arthur Henderson, Labour, trade unionist turned statesman who, while trusted by both France and Germany, no small feat, may have been in waters too deep and too treacherous for his compassionate nature; Sir John Simon, Liberal, returned from studying the problems of India and reluctantly endorsing protection who may have been too skilled in the arts of compromise or, as one critic claimed, of fence-sitting.[3] Perhaps, and, more likely, the very complexity of the changed international scene required leadership, vision, and resolve to guide the British public, and politicians, away from too great sympathy towards Italian and German claims and to separate legitimate or reasonable claims firmly from illegitimate and unreasonable ones.

One British leader, not in the government, but much before the public in those days, promoted an old solution to Britain's economic problems. Lord Beaverbrook, Max Aitken, the Canadian-born press magnate, publisher of the *Daily Express*, the *Sunday Express*, and the *Evening Standard*, argued for something he called Empire Free Trade. This notion, really neo-mercantilist in concept and, in essence, similar to Joseph Chamberlain's imperial *zollverein*,[4] would have created an imperial trading bloc which, behind tariff barriers, would permit the freer flow of goods within the Empire and restrict access of goods from the rest of the world. This proposal was hardly a solution likely to appeal to the dominions, themselves in serious financial difficulties because of their relatively weak positions in the world economy. Yet, the idea was carefully considered, and speedily scrapped by the dominions, at the Imperial Conference in Ottawa in 1932.

While the Labour Government and the National Governments searched for economic solutions to Britain's plight and while successive leaders worked through the League of Nations for collective security in Europe, Britain also took the lead in pursuing world disarmament. Naval conferences among the powers established ratios for the size of fleets each could build. The culmination of efforts at disarmament came at Geneva in the winter of 1932 when the greater and lesser powers of the world met under the chairmanship of Arthur Henderson. No effective agreements could be reached.

These, in brief, were some of the elements in the world and in the country from the end of 1928 through to the spring of 1934. Even as he observed all that was going on, Keith continued his work and activities. The various aspects of that work and of those activities must be considered. He produced scholarship in Sanskrit and Oriental studies. He became directly involved in the India Round Table Conferences and Indian affairs between 1930 and introduction of the Government of India Act in 1934. He published works in law beyond updating Dicey's *Conflict of Laws*, and he became directly involved in advising on the law in two marriage cases, that of the Inverclydes and that of the Campbells. He wrote extensively on imperial constitutional law and increasingly on international affairs. He followed with particular interest the turn of events in the Irish Free State which brought De Valera to power. In the last year of this period under consideration, he had to cope with the reorganisation of his domestic life after his wife's death.

Sanskrit and Oriental Studies

In these years, his principal contributions in the field where he held his title and chair can be found in various journals and in several *festschriften*. In addition, he continued the laborious process of working, as he had the time to be in London, at the identification and listing of Sanskrit and Prakrit manuscripts in the Library of the India Office. Completion of that task ultimately resulted in a catalogue that was finally published in 1935.

It is interesting to note that by 1932 he had re-established his relationships with the Royal Asiatic Society and was willing, once again, to write reviews and to contribute articles to the *Journal*. The volume of his work was not what it had been in his earlier association, yet it is significant that he was reconnected to the principal journal for his speciality. It is clear that he was industrious in reading journals and books in Sanskrit and Oriental studies. In the six book reviews which he contributed to the *Journal* between 1932 and 1934, he cited the various works which were related to the specific book under review. He knew what was being written, argued, and theorised. For example, he expressed dubiousness about Charpentier's interpretation of the doctrine that Brahman equals cosmic fire as being too closely dependent upon Hertel's theories, which Keith also doubted.[5] Generous when he concurred and when he accepted the significance of a work, he was forthright in saying so as, for instance, with respect to W Caland's translation of *Pañcaviṃśa-Brāhmaṇa*: 'It is invaluable to have the contents of the text made effectively available'.[6] After indicating the places where he differed in interpretation, he continued: 'But difference of opinion, one is glad to note, is only possible because of the real knowledge of the two texts which we owe to the tireless energy and deep insight of the distinguished author'.[7] Again, he was enthusiastic when he reviewed Bloomfield and Edgerton's *Vedic Variants*:

> The work ... is of fundamental value for the progress of Vedic studies. It forms an indispensable adjunct to the elucidation of the history of the Vedic texts and the determination of their meaning and their interrelations.[8]

He wrote a sympathetic review of a work by an old correspondent, Sylvain Levi, whom he described as 'so admirable an interpreter'. In reviewing *Matériaux pour l'Etude du Système Vijñaptimātra*, Keith expressed his appreciation of the book and especially of the fact that it was based, in part, on manuscripts which Levi had found in Nepal: 'The work therefore forms an indispensable contribution to the study of a historically most important system, which already has had the good fortune to be studied by Professor Louis de la Vallee Poussin'.[9]

The one article which Keith contributed to the *Journal* in the period was published in 1933, 'The Origin of the Aryan Gods'.[10] In this, he made reference to the work of Rudolph Otto, a German scholar, who rejected the notion that the gods were created by ancient people in response to natural phenomena. Keith argued that there was limited use in worrying about the origins of religion; what was critically important for the scholar was to know what religious beliefs undergirded religious practice and ceremonies at a specific historic time and, he wrote, 'These may be very different from the opinions to which they should logically have advanced.'[11] Keith was not very supportive of elaborate explanations for origins but rather argued that Vedic texts themselves yielded sufficient clues:

> But it is plain that he [Otto] under-estimates the importance of two clear facts. In the Vedic literature we have the product of a time of active religious thought and of a marked tendency to pantheistic conceptions, and of a period when there was a widespread belief in the existence and activity of spirits of the dead. There is nothing in the litany which cannot be explained when these facts are borne in mind, nothing which requires us to go back to the making of religion and the working of the numinous fancy of primitive man.[12]

In addition to his work for the *Journal of the Royal Asiatic Society*, Keith contributed a limited number of articles and reviews to other journals. He wrote two articles dealing with aspects of Buddhist belief for the *Bulletin of the School of Oriental Studies*. As well, he wrote for a journal published in India, *Indian Culture*, and did a review in the *Annals of the Bhandarkar Oriental Research Institute*.[13] He corresponded on Sanskrit and Oriental matters with colleagues in various parts of the world.[14]

In these years, he contributed pieces to five *festschriften*. One which must have given him particular pleasure was for the book honouring Lanman at Harvard; for that, Keith wrote: 'Daṇḍin and Bhāmaha'.[15] In the book honouring G H Ojha published in Allahabad, he wrote: 'The Aryans and the Indus Valley Civilization.'[16] For a book in honour of Sir George A Grierson, published in Lahore, he contributed: 'The Grouping of Indo-European Dialects'.[17] He pursued a similar theme in 'The Home of the Indo-Europeans' in a book honouring C E Parry, published in London.[18] He drew from his work in philology and language for the essay, 'The Etymology of Guna' in the volume which honoured K B Patthak, published in Poona.[19] Keith's works in these various articles reflected the range of his interests. Further, the fact that he was invited to contribute to several such compilations is, itself, an indication of the esteem with which he was held in the field.

Indian Round Table Conferences and Indian Affairs

It was not only by the language, religion, and philosophy of ancient times that Keith was connected to Indian affairs; it was, as well, by the current political scene. While Keith felt that his knowledge of classical patterns of Indian thought and belief did provide some insight into contemporary Indian matters, he knew that his more recent exposure to Indian politics through his membership of the India Office Study in 1919, his collection of documents on Indian policy published in 1922, and, especially, his writings on imperial constitutional law were the reasons why he was approached to become involved in the First Indian Round Table Conference in November 1930, and, as well, in the subsequent developments that led to the introduction of the Government of India Bill in December 1934. These were years when Keith had direct involvement in a significant imperial matter.

If India was the jewel in the crown of the British Empire, then Keith welcomed the opportunity to be involved in moving her from a semi-lustrous past under British aegis into a sparkling future under her own political authority. He approved all the evidence of improved status for India that had come through the war, the treaties, the Imperial Conference, the League of Nations, and elsewhere. He was pleased with the Montagu–Chelmsford proposals, but felt that they did not move India quickly enough to responsible government.[20] When Sir John Simon, on behalf of the second Labour government, went out in 1929 to undertake an inquiry into the future constitutional status of India, Keith applauded the report's conclusion which called for dominion status in the immediate future. It was, in fact, the fate of that report in the context of political uncertainties in Britain and the emergence of Gandhi to power in the Indian nationalist movement that led to the series of conferences and negotiations which ultimately resulted in the Government of India Act, passed finally in July 1935, legislation which, again, regrettably Keith felt, fell far short of the goal of the Simon Report.

It is important to note the way in which Keith became involved in Indian affairs. It was not the India Office or the Government of India or any department of the British government which sought him out; rather, it was the Associated Chambers of Commerce of India and Ceylon which did. Their leaders headed by E P Benthall, President, with the full support of Sir Hubert Carr, prominent in British-Indian trade and active in the European Association, India, approached Keith in the autumn of 1930 through Hugh Molson, a Conservative MP, who served as Secretary to the European Delegates to the First Round Table Conference. On the basis of *Responsible Government in the Dominions* and Keith's various writings on merchant shipping, Benthall, Carr,

Molson, and their colleagues felt that Keith was the best person available. The letter inviting him to assist their cause made it clear that they would be willing to retain him in either of two ways:

> Should you regard this as falling within the scope of your work as a Barrister, we should, of course, be prepared to have you instructed through Solicitors. If, on the other hand, you advise us in your capacity as an expert on Imperial Constitutions, I should be, I think, competent to put before you all the materials upon which your advice would have to be based.[21]

Keith accepted in his role as barrister, but, in fact, he functioned both quite formally in response to instructions provided by solicitors, Denton, Hall, and Burgin primarily and, on occasion, Sanderson, Lee, and Company, and quite informally as Carr or Molson or Benthall or others would write and ask for opinions. His response to instructions from solicitors and from leaders of the Associated Chambers was always prompt, extensive, and evidential. He wasted no time in addressing the various queries which were put to him.[22] As needed, he went to London to meet with the men who had retained his services, with officials at the India Office, and with participants in the Round Table Conferences. In the years between the fall of 1930 and the spring of 1934, he was paid legal fees, amounting, probably, to something between four hundred and five hundred pounds.[23] Practising as a barrister clearly was not a volunteer activity for him, but, rather, one for which he received appropriate compensation.

While he gave opinions on a variety of matters which concerned the Associated Chambers of Commerce as the prospect emerged of political power in India shifting from the ultimate authority of the British parliament through the India Office, the Government of India, and the Viceroy to the authority of an Indian parliament resting on an expanded degree of suffrage, there were two very specific questions which were central and crucial: under such a new regime, what sort of protection would there be for European companies chartered in Britain or in India which conducted their business in pounds sterling; could such companies be discriminated against in favour of Indian-controlled companies doing business in rupees and, if so, could not constitutional provisions be enacted to preclude such a result? The second was equally important: what was the relationship between being a British subject transacting business in India, as it existed under the present regime, and being a British subject required, under one set of Indian nationalist proposals, to become an Indian citizen in order to transact business and participate in political life?[24]

Keith's position on these matters was consistent with his analyses of the ways in which responsible government had transformed dominion status. He argued, and, indeed, persuaded the delegates of the Associated Chambers to accept his view, that, on the first question, there was every likelihood that a nationalist government with the full authority of dominion status would discriminate. The approach, then, was to avoid trying to write entrenched clauses into a constitution which, he pointed out, had not been very effective in the case of the Irish Free State, especially since those clauses would undoubtedly be subject to interpretation through a Supreme Court in India but, rather, to accept that, when dominion status was granted, India would become *vis-à-vis* Britain just like other dominions. Thus, India and Britain should draw up an agreement, and he prepared numerous drafts along this line, setting out the principles for commercial relationships that would obtain between the two countries, such an agreement would include a clause providing for arbitration of disputes or differences of interpretation through an inter-imperial body, essentially the Judicial Committee of the Privy Council expanded to include several Indian, not English, judges on the imperial panel. It is interesting to find Keith consistently arguing the value and validity of inter-imperial arbitration. 'Reservation implies a superior party which cannot last indefinitely, arbitration an equality which is a permanent condition.' He had used the same reasoning a decade earlier in the Brisbane Tramways case. Unfortunately for his views, the Law Officers, whenever they were consulted on the matter, indicated their preference for regular courts and legal proceedings. Keith pointed out, on many occasions, why he favoured arbitration over court proceedings as more likely to achieve equity in inter-imperial matters:

> The whole point is this, that a Court interpreting an international or Inter-Imperial-convention is not bound by the narrow rules of legal interpretation which compel Courts in interpreting Acts of Parliament to apply a literal interpretation.[25]

On this point, Keith held a solitary view. The Law Officers, and others who might have done so, did not support his concept. His was a creative idea which came, however, at a time when, perhaps, too many other rapid changes in imperial relationships were occurring. It was a significant proposal to continue the gradual transformation of the Judicial Committee of the Privy Council into a real imperial court of appeal and free it from its too constricting relationship to the British government.

On the second issue, that of being a British subject or a citizen of a dominion, Keith was equally clear. He felt there was no higher status than being a British subject; that that was the common element which held the British Commonwealth of Nations together. He saw no conflict between being a British subject located anywhere in the British Empire or Commonwealth, with there being subsidiary requirements for residence, for suffrage, for taxation, for eligibility for certain benefits, and the like. Those local requirements, he felt, were perfectly consistent with the commonalty of being a British subject under one King anywhere within his realms. He saw the efforts of the Irish Free State to introduce a special citizenship as awkward and as illustrative of the way the matter should not be handled. In the particular instance of India, Keith saw a further complication: how were subjects of the princes in the various native states to be considered? Keith felt that the princes could not allow their subjects to become Indian citizens. Being a subject of a common imperial monarch was a comprehensive status, in his view, and handled the matter for subjects of the princely states, for Britons domiciled in India, and for native-born Indians of all castes and all religions. What should exist, he argued, ought to be a continuation of the reciprocity which then existed: subjects of His Majesty who were Indian-born could come to Britain, could establish residence in Britain, could enter into political life in Britain including the franchise. Why, he reasoned, would not the same status obtain, in the reverse, in the new India? There would, then, be exactly the same relationship for Britons who went there to live or to engage in business as for Indians in Britain. At several points, he put his views.

> An Indian British subject is free to visit England, to obtain the franchise by mere residence, to hold any office, and to acquire an English domicil. Why, therefore, should India say that you can have rights, but only if you call yourself an Indian citizen? Is the title British subject not enough? The average Englishman is proud of his allegiance. Citizen to him connotes a republican form of government.[26]

Fully cognisant of the power of national aspirations in the dominions, he still believed that, in this instance, the commonalty of British subject would suffice. In the event, of course, it did not. His guiding principle was that of equality and reciprocity among the parts. Yet, the pull for each dominion, following the Irish model, to begin to define its own requirements for citizenship was too great to withstand the concept of commonalty and, in his view, carried equality too far. A dualism set in which, soon, Keith would describe in his works, even as he lamented its existence.[27]

He continued his work for the Associated Chambers over several years. He argued his positions and was successful in enlisting support for them at least in the processes of bargaining that occurred during the Round Table Conferences and the Joint Select Committee after the matter came before the British parliament. In the course of this work, he had considerable discussion and correspondence with his oldest brother, William J Keith, who became involved in commercial matters because of the interest of the Chamber of Commerce in Burma where he, of course, served. William came in to Crawfurd Road from St Margaret's in Dunbar to consult with his brother. Notes that remain indicate that the meetings were cordial and mutually helpful.[28]

When the Joint Select Committee of parliament was considering Indian constitutional issues in 1933, Keith still was retained by the Associated Chambers. In addition, he wrote directly to several of the key persons who were involved in that stage of the process. He continued to press his concept of inter-imperial arbitration and to argue for avoiding the creation of a separate Indian citizenship. He wrote to Lord Reading, to Stafford Cripps, to Herbert Samuel, to Lord Rankeillour, and, of course, to Molson. His comments were precise and helpful, at least his correspondents acknowledged them as such.[29]

In his work on Indian constitutional affairs during these years, he brought a vision of India and her future relationships within the British Commonwealth of Nations that was still premature in the 1930s. He deplored, for example, the ways in which the India Office continually slowed the movement toward dominion status. He saw that India must be raised quickly and confidently, to that status of equality, for that is what it amounted to after the Imperial Conference of 1926. This passage from a letter to Molson in September 1931 gives the flavour of Keith's sentiments:

> I noted with much regret the apparent desire of the India Office to evade the promise of Dominion Status as the ultimate goal of Indian progress. It may have been unwise to give the promise but I have always assumed that it was made in good faith, and have so assured Indian correspondents of whom my membership of the Crewe Committee have always brought me a number. Nothing will do us more harm in India than bad faith in this matter, and I hope that the delegates [that is, of the Associated Chambers] will at least avoid in any way seeming to be hostile to Dominion Status. No one can seriously believe that India can be kept in the Empire by mere force, and I am sure that the interests of Europeans [that is, British Indians] will suffer severely at no distant date if they are held to be implicated in any attempt at repudiation. ... This is, I think, essentially a time for long views as opposed to a mere enforced settlement which would contain in itself the certainty of early denunciation, on the score that it violated the principle of equality.[30]

The short view prevailed, however. His advocacy of the long view which would bring India, he hoped, speedily and co-operatively into equal relationship with Britain was not necessarily a popular one. Certain members of parliament, Churchill included, used the Indian constitutional reform to prop up their political destinies as much as the destiny of the Empire.[31] Keith made use of the press as a way to carry his arguments to the public. He was even accused of advocating 'the abandonment of British control over India' by a correspondent to *The Morning Post*. In response to a letter from the editor, he wrote back, at the end of May 1933, on his position:

> I need hardly say that I have never suggested the abandonment of British control over India. On the contrary, I have consistently held that the Simon report should have been put into operation, as the retention of central control would have saved the situation and permitted orderly evolution of capacity for self government; that the substitution of the idea of creating a conservative central legislature and government by using the States is unwise, for the States will not successfully play the role assigned to them; that the alleged safeguards are utterly valueless and that the government in putting them forward doubtless acts with honesty but nonetheless with incredible lack of judgment; and that the attempts to safeguard the interest of British commerce as set out in ss. 122–4 of the White Paper are valueless.[32]

In the context of all else that Keith wrote in those years about India, this letter makes it clear that he wanted orderly, yet speedy, transition to responsible self-government with dominion status. His criticisms of the provisions on commercial safeguards came from his belief that constitutional restrictions would never work nearly as well as a negotiated agreement between two equal parties. His feeling that bad faith in the movement to dominion status would seriously impair British–Indian relationships was well-grounded for that status was achieved only after continued turmoil and after the Second World War, far too remote in time and events and far too tragic in the process of partition to have provided for the 'orderly evolution' which Keith had desired.

It is perhaps not surprising that Keith began, concurrently with his legal consulting on the Indian constitution for the Associated Chambers of Commerce, to compile his knowledge into another book. The genesis of that work which came out in the year following the passage of the act creating the new Indian constitution was rooted in the detailed investigations he carried out in connection with the Round Table Conferences and related matters. *Constitutional History of India, 1600–1935* contained insights related not only to the past but, as well, to recent events.

Writing and Practising Law

It is clear that Keith made good use of his preparation in law as he consulted with the Associated Chambers of Commerce of India and Ceylon about the development of a constitution for India. Obviously, he also drew upon his detailed knowledge of imperial constitutional law, especially as that might be applied in a different setting. In these years, in addition, he expanded his work in law in two other ways: he wrote three books on aspects of English law, carried through another revision of the book which Dicey had entrusted to him, and prepared a new edition of another standard work on English law. The other way he was involved arose primarily because of his membership of the bar both in England and in Scotland. He was retained in cases which involved two Scots families.

It is apparent that, in these years, his interests in law increased. He prepared two works in 1930 which were published the following year: *Elements of the Law of Contracts* and *An Introduction to British Constitutional Law*. He undertook those specifically at the request of officials at the Clarendon Press. They had, of course, published many of his books both in imperial constitutional law and in Sanskrit. They well knew his prodigious energy, as K K Sisam wrote to J L Brierly in March 1930:

> Would you object to that extraordinary man Keith, who can do anything in a short time, being asked to try his hand on a short book (30,000 words or so) on Contracts—I mean the principles for those who have not swallowed Anson whole? I remember you thought this was impossible of execution when we talked of it, but it would be a great seller if it were reasonably good; and Keith has a lion's courage.[33]

In due course Chapman put the proposal to Keith who responded promptly: 'It is very kind of you to suggest so pleasant a vacation task.'[34] By June, Keith had completed the manuscript and left Sisam almost wordless: 'That extraordinary man Keith has done the little book on Contracts—it looks to be of the right length and standard.'[35] He then wondered whether there might not be another book which Keith could undertake 'to keep him out of mischief'. He mused about the possibility of asking him to rework Anson and finally suggested inviting him to undertake a book of about the same length as the one on contracts, this time to deal with British constitutional law. And Keith quickly produced it. Neither book turned out to be the seller which the press hoped for, but both books continued in print for a considerable period of time. To each, Keith brought power of analysis, exposition, and, because it was specifically stipulated, compression. Each was designed for students studying law.

A year later, in 1932, he brought out the fifth edition of *A Digest of Law of England with Reference to the Conflict of Laws*, the book which he had inherited from Dicey. In fact, this was to be the last edition which Keith undertook of that work. He brought to the task his usual ability to capture the essence of the law through the citation and illustration of cases. This edition saw nearly a thousand new cases included with resultant reductions in other parts of the text. Reviewers found it still to be of particular value to those lawyers who were interested in the detailed problems of conflict of laws. They also felt that this edition simply indicated the increasing complexity of such matters rather than any movement in the direction of simplification.[36]

Between the fourth and fifth editions of this work, Keith received an inquiry from Frank B Edwards who wanted to know about how he had come to be involved with Dicey and to have received the commission to carry on revisions. Keith explained:

> Curiously enough I never knew Dicey until after I had left Oxford, when he wrote to ask me some points in colonial laws, and thereafter we used to correspond from time to time, and finally at his very pressing request I took on the task of editing his Conflict of Laws. It is rather a curious instance of a very sincere friendship based almost entirely on letters, for a series of chances prevented me ever availing myself of his many invitations to stay at Oxford.[37]

It is strange that the men never met, in view of the lengthy correspondence which they carried on. But, in spite of never having had a direct conversation with him, Keith was an admirer of Dicey's work: 'I had a very high opinion of his abilities, and perhaps most of all of his amazing lucidity a result which,' Keith admitted, 'I have never achieved.'[38] Certainly, Keith more than fulfilled his legacy from Dicey by seeing that classic work through three successive editions.

The two other legal works which Keith brought out, at this time, included one which did for the dominions the sort of exposition he had undertaken for Britain itself: *The Constitutional Law of the British Dominions*. For this, he moved to a different publisher, Macmillan. The book was considerably longer than the similar one for Britain, but that reflected, in part, the greater complexity of finding guiding principles for all of the dominions, especially in view of the changes which the Union of South Africa and the Irish Free State had introduced. It reflected the changes which arose from the passage of the

Statute of Westminster.[39] For the last legal work he produced in this period, Keith undertook for Stevens and Sons, the principal publishers of law books, the task of revising and rewriting E W Ridges' standard treatise, *The Constitutional Law of England*. Published in 1934, this was the fifth edition of the work which Keith would see through another two in subsequent years. Again, he committed himself to keeping another classic work current. He intended that these works be available for lawyers and others in terms of the most recent cases and formulations.

For some persons, writing about law might be sufficient; for Keith, however, when he had the opportunity, once again, to become directly involved in practising law he seized it. In the autumn of 1932, he received a letter from Harry G Abrahams a member of Michael Abrahams, Sons and Co, one of the numerous law firms in London which dealt in divorce matters. Abrahams wrote to ask whether Keith would be willing to advise about Scots law as it might apply in two cases concerned with marital problems, one that of the Inverclydes and the other that of the Campbells. Keith readily accepted the offer to participate and for several months during the winter of 1932–3 was heavily involved in the cases, especially the latter.[40]

The former case involved the marriage between June Tripp, an actress, and John Alan Burns, the 4th Baron Inverclyde. His first marriage had lasted only two years, and he had been granted a divorce in that instance. The heir to substantial money from the Burns Steamship Company and from Cunard, he took his second wife in March 1929. Lady Inverclyde found her marriage in difficulty because her husband seemed unwilling, or unable, to fulfil his obligations. In 1930, she sued in an English court, but without success, to have the marriage nullified 'on the grounds of the impotence of the man'. The court found for Lord Inverclyde on the grounds of domicile, citing among other authorities, relevant passages from the fourth edition of Dicey's *Conflict of Laws*.[41] Following that decision, Lady Inverclyde decided to pursue the matter in Scotland. As Abrahams described it to Keith:

> We have been consulted ... as to whether the Scotch Court would entertain a suit for nullity brought by the wife on the ground of her husband's impotence or non-consummation, or alternatively whether in the event of the husband bringing a suit for desertion the wife could successfully cross-petition for a Decree of Nullity, and whether if a Decree of Divorce was pronounced an Antenuptial Settlement on the wife made by the husband could be varied by an Order of the Scotch Court.[42]

Keith explained the details of Scots law which strongly supported marriage bonds and took a dim view of separation and divorce. He advised that the initial view of a Scots court would be to determine whether or not any attempt had been made at reconciliation. To that end, he edited a letter drafted by Abrahams which Lady Inverclyde sent to her husband on 27 November.[43] The letter yielded neither consummation nor satisfaction. Keith, then, urged another try and drafted the letter which she sent early in December: 'I need hardly say that I am very willing that it should be generally known that I have taken the initiative in seeking reunion, and I felt sure that your action in granting of my request would meet with wide approval.'[44] Skilled though Keith's words were, they did not achieve the desired result, in the sense that no reconciliation occurred. Keith received payment of twenty guineas for his part in the affair. Several years later, Lord Inverclyde sued his wife and was granted a divorce.[45]

The other case was more important because of the prominence of the parties involved. Keith came into this case, again, as a specialist in Scots law. Abrahams also worked through Allan, Dawson, Simpson and Hampton one of the legal firms in Edinburgh. Keith was in extensive correspondence with Abrahams in London and, as well, in regular contact with William Allan in Edinburgh.

The Defender was Ian Douglas Campbell, at that time, the heir presumptive to the Duke of Argyll and, subsequently, the 11th Duke. A playboy of the western world, at least of Paris, London, and other places where attractive women could be found, his first marriage was to Janet Aitken, daughter of Lord Beaverbrook. They had married in 1927 against the advice of her father; a daughter had been born to them a year later. From early in the marriage, apparently, their relationship had turned sour. He carried on his affairs; she took refuge with her father. By 1931, the marriage was over, and it was just a question of how to terminate it. He wrote to her on 3 May:

> This intolerable farce must stop. Since you have made a complete mockery of loyalty and decency I am taking effective steps to put an end to your comedy. Your prattle about 'business arrangements' is, if anything, more contemptible than any of your former excuses. To attempt to pick up the pieces now would be as stupid as it would be physically nauseating.
> I am going abroad. ... I will provide you with ample grounds for divorce.[46]

At that time, divorce laws in England were as strict as those in Scotland. Adultery had to be proved in order for divorce to be granted. It is that fact to which Campbell referred in his final sentence.

The first question about which Keith was consulted had to do with where the divorce proceedings should take place, in London or in Edinburgh. Campbell was frequently in France for lengthy periods of time and attempted to claim domicile there. Indeed, the idea of a French divorce had some attraction for his wife as being, perhaps, simpler and, certainly, less public. Keith advised against pursuing that route. Since Campbell's lineage was unquestionably in a Scots family and since the estates to which he was heir were also unquestionably in Scotland, Keith concluded that, also unquestionably, the case would fall under the divorce laws of Scotland rather than those of England. Clearly, adultery had to be established in a way which the courts would accept. Under direction of Janet Campbell, Abrahams hired persons to watch Campbell's comings and goings in Paris and London and to secure testimony from persons who witnessed his activities with various women. Abrahams reported the results of that surveillance in great detail to Keith:

He [Campbell] passed the greater part of yesterday up to mid-night in the company of his inamorata with whom he went to several second rate restaurants and drove her about in several taxis. He also went with her to a night Club where they had drinks. He of course knows she is married. ... Although there is ample evidence of a great intimacy between two married people which may be of a sexual character, indeed Campbell seems to pass nearly all his time in London with this woman going about with her to resorts which are hardly fitting to their station and drinking with each other, occasionally kissing and cuddling but I suppose that even Scottish Judges though perhaps stricter in their views on morality than English ones would be likely to find that a man and woman may do such things without it necessarily following that their relations are absolutely adulterous.[47]

To this evidence, a great deal more was systematically added to complete the picture, in so far as that was possible, that Campbell and Mrs Betty Pawson must have engaged in adultery. From the reports assembled, it is clear that Campbell did honour his promise to provide 'ample grounds for divorce'. Keith was explicit on what that involved: 'Adultery demands opportunity *and* guilty intention; Mr Campbell's actions (accepting our essential witness to be correct) is compatible with and strongly suggests a simulation of adultery.'[48] Therefore, Keith, satisfied that the case had suitable evidence, in consultation with Abrahams and Allan, prepared the text of the first Summons which was served on Campbell on 9 January 1933.[49]

However, by the time that Campbell received that Summons, he had been in contact with his wife on the 7th, indicating that he wished Mrs Pawson's name kept out of the affair and that he would provide alternative evidence on which to base the divorce action. He called again a day later with the same message. Then, in a very visible manner, he spent the better part of the weekend of 14 January at the Hotel Metropole with Miss Margaret Black. Abrahams had his man watching them, collecting evidence, and reporting it all. As Abrahams detailed all this to Keith, he included surmises about the length of time they needed to be by themselves in a hotel bedroom for intercourse to have occurred. Abrahams was certain that it had and that, therefore, an additional Summons should be prepared naming Margaret Black. After some exchanges with Abrahams, Keith did prepare a Supplementary Summons on those lines and that was served on Campbell on 24 January.[50]

It was the preparation of that additional Summons which began to worry Keith. He became deeply troubled and fearfully convinced that the Court in Scotland would look at the telephone calls of Campbell to his wife as evidence that Janet Campbell had agreed to withdraw the Summons based on adultery with Betty Pawson and, instead, to proceed with a Summons based on the new evidence of adultery with Margaret Black. Further, he feared that Campbell himself might allege that some such agreement had been struck. Keith moved into action. He expressed his worst fears to Abrahams[51] and then wrote a lengthy letter to Janet Campbell sending a copy with a cover letter to Beaverbrook.[52] Keith was certain that he must have a direct interview with Janet in order to find out precisely what she said to her husband in the telephone conversations. He also made it clear that Abrahams should have advised her, when she went there to tell him about the calls, to write a letter to Campbell denying that she had ever consented to any arrangement which would keep Betty Pawson's name out of the case. The absence of such a letter, Keith feared, would seem to indicate collusion in arranging such open and flagrant adultery. Keith requested Janet Campbell to come to Edinburgh to meet with him, basing his request on the initial stipulations of Abrahams that Keith might talk directly with her if the occasion warranted it. She refused to come even in response to a second request. Keith finally agreed to come down to meet with her; Beaverbrook arranged for Keith to be picked up by motor in London in order to have that conference with his daughter.[53] Keith was never fully satisfied that she was innocent of such collusion. In any event, the case was heard in Scotland and the decision of Lord Fleming differed from Keith's understanding about Campbell's domicile: the Court found that 'the respondent, at the time that the petition was presented, was not domiciled in Scotland' and that, therefore, it lacked jurisdiction in the matter.[54] Keith then withdrew from the case which, later in 1934, resulted in the divorce of Ian Campbell from Janet Campbell on the obvious grounds of adultery.[55]

Imperial Constitutional Issues and International Affairs

While Keith applied his legal knowledge to Indian affairs, to writing and editing several books in law, and to advising on two marriage cases, he, at the same time, continued and expanded his work on imperial constitutional issues and on international affairs, especially as they were connected. These years were ones of significant change on the imperial front. Keith studied, analysed, and wrote about each of the stages which led to the development of legislation to establish, in formal terms, the changed relationships among Britain and the dominions.

How was such change brought about? The Imperial Conference of 1926 had, in that famous passage crafted by Lord Balfour, enunciated the principle of equality of status for the United Kingdom and the Dominions.[56] But that statement had no legal standing of itself and especially since only one dominion parliament acted upon it.[57] The ambiguities of the Balfour statement had to be addressed and, to the extent possible, clarified in subsequent meetings of specialists from Britain and each of the dominions. These sessions, especially the Imperial Conference of 1929 on Dominion Legislation and Merchant Shipping and the Imperial Conference of 1930, led to the formulation of the Statute of Westminster which was passed by the parliament of the United Kingdom, that is, the Imperial Parliament, in 1931.[58] That statute gave legal effect to equality of status as Britain, in fact, eliminated the power of the imperial parliament to legislate on behalf of the dominions unless one of them made some specific request, repealed the Colonial Laws Validity Act of 1865 so that dominion legislation could no longer be illegal on the ground of repugnancy to British statute, removed territorial limitations on dominion legislation which was of particular importance for merchant shipping legislation, restated the centrality of the Crown as the symbol of imperial unity, and provided for dominion action on any change in succession to the throne.

Keith understood all of the various steps involved in this process. Through articles in journals, letters to newspapers, books, and correspondence, he pointed out particular issues and problems, explained the meaning of specific phrases, and interpreted these changes to the public. In every issue of the *Journal of Comparative Legislation*, he had an article, 'Notes on Imperial Constitutional Law', in which he kept readers informed about each of the changes involved in the major movements of redefining imperial relations and, as well, about specific imperial issues that arose. From time to time, in addition, he contributed an article which addressed one particular point as, for example, that on the Imperial Conference of 1930. In numerous letters to *The Times* and *The Scotsman*, he told the public about developments. Often these letters brought some response in the columns of the paper. Through this forum, Keith was the principal contributor in these years to public consideration of imperial changes.[59]

In 1929, he brought out two books which gave an analysis of the steps that had been taken to that time. In one, *Dominion Autonomy in Practice*, a rather brief book which was an expanded version of one he wrote in 1921 under a similar title, he was quite explicit about its purpose: 'It is the aim of this edition to state the present practice as regards the autonomy of the Dominions with special regards to the Imperial Conference of 1926 and its consequences.'[60] In the space available, he did sketch those changes and, more importantly, some of the limitations on autonomy which still existed, especially in the area of international affairs and foreign relations.

In the other book, *The Sovereignty of the British Dominions*, he developed at considerable length the nature of sovereignty and of the remaining limitations. In this, he provided a substantial analysis of the Imperial Conference of 1926, and then proceeded to examine both internal sovereignty and external sovereignty. For each form of sovereignty, he traced the way it had been achieved essentially as a result of the logic of responsible government before he discussed, in some detail, the various limitations which still existed on both forms of sovereignty at that time. He demonstrated that internal sovereignty was more fully achieved than external, in part because of great variations in size, population, location, and resources among the dominions. External sovereignty involved world affairs and, particularly, European affairs where British interests, in contrast to imperial interests, were dominant. He clearly recognised and emphasised the importance of both the Union of South Africa and the Irish Free State as bringing into imperial circles strong impetus for change in the direction of expanded sovereignty for the dominions. He was clear about his intention, throughout the book, to identify those places where further study and further action were needed. He felt this was necessary especially with regard to clarifying the international standing of the dominions. He indicated the very considerable problems involved in their achieving a standing independent from that of the Empire. He discussed the complexities of the way in which the Treaty of Versailles had been signed, of the way in which the British Empire membership of the League of Nations had been worked out, of the ways in which the dominions had, and had not, been involved in the Chanak crisis, the Lausanne Conference, the Locarno Treaties, and the like.[61] He was particularly critical of the United States for its lack of understanding of the ways in which the status of the dominions had been substantially changed through the war and through the imperial conferences following it.[62] Running through all this analysis, Keith pointed out the difficult paradox of having imperial unity exist under one King and one Crown, yet, at the same time, having real diversity exist in the varied degrees of interest, intent, and involvement which the dominions brought to imperial affairs. One reviewer characterised the book this way: 'It is an extremely valuable work, and not least in the fact that it is written especially for the citizen to read and not merely for the specialist to criticise.'[63]

In the same year in which Keith brought out these two books with a focus on dominion status, he undertook the sixth edition of Henry Wheaton's *Elements of International Law*, for Stevens and Sons. It is interesting to note that he drew upon his revision of Wheaton's work as, in the other two works, he analysed international issues that affected dominion status. In the revision, he expanded on the work, substantially enlarged it, and, in typical fashion, rewrote much of it. It, too, was one of the standard works in international law. The fact that he was willing to undertake this revision when he had the other works in hand is indicative not only of his considerable energy but also of the ways in which he saw imperial affairs and international law entwined. It is not surprising that, in the letters he wrote to the press in these years on international issues, he was much concerned with the status of the World Court and the relationship of the dominions to it. He was eager for the Empire to establish some form or way to arbitrate disputes involving the dominions, India, and the United Kingdom rather than have them be considered international in scope and under the jurisdiction of the World Court.[64]

During 1929 and 1930, he undertook a rather different, yet related project. He was troubled that the *Cambridge History of the British Empire*, the first volume of which had just come out at that time, appeared not to provide sufficient clarification or elucidation about significant constitutional developments and precedents in the old Empire in the years prior to the American Revolution. In the autumn of 1929, Keith wrote to Chapman with a proposal to write a book on the constitution of the British Empire from 1600 to 1776. In his letter, he indicated that American scholars had produced very substantial material and 'often excellent research' on colonial matters 'but their books are either monographs on special aspects or concern themselves also with general history'.[65] Chapman consulted with the faculty in history at Oxford and pressed them to determine whether such a book was desirable; if so, to suggest its focus and, particularly, to indicate an appropriate length. Chapman was emphatic on this latter point; he wrote to G N Clark:

> If I merely write, 'My dear Keith, how long a book do you propose?', I think his Highland sensitiveness may cause him to smell reluctance and he may reply, 'Dear Chapman, I propose to write nothing.'[66]

Clark and his colleagues affirmed the need for such a book, made some suggestions about focus, and indicated an appropriate length.[67] Based on these guidelines, Keith eventually agreed to write a book of about 150,000 words and give particular attention to the colonies in the West Indies as well as dealing with those in North America. It is worth noting that Keith understood this book would be quite different from his other works on imperial constitutional law since it covered a period that was finished, not in evolution. As he wrote in a postscript to a letter to Chapman, 'It will be a new and not unpleasant experience to write without the feeling that each day sees developments in Dominion autonomy which tend to render one's work behind the times ere it is issued.'[68] *Constitutional History of the First British Empire* appeared in 1930. In it, Keith provided a clear and useful analysis of imperial constitutional developments from the time of Elizabeth I to that of George III. A reviewer of the book praised it as filling the need for a textbook on imperial constitutional history 'in the most competent manner by this compressed but masterly survey'.[69] Keith drew upon his knowledge of the West Indies, acquired first-hand some years earlier in the Colonial Office,[70] to provide detailed analysis of a wide range of constitutional points about which the same reviewer commented, 'Many and nice are the constitutional questions which arise as the story is unfolded.'[71] Keith sent a copy to Mackenzie King, as well as to many other persons. King was delighted to receive it and wrote back a warm, cordial letter in which he repeated his admiration for Keith's work:

> How you ever managed to do the amount of research required to produce such a volume is something which passes my comprehension. The debt which those of us who are in public life owe to scholars like yourself is one which no words can begin to express.[72]

The quality of Keith's work was recognised when, in 1931, the Royal Empire Society selected it from among fifteen publications as the work to receive its gold medal 'for the best book published recently on any subject dealing with economics, history, politics or science within the Empire'.[73] The work has stood the test of time; it still appears in bibliographies of American colonial history as well as of imperial constitutional history.

No sooner was that work out of the way than Keith was ready to start on the next. He had arranged with Humphrey Milford to assemble documents to illustrate the transformation of dominion status from the war through the Statute of Westminster and to plan that work to parallel the earlier collection on colonial policy. Keith completed that editing and compilation in time to send it off with a letter to Milford on 27 November 1931, four days before the Statute of Westminster took effect. Such timing! There is no question but that the charge sometimes levelled at Keith that his works attempted to keep pace with current changes in dominion status was often an accurate one.[74] In this instance, it was quite intentional that the work should be issued just as quickly as possible so that, in addition to his longer works, scholars and others concerned about such matters might have a convenient collection of documents. He wrote to Milford, 'It would be best to get the book out as soon as possible after the passing of the Statute of Westminster when people would be interested in seeing what brought about the passing of that measure.'[75] He also felt that it might sell best with that sort of timing. The book did come out in 1932 in the *World's Classics* series: *Speeches and Documents on the British Dominions, 1918–1931: From Self-Government to National Sovereignty*. Reissued through several printings, it was, indeed remains, an extremely useful collection of documents.[76] And fully the most significant part of it is the introduction in which Keith summarised in clear fashion, and more briefly than in his major books, the course of developments in dominion status in those years.

In addition to contributions to the *Journal of Comparative Legislation*, letters to the press, and publication of books, Keith was invited to use his knowledge of constitutional developments to write in other places. He prepared an article interpreting the Statute of Westminster and analysing its implications for a German audience in *Zeitschrift für auslandisches u. internationales Privatrecht* which appeared in the issue of January 1932. Further, he was invited to prepare an essay for a Chatham House book, the Royal Institute of International Affairs, *Consultation and Cooperation in the British Commonwealth*.[77] This book was published in 1934 with Keith's essay, 'On the Constitutional Development of the British Empire in Regard to the Dominions and India from 1887–1933', serving as the introduction. In that essay, he provided a very compact analysis of the shifts which had resulted from successive Colonial and Imperial Conferences, ending, of course, with the major changes of the Statute of Westminster. It was a useful summary. In both these contributions, he brought his powers of analysis and exposition to bear so that each essay fitted effectively into the setting for which it was designed.

On the international front he watched and commented on, among other issues, the changes that occurred in British relations with the Soviet Union, with Egypt, with the mandate system and particularly with the British mandate in Palestine and the South African one in South West Africa, and with oil resources and British interests in Persia. On all these issues, he wrote letters to the press and, frequently, became involved in a continuing controversy.[78] For example, in late May and early June 1934, after he had written virtually nothing in the months following his wife's death, he engaged in exchanges in *The Times* with W H Stoker with respect to South African policy in South West Africa. While Keith did not agree with the aims of the South African government with regard to native policy, he was, nonetheless, always supportive of the text of the actual documents in every case. In this instance, he differentiated the fine line that existed within the wording of the mandatory clauses which prohibited annexation but which permitted treatment of the territory as 'an integral portion of the Union of South Africa'. On the basis of that distinction, Keith argued that the policy of Smuts' government was proper and pointed out:

> General Smuts would have preferred annexation out and out, but he accepted the compromise which gave him power to treat South-West Africa as an integral

part of the Union. The proposal to give the territory provincial status, therefore, violates no right of the native races: its expediency at the present time is more open to question.[79]

Stoker, extremely interested in the rights of Germans and less interested in native rights, disagreed with Keith's interpretation of the mandatory clauses. Yet, Keith had set out quite accurately the meaning of those clauses even though he might have preferred to have them drawn in a different manner. He knew, in this instance, not only what the text stated but also, from his study and direct knowledge about the Versailles Conference what the arguments and meaning behind it had been since it involved the creation of the Class C mandate specifically for this particular case. This is but one illustration of the way in which he conducted correspondence in the press during these years.

His interests in native affairs were long-standing.[80] This interest was most particularly directed to matters in South Africa. It was not just the matter of the Union government seeking to incorporate the mandated territory of South West Africa that was of interest to Keith but, in addition, he was concerned about the condition of the protectorates (Basutoland, Bechuanaland, and Swaziland) that still lay within Union bounds but which were directly connected to the Crown through the office of High Commissioner. Somewhat analogous to the native states in India in their constitutional status as being related to the Crown through treaties and being separate from the political entities within which they were geographically located, the protectorates were radically different in their actual condition. Basutoland, Bechuanaland, and Swaziland, were all areas organised on a tribal basis and represented a principal source of contract labour for South African mines and industries. The Crown, that is, the British government, had pledged to maintain and protect these areas even though a clause in the South Africa Act made provision for their transfer to the Union at some unspecified future time.[81] It was the aim of the Union government to seek to replace British control of the protectorates by having such control assigned to South Africa. Hertzog, particularly, had raised that prospect. In June 1934, the British government created a parliamentary committee chaired by Lord Selborne to study the matter of the protectorates and to develop guidelines for transfer, if that were to take place at all. Keith received an invitation from John Harris, Secretary of the Anti-Slavery and Aborigines Protection Society, to join a committee that was being created outside parliament to bring specialists together to assist in drafting materials for the parliamentary committee. Keith accepted the invitation and worked with Harris and others in preparing recommendations. To this work, he brought his detailed knowledge of imperial constitutional law, of the situation in South Africa, of international law and, as well, his long-standing conviction about the necessity of the British government providing adequate protection of and support for native rights. He had felt, for years, that Britain had abdicated its responsibility for natives when it handed over all control on native policy to the four colonies and then to the Union government in South Africa; he was eager that Britain, having abdicated once, should avoid a similar abdication in regard to the protec-torates.[82] Harris acknowledged Keith's role: 'I enclose a copy of the mem-orandum for the Parliamentary Committee, in the preparation of which we had your kind help.'[83] The proposals reflected Keith's convictions that Britain had a legal and a moral responsibility to maintain the protectorates in order to ensure adequate protection for natives.[84]

Irish Free State Issues

Clearly, in these years, Keith found that South African affairs posed an important cluster of imperial and international issues, especially in view of the fact that mandates came under the aegis of the League of Nations. Yet, it was nearer to home that he was forced to give particular attention to constitutional developments as the Irish Free State continued on its persistent course of seeking ways to incorporate republican forms into its laws and its practices. The two dominions differed in many ways but especially in the source of internal pressure on the governments of the day to change positions. In the Union of South Africa, political dynamics stemmed from the con-servative right, especially Afrikaners, who supported an increasingly restric-tive racial policy and separatist programme; in the Irish Free State, by contrast, political dynamics stemmed from the radical left, the republican wing, the actual opposition to Cosgrave's government, led by De Valera which, for the first five years of the new regime, carried on that opposition outside the Dail.[85]

The British Government found itself having to deal with rapid changes in its relationships to the Irish Free State, particularly after 1927 when De Valera, on whatever basis he judged reasonable, entered the Dail after taking, or perhaps not taking, the oath. For the next years, now inside the legitimate government of the Free State, he pressed Cosgrave to seek increasing sep-aration and differentiation in relationships to Britain. The arena was, of course, that of the specialist conferences leading up to the Statute of Westminster, a statute which it could reasonably be expected both the South Africans and the Irish would interpret as liberally and broadly as possible. By 1932, De Valera and his party had secured a majority in the Dail so that he, a long-time opponent of the Treaty, a long-time critic of the existence of any evidence of the Crown in the Free State, a long-time advocate of a republic for Ireland, became the President of the Executive Council. His programme was, in fact, a continuation of that which Cosgrave had initiated: to weaken all evidences of the British connection in the Irish Free State, yet to maintain all the advantages of association within the British Commonwealth of Nations, especially access to British markets. By the time De Valera took over power, Cosgrave's government had already achieved significant gains for the Free State both through advances in dominion status by way of the Imperial Conference and subsequent legislation and through direct negotiation or unilateral action affecting Britain.[86] It was Cosgrave who, by 1931, had abolished appeals from the Free State to the Judicial Committee of the Privy

Council, had eliminated the Crown from the civil service, the armed forces, postage, justice, and the like. Further, he had, with concurrence from Britain, created an Irish Seal to replace the Great Seal.[87] What De Valera did was to initiate a programme to speed up the completion of the process.

The British minister who had to respond to Irish initiatives was James H Thomas who served in the National Government as Secretary of State for Dominion Affairs from 1930 to 1935. A former train driver and member of the executive of the National Union of Railwaymen, he had been in the first Labour government and, by this time, had held various cabinet posts. In Keith's view, Thomas simply did not understand the complexities of the constitutional basis for the British Commonwealth of Nations and was singularly ill-equipped and poorly advised to deal with Irish matters.[88] It might have been anticipated that a minister from Labour might have a more sympathetic or, at least, pragmatic view of relationships with the Free State. That was hardly the case, for Thomas viewed the Anglo-Irish Treaty of 1921 with a sanctity that heartened the most conservative members of the House of Commons.

De Valera's programme was straightforward in its intent and in its stages. As soon as he could, he used his power as President of the Executive Council to whittle away the authority of the Governor-General, the link to the Crown. He insisted on dismissal of James McNeill as Governor-General and, in the new appointment of Donald Buckley, he reduced salary and provision for housing. He maintained that the Treaty was simply a *de facto* agreement which he would use for the time being but promised that at some subsequent time he would submit the form of the Constitution to the voters. In the spring of 1932, he introduced an amendment to the Constitution which called for the removal of the Oath of Allegiance and for the payment of land annuities to the Free State Government rather than to the British Government.[89] Both actions appeared to contravene the terms of the Treaty. To these propositions, Thomas, on behalf of the British Government, responded in irate and legalistic language. The result was the initiation of a trade war between the two members of the British Commonwealth of Nations: the Free State restricting access of British goods into the Irish market; Britain responding in kind.[90] Without those two matters resolved, De Valera took the next steps in the fall of 1933 with three amendments to the Constitution: to transfer from the Crown to the Executive Council the formal recommendation for monetary appropriations; to delete the power of the Governor-General to withhold assent or reserve bills; and, to make formal what was already practice, to eliminate appeals to the Privy Council.[91]

Thomas was unable to find any effective way to respond to this whole programme. The trade war, in the context of world depression, was as injurious to Britain as it was to the Free State. Coercion was not an option. Britain had earlier insisted at the League of Nations, and successfully so, that the Anglo-Irish Treaty was not international in the sense that any portions of it or any actions flowing from it could be submitted to the World Court. Although Keith and others had been interested in an inter-imperial structure for arbitration, such a body had not really come into existence.

What is of considerable importance in all these matters is that Keith's authority was primarily on the side of the Irish Free State. He based his judgements on the texts of documents, on the precedents that had occurred, on the interpretation of the Statute of Westminster, on the constitutional position that Canada had gained, and on his belief that reasonable men ought to be able to find some rational way out of such a legal impasse. He wrote extensively to the press. He wrote to influential members of the Labour Party such as Sir Stafford Cripps, of the Conservative Party especially the Attorney-General, Sir Thomas W H Inskip, of the Liberal Party such as Simon and Samuel.[92] While his correspondents did not necessarily agree with him, they acknowledged the value of Keith's views on the issues and Inskip asked his opinion on a number of specific points. Keith permitted himself to be interviewed for quotation by the Irish News and Information Bureau which subsequently published the interview and three of his letters to the press as a booklet. In the introduction, Henry Harrison, the editor, queried:

> How many are there, either in Britain or abroad, who have been aware so far of the fact that one of the most distinguished of British jurists has severely criticised certain of the legal conceptions and arguments contained in the British case as formulated by the Secretary of State for Dominion Affairs?[93]

Keith's main points which he elaborated in some detail were that Thomas was wrong to make the oath an issue of substance which it really was not. If Canada, Keith argued, wanted to remove an oath, and sent a petition to that effect to the imperial parliament, would not, under the terms of the Statute of Westminster, the British government be bound to carry it through? If that was so for Canada, then, under the Treaty of 1921 which gave the Free State the same status as Canada, that certainly had to be equally true for the Free State. While there had been agreements after 1922 about the land annuities, those agreements had been couched neither in a form which was approved by the respective parliaments nor in the form of an international treaty. Their meaning, thus, could be open to doubt and, here Keith repeated his proposed solution: since there was substantive material they should be placed for arbitration before an inter-imperial body. So far as amending the Constitution of the Irish Free State to place authority for appropriations requests with the Executive Council, there was good precedent for that and, as Keith pointed out, any Australian state could achieve that result without question. Restricting the Governor-General from withholding assent or from reserving Bills? That was the logical result of actions by the Imperial Conference of 1930 translated into the Statute of Westminster. As for appeals to the Privy Council being eliminated or restricted, that, too, rested upon sound precedents from Canada and De Valera's move to amend was simple formality, fully consistent with Cosgrave's earlier decision. What Keith wanted was to have the substantive points addressed and answered. He saw the chief substantive point to be the relationship that ought to exist between Britain and the Irish Free State and their mutual role in the British Commonwealth of Nations. Three passages from Keith's published letters convey his views and the tone of his comments:

> I fear that our Government, after swallowing a camel, is straining at a gnat in its fulmination against Mr de Valera.[94]
>
> Mr Thomas has evidently forgotten that Lord North and George III lost the British Empire in America by inability to surmount a rigid legalism and to apply constructive imagination to refashioning Imperial relations.[95]
>
> I have never pretended to think that the changes in Imperial relations of 1926–1931 were wholly wise, agreeing in this with the statesmen of Australia and New Zealand and of certain Canadian authorities, but what has been done cannot be undone, and this point [the abolition of appeals to Privy Council] seems now clearly within Irish power.[96]

What, perhaps, is even more surprising is that Keith argued, both publicly in his published letters and privately in correspondence to key political figures, that the British Commonwealth of Nations should be adjusted in its constitutional structure in order to incorporate a republic.[97] He pointed out, for example, that the charters granted by Charles II to Connecticut and Rhode Island were sufficiently republican in form to carry both of those colonies into statehood in the American republic where they continued as the basis of state government until the nineteenth century. If that could happen by royal grant in the seventeenth century, certainly, sensible leaders, perhaps wiser through experience, ought to be able to find, in the twentieth century, a solution to the republican aspirations of the Irish Free State, particularly in light of the *de facto* republic that had been created there during the 1920s. On 15 November 1933 in a published letter, he wrote: 'It seems to be a confession of bankruptcy of British statesmanship to deny the possibility of a formal republican constitution within so strange an edifice as the British Commonwealth of Nations.'[98] A day later, he made the same point in a letter to Sir John Simon: 'I cannot really believe that you and Sir T Inskip could not manage to fit a formal Republic into the Commonwealth.'[99] That view, of course, found no support among British leaders. It took the devolution of Empire after the Second World War for a solution to that problem to be found. Keith posed the argument a bit too early for it to be acceptable or even to be considered seriously.

Death of Margaret Keith

There is little question that Keith found the six years after 1928 productive and rewarding. He continued his respected scholarship in his principal field, expanded his writing and influence in the areas of law within England and Scotland, of imperial constitutional developments, and of international relations, and gave particular attention to the complexities of the Irish situation. Awards and recognition were his as scholar and sage.

Yet, the period ends on a sad note. On 25 March 1934, Margaret Balfour

Allan Keith, fifty-eight years old, died at Crawfurd Road. The death certificate indicated that she had a heart condition which was the apparent cause. In the obituary, she was described as 'dearly beloved wife'.[100] Her funeral was held at the Grange Cemetery in Edinburgh, not too far from the house where she had lived since 1920.

For a person like Keith, dependent on someone else to attend to the essential details of daily life in order to be freed, totally, for intellectual life, the loss of his wife must have been a severe tragedy. She had organised the household for years. She had provided on-going support for his work in such ways as proof reading, sharing ideas, and typing, support which he regularly acknowledged in the introductions or prefaces to his books. She had made arrangements for housing, for travel, for holidays. She had attended to the entertainment of friends and distinguished visitors. She had provided companionship to him. She had read mysteries to him while he worked. She must have listened to him talk about his concerns, worries, hopes, and ideas.

The ending of any lengthy relationship always poses great difficulty for the survivor. Keith must have felt the loss severely since they were in their twenty-second year of marriage and, of course, had known each other considerably longer than that. In the absence of any direct documents, no one can know for certain what went on inside that marriage. It seems entirely possible that what was initially a marriage of convenience, certainly for both, may have evolved into a marriage of real affection and support. There are only clues to Keith's feelings for his wife. The inscription that he wrote, or chose, for the handsome gravestone may provide one clue; in Latin, appropriately, it expresses a sensitive sentiment: 'What shame can there be in the longing for so dear a head?'[101] Another clue to Keith's feelings may be found in a letter he wrote to his sister, Nan, on the third anniversary of Margaret's death: 'You are right regarding 1934. That was a disaster for me which nothing can substantially diminish. ... But we cannot control these things, and all we can do is to cope with them to the best of our ability, with the aid of sympathy of others.'[102] The only other clues can be found in Keith's concern that her grave be well tended and have flowers placed on it as well as in the frequency with which he visited the cemetery.[103]

Loss, tragedy, and disruption: all these were true. Keith was left, of course, with the servants, whom Margaret had trained to his ways, yet he had to determine his next steps. Within a short time, he reached out to a member of the family and contacted his younger sister, Nan Dewar, widowed for six years, and invited her to come to Edinburgh. Her older child, a daughter, was in her late twenties and no longer at home, but her younger child, a son, was still in his teens with school and university ahead of him. Yet, Nan, somewhat surprised at the invitation apparently since there had not been ongoing, close relationships between them, agreed to take on the responsibility for her older, distinguished brother so long as she could maintain a flat in London where her son might come during school holidays.[104] Keith was satisfied with these arrangements.

The period of late March, April, and May 1934 is a time when Keith wrote few letters to the press. His work seemed to come to a brief halt until his domestic life could be reorganised. By the end of May, he and Nan appear to have worked matters out so that he might continue his usual routine of going to London in the early summer. This time, however, when he went up to London, or 'to town' as he called it, he started the new pattern of using her flat in Kensington rather than a hotel. His correspondents soon came to know the address of 10 Porchester Court W2 as well as that of Crawfurd Road.

When he returned to Edinburgh later in 1934 to cope, again, with the loss of his wife, it was Nan who arrived to take responsibility for the management of the household and to fill the role of companion. She remained with him for the next decade, until his declining health resulted in death. It is to that final period of his life that analysis now must turn.

CHAPTER 12

Commentator and Participant, 1934–1944

In the ten years from the death of his wife until his own death, after a period of progressive illness, Keith continued to write about and to work vigorously for those causes and issues which he believed to be of major significance to Britain and the western world. He was forthright as a critic and commentator, a 'keen controversialist' one person labelled him.[1] Indeed, until the last year or so of his life, it would be hard to know that he had any illness at all judging from the public record since his activity continued unabated in letters to the press, in the preparation of books, in articles for journals, and in correspondence.

From 1934 onwards, as Britain lurched towards an economic recovery of a sort and towards the outbreak of war, Keith found that there was much to criticise and to comment on both nationally and internationally. He continually chastised Britain's leaders, and would-be leaders, for their apparent unwillingness to confront national and world issues as he felt they should.

It must be said in partial defence of those whom Keith severely castigated that all such issues were complex because Britain was in a time of considerable difficulty and uncertainty.[2] A world power of the first order, at least so it appeared to leaders of the world at the League of Nations and elsewhere, in fact, Britain had been seriously weakened and profoundly transformed as a result of the First World War. From the perspective of hindsight, it is now clear that Britain had become a second-rate power by that time, a power whose commitments exceeded her resources. It would have taken some extraordinary vision and leadership to move Britain into the realities of her new role in the world. Britain lacked the military muscle, the political will, and the support of the public to translate platitudes about peace, collective security, and international order into effective policy. Certainly, none of the prime ministers of National governments, Ramsay MacDonald and Stanley Baldwin and, after 1937, Neville Chamberlain, could provide that sort of vision and leadership. Shuffling of office was no substitute for clear, vigorous statesmanship. Unemployment, labour unrest, and rearmament remained as continuing domestic problems. And Chamberlain whose principal interests were in social reform and social policy was fated to lead Britain in a crucial and tragic international role for which he was singularly ill-equipped.[3]

In those years of gloom, the joyous celebration of monarchy with the Silver Jubilee of George V in 1935 proved but a temporary respite. By the next year, even the monarchy appeared problematic, for the moment, as the country plunged into a constitutional crisis with the accession and ultimate abdication of Edward VIII at the end of 1936.[4] The romantic dimensions of the affair held public interest, to be sure, far more than speculations, analyses, and concerns about the changed nature of the monarchy and Crown, a change which became quite clear when the Union of South Africa, Canada, and the Irish Free State all acted to establish an accession date for George VI in those dominions different from that in the United Kingdom. Was it resolutions that finally divided both Crown and kingship? Not really, for the actions taken by those dominions were simply a logical outgrowth of the principles enacted in the Statute of Westminster. Dominions seeking looser association within the British Commonwealth of Nations successfully achieved that goal.

Keith could certainly be expected to comment on and to explain these changes in dominion status, and he did. However, his principal concerns in those years rose from the international scene especially as he saw the connection between British foreign policy and British domestic politics in constitutional and legal terms. Events on the international front offered little hope, but rather led to dilemma after dilemma. That was clear to persons who lived then as well as to persons of later generations. Hitler, rising to power in a revived, vigorous, and increasingly totalitarian Germany, challenged the Versailles settlement at virtually every significant point. With a claim to *lebensraum* and, particularly, to the incorporation of all Germans into the Third Reich, this latter an ironic twist for those who had drawn the Treaty of Versailles on the principle of national self-determination, he successively, and successfully, remilitarised the Rhineland, annexed Austria, and dismembered Czechoslovakia. When he invaded Poland in September 1939, war resulted, a war which Keith and others anticipated and feared, but felt could have been avoided with effective leadership from Britain.[5]

But it was not just Hitler and Germany. It was Mussolini and Italy as well, seeking, in a romantic but real sort of way, to return the Mediterranean to *mare nostrum*, the centre of the world as in Roman times. That, necessarily, posed challenges to Britain as the dominant power in the Mediterranean with her lifeline to the East threaded through Gibraltar, Malta, the Suez, and the Red Sea. Mussolini could not move except to counter Britain. His invasion of Abyssinia in the spring of 1935 challenged the League of Nations and Britain. Perhaps Britain's ineffectual response to that invasion, more than anything else, let the dictators know about Britain's lack of resolve and the ineffectiveness of collective security.[6]

And the brave new world of the Soviet regime continued its way under the dictatorship of Stalin who set loose brutal and bloody purges to guarantee orthodoxy and eliminate controversy. Britain's traditional scheme of maintaining the balance of power led her to support Mussolini, obviously a fascist dictator running a ruthless regime, against Hitler and led her to court the Soviets in hopes of achieving a balance on the eastern front. But all hopes of achieving any such balance collapsed in August 1939, when Hitler struck the non-aggression pact with Stalin, thus sealing the doom of Poland and gaining guarantees in the east.[7]

In many senses, the war had been foreshadowed in the Spanish Civil War. That involved not just factions in Spain but men and weapons from Hitler's Germany, Mussolini's Italy, and Stalin's Soviet Union as well. That posed further problems for Britain and France, especially which side to support since either side would ally them with one of the dictatorships. In the event, the Spanish generals led by Francisco Franco won and another fascist regime, distinctively different however, came into power.

Can it be any surprise that Keith with his beliefs in the sanctity of treaties, the efficacy and ultimate morality of law, the possibility of arbitration of international disputes, and the necessity for rational analysis of issues would be profoundly disturbed by the series of events which unfolded in these years? What a litany of disasters! He devoted his mind and his energies in the futile attempt to point out what should be done, in sharp contrast to what was being done. International debacle and national disorder provided the context in which he lived out the final years of his life.

During those years, he was exceedingly fortunate to have his younger sister care for him. Nan took over the organisation of the household and the direction of his affairs: hiring and supervising servants and secretary, seeing to it that materials on which he was working were put in the proper places, doing some of the typing, arranging for his travel and holidays, reading to him as he worked in the evenings, listening, in all probability, to him fulminate about the inadequacies of leadership in Britain, helping to clip and arrange newspaper materials, assisting in the preparation of books, and, most import-antly, providing continued companionship.[8] With much of the temperament of her mother, she persuaded and wheedled persons to her will and way. Yet, she must have felt considerable strain in caring for her brother since she still had responsibilities to her youthful son. She had the complex tasks of making certain that Keith's household would continue to run smoothly during those weeks when she needed to be in London in her own home, there making certain that she also provided for her son's needs. Keith was solicitous for the welfare of his nephew. In the summer months, of course, Keith joined her in London or on holiday, usually at Eastbourne.[9] Judging from the correspon-dence that remains from Keith to Nan, he appreciated the role that she was willing to play; from a letter of March 1937: 'I am very far from failing to realise how much you have done, despite our almost complete diversity of natures, to render life tolerable.'[10] He felt free to express to her his anxieties about health, about the work on which he was engaged, about their domestic arrangements—'I confess the advent of a new damsel is a bore', about the problems of life—'I have just sent off my income tax return, which adds to one's gloom', and about the great loss he underwent in his wife's death.[11] Clearly, it was Nan who sustained his life and work during these years.

In order to understand his work during this time, it will be necessary to examine several different aspects. He continued in his post at the University and from that position achieved recognition in many ways for his varied contributions. He studied and wrote about the changes which occurred in the British Commonwealth of Nations and dominion status. He became

13 Nan Balfour Keith Dewar, *c.* 1936. Photograph courtesy of Mrs J Walcot Burton.

increasingly convinced that the constitution was severely threatened and that civil liberties, won, often at great cost, over such a long period of time, were being eroded. He was a persistent critic of foreign policy so much so that he became actively involved in the lobbying that was organised to protest against British policy towards Italy after the invasion of Abyssinia. After 1942, he found his physical condition weakened but continued his mental activities. With splendid support from his sister, Nan, in caring for the household and in assisting him in all ways, Keith lived a full and productive life, although not necessarily cheerful, almost to the time of his death.

Edinburgh University, Professor and Scholar

As Regius Professor of Sanskrit and Comparative Philology and as Lecturer on the Constitution of the British Empire, Keith continued to fulfil his dual responsibilities to Edinburgh University through teaching, examining, research, and writing. In many ways, he was better known outside the University than within it. By this time, he had ceased to have anything to do with University affairs other than responsibilities for his courses. He never attended meetings of the Senatus; he took no particular interest in any of the issues until the outbreak of war when he became concerned to be certain that students knew about its causes.[12] In effect, while he met his classes, his reputation rested not on teaching but rather upon the books and articles which he had published.

None of the classes ever enrolled many students. In his later years, Keith met those few students who read with him in any of the subjects at Crawfurd Road.[13] He wrote to Nan in October 1938 about his teaching responsibilities:

> My Comparative Philology boy has duly turned up, to my utter disgust. It is too annoying and I apparently am to have one Sanskrit pupil only, the youth I had two years ago, who failed completely in his examination work.[14]

Yet, for those students who did read Sanskrit, Keith provided effective instruction, typical of that given in those days. Students prepared exercises based upon vocabulary, grammar, and literary passages. In the classes, students recited materials they had prepared. Keith took the recitations, made corrections, provided explanations, and indicated the next steps. At the end of the course, students sat examinations. One student of those years who took the class remembered that Keith always arrived with a large bundle of mail which he proceeded to read through and to prepare answers for while students recited their exercises. 'The amazing thing,' recalled the student, 'is that he never missed an error and never failed to give corrections!'[15] Those who studied Sanskrit under his direction and who did the work laid out by him were able to score well in examinations; some went on to continue their studies successfully on the basis of the foundation they had received from Keith.

One of the students who took the course on the Constitution of the British Empire during those years, and won the Margaret Balfour Keith Prize for her performance on the examination, recalled that there were only four students. They met around a blazing fire in one of the Retiring Rooms of the Old College. She described the course:

> I must admit that I found the Course dull—the lectures being confined entirely to the constitutional framework of the Dominions, Colonies and dependencies of the British Empire. They were dictated, more or less, in a rather flat tone and precise manner, in due course to be regurgitated in examinations. I was given to understand that there was no living person so well-versed in these constitutional details and the negotiations leading to them as the Professor.[16]

Keith himself described the class as being concerned 'with many difficult legal issues'.[17] It is fair to assume that students heard his ideas; in a note to Nan on 8 December 1936, he stated, 'My class asked me to explain the position of the King, and I did so at length!'[18] Likely, too, students heard a considerable amount of the text from the most recent works that he was then writing.

In the field of Sanskrit, Keith continued to produce materials, primarily articles and reviews. He did finish one complex task for the India Office, that of working through nearly 1,600 manuscripts. That task resulted in the only book he published related to Sanskrit in this period: *Catalogue of Sanskrit and Prākrit Manuscripts in the Library of the India Office. Volume 2. Brahmanical and Jaina Manuscripts*. Published in 1935, that catalogue was, and continues to be, an important addition to the inventory of such manuscripts available to scholars. In order to complete it, Keith had had to invest substantial time in the project over several years.

In addition to that, he continued writing reviews and an occasional article for the *Journal of the Royal Asiatic Society*. From the reviews, it is obvious that he continued to do a substantial amount of reading since he was able to provide not only critical comments but also bibliographical points in the course of the reviews. His contributions continued right into 1941. In addition, almost to that same year, he wrote articles for *Indian Culture* and the *Indian Historical Quarterly*. As in the earlier period of his life, he was invited to contribute articles to various commemorative volumes with the last such article dealing with a subject of long-standing interest to him, 'Pāṇini's Vocabulary', which appeared posthumously in 1945 in *Bhārata-Kaumudī: Studies in Indology in Honour of Dr. Radha Kumud Mookerji*.

In several significant ways, in those years, Keith was honoured publicly for his extensive contributions to Sanskrit and, as well, to constitutional and legal studies. Such honours reflected, of course, his extraordinary intellectual achievements. Yet, clearly these rested upon the fact that, in his role as professor and lecturer, he was freed to devote time to such work. He had a continuing and dependable financial base combined with minimal responsibilities, only two terms of instruction and few students at that, which provided the security to make scholarly production readily possible. In a very real sense, all the honours which he received honoured Edinburgh University at the same time, since it supported him, to be sure, although never as generously, in financial terms, as he felt he deserved.

He was honoured in three significant ways. In 1935, he was elected as a Fellow of the British Academy, that group of three hundred British individuals selected because of their unusual contributions to various areas in the intellectual realm. Similarly, he was elected in the next year as a member of the American Philosophical Society, an organisation founded by Benjamin Franklin, one of the geniuses of the eighteenth century, to recognise distinctive intellectual contributions. Not restricted to citizens of the United States, it included scholars and other noteworthy people from around the world. Keith accepted both of these honours, although he resigned from the British Academy in 1939.[19]

In June 1936, he accepted the honorary degree of Doctor of Laws from Leeds University. Offered honorary degrees earlier, he had been indifferent to them and, also, reluctant to travel to have them awarded in person. When he received the letter from Leeds proposing the degree, he reacted negatively at first; he was dubious about whether or not he wanted to be troubled to make the trip and to participate in the ceremony.[20] Finally, he decided to attend and take the degree. He received full instructions from the Vice-Chancellor and the Registrar for the ceremony. On 29 June, he was awarded the degree. In a letter the following day, the Vice-Chancellor sent a copy of the citation to Keith; he kept that citation.[21] Whoever wrote it, while using the rhetorical flourishes customary for such occasions, was, however, quite perceptive about the ways in which Keith deserved to be honoured for his unusual and unique life and contributions:

> It is rarely that we find united in a single individual the wide scope, and at the same time the power of detailed exposition, which distinguishes the work of Arthur Berriedale Keith. The titles of the posts which he holds at Edinburgh University ... though sufficiently impressive by their very variety, give but an inadequate idea of the range and quality of the achievement by which they are supported, an achievement not merely academic in the narrower sense, but one of active personal participation in the great fields which he has chosen. ... He has applied an unrivalled knowledge of Constitutional law to the intricate problems affecting the Empire as a whole, as well as its constituent parts; though this is, for him, but one department of a field embracing the whole history of our constitutional and legal relations, both internal and international. He has established himself as an authority in those domains by a long series of published works, which leave unelucidated hardly any aspect of the great problems involved. ... His eminence as a scholar in the ancient languages and literature of India was foreshadowed in his student days at Oxford: it has been confirmed and illustrated by a number of works rivalling his achievements in the field of law. ... It is with peculiar satisfaction that we welcome to this University one whom we may rightly regard as the chief ornament of Scottish learning, cast in the mould of the Schools of England.[22]

Thus did an English university select and honour a distinguished member of a Scottish university. Keith was not insensitive to the recognition.

Tensions in the British Commonwealth of Nations

During this period, Keith followed changes in the British Commonwealth of Nations with interest and concern. He examined, analysed, and wrote about such issues as the continuing matter of the status of the protectorates in relation to the Union of South Africa, the final stages in the Government of India Bill, the Irish Free State under De Valera testing the definition of dominion status through designing a new constitution with no reference to the Crown in it, on-going questions about dominion rights to secession and neutrality, and the increasingly troublesome quandary about the role of the dominions in defence. As one of the principal persons respected for his authority on imperial constitutional affairs, he accepted responsibility for interpretation of those issues and events which created tension and change within the British Commonwealth.

Not only did he continue the practice of setting out his views in letters to the press in these years but also he assembled certain of those letters into form for publication. He prepared the first of three such books in recognition of his wife's special contribution to his work. *Letters on Imperial Relations, Indian Reforms, Constitutional and International Law, 1916–1935* appeared in 1935. Keith dedicated the book to her and took the occasion to acknowledge his indebtedness:

> These letters were written for the most part at the suggestion of my wife; in all cases their contents formed the subject of discussion between us, and they were approved by her in the final form. Copies of them were preserved by her with the intention of publishing them after my death. In no part of my work did she take a greater interest, and I publish them now in her memory as some slight acknowledgement of twenty-one years of constant help.[23]

For the other two collections, *Letters and Essays on Current Imperial and International Problems, 1935–1936* published in 1936 and *The King, the Constitution, the Empire and Foreign Affairs: Letters and Essays, 1936–7* published in 1938, he relied on his sister to assist in the selection and preparation of the letters. The three collections include some 250 letters and provide a convenient way to follow Keith's ideas on the wide range of issues.

In addition to the collections of letters, Keith published two substantial books in the area of imperial constitutional law and relations during this period. *The Governments of the British Empire* in 1935 and *The Dominions as Sovereign States: Their Constitutions and Governments* in 1938. In both of these works, Keith reviewed current themes and issues in the development of dominion status and in the relations among the dominions and Britain. Especially in the first book, he described the nature of the basis for government in each of the dominions, colonies, and, as well, in India, set out the constitutional and political structure of each in some detail, and, in the process, affirmed the adaptability of British constitutional development and practice. One reviewer commenting in favourable terms about the book as 'first and foremost a work of reference' went on to commend Keith for his sense of historic developments: 'But he has never allowed himself to forget that the facts have themselves been shaped by circumstances, and that as the circumstances are still changing the process continues.'[24] The second book was addressed to that continuing process since the circumstances, especially around the abdication, led to considerable change. In the attempt to keep information current, he brought out that book with considerable material on very recent matters.

What then were some of the issues and what were the bases for positions that Keith took? It is necessary to examine several in order to understand his thinking.

One issue which Keith continued to find troublesome was the matter of the protectorates in the Union of South Africa. When the Status of the Union Bill was under consideration in 1934, he accepted it as a logical outgrowth of the Statute of Westminster. Further, he accepted on the same basis, the Royal Executive Functions and Seals Bill of that same year which certainly turned the Crown into a divisible one since, after the enactment of that bill, all Crown authority within the Union of South Africa would be exercised by the Governor-General in Council, that is, his advisers in the South African Government, without any reference to Britain. It was this precise point which Keith now took as he opposed, in the strongest possible terms, any transfer of the protectorates to the government of the Union. In his letters to the press, he argued the case vigorously: since, regrettably, the Crown was now divided by statute of the Union of South Africa, legal as such action undoubtedly was, he wanted the public, members of the British Government, and Parliament to know that the Crown which guaranteed protection for natives in those territories was the British Crown, not the South African Crown.[25] It is significant to note how he accepted the divisibility of the Crown only to draw a conclusion from that fact totally different from the conclusion drawn by Hertzog and his colleagues in the Union. But he went beyond writing. He joined in the protest organised by the Anti-Slavery and Aborigines Protection Society. At a meeting of the society at Caxton Hall, London on 18 June 1935, Keith was present to make a speech explaining the constitutional points at issue and, then, to give support to a resolution which he had prepared in somewhat more diplomatic tone than his speech:

> This meeting desires to record its conviction that in view of the vital constitutional changes since the passing of the South Africa Act, 1909, the transfer of the administration of the High Commission territories in South Africa to the Government of the Union of South Africa cannot be carried out except with the goodwill and co-operation of the inhabitants of those territories.
> This meeting welcomes the decision announced by the Secretary of State for Dominion Affairs to extend co-operation between the Union Government and the Administration of the Territories over as wide a field as possible, and desires to urge upon His Majesty's Government the importance of combining a policy of economic progress with the systematic development of those elements of self-government which are implicit in the tribal constitutions of the territories.[26]

In that resolution, he injected a new principle, that is, that transfer could only occur with the assent of the inhabitants. For this, he reasoned from precedents in India in the relation of inhabitants of the Indian States to the new federation. Crown responsibility, that is the responsibility of the British Crown, continued to exist towards inhabitants of the protectorates, as in the Indian States, and even if at some subsequent point transfer were thought desirable, the Crown of the United Kingdom at least through the Judicial Committee of the Privy Council must remain available to natives. Keith saw the entire issue as 'one of the moral obligations of the Crown'.[27]

While he was troubled about the ways in which the Union Government had extended the legal basis of dominion status, he still felt that such status should be the immediate goal of British policy in India. He followed with great interest as the Government of India Bill made its way through successive legislative stages in order to become statute in the summer of 1935. Throughout that process, he continued as a legal consultant to the Associated Chambers of Commerce of India and offered advice as he was asked to.[28] When the Act was finally passed, he was pleased that some of the goals for which he had worked were, in fact, achieved in the legislation. He remained disappointed, however, at what he felt was a lost opportunity for Britain to extend effective responsible government to India and to insist upon the introduction of democratic procedures into the Indian States. He saw such lost opportunity as detrimental to assisting moderate political leaders in India to maintain the imperial connection. Typically, he held that position in 1935 and still held it some years later as, for example, he pointed out in a letter of 23 October 1939 after the war had started:

> They [the Ministry] are, I fear, missing an opportunity to secure Indian goodwill, and of course outsiders in neutral countries cannot be impressed by our anxiety to aid the Polish oligarchy when coupled by a negative attitude in India. In the long run our refusal to insist on democratic institutions in the States is a definite act of failure of duty towards their peoples, for the States are upheld in autocracy and often misgoverned by the protection of the British Crown.[29]

Concurrent with his work for the Associated Chambers of Commerce and with his comments and analysis about the Government of India Bill, he engaged in the preparation of a study of the constitutional development of India. In that book, he incorporated much of the material and many of the insights he had gained in direct work on Indian matters. In many senses, it was a continuation of the collection of documents he had put together after the India Act of 1919. *A Constitutional History of India, 1600–1935* remains a magisterial survey of that subject. He took, as one reviewer rightly observed, a legal approach to the material which meant that he continually asked questions about documents and evidence. He ended the book, logically from his view, with an elaboration of the reasons why dominion status should be extended to India, particularly by recapitulating successive pronouncements, statements, and promises. The work had an immediate use when war broke out and the British government found itself, with little success, still searching for an effective Indian policy; Keith had already described numerous lost opportunities. When a mission was undertaken by Sir Stafford Cripps in 1942, Keith felt it promised too little, too late, and, moreover in the crisis of war, too much still in the future. Keith was harsh on Cripps for proposing, on behalf of the British Government, deferred dominion status and was critical of many details of the proposals.[30]

In addition to South Africa and India, Keith followed with particular interest the sequence of events in the Irish Free State in the years of De Valera's ascendancy. Keith had clearly understood De Valera's aims and the politics of his position.[31] While he was not necessarily sympathetic to them as offering the best approach to the development of dominion status and of common interests among members of the British Commonwealth, yet, he felt they were appropriate, in part, because he understood that the Irish Free State in its constitutional development had to be decidedly and distinctly different from the other dominions. Further, he supported the legality of the various steps that De Valera took.

Keith, therefore, watched with great care a case which went before the Judicial Committee of the Privy Council and which was designed to test the legality of the formal step that De Valera had taken in 1933 to abolish such appeals. The Privy Council on 6 June 1935, in the case of *Moore v. Attorney-General for the Irish Free State* decided that the act which the Irish Free State had passed to eliminate appeals was valid.[32] Keith accepted that as the correct decision in terms of the status which dominions had achieved by that time. But, in letters to the press and to Gerald Fitzgibbon, a judge in the Irish Free State, he expressed deep concern over the grounds on which the Privy Council had based its decision. He criticised the justices for ruling that the Statute of Westminster overrode the terms of the Anglo-Irish Treaty of 1921 and, thereby, opened the door for De Valera and the Dail to modify any of the terms of that Treaty.[33] Keith felt that there was ample precedent for dominions abolishing or restricting appeals to the Privy Council and that the decision could just as well have rested on the basis of precedent. While he had no difficulty with the Free State taking steps to abolish the office of Governor-General, indeed, felt that such a move would be sensible since the office had been stripped of any significance after the decision of the Imperial Conference of 1930 which called for only persons named by dominions to be appointed to such offices and, also, from the ways in which the Free State had reduced the office almost to the point of ridicule, he was troubled about the unilateral power which the Free State would now have, flowing from the decision to amend or abolish other provisions of the Constitution and, implicitly, the Treaty. Especially, he was concerned about provisions that established the constitutional basis for the government of the Free State and that dealt with British use of naval bases and with the stationing of British troops in the Free State. Further, he felt that the decision of the Privy Council created a legal paradox. He set out that problem in a letter of 22 June 1935, to *The Morning Post*:

The Privy Council has ruled that under the powers of legislation accorded by the Statute of Westminster the Free State Parliament is able to repeal any provision of the Constitution enacted by the Constituent Assembly, including the clause which made the terms of the Irish Treaty the paramount law of the Free State.

Now the Supreme Court of the Irish Free State, in a decision of December 1934, ruled that the Constitution is the supreme law of the land and cannot be overridden by legislation, so that as, the Constituent Assembly made the Treaty part of the supreme law of the land, the Parliament cannot legislate contrary to it.

It follows, therefore, that as, since the abolition of the appeal, the Irish Supreme Court has been in no way subordinate to the Privy Council, the highest Courts of the United Kingdom and of the Free State take diametrically opposite views of the Treaty; the former asserts that it does not bind the Irish Parliament, the latter that it does. Presumably, however, the Irish Court will feel unable hereafter to maintain its earlier attitude in view of the obvious difficulty of it insisting on the existence of a fetter on Irish legislation which the Privy Council has denied.[34]

Also, he shared these views privately in correspondence with Fitzgibbon who, in turn, added information about the ways in which Irish justices understood the Privy Council's decision.[35]

Few, other than legal experts, were troubled about the paradoxes and the technical difficulties with the decision. De Valera and his colleagues in the Free State accepted the decision as giving them legal power, unilaterally, to modify the Constitution and the Treaty. Keith anticipated this when he criticised the Privy Council for its lack of precision in stating the grounds for its decision:

> But it is most unfortunate that by failing to adhere to the established terminology it has put it in the power of Irish Republicans to argue that the highest tribunal in the Empire has declared that the Statute of Westminster has given the right to abrogate the treaty.[36]

While Keith continued his criticism of the grounds for the decision as creating a murky sort of legal context, he understood the politics of the matter quite clearly. Again, it is important to note, he suggested that somehow or other the government of the United Kingdom and the other dominions ought to find ways to reconcile De Valera's republican goals and moves, now further strengthened legally by the decision of the Privy Council, with the continuation of the British Commonwealth of Nations. Excerpts from several of his letters make his views clear:

> We have been offered by Mr De Valera the association of the Free State as a Republic with the British Commonwealth of Nations and security from attack based on Free State territory. ...[37]

> Is it wise to refuse to negotiate with Mr De Valera while he is still prepared to offer, if the Free State is permitted to adopt formally Republican status, to accept association for certain purposes with the British Commonwealth of Nations,

and to guarantee that Irish soil shall not be used as a basis of attack on the United Kingdom? ...[38]

But it may be permitted to hope that the unbending attitude of Mr Thomas is not the last word in British statesmanship, and that a Government which has jettisoned the Treaty of Versailles may yet find it possible so to modify the Treaty of 1921 as to render otiose such speculations as these. If Germans deserve generous treatment, why should it be denied to a people who, unlike the Germans, have suffered much wrong at English hands?[39]

Part of the reason that Keith was not persuasive is that some of his critics could not understand how, on the one hand, he could be so critical of the decision of the Privy Council as giving legal foundation to De Valera's likely next moves and, on the other hand, could be so critical of the British government for its inability to find some way to reconcile a republic within the British Commonwealth. Keith was consistent in advocating some solution to Irish republican aspirations which would guarantee Irish continuation within the Commonwealth. But, if the Treaty of 1921 had sanctity, and if it insisted, however wrongly perhaps, on the continuation of the Crown in the Free State, how was a republic then possible? As noted earlier, Keith was essentially pragmatic in his approach to matters and he simply felt it would be wise British policy to find a negotiated solution to a republic within the British Commonwealth.

In these years, other aspects in Irish-British-Commonwealth relations interested Keith. For instance, he found the matter of Irish citizenship of particular importance. Subsequent to the decision in *Moore v. the Attorney-General*, De Valera and the Dail enacted the Irish Nationality and Citizenship Act in 1935 together with the Irish Nationality and Aliens Act.[40] There was precedent for such action in legislation passed earlier in the Union of South Africa. Difficulty, however, rose, as in so many ways in Irish-British matters, from the proximity of the Free State and the United Kingdom. While Britain maintained the stance that any person within the Commonwealth and Empire was a British subject and entitled to whatever British subjects might claim, enactment of restrictive legislation in the Free State did not provide such large reciprocity or permit easy access for British subjects, especially those in the United Kingdom, into that dominion. Keith saw the acts as perfectly legal but as another impediment in the concept of the sort of desirable association in the British Commonwealth. He argued for some sort of bilateral agreement with the Free State around this, as around the larger issue of the republic.

It was somewhat quixotic that it was the abdication of Edward VIII in December 1936 that gave clear opportunity for De Valera to take another important step in ending the presence of Britain and the Crown in affairs of the Free State. While he had been working on the prospect of substantially removing the Constitution of 1922 and had often made clear that he accepted it only on an *ad hoc* basis, he saw the abdication as the context for initiating a new constitution for the Free State. Under the Statute of Westminster, any change in succession to the throne required action by each of the dominions.

On that basis and in a most non-republican way, De Valera set the accession date for George VI so far as that would affect the Irish Free State as different from the date in the United Kingdom.[41] He then proceeded to have a constitution prepared which eliminated all references to the Crown, a constitution which went before the voters and then into effect in 1937. In this constitution, De Valera achieved what he had been seeking since the great debates on the Treaty: for all practical purposes, the Irish Free State, renamed as Eire, was a republic internally yet, for external purposes, it remained within the British Commonwealth of Nations which had the monarch as its head and as its symbol of unity and, moreover, used that monarch to accredit its diplomats.[42] Fitzgibbon wrote to Keith in December 1937, to tell him about taking oath as a justice under the new constitution; he found it a curious proceeding but had no doubts about its legality.[43] Interestingly enough, Keith had no difficulty either about the legality of the new Constitution or about the status of Eire within the British Commonwealth. Since British politicians had been unable to find a satisfactory solution to Irish aspirations, the Irish had solved the problem themselves, and on their own terms.

Interestingly enough, it was the government headed by Chamberlain which, after all these changes had occurred, decided to negotiate with De Valera. By early 1938, all the issues which had been troubling relationships were settled, with the exception, of course, of Ulster. These settlements even included handing over to Eire the British naval bases along the south coast.[44]

The coming of war in September 1939 put a further strain on Irish-British affairs. De Valera took that occasion to declare neutrality.[45] Britain could not re-establish its control over naval bases which the Admiralty considered vital to Britain's security.[46] Keith found the position of neutrality, especially after Britain had accepted the constitutional changes in the Union of South Africa, to be, regrettably, legal, if illogical. Eire, as another dominion, had control of its own affairs. Internal controls were long established; external controls more recently. External control included the right for dominions to decide about the degree to which they would become involved in war. He had hoped that, in the particular context of confronting Hitler and Mussolini, Eire would respond positively. He, and others who had led to the settlement of Irish claims, were disappointed. In fact, Eire maintained neutrality throughout the course of the war.[47]

Malta Appeal and Tanganyika High Court

While his interests in Eire continued throughout this period along with those involving South Africa and India and while he wrote extensively about all those matters, he became, in 1938, a direct participant in the problems of Malta, a small but vital part of the British Empire especially in that time of Italian ambitions in the Mediterranean. The case which came to the Judicial Committee of the Privy Council concerned constitutional relations between Britain and that colony. Gerald Strickland, by that time successful in becoming a peer, was at the centre of the appeal and the dispute. Strickland and Keith had been friends and correspondents for something over thirty years, from the days when Strickland was a governor in various of the Australian colonies and Keith a clerk in the Colonial Office.[48] During those many years, they had seen each other and continued to write. Strickland was always interested in abstruse constitutional points and Keith, with similar interests, welcomed the chance to explicate. After Strickland had completed tours of duty as governor in various colonies, he returned to Malta, became directly involved in Maltese politics as one of the framers of a constitution for the colony in 1921 and then as a member of the Legislative Assembly, and served as Prime Minister and Minister of Justice from 1927–32. He had also served in the British House of Commons in the mid 1920s. Living his life between Britain and Malta, he had opportunities to participate in political and constitutional matters in two arenas.[49] By the time the Malta appeal came to the Privy Council, Strickland was in his late seventies and had become somewhat hard of hearing. Thus, he turned to Keith as a prominent constitutional expert to assist him in carrying the appeal forward in the best possible legal terms. Keith welcomed the opportunity to put his constitutional and legal knowledge about the Empire to practice.

The case was just the sort of one that would interest Keith. In the spring of 1938, he started to respond to Strickland's letters to determine the ways in which he might be of assistance.[50] He had, of course, first to understand the variety of issues that were involved. Fundamentally, the case rose out of action by the Secretary of State for Colonies, Malcolm MacDonald, following passage of an act in Parliament about Malta, in issuing new Letters Patent for the government of Malta in 1936, the effect of which was to withdraw the Legislative Assembly from operation and then to legislate for Malta through the reintroduction of Crown Colony government, that is, by the Governor in Council.[51] Malta's serious problems with its mixed population and religions was reflected in party strife and in the inability to establish effective government; that, at least, was part of the argument put forward for suspending, and then abolishing representative institutions. The specific issue on which the case rested was the legality of customs duties levied by action of the Governor in Council.

The case had gone through various stages within the courts of Malta before leave was granted to appeal to the Judicial Committee of the Privy Council. Keith immersed himself extensively in the case and assisted in the preparation of various documents to sketch out the basis for the appeal. He was retained in his capacity as a Barrister to work with Blout, Petrie, and Co from whom he received instructions and questions.[52] As with all legal matters which he handled, he was confident that he had a grasp of the fine points involved and he proceeded to write them out at considerable length.

Keith played two related roles in this case. In the first, he was the person who prepared the legal argumentation which, in written form, went before the Judicial Committee of the Privy Council. In the second, he actually presented the oral arguments of the case before the Privy Council when it sat in late June 1938.

For the written legal arguments, Keith drew upon his enormous knowledge of constitutional law, legal cases, and precedents. He assembled what he believed to be a convincing argument. He saw the central issues to be two: the competence of the Crown to legislate by Orders in Council given the basis upon which Malta entered the Empire, and the right of the Crown to withdraw representative institutions once granted particularly in the absence of any local request for that to occur. The briefs that he prepared were extensive.[53] He studied the ways in which Malta had entered the Empire and made a particular point of the fact that this was not annexation by conquest or by cession but rather was annexation by request of the Maltese. This, he argued, made a significant difference to the way in which the Crown must function. He raised no question about the Crown's authority and power to legislate for 'peace, order, and good government' of Malta, as for any area under the Crown, but he did have serious reservations about the constitutionality of the Crown granting representative institutions by Letters Patent in 1921 and then, unilaterally, withdrawing those institutions fifteen years later, without any request from the Legislative Assembly to have that occur. Can the Crown having once limited its prerogative by grant of an Assembly reverse that process? He argued that the Crown could not and that, therefore, the specific customs tax in question was illegal because it was enacted by an unconstitutional body.

In his second role, Keith, as it turned out, was selected to make the oral presentation of the case. There had been considerable correspondence with Blout, Petrie, and Company, with Strickland, and with the Clerk of the Privy Council to determine what was appropriate in the particular circumstances. At one point, it appeared that Strickland would make the presentation himself but he withdrew from that idea on the basis of his hearing. It was finally the Clerk who indicated that, of the options, Keith might, if they wished, present the case. That was decided upon by those bringing the appeal. Keith did the best job he could in presenting the arguments.[54] He certainly spent considerable time in preparation and, after the first day's presentation did not go as effectively as he hoped, plunged into further preparation for the next day. The report of his presentations seems to indicate that he argued his points well. But one observer reported that Keith 'made a deplorable impression. The judges said, Who is this man? We have no idea what he is talking about.'[55] The decision of the Privy Council went against the appellants. Keith was disappointed but not surprised. He wrote to Strickland on 24 June:

> I was sorry not to see you for a moment last night and to say how much I regretted the result of our case, inevitable as it was from the first, since we had to ask the Committee to declare that an Act of Parliament deliberately passed in order to destroy the rights of the [constituents] to constitutional government had failed to accomplish its purpose. But I admit that I was surprised to find the Committee so anxious to uphold the highest claims of prerogative without hesitation or stint. But most of all was I surprised at the anxiety to find that Malta fell under the control of the British Settlement Act, 1887, against the claim of the Attorney General that Malta was as a ceded colony not within the terms of the Act.[56]

The matter did not end with that decision, however. Strickland continued to pursue it through the House of Lords and, in fact, was instrumental in carrying a fourth and fifth appeal in 1938–9 as well as in 1940. In each of those cases, Keith wrote and provided work in drafting materials.[57] He did not, however, present oral arguments for each appeal.

Perhaps the most valuable outcome of the third appeal on which the negative decision was given on 24 June 1938, was the announcement on 29 July, a few weeks later, by MacDonald in the House of Commons extending representative institutions to Malta.[58] Strickland wrote quickly to Keith and commented that it was 'a liberal (vy. generous) constitution' and 'It follows that our labours have not been in vain'.[59] The restoration of a Legislative Assembly to Malta was timely and helped to secure better local support during the course of the war which followed the next year. Yet, volatile Maltese politics continued. Keith, in any event, could feel, rightly, that he had helped in some substantial way to call the attention of the Colonial Secretary to the importance of representative government and of constitutional practice with respect to Malta. Strickland's daughter Mabel, in one of numerous expressions of thanks, indicated, in a note of 12 August, that MacDonald had, in fact, visited Malta and 'was I think impressed by all he saw'. She went on to observe, 'I gather that the Colonial office is horrified at yours and father's independence. This of course delights me.'[60]

During the course of the war, the Colonial Office found that it had to turn to Keith's expertise with respect to a case which arose in Tanganyika. This was a continuation of opinions he had given some years earlier to Justice B A K McRoberts about matters involving the Chagga tribe. In September 1941, McRoberts wrote through the Colonial Office to Keith to seek assistance.[61] The issues involved interpretation of mandatory clauses, of land laws, and of tribal law. McRoberts asked for Keith's guidance since there was so little known about indirect rule and the ways in which it could be related to the courts. He wanted to know whether there was anything in English law related to local authorities which might have any bearing on matters in Tanganyika. As usual, Keith studied the matter, assembled available evidence, and wrote back within a matter of days of receiving the inquiry. In the final paragraph when he apologised for the delay in responding, he indicated that when McRoberts' letter arrived, he had, in fact, been engaged in preparing an opinion 'to be telegraphed to India on a very vexed problem concerning the rights of Indians in respect of migration to Burma'.[62] Yet, his response to McRoberts was clear, detailed, and filled with citations to support his points.[63] His major suggestion was that the High Court of Tanganyika like any other high court in the British Commonwealth had common law, equity, and statutes to guide it in its decisions, plus having the terms of the mandate clauses and the existence of native law. With all that, he urged a rather pragmatic approach with significant respect for native law. In due course, McRoberts wrote back to express appreciation:

> You have told me just what I wanted to know, and you have given me lines which I can follow now without difficulty. I was particularly pleased with what

you said about the right and duty of the High Court not to be excluded from
the native system of law, when that law has been made part of the law of the
land.[64]

In giving assistance to justices and law officers, Keith continued to make some
practical contribution to the British Commonwealth of Nations and Empire.

Interpreting the British Commonwealth of Nations

During the last decade of his life, Keith certainly played an important role in
elucidating dominion status and in interpreting the nature of the British
Commonwealth. He watched as leaders in the Union of South Africa and in
the Irish Free State, Eire, extended the definition of dominion status. He saw
the emergence of the right of secession although he never accepted that a
dominion might employ that unilaterally.[65] While he lamented the potential
of neutrality by a dominion, he saw that become a reality as war broke out.
He had opportunities to participate directly in certain matters as in the passage
of the Government of India Act, in the Malta appeal, in response to inquiries
from courts in India, and in advice to the High Court in Tanganyika.

When the British Council, as part of the war effort, decided to put together
a series of pamphlets describing various aspects of British life, Keith was invited
to prepare the one on the British Commonwealth. It was published in 1940,
The British Commonwealth of Nations: Its Territories and Constitutions. In many
ways, it was fitting that this was his final work on the Commonwealth.
Restricted in scope and space, Keith yet managed to provide a lucid, accurate,
and useful description of the British Commonwealth and Empire in just under
fifty pages. He organised it into four principal sections: territories, creation
and history, constitutions, and systems of law. To that, he added a postscript
when the pamphlet was brought out, along with all the others in the series,
in hard cover in 1941 under the title, *British Life and Thought: An Illustrated
Survey*. In each of the sections, he provided concise material and, in his usual
style, pointed out recent changes. For example, he interpreted the term itself:

> Of late years the term 'British Commonwealth of Nations' has come into both
> official and private use as a synonym for 'British Empire'. The choice of name
> is not arbitrary; it is felt to be more appropriate to describe a grouping of peoples,
> which now rests essentially on a voluntary basis, than the older name with its
> suggestion of the rule of Britain over subject races.[66]

He made it clear that this was an umbrella term and went on to establish the
various categories underneath it. In the section on the constitutions, he
pointed out the two principles upon which British policy rested: that Britain
ruled 'for the primary purpose of the benefit of the people' with, indeed, a bias
toward their welfare and 'that the first principle can best be carried out by
giving to the people in each territory as far as is possible the power to order
their own affairs'.[67] He went on to use those principles to summarise the

various forms of constitutions and governments that existed. Further, he related those principles to the wide variety of legal systems found within the British Commonwealth. Suitable to the purposes of the series, Keith stressed the beneficence and the positive achievements of Britain in imperial development. The fact that he was invited to write the pamphlet was public recognition of the prominent place that Keith held as a pundit on imperial matters.

CHAPTER 13

Critic and Activist, 1934–1944

In the last ten years of his life, in addition to receiving recognition for his scholarly work in several fields, to analysing changes as they occurred in the constitutional basis, structure, and actual operation of the British Commonwealth of Nations, and to participating directly in several imperial matters, Keith was deeply troubled about the international scene and about the ways in which Britain, he felt, was not fulfilling its responsibilities. He was convinced that both Stanley Baldwin and Neville Chamberlain, out of their ineptitude, particularly the latter, had created a crisis in the constitution in Britain and had aggravated the crisis in Europe, rather than alleviating it. Out of the depth of his concerns, Keith did more than simply write letters to the press or to individuals from the seclusion of his home in Edinburgh or Nan's flat in London, although he did write, seemingly, in a never ending stream. In fact, he became actively involved with three organisations that, in various ways, criticised the Government: the Abyssinia Association, the London Group on African Affairs, and the National Council for Civil Liberties. Leaders of those organisations turned to Keith because of his knowledge, particularly of constitutional and international law, of his writings critical of the Government, and of his demonstrated concerns with justice.

In those years, Keith identified three events in the international sphere as forming the central and crucial steps leading to the disaster of war in the autumn of 1939: Hitler's accession to power as Chancellor of Germany on 30 January 1933; Mussolini's full-scale invasion of Abyssinia on 3 October 1935; and Chamberlain's agreement with Hitler, arranged under Mussolini's aegis, at Munich on 29 September 1938. To each event, he felt the British Government made an inadequate, inept, and, often, illegal response. He was forthright in his criticism both at the time of the event and later from the perspective of the tragedy of war. Once war broke out, he saw further threats to civil liberties and the constitution. Keith left his own chronicle of despair about all those events which framed the decade in many letters to the press, in articles to the *Journal of Comparative Legislation*, in correspondence, and, perhaps best elaborated, in a rather critical and controversial book published in the first year of the war, *The Causes of the War*.

In order to follow his thinking on these national and international issues, it will be helpful to look at three more aspects of his work during this decade. He wrote extensively about the nature of the British constitution and especially about the ways in which he saw it in crisis and under strain. He wrote and worked actively on international matters of peace and justice related to the cardinal events of the years. In addition, he was troubled about the effect of constitutional strain upon civil liberties which, during the war, were, he felt, severely threatened by what he, and others, saw to be unnecessarily repressive measures. In some ways, it is curious that he developed the reputation of a recluse during this time when, in fact, although he had ceased doing anything with University matters or party politics, he was so actively involved with such a range of persons and of issues right up to the time that his health began to fail.

The Constitution under Strain

In 1942, Keith brought out a pamphlet in which he stated his views about why and how the constitution was threatened. In this, *The Constitution under Strain: Its Working from the Crisis of 1938 down to the Present Time*, he built upon, and expanded, the final chapter which he had written in 1939 for his book on the British cabinet. Certainly, the title he chose reflected one theme which he saw as of primary concern in these years, that is, the ways in which, under successive leaders, the constitution had been twisted and turned in what he thought were dangerous new ways.

Before analysing his concerns, it is necessary to indicate the importance he placed on his works in the field of constitutional law in those years. That pamphlet, with its focus and theme, epitomised the work that Keith did. Perhaps it was because he was so concerned about the condition of the constitution that he wrote so many books in this area. Indeed, the largest number of books he wrote in any category, at that time, dealt with constitutional matters. Including that pamphlet and another written for the Historical Association in 1942 on *Federation: Its Nature and Conditions*, he produced eight works on constitutional affairs.

Of that number, two books were editions of classic works in the field. In 1934, at the request of Oxford University Press, he undertook a revised edition of the two lengthy parts of Volume II, *The Crown* of W R Anson's *The Law and Custom of the Constitution*. In 1939, he brought out the seventh edition of E W Ridges' *Constitutional Law of England*. In revising both works, he included materials which dealt with current constitutional issues even as he retained the principal argumentation and structure of the original work. Further, he made major additions describing in some detail changes in the British Commonwealth of Nations and the British Empire. Readers handling the new editions would most certainly find out what Keith identified as the critical constitutional matters. He explained the issues, cited the statutes and law cases, and interpreted the effects. While the works themselves are long and cover a wide range of information, Keith's comments which are readily identified in the sections he added are often quite concise and clear.

The other four works covered various aspects of the constitution. He addressed two books very much to the particular issues of the day which rose from the death of George V and the accession of Edward VIII: *The King and the Imperial Crown: the Powers and Duties of His Majesty* and *The Privileges and Rights of the Crown*. When Keith brought them out in April 1936, he could not know about the further constitutional crisis that would arise later in the year around the abdication. What he was anxious to do was to explain the ways in which changes in the status of the dominions and in the constitutional basis for the British Commonwealth of Nations had a bearing on the actual manner by which the Crown functioned both in the British Commonwealth and in the United Kingdom. He was concerned that the nature of these significant constitutional changes be made very clear, and he felt that he was especially suited to undertake that task. He understood, as noted earlier, that the Crown had become divided through legislation in the Union of South Africa and the Irish Free State and that, therefore, the relationship of the Crown, under advice from the British cabinet, was distinctly different from the Crown, under advice from a dominion cabinet. This was especially true since, after the Imperial Conference of 1930, the Governor-General ceased to represent the Crown in its British aspect since the monarch filled that office only on advice of the dominion government involved.

By contrast, two books were primarily historical: *The British Cabinet System, 1830–1938* and *The Constitution of England from Queen Victoria to George VI*, a work which took two volumes. In these, Keith traced, and analysed, the ways in which the constitution had changed, the precedents under which it functioned, and the manner in which it currently operated. Yet, he did more than that, for in each work he pointed out the ways in which the present situation of the constitution was unsatisfactory because of the manner in which the government of the day either ignored proper precedents or took steps which were improper. This sharply critical stance characterised *The British Cabinet System*. Officials at the Oxford University Press were troubled by that stance. When, in addition, their readers advising on whether the book should be published found a considerable number of inaccuracies in the text and judged the writing to be 'slipshod, sometimes even ungrammatical', they decided to reject the book after they had initially accepted it, unless Keith would undertake extensive revisions.[1] That took courage on their part for Chapman and others knew from long experience how sensitive Keith was about his work. That rejection together with a misunderstanding over the terms on which he had offered the book to the press led to a rupture in relationships that was never repaired. In a very formal note, Keith wrote to Chapman on 27 July 1938:

> Sir,
>
> I have to acknowledge the receipt of your letter of the 25th inst., and to say that the fact that my work was immediately accepted without criticism and on most favourable terms by a firm of the highest standing affirms complete confirmation of the dishonourable character of the action of the Delegates in the matter.[2]

Stevens and Sons, whom Keith knew through earlier experience, published it. The book had mixed reviews, but a long life. It remained in print for several years. After the war, N H Gibbs prepared a second edition in 1952; he deleted much of Keith's vitriol and added material about the War Cabinet, but retained Keith's basic analysis and general conclusions.

Those are the eight books and pamphlets where Keith set out his concerns and ideas on constitutional matters. What Keith made clear in these works was that, while the Crown as a symbol of the unity of the British Commonwealth of Nations was a fragile symbol, it did have a legal, constitutional, and functional reality that was of great importance. Keith provided readers with a wealth of information, with extensive citation, and with fine points of detail. And, to be expected, he provided readers with his interpretation of constitutional points that were troublesome, especially in the current scene. In addition, of course, he dealt with specific issues in numerous letters to newspapers and many of those were reprinted in the three books which have been mentioned earlier. He had no hesitation in quoting from himself in all his works.

What were the constitutional issues that he felt of major importance in these years, and why did he feel that the constitution was under strain? There are so many points that he found troublesome and so many are interrelated that it may be helpful to discuss the principal ones, roughly, in chronological order.

As the period opened, Keith continued to be exercised about what he felt was the total inadequacy of the position which Ramsay MacDonald held as Prime Minister in the National Government, the post he had held since 1931. Keith criticised MacDonald for holding on to the office after colleagues in the Labour Party had turned against him and voted him out of that party and, especially, after he lost a seat in 1935 and one had to be found for him. How, Keith wondered, is it possible for a man to be Prime Minister on a personal basis, rather than a party basis, in the third decade of the twentieth century?[3] The reality, of course, was that the National Government which MacDonald headed had overwhelming support in the House of Commons in spite of the peculiarity of his position *vis-à-vis* the Labour Party. So long as the Conservative Party, since that was the real core of the National Government, supported MacDonald and so long as Baldwin wished it that way, he could remain in power.[4] All that seemed to Keith to be a clear indication of the way in which cabinet government ought not to work. And he wasted no words in pointing that out:

> In 1931, the retention of Mr R MacDonald was due to the policy of Mr Baldwin who preferred to create a national ministry instead of insisting on his clear right to become Prime Minister. In 1935, the time had plainly come for Mr Baldwin to stand out as the real master, his nominal superior having a mere nominal following in the country.[5]
> [On MacDonald meeting Mussolini at Stresa, April 1935] The Premier, however, since his retention of office at the cost of his principles and his colleagues, had lost moral authority, and doubtless feared to challenge in person the fiery earnestness of the Duce.[6]

It was not only MacDonald's leadership that Keith criticised but also the fact that the National Government commanded an overwhelming majority in the House of Commons. Obviously, MacDonald and Baldwin could not be held responsible, in one sense, for the fact that voters affirmed the Government; indeed, the National Government would have ceased if the voters had acted differently in the general elections of 1931 and of 1935. But, in both instances, voters gave full support to the Government, so much so, that Keith saw the lack of an effective Opposition in the House of Commons as a serious danger. In his book on cabinet government, he developed this line of argument by pointing to the necessity for a Government to be certain that the rights of the Opposition were carefully safeguarded; the lack of effective Opposition weakened the constitution. A Government with so much power in its hands and led, in his view, by a discredited Prime Minister, was likely to order the business of the day in a manner which precluded careful consideration of various aspects of legislation. Why should such a ministry bother to take time for debate? Keith felt that, in some senses, such unrestrained power in the hands of the National Government was almost as dangerous to constitutional government in Britain as Hitler's absolute control of the machinery of the Weimar Republic was to German democracy.[7] Such power meant that successive Prime Ministers did not need to tell the country or the Commons what was going on in the world. Keith wrote in *The Causes of the War* on this point:

> In Britain indeed the supremacy of the Conservative Prime Ministers was untroubled by any serious opposition; the Labour party was annihilated by the election of 1931, while that of 1935 merely raised its numbers sufficiently to make it effectively vocal but impotent. The Liberal leader had a fractional following. But Mr Baldwin, despite his great skill in managing Parliament, and though he was virtually Prime Minister before Mr Ramsay MacDonald retired from a situation which he had ceased to guide, was not an expert in foreign affairs, and he held the fatal doctrine that it was not the duty of a leader to warn his people of the dangers into which they were falling through lack of defence preparations lest this might cause loss of by-elections, or still worse, of a general election.[8]

Of course, as he reviewed those years from the perspective of the war, he was convinced that he had made a correct assessment of the situation earlier. If there had been effective Opposition, Keith felt that some egregious blunders must certainly have been avoided; in the absence of such constitutional balance, the Government could make serious mistakes and survive, and it did.

It was, Keith felt, because of such imbalance in the normal working of the constitution that the National Government could readily disregard the results of the Peace Ballot of 1935. That was an extensive poll of public opinion, the most extensive taken of the British electorate up to that time, which involved the views of some $11\frac{1}{2}$ million voters. It was organised by the League of Nations Union. The results were significant: some 11 million respondents supported Britain remaining in the League of Nations; more than 10 million favoured the use of 'economic and non-military measures to stop an aggressor'; $6\frac{3}{4}$ million supported the use of armed force, if necessary, against aggression.[9] Keith felt the result a clear direction for Britain in its foreign policy: remain in the League of Nations and use its authority, halt aggression by all means short of military measures but, if necessary in the final resort, halt it with force. 'No Government could ignore this clear proof that the country was in favour of a policy of sanctions by the members of the League'.[10] Yet, the Conservative Party had urged electors not to bother filling out the questions for the Peace Ballot. Was it any wonder, Keith reflected, that the National Government could act with such blatant disregard for its results?

Events in the fall of 1935 which culminated in Italian aggression in Abyssinia seemed to Keith to be full evidence of the constitutional dangers rising from a Government with unrestrained power. He sharply castigated Baldwin for the ways in which the Government ignored implications of the Peace Ballot and pursued steps which violated obligations under the Covenant of the League of Nations.[11] The denouement arrived in December when Sir Samuel Hoare, then at the Foreign Office, and his opposite number in France, M. Laval, attempted to carry an agreement on Abyssinia which, in effect, scuttled the League. It was only after the Cabinet had approved the plan that Baldwin belatedly realised that public opinion would not support such blatant disregard for the League of Nations.[12] Hoare was replaced as Foreign Secretary by Anthony Eden but, as Keith pointed out, then and later, the policy did not really change:

> The obligation to impose sanctions which arises under Article 16 of the Covenant is imperative and categorical. If Britain decides to hold that it is not bound to give effect to it, it can do so only on the ground that no treaty need be respected unless it seems convenient to do so. That means the complete collapse of the Locarno Pact and the efforts to establish a system of collective security.[13]

Certainly, Keith reasoned, a Government which was in a more effective parliamentary position, that is, with a clear Opposition, would have had to be more attentive to public opinion. As it was, Hoare's departure failed to remove the damage of his actions: 'He [Hoare] had, in fact, not secured immediate victory for Italy, but he had destroyed the chance of an effective oil sanction, and he had undermined sanctions as a whole.'[14] For Keith, such a fundamental error in British foreign policy was clear evidence of the nature of the crisis in the constitution.

Further strains appeared in the next year when the United Kingdom, the British Commonwealth of Nations, and the British Empire experienced a change in monarch. In the thirty-five years after the death of Victoria, the office of King and the functioning of the Crown had been modified, particularly through changes in Britain's relations with the dominions. While some of that took place during the brief reign of Edward VII, most of the changes came during the reign of George V. In a particularly warm and moving letter published after the death of George V in January 1936 in the *Manchester Guardian*, Keith traced those changes:

> So long as the Imperial Parliament could be regarded as supreme over all the

Dominions of the Crown, the tie of allegiance as the source of Imperial unity might be deemed of minor consequence. With the laying down of that supremacy under the Statute of Westminster, 1931, and the surrender of control of foreign policy by the British Government since the creation of the League of Nations, with the Dominions and India as full members, the Crown has stood forth as the one essential link of unity. It is in virtue of our personal relationship to the King that we enjoy a common citizenship with the nationals of the other units of the Commonwealth; for subjection to Parliamentary control as a basis of unity is substituted equality in loyalty. To the welcome accorded to the change in the Dominions special strength was given by the fact that, by King George's personal visits and by those of the Prince of Wales and other members of his family, monarchy had ceased to be a distant abstraction to dwellers overseas.[15]

Keith also indicated that the King occupied an 'unparalleled position ... in the minds and hearts of his people' and that 'monarchy has shed something of its divinity, but it has shown instead a deep humanity';[16] all these changes, he saw, were a tribute to the effectiveness of the late monarch. The transition in kingship in January 1936, was the first to occur under the changed relationships among the United Kingdom and the dominions and Keith, quite obviously, was concerned to follow the ways in which that transition differed from the last which he had observed in 1910 from the vantage point of the Colonial Office. And there were profound differences, as discussed earlier, as the dominions treated the succession in distinctive legal instruments.[17]

The logical question, of course, was whether Edward VIII, however pro-claimed in the Union of South Africa or Canada or the Irish Free State, would be able to fulfil the new role for monarchy. That, naturally, was a question which Keith pursued. Initially, all the evidence seemed to indicate an affirm-ative response. Yet, as the year of 1936 unfolded, it became apparent that all areas under the British Crown were to be plunged into a constitutional crisis over the King's desire to marry Mrs Simpson, an American twice divorced. That Mrs Simpson was a commoner with no ties to any line of nobility posed a certain problem which could have been resolved rather easily through granting her a title; that she was an American socialite presented another problem but no real impediment to marriage. The central issue was her divorced status. That became, as it turned out, the insurmountable obstacle. A question of legal standing in England remained about the first divorce she had received in the state of Maryland while she only received the second divorce in England late in 1936. But, for Keith and other lawyers, the critical question was the status of the first divorce:[18] If it were not legal in England, then how could she remarry legally even if the second marriage also ended in divorce? And, quite in contrast to the latter part of the twentieth century when divorce is readily available, in that time it was difficult to achieve in English courts and, when achieved, it certainly resulted in a status that the public frowned upon. The continued role of the monarch as titular head of an established church which did not recognise divorce further compounded the dilemma. The fact that royal marriages required the assent of the Cabinet, as representing the people of the kingdom, created the practical obstacle to the royal marriage since Baldwin, under substantial pressure from the Archbishop of Canterbury, found that he could not support the proposition of the King marrying Mrs Simpson, even if it were to be a morganatic marriage.[19] Under the particular political configuration in the House of Commons, if Baldwin were to resign on the issue, no other person could command a majority to form the Government. Dissolution would have to result with the likely outcome that no ministry would have come to power which would have advised in favour of the marriage. Keith followed all these steps and stages with intense interest and grave concern. He wrote to newspapers and explained the various legal points involved.[20] Because of his prominence, he was invited by the National Broadcasting Corporation in America to make a broadcast outlining the issues involved in the matter. He did that on 8 December 1936, and repeated the text in a letter to the *Manchester Guardian*. He made a sympathetic statement of affection and support for the King: 'The popularity of our King is unparalleled in our history and in his present position he commands unstinted sympathy.' He acknowledged Mrs Simpson as 'charming, cultured, and a hostess tactful and distinguished'. He sketched out the legal basis for objection to the marriage and then indicated the three options the King had: insist on the marriage which would be 'a disaster to the nation', which would 'discredit constitutional monarchy', and which would 'divide the country into monarchists and anti-monarchists'; abdicate which would be 'without precedent in our history' and which would create challenges with respect to the dominions, especially the Irish Free State 'the opportunity which it could hardly avoid taking of raising the whole issue of the connection of the State with the British Crown'; or give up the marriage project in favour of kingship which was the 'sacrifice' that Keith, and many others, hoped the King might take.[21] After painful searching, Edward VIII chose love, marriage, and abdication. He broadcast his decision to the nation, and the world, on 10 December 1936.[22] That solved the constitutional crisis for the moment although Keith felt that the abdication 'gravely weakened the position of the Crown, and may prove to have reduced the Crown to mere ornamental and symbolic functions'.[23] Keith was absolutely correct, as has been earlier discussed, that the abdication would lead to further separate action by the various dominions on the accession date for George VI and to De Valera bringing in a new constitution for the Irish Free State.[24]

No sooner was Keith finished interpreting the abdication crisis than he became concerned about the changes that were proposed for the coronation oath that George VI agreed to take. This was the text:

> Will you solemnly promise and swear to govern the peoples of Great Britain, Ireland, Canada, Australia, New Zealand, and the Union of South Africa, of your possessions, and the other territories to any of them belonging or pertaining, and of your Empire of India according to their respective laws and customs?[25]

Here, again, Keith was very conscious of the ways in which the Statute of Westminster had changed relationships between the United Kingdom and the dominions. Since this was the first coronation after that statute, he felt that particular attention needed to be given to the precise formulation of the oath. While he supported an oath that reflected the equality of the dominions and the United Kingdom, he had grave difficulty with accepting that the British Cabinet could determine a change in oath without giving it effect through legislation and, under the Statute of Westminster, concurrent legislation enacted by all parliaments of the various dominions. He followed his customary practice and set out his concerns in letters to newspapers.[26] Without such legislation, Keith maintained that the coronation oath was illegal. Even after the event, he maintained his position and argued that the way the oath was created further weakened the role of the Crown in the constitution:

> Further, the acceptance by George VI of the new form of the Coronation oath, despite its patent illegality, must be regarded as the admission of the doctrine that in legal issues the King must accept the advice—however unsound—of his ministers. ... The possibility of the Crown continuing to serve as a safeguard to the Constitution must, therefore, now be reckoned doubtful.[27]

Coronation, as well as abdication, then, provided specific points at which Keith brought his knowledge of law and of developments in the British Commonwealth to bear as he saw in both events serious threats to the constitution.

One other matter involving monarchy soon emerged, that of the nature of regency. The desire of the Government was to make continuing provision for a regency through statute rather than having to create something on the specific occasion of need. This desire really grew out of episodes in the reign of George V when his health faltered and there was no clear procedure for an alternative mode of exercising the kingship. Keith became concerned about the issue and its relationship to constitutional precedents and practice. As the Regency Act, 1937 started on its stages to become statute, Keith noted that it contained a serious defect.[28] In listing those persons who must certify that the monarch was incapacitated to exercise royal functions, the initial draft included the prospective regent, that is, the person next in line of succession. Perhaps with recollections of earlier history in the Hanoverian family, Keith insisted that the prospective regent must not be in such a position. He wrote to the press and other persons. On this occasion, the Government took his point so that the statute when it was finally enacted omitted the prospective regent from that list.[29]

But it was not only constitutional matters related to the monarchy which attracted Keith's attention. Given the fact that he was antipathetic to the National Government throughout its life, at least until it was transformed under Winston Churchill in 1940, he saw British policy with regard to the Spanish Civil War as yet another way in which the constitution was put under strain. That war started in the summer of 1936 and continued until the spring of 1939.[30] Led by General Franco, the rebels against the Spanish republic waged, in effect, not merely a civil war but an international war, with German and Italian support for Franco and Russian support for the republic. British policy towards that conflict was inseparable from that towards Italy, the aim of which was to treat Mussolini as trustworthy and to accept his aggression in Abyssinia. That link, in Keith's view, made it utterly impossible to find a reasonable and honourable way for Britain to assist in stopping the carnage throughout Spain and in bringing the civil war to a conclusion. Italy could not be trusted. Complex negotiations to that end in February 1938 proved fruitless with the principal result being the resignation of Eden from the Foreign Office. As Keith described the event later, it was clear that he felt sound constitutional practice had been violated:

> He [Chamberlain] hastily summoned a Cabinet for the 19th, and on the 20th the Cabinet decided to yield to the Italian ultimatum [to talks without any withdrawal of Italian troops as evidence of good faith], without even waiting for the formal reply to the question asked by the Premier—whether Italy would accept the British formula for withdrawal of troops. Mr Eden resigned at once.[31]

When Britain recognised the legitimacy of Franco's government in February 1939, Keith's ire was virtually unrestrained. The Government recognised Franco before the matter was put to the House of Commons. How could this be? Clearly, that was inappropriate and improper.[32] Yet, after the event, the House approved the action, simply another illustration to Keith of the dangers of a government holding such a powerful majority. Further, he pointed out that Chamberlain had not given full information to the House when he got approval for the final agreements arrived at in 1938.

> One painful episode was to follow. It soon proved that Italy, though withdrawing after a long delay, and not forthwith as promised, was handing over to Spain large quantities of war material, which obviously could only be needed in order to strengthen General Franco if Italy were to war on France and called on his aid to menace the French frontier. The Premier had to admit on 7th and 12th June [1939] that this action was not inconsistent with the Italian undertaking, showing clearly that he had misled the Commons when securing its imprimatur for bringing the agreement of 1938 into operation. It was clearly a most deplorable incident, for the Commons were wholly misled, and it has necessarily created doubt as to the accuracy and fullness of any statements of the Premier. From that high office candour is essential if respect is to be paid, and on foreign opinion such a confession has even more serious effects than in Britain.[33]

Misleading the Cabinet, misinforming the House, and, moreover, misdirecting British policy; Keith felt that all these actions characteristic of Chamberlain's exercise of power threatened the constitution.

It is, therefore, no surprise to find that Keith was appalled at the Munich arrangements that Chamberlain made in the fall of 1938. International disaster and domestic constitutional crisis combined in the event. Why? Keith put it directly:

> Mr Chamberlain had created a constitutional innovation in concluding the Munich Treaty without obtaining the royal sanction or Cabinet approval, or submitting it for acceptance of Parliament. Moreover, he had negotiated it

without the presence of the Foreign Secretary, and he presented it for acceptance to his colleagues in conditions in which rejection was impossible.[34]

In many ways, that was the precise sort of constitutional crisis which Keith had feared all throughout these years. With the Prime Minister backed by an overwhelming majority, with a virtually non-existent Opposition, and with a leader having little regard for his colleagues, Commons, or constitution, such a crisis, in Keith's view, became all too possible. In the Munich agreements, every constitutional safeguard which should have prevented such action was blatantly ignored. As Keith pointed out in his book on cabinet government, the theory of the constitution required that foreign policy be related to the electorate, that is, responsive to the House of Commons; conducted through the proper department of state, that is, the Foreign Office and the Foreign Secretary; be reviewed by the Cabinet; and, all of this, be undertaken with the knowledge and concurrence of the Crown.[35] None of these was operative in the Munich agreement. Bitterly critical of Chamberlain, Keith wrote:

> Lack of familiarity with foreign issues until old age and the limited outlook of a successful business man have rendered his control of external policy disastrous to his country and to Europe.[36]

His criticism was intense and his prophecy accurate that, 'Munich will undoubtedly be ranked by historians as marking the definitive acquisition of hegemony in Europe by Herr Hitler'.[37]

Further, Keith felt that the fact that Parliament was in recess while Chamberlain was manoeuvring with Hitler in the fall of 1938 presented a further threat to the constitution. In *The Constitution under Strain* he proposed that there be some mechanism established for the Speaker to summon the Commons on petition of a certain number of members as one way to ensure that such flagrant violation of constitutional practice could not occur in the future.[38]

These issues, culminating in Munich, indicated the ways in which Keith perceived the constitution was under serious threat and strain. He invested considerable energy in those years in trying to get responsible persons to understand the nature of the threats and to take appropriate steps to head them off. The patent hostility he displayed to all members of the National Government made it difficult for them to listen to his concerns and criticisms. Keith was not prepared to suffer with much charity those whom he considered to be foolish and inept, especially when they had power over the destiny not only of people in Britain and the British Empire but, in his judgement, in the western world as well. While Keith diagnosed the creaks and strains of the constitution during the days of the National Government, he saw even more threats with the outbreak of war.

Critic of Foreign Policy

It is obvious that Keith's view of threats to the constitution during this decade under consideration included both those that arose from domestic issues and, as well, from foreign matters. In his response to all threats, crises, and strains, he was unstinting in his criticism of successive leaders of the National Government. But, it was their tragic inadequacy in international relations which Keith felt to be their principal fault.

He addressed those faults, as has been discussed, through letters to newspapers and through personal correspondence. In addition, he compiled a collection of documents reviewing the principal international developments in the two decades after the end of the war. He brought that out in the *World's Classics Series* as *Speeches and Documents on International Affairs, 1918–1937*. He hoped that by compiling the principal documents following the Treaty of Versailles, he might be able to influence those who made policy to understand, and halt, the direction in which events were leading. He minced no words in his prefatory remarks about the dangers of German remilitarisation of the Rhineland or about the collapse of the League of Nations or about the appeasement of Italy over Abyssinia. Alas, his efforts to alert and to warn were too late, too ill-focused, or too acerbic to give any impetus to change the direction of British foreign policy.

The other book which he wrote dealing with international affairs was *The Causes of the War*. He completed that during the dark winter of 1939–40. Since it was brought out in May, he added, in his usual effort to keep his works current, a section on Churchill's coming to power and the way in which he recast the ministry.[39] In this book, which in many ways is utterly immoderate, Keith provided a clear record of the way in which he looked at matters. It is certainly not necessary to agree with all his analyses or conclusions or allegations, but it is necessary to examine the book in order to understand the ways in which Keith placed responsibility for causing the war. It is also important to remember that his concern for locating responsibility was, in part, a reflection of Article 231 of the Versailles Treaty in which the Allied, victorious powers insisted on a clause by which Germany was forced to accept responsibility for causing the War of 1914–18. Without waiting for the end of the war which started in September 1939, Keith provided his own analysis of causes and made his own assignment of responsibility.

Organised around six chapters and a postscript, Keith progressively presented his understanding of why the war came; the general nature of aggression and the ways in which it might be restrained; the specific reasons for German aggression, especially as they flowed from the settlement at Versailles; the efforts made through alliances and the League of Nations to achieve collective security and 'the rule of law'; the collapse of collective security, the League, and, thereby, effective international law; the specific steps that Hitler took from 1935 to 1939 to remilitarise Germany, to reoccupy the Rhineland, to achieve the Austrian *anschluss*, and to dismember Czechoslovakia; and the particular ways in which Britain, Germany, and the Soviet Union sought either to threaten or to guarantee Poland with tragic results in September 1939. In the preface to the book, Keith identified his purposes and laid out the line of argumentation he would pursue:

> It is the aim of this work to trace the motives which have induced the German

people, under the leadership of a man of disordered genius, to enter into a course of action aiming at world hegemony at the expense of the liberty of thought and action of other peoples, and to indicate the causes of the disintegration of the machinery which was created after the Great War in the hope that its operation would save the world from the recurrence of that grievous disaster. It is doubtless difficult, at a time when German atrocities in Poland and Czechoslovakia, and Russian aggression on Finland, have shocked the public conscience of Europe and America, to escape the tendency to deny or minimize the grievances of Germany, and to ignore or gloss over the errors of the Western Powers. ... It is, I think, plain that war might have been avoided had western statesmen understood earlier and appreciated the candid revelation of himself given by Herr Hitler in *Mein Kampf*, and had realized that they must not judge him by the standards of everyday political life. It might also have been prevented, had Herr Hitler ever understood the British character in its fundamental soundness, instead of believing that it was expressed in the social groups frequented by Herr von Ribbentrop or even by the most determinedly pacifist of British Prime Ministers. Nor would it have been inevitable, if the British people had realized that great possessions entail great responsibilities; that a realm acquired by heroic activities cannot be retained by inertia; and that, while peace may seem to the inhabitants of a satiated country the obvious ideal for man, dwellers in less happily situated lands may see in war the legitimate means of wresting from those unworthy to retain them the living spaces requisite for the life and expansion of a race with higher ideals. If historians ought to place on Germany the major responsibility for the present conflict, they ought nevertheless to add that, had Britain and France remained faithful to their traditions, and had they honourably fulfilled their clear obligations, the conditions which invited German aggression would never have been presented. The war will have been fought in vain if the peoples do not emerge from it determined that they shall never again allow themselves to surrender principles of international obligations for selfish reasons of immediate advantage.[40]

Keith's was one of the first books to begin to look at the causes of the Second World War, an issue that would be considered in the decades after it finally concluded.[41] Many of the issues that he addressed and many of the positions he took have been supported by others who have had opportunity, in more recent times, to examine the relevant documents more directly. Of course, others disagreed with the harshness of his criticisms at the time and subsequently.

Within his analysis, Keith developed arguments about the nature of Hitler and the Nazi regime; they turn out to have been quite accurate. Early, Keith understood that Hitler was different from the usual, rational statesman with whom it would be possible to negotiate. He read and studied *Mein Kampf* and accepted it as one statement of Hitler's aims and ambitions and, as well, as a source to understand Hitler's motivations and ways of perceiving the world. From that written record, Keith could see the ways in which Hitler was moving to bring about a 'German Renascence'. He accepted, in the manner of Keynes,[42] that there were legitimate elements in Germany's complaints about the settlement at Versailles, especially reparations. He felt that the

Western powers should have accepted and resolved those legitimate complaints quite quickly and directly rather than allow them to become festering sores in the German body politic. Yet, he rejected the simplistic explanation about the cause of the war as rising from the actions of a 'homicidal lunatic' or a 'mad dog'. While Hitler might possess those characteristics, Keith recognised the complexity of causation of the war as going beyond the action of any single individual, totalitarian dictator though he might be.

In Keith's view, a careful study of the history of the inter-war years confirmed the complexity of causation. Hitler could not, any more than Mussolini or Stalin or Daladier or Franco or Baldwin or Chamberlain or Franklin Roosevelt, function unilaterally in some sort of international vacuum. All states were interrelated most obviously in economic terms but, as well, in international law, international relations, and international politics. No state, not even the United States of America then at the height of its isolationist years, existed outside the international orbit. So, reasoned Keith, to look for the causes of the war required examining the whole pattern of international relations from 1918 onward, and acknowledging the few successes, such as the concept of the League of Nations and the thrust of the Locarno Treaties, while dissecting the many failures, such as Italian seizure of Corfu or Japanese aggression into Manchuria or Italian aggression against Abyssinia or, and Keith's list went right on, German and Soviet aggression on Poland. How to account for the successes? How to account for the failures? Keith saw that the only way to arrive at answers, and in that process find the ways to avoid war in the future, was to analyse the sequence of events. He perceived British policy to be of major importance in those inter-war years and, here, as may be expected, he was bitterly critical of the National Government.

In his books and in numerous letters and articles, he dealt, almost in an encyclopedic fashion, with virtually every international issue of significance, for example, from details of British operation of the mandate in Palestine and of British policy in the Middle East or of details of the Spanish Civil War or Japanese policy in Manchuria to details of the Covenant of the League of Nations; the list is endless.[43] Yet, as he followed events in those years and as he reflected on them in the first year of the war, and in later years, as well, he became increasingly convinced that the central event which caused the war was the abject and total failure of the British Government in concert with other powers through the League of Nations to resist and halt Italian aggression into Abyssinia. If there was one scene which, perhaps more than any other, symbolised the tragedy and pathos of that dishonourable failure it would not be Italian airplanes bombing Abyssinians armed with spears, horrendous though that was, but rather would be the speech which Emperor Haile Selassie delivered, 'a noble address' before the League of Nations in Geneva on 30 June 1936.

> I, Haile Selassie I, Emperor of Ethiopia, am here today to claim that justice that is due my people and the assistance promised to it eight months ago ... None other than the Emperor can address the appeal of the Ethiopian people to those fifty-two nations ... What are they willing to do for Ethiopia? What measures do

they intend to take? Representatives of the world, I have come to Geneva to discharge in your midst the most painful of the duties of the head of a State. What answer am I to take back to my people?[44]

Driven out of Abyssinia, appealing to the world for justice and support, Haile Selassie found no answer to take back, only the record of the manner in which the powers had searched for a way to appease Mussolini through imposing sanctions half-heartedly, permitting Italy still to have access to the Suez Canal, and devising various schemes to partition Abyssinia. The Emperor went on from Geneva to London in exile, the first of many rulers and governments to do so as the dictators moved forward.

For Keith, then, the policy of the British Government in 1935–6 was instrumental in ending any serious attempt to maintain collective security. The lesson of the collapse of collective security if not fully understood by the western powers was, Keith observed, well understood by Hitler and Mussolini. From then on, they knew that the western powers would not resist aggression. From then on, the dictators held the initiative. From then on, the dictators were able to pursue their aims, individually or through the Axis, unencumbered by any regard for international law. From then on, the dictators needed to pay no attention to resolutions, diplomatic warnings, or newspaper editorials. From then on, the dictators had strategic power, while they might not yet have had effective military power, to mesmerise leaders in Britain and France. Since, in Keith's analysis, the western powers had violated international law in their response to Italian aggression, it was not likely that the dictators were prepared to abide by it.[45]

Keith argued at the time of the Italian aggression and in subsequent years that, in the final analysis, Britain carried primary responsibility for the events that followed. As one of the victors in the war of 1914, as one of the designers of the provisions for collective security in the Treaty of Versailles, as one of the permanent members of the Council of the League of Nations, as one of the great powers in the world and still the greatest naval power, Britain, he felt, had to play a central part in maintaining peace. Whether it was because of desire to woo Mussolini as a balance to the threat of Hitler or because of an inability to see the importance of obligations to collective security, the Government initially led by MacDonald and then by Baldwin failed to lead Britain along international paths of honour and justice. Britain did not, or was unwilling to, honour her international obligations to participate in collective security, obligations which she had formally accepted through the Covenant of the League of Nations, through the Locarno Pacts, and through the Paris Pact. While he made this point repeatedly, he put it succinctly in *The Causes of the War*:

The episode of Ethiopia destroyed collective security, and took all reality from the political part of the Covenant. The failure of the League members to keep their obligations demonstrated that public faith could no longer be trusted, and that international obligations were all facultative. No Power which violated an obligation under the Covenant could be expected to maintain faith in other things, nor was any other Power bound to keep faith with it. Britain, which had since 1919 founded her policy on collective security, had thrown it away and ruined her reputation in and outside Europe for honourable dealings.[46]

As Keith reviewed that shameful episode, no British leader was spared his opprobrium, not even the monarch:

[Chamberlain, Chancellor of the Exchequer, deciding in 1936 to end sanctions] His view was very natural in a plain businessman, vexed to see money being spent uselessly, and an excellent customer, alienated for the sake of a number of black people, accused of being slave holders and traders, who would be better off under the Duce.[47]

[Hoare, Foreign Secretary] ... palpably it was his desire to placate the Duce that led him astray, and made him an easy prey to the arguments of M. Laval, to whom France owes ultimately her implication in the present war. He thought, quite wrongly, that the war would be slow, and that compromise would be inevitable.[48]

[Baldwin, Prime Minister] ... so also the prolonged period when Mr Baldwin's government was induced from the fear of losing by-elections to postpone the necessary process of rearmament to confront the menace from the ever-growing strength of German preparations must be deemed not merely to have increased the risk of war, but to have been a prime cause for the defiance of the League by Italy[49]

[Eden, Foreign Secretary, advocating withdrawal of sanctions] Mr Eden shared in the debacle; a young minister, he lacked the courage to resign, and remained in the ministry in an ambiguous and undignified position, after Mr Chamberlain succeeded Mr Baldwin and took into his hands control of foreign affairs, until he was discarded in 1938. His reputation suffered an irreparable blow[50]

[Chamberlain, Prime Minister, and Lord Halifax, Foreign Secretary, on Anglo-Italian Accord, 1938, and their trip to Rome, January 1939] But solemn undertakings do not mean much in the mind of a business Premier, and a High Church Anglican conscience is capable of strange feats. ... To add to the completeness of British humiliation, Mr Chamberlain and Lord Halifax went on the bidding of the Duce to Rome on January, 11, 1939, to toast the new Emperor of Ethiopia. It was perhaps a fitting reward of an act of repudiation without parallel in modern British history that the Duce imparted nothing to his guests of his fixed intention to seize Albania.[51]

[On George VI] The Anglo-Italian Accord ... involved a promise to break the League Covenant's prohibition, despite the embarrassment that what George V had solemnly undertaken was to be repudiated by George VI, whom the country had welcomed as one to walk in the ways of his good and highly honoured father.[52]

Those passages provide some flavour of the depth of feeling that Keith had about the matter. They also display Keith's polemical talents and his invective at its best, or worst. Such assertions and such wide-ranging condemnation made it difficult for some to take seriously Keith's analysis which, in the main, has stood up over the years.[53]

It was out of his deep concern over British policy on Abyssinia that he became involved with two organisations created to provide pressure on the British Government to alter its policy and to provide justice for Haile Selassie and his people. One organisation was the Abyssinia Association which was headed by three Presidents: Sir Norman Angell, Sir Hesketh Bell, and Sir George Paish. It had widespread support from individuals in the various political parties, both those in Parliament and in the country and from leaders of the churches. Professor Stanley Jevons served as the Hon Treasurer while Muriel Blundell was the Hon Secretary. The other was a weekly newspaper, New Times and Ethiopia News. Its first issue came out on 9 May 1936, the day on which Mussolini proclaimed sovereignty over Abyssinia. Its editor was E Sylvia Pankhurst, freed by success from her efforts on woman suffrage to give her great energies to confronting injustice in another area. Muriel Blundell at the Abyssinia Association and Sylvia Pankhurst at New Times and Ethiopia News became Keith's correspondents.[54]

What role did he play in the organisations? For the former, he provided, as requested, analysis of various documents that Blundell wished to send to the Government or of various international documents that had relevance to the case. She also wrote a substantial amount of material, some of which she sent along to Keith for his opinion and for his judgement about the line of argumentation. At certain points, during 1941 after British and Abyssinian troops had defeated the Italians so that the Emperor could return to Addis Ababa, Blundell felt his opinion of such urgent importance that she tele-graphed to elicit it.[55] When the Association needed a prominent name for a petition or for raising funds for Abyssinia, Keith was prepared to associate himself with such causes, even though his financial contribution might be small.[56] In every way available to him, he was eager to work with the Association to see that British dishonour and humiliation might be turned into British honour and atonement.

For New Times and Ethiopia News, Keith functioned in a style which had become second nature to him by that time. He wrote letters and articles on a regular basis.[57] Since Pankhurst was clearly desirous of influencing British politics and policy, she held a number of conferences in co-operation with the Abyssinia Association. When he could, Keith attended; when he could not, as in the summer of 1942 because he was in hospital, he wrote. His first letter was in September 1937 while his last was published in November 1943. Since Pankhurst held a view similar to Keith's about the inadequacy of the Government, he could be sure of a warm reception for anything he wrote on Abyssinia.

The principal questions which Blundell and Pankhurst and their supporters had to address following May 1936 were those about the future.[58] The fact of the matter was that the British Government had recognised Mussolini's conquest of Abyssinia and had acknowledged the addition of the title, Emperor of Ethiopia, to the royal style and titles held by the King of Italy. While they could continue to criticise the complicity of the Government in those matters, they focused initially on trying to persuade the Government to reverse itself, especially as events unfolded to make increasingly clear the injustice of British policy. But, after 1939 when Britain was at war, they recognised that there was little likelihood of getting the Government to reverse those actions; they, then, turned to questions about British policy towards Abyssinia if and when Italian forces there were defeated. Here, Keith made particular contributions as he wrote about his understanding of international law and its application to such matters as concessions of timber and mineral rights made by the Italian government through its controlling power in Abyssinia. Should those concessions still be honoured? Keith argued negatively since Italy had conquered militarily and, therefore, only those concessions made by the Abyssinian government prior to the conquest had standing.[59] Not all agreed with his arguments. One lengthy and controversial matter which Keith opened up was the nature of the total settlement which might be arrived at following the war, of which Abyssinia, naturally, would form a significant part. He sketched out the need to restore Abyssinia and perhaps to assign some of the adjacent Italian territory to her. One of the longest pieces that Keith published in *New Times and Ethiopia News* was the document he sent to Eden under the date of 14 October 1941, in which he pleaded to know why Britain had not re-established full diplomatic relations with Ethiopia, especially since the Emperor had, by that time, been back in power from May.[60] How could Britain act as if Abyssinia was going to become a British protectorate? Did not Britain have the responsibility to ensure Abyssinia's full independence and to restore full diplomatic relationships? If those steps were not taken, Keith asked, how could India expect much from British promises and how could the world believe that Britain really supported the principles of the Atlantic Charter? The minute in the Foreign Office on Keith's letter noted that he was 'a prolific writer, an authority on constitutional law and a champion of the "black races". He has been bombarding the Press with letters on the "wrongs suffered by Ethiopia" ... A soft answer, which will leave as little opening as possible to the Professor's propensity for inconvenient argument, seems desirable.'[61] Only at the end of October did Eden in a 'soft answer' acknowledge receiving the memorandum. When, finally, Britain did reach an accord with Abyssinia on 31 January 1942, Keith welcomed it as helping to clear up certain legal matters. He wrote a long analysis of the terms of the Agreement in which he identified certain details that required further attention. In the main, however, he found it satisfactory with one major reservation: it was drawn between HM Government and the Emperor. 'The agreement should have been concluded as one between the King-Emperor and the Emperor of Ethiopia, and it is unfortunate that the Foreign Office should have been guilty of this breach of courtesy.'[62]

In his relationships with the Abyssinia Association and *New Times and Ethiopia News*, Keith continued to align himself with those who shared his views of justice and injustice, of international order and the dangers of breaking that order, and of concern for peoples in the world who, like those in the protectorates of southern Africa, were not yet developed in the ways in which the western world had become and for whom, therefore, powers in the western world had particular responsibility. For him, Abyssinia was the test case in determining whether or not collective security could work and whether Britain had the will to make peace secure; and Britain failed the test.

From his perspective, Chamberlain as Prime Minister simply carried forward a policy of conciliation and appeasement of the dictators, a policy which, Keith concluded, had already been discredited and which could only lead to further disaster. In his letters to the press, in his correspondence, and in his book, *The Causes of the War*, Keith described Chamberlain as making bad policy worse by the ways in which he bent the constitution, as already discussed, in which he naively, and with no experience, engaged in personal diplomacy, and in which he continued to believe, with increasing evidence to the contrary, that Hitler was a rational ruler who would honour solemn agreements.[63] In his view, Chamberlain carried considerable responsibility for causing the war. When Chamberlain accepted terms, which he had denounced earlier, for the dismemberment of Czechoslovakia at Munich, Keith saw that as merely another in the series of disastrous steps taken under the policy of appeasement. He presented a severe indictment of Chamberlain:

> The Premier glorified his magnificent service to the world by securing peace, asserted his belief in the security and happier future of Czechoslovakia under the proposed guarantee, and on 6th October, in replying to the debate, made the deliberate assertion that 'We had no treaty obligations and no legal obligations to Czechoslovakia.' This deliberate denial of all binding force of the League Covenant, Articles 10, 16, and 20, is the classic repudiation by Britain of the binding nature of the most solemn treaty ever concluded by her only nineteen years earlier ... It is idle to pile up lists of treaty violations by other Powers on the assumption that Britain has not been guilty of equal violence of law and morality. ... There is no more bitter comment on the action of the Premier that we fight to-day without effective allies to undo a wrong for which we and France bear a deep load of blame.[64]

At the time, he wrote to his friend, Strickland, in hope that he might make some statement or inquiry in the House of Lords. 'I am not proud of our PM's performance and I think a new guarantee to Czechoslovakia meaningless, for we could not possibly honour our obligation if aggression took place.'[65] In one of his letters to *The Scotsman* about Munich, he included the monarch among those who had not prevented the debacle: 'We have every reason to regret that in this essential crisis of European affairs the wise control of King George V should have been lacking.'[66] Interestingly enough, that brought Keith a query from the Private Secretary to George VI to ask what he thought the King might have done under the particular circumstances. Keith, of course, responded with suggestions about the ways in which residual powers of the Crown might have been used.[67]

The final failure of Chamberlain's policy became conclusive in the summer of 1939 when Britain was unsuccessful in achieving an agreement with the Soviet Union, while Germany was successful. On the basis of that, German aggression into Poland became the final event for which Chamberlain could no longer apply the policy of appeasement. Ultimately, that aggression had to be resisted with force and Chamberlain, the social reformer, the pacifist, the appeaser, became the uneasy leader in war. 'No British Premier, perhaps,' Keith wrote, 'could have been less well fitted to deal personally with men of enthusiasm and purpose for the aggrandisement of their peoples, such as Signor Mussolini and Herr Hitler.'[68] Keith welcomed the change in the British Government which came in May 1940, although he was critical of Churchill for retaining in the War Cabinet the two persons principally responsible for the fatal programme of appeasement, Halifax at the Foreign Office and Chamberlain, himself, as Lord President of the Council.

Before turning to the final area of Keith's activities in this decade, it is necessary to add a brief comment about other dimensions of *The Causes of the War*. Some of the quotations included above are clear evidences of Keith's invective. But, it was not just intemperate invective which characterised the book. It was, as well, the comments that Keith gratuitously included on all sorts of matters throughout the book. It is possible to compile a list of Keith aphorisms:

The most learned men do not seek the fame of such learning, but pursue it disinterestedly.[69]

A society which contained only individuals content with equality would be essentially stagnant.[70]

It is easy to understand atheism and agnosticism, but the return to pagan German worship is beyond the comprehension of sane humanity.[71]

[On Nazi Secret Police] The modern form of the inquisition is as vigorous as and probably more effective than the old.[72]

[On Chamberlain] A business man imbued with the ideals of pacifism ... held that, just as in business it is best to cut losses, so in public affairs it was desirable to retire with the minimum loss from commitments which had proved inconvenient to keep.[73]

[On the League of Nations after Corfu] It was from this time that opinion generally, which had regarded the League as indicating a new orientation in public morality, began to stress the view that the League had been adapted by the great Powers as a means of furthering purely selfish ends by clothing their decision in their private interests in the guise of international justice.[74]

Popularity should not be bought by pandering to popular feeling[75]

Moreover a pestilential deluge of defeatist propaganda was poured forth from renegade British, mostly females resident in Italy, for which the only charitable explanation is fear of Fascist reprisals on their worthless selves.[76]

[On Chamberlain] Small souls and great destinies are ill combined, and the virtues of business life are inadequate for high politics.[77]

[On Franklin Roosevelt, 1937] The President, it is clear, shares the pathetic delusion of his countrymen that noble sentiments have power to control events.[78]

Mr Chamberlain and M. Daladier dictated as destructive a peace to Czechoslovakia as was ever dictated by a conqueror.[79]

... evil communications corrupt good manners[80]

... charity covers a multitude of sins[81]

There are as dangerous ideologues in Britain as in Russia.[82]

With how little wisdom the world is governed![83]

But, in other areas of the book, Keith became presumptuous and preposterous.
He undertook to deal with everything, for example, from the position of
conscientious objectors to preaching in the Church of Scotland, to newspaper
publishers either supporting or not supporting Government policy, to upper
classes in Britain and their relation to political figures, to the dangers of
Anglo-Catholics in high places, to comments about German characteristics,
to the origins of Aryans and so on.[84] In too many ways, Keith lost the force
of his argument through inclusion of a life's collection of asides.

Yet, Keith was simply one of the outspoken critics of the government's
policy of appeasement. He believed and hoped in the power of public, rational
debate. He documented the times and places where Britain failed. For that
role, he must be acknowledged as having made a substantial contribution to
discussion of foreign policy.

Concerns over Civil Liberties

As Britain gradually approached war, Keith became involved with several
matters in the area of civil liberties. Justice, equity, and fair treatment as the
core of civil liberties, he had these as old concerns. As long ago as his days
on the staff of the Colonial Office, he had been troubled about the ways in
which Britain paid insufficient respect to the civil liberties of the people under
imperial rule; he had protested about abuses of flogging, about sentences and
executions carried out under court martial, and about inadequate conduct of
British responsibilities in the South African protectorates.[85] Now, with clouds
of war on the horizon, he worried about the ways in which a Government
which had such enormous, unchecked power might threaten civil liberties.
If the Government had erred in its international relationships, might it not
also be likely to err in domestic policy and so jeopardise hard-earned rights?
Keith associated himself with some groups that were prepared to take up the
cause to protect civil liberties. He saw the defence of civil liberties as being
important both in the broad setting of Empire and in the specific setting of
the United Kingdom itself.

Among other organisations, the London Group on African Affairs was
particularly active at that time about issues of civil liberties that rose from
the Empire. Keith's concerns were well-known because of his earlier involvement with the Anti-Slavery and Aborigines Protection Society. Under the
aegis of both groups, several leading public figures were enlisted to make a

public statement about discrimination that was practised by hospitals and similar institutions against coloured medical students, both doctors and nurses. When the letter of protest was published in *The Times* in February 1938, Keith's name headed the list. The language was strong; the charges of discrimination were substantiated; the plea for corrective action was forthright:

> To make what is practically a colour bar among medical students and nurses creates bitterness and has unfortunate effects overseas. ... In view of the fact that India and the Colonies form such a large proportion of our Empire population, may we ask for policy in this matter to be reconsidered and for public opinion to express itself in favour of the removal of barriers other than those concerned with character and ability. We must face up to these difficulties if our Empire is to maintain its unity and strength and to become a real Commonwealth of Nations.[86]

It would be entirely in character for Keith to permit his name to be first among the signatories. That was precisely the sort of injustice that he felt was grossly unfair to persons of colour throughout the Empire. If Britain were ever to protest against Nazi racial policies, then Britain had better attend to her own policies and attitudes about racial groups, particularly since the Empire was overwhelmingly non-white.

With full awareness of Keith's bias for fairness and just treatment, F S Livie-Noble, Secretary of the London Group on African Affairs had full confidence of a favourable, helpful response when, in February 1939, he wrote to ask for assistance with a petition from the Paramount Chief of the Swazis. Keith had earlier given a legal opinion on certain issues affecting the Swazis. For that, Chief Sobhuza II had expressed thanks in compelling words: 'Please give to Professor Berriedale Keith my deepest gratitude and that of the Swazi nation. He has not seen us and yet he loves us—he loves humanity and therefore we praise him.'[87] In his letter, Livie-Noble asked Keith to examine a substantial body of materials which Chief Sobhuza II had sent to London together with a petition to the King in Council. His specific request was that Keith help the Chief fashion the petition, if Keith felt the case had any merit, so that it might receive a favourable hearing. Keith went to work on the case. He studied the materials and the draft petition that the Chief had prepared. Keith certainly felt the case had considerable merit because it touched one of his deep concerns about the threat that the British Crown might, in Keith's view, abdicate its responsibility for law and order, for just and fair treatment on behalf of Swaziland by acceding to demands of the Union of South Africa to assign administration of the protectorate to that government. That should not happen. But, short of that, the Swazis had a list of specific grievances for which they sought redress. These involved the assignment of land, revenue, and mining concessions away from Swazi control. Keith remodelled the petition and improved its focus substantially. He advised against sending it to the King in Council in favour of presenting it directly to the King. He also advised that the Chief find some Members of Parliament to take up the cause.[88]

Keith made it as clear as he could that he would continue to speak against any incorporation of Swaziland into the Union of South Africa. Unfortunately, in the turmoil of 1939, the petition had no effective result. When Britain entered the war, and when the Union of South Africa finally joined in, Britain's continued responsibility for the protectorates became increasing tenuous.

Another organisation where Keith continued his work and association was the National Council for Civil Liberties. Founded in 1934 with E M Forster as President, it had as its principal focus the identification of threats to basic liberties of the press, of speech, of assembly, of petition, and the like, liberties which had been painfully achieved throughout the seventeenth century and which, frequently, were threatened by new forms of power and of new technology.[89] It developed a programme of public information and it aimed to exert appropriate pressure on Parliament. George Orwell and other figures more on the left of the British political spectrum were members and supporters. At the time the war came, Ronald Kidd was Secretary, Sylvia Crowther Smith, Assistant Secretary, and Nancy Bell, National Organiser. All of these officials corresponded with Keith.

From time to time, they asked him to undertake certain tasks for the National Council as, for example, in the spring of 1935, to meet with a delegation from the Gold Coast and assist its members in preparing a statement of grievances to lay before Parliament.[90] But, it was in the early years of the war that Keith became quite active in working with the National Council in protesting against actions of the Government restricting liberties under pressure of war and, as well, in looking to the world after the war ended to identify those civil liberties which Britain ought to be certain to extend to the Empire. In July 1939, Kidd sent Keith a copy of the Prevention of Violence Act and asked Keith to study it, to comment on it, and to indicate the ways in which it was threatening to civil liberties. Keith responded quickly and sympathetically to the concerns.[91] And, in his usual manner, he wrote to the newspapers at the same time and pointed out some of the issues and dangers. When the National Council organised a conference for the spring of 1940 on Colonial Civil Liberties, Kidd wrote to ask whether Keith would be on the Executive Committee. Keith was willing to do that and took considerable interest in the work of the Conference.[92]

Later during the summer of that same year, Keith felt very directly the hand of censorship. One of the letters he wrote to the *Manchester Guardian* dealing with the Empire and the War Cabinet was fully printed, but when one of the news agencies sent copies, as usual, to newspapers in the dominions and the colonies, some censor had the temerity to delete portions of it. An official of the news agency sent the relevant materials to Kidd who promptly wrote to Keith. It is fair to assume that, in the act of censorship, Keith saw his worst fears realised: a Government, unrestrained in effective constitutional terms for many years, now, under the crisis of war, with ever fewer restraints, could stifle freedom of the press. He wrote right away to Duff Cooper at the Ministry of Information and asked for an explanation.[93] Threats to civil liberty of the press had moved from the general to the particular; Keith wanted to know how such censorship could occur. He persisted until he received a response which acknowledged the error, and apologised for it. When Kidd received a copy of the correspondence, he wrote asking for permission for National Council to use it and, also, suggesting that Keith write a letter about it to *The Times*; Keith granted the permission and did write the letter.[94]

In relation to the project of the National Council in devising a programme of civil liberties for colonies, Keith played a significant role. He was part of the Conference on the matter in 1940 and continued his interest in it. He saw the draft entitled, 'Minimum Programme of Civil Liberties in the Colonial Territories', through several versions even though he complained at one point that the committee had already spent too much time on it.[95] Each version he edited profited from the specific, detailed observations and suggestions that he made. He refined the structure of legislation to be proposed as 'An Act of Parliament to Promote Freedom and Racial Equality in the British Colonial Empire'.[96] The proposal included a listing of the specific points for freedom and equality including such matters as franchise, office holding, immigration, and the like. Keith was not hopeful about any action on the proposal: 'Unless the political atmosphere changes very considerably, I doubt if much more would be acceptable to the majority of the House.'[97] All of this work represented a significant attempt to influence public opinion and official thought in positive ways. Keith, in many ways a committed civil libertarian, supported that effort.

In the autumn of 1941, he was engaged in another aspect of the work of the National Council. From the Prevention of Violence Act, the Government moved to restrain individuals through Defence Regulation 18B. This, in effect, stripped persons of the usual protection of law, of habeas corpus, and of other rights on the grounds of the emergency of war. Keith, while he recognised the realities of war and the need for security, felt, however, that extension of executive authority which he judged to be needless should be restrained. For the National Council, he wrote several short papers dealing with Regulation 18B which he judged not only a needless extension but also a dangerous intrusion on the rights of individuals since a person could be detained and interned without an opportunity to plead a case. 'On the other main issue,' Keith wrote, 'the propriety of the grant by the legislature to the executive of the power of preventive detention of indefinite duration of persons deemed dangerously opposed to the national effort, it is possible to feel grave uncertainty.'[98] It was on the basis of his concern and his writing that Keith was invited to give the address opening a conference on wartime legislation under the title, 'The Constitutional Status of the Emergency Powers (Defence) Acts and Defence Regulations'. The National Council for Civil Liberties held that conference on 23 November 1941; it is unlikely that Keith accepted the invitation to present address.[99]

In these, as well as through his continuing comments in letters to the press, Keith became actively involved in the cause of civil liberties.[100] This concern was scarcely one for which he would find much public support. But, he never was concerned about public opinion towards himself. Rather, he was deeply concerned about the issues which he addressed and he hoped that some persons might see the significance of the issues. In his view, the defence of civil liberties was as important in war, perhaps even more so, as in peace, especially when, in his view, the constitution was already under very considerable strain.

Last Years

With concerns over civil liberties, over the condition of Abyssinia, over the strain of the constitution, over the continuing changes in the British Commonwealth of Nations, Keith found ample material to engage his mind and energies in the final decade of his life. In all the ways he could think of, including becoming actively involved with several organisations, he shared his anxieties, ideas, insights, knowledge, and opinions with the general public and with a wide range of individuals from all levels of society and from many different positions. He maintained his vigorous life as long as he could.

Several letters that he and Nan exchanged from 1936 onwards provide most of the limited material that is available in which he talked about himself or his feelings. In those, he dealt with a variety of household matters that he hoped Nan would attend to. He confessed that he paid very little attention to how she paid the bills and was grateful that she attended to them.[101] He indicated his willingness to help in the support of her flat in Kensington, or he would agree to her selling it; whatever she wished, he would approve. He enjoyed going to the flat: 'Though your flat appeals so much to us, many people probably prefer other localities. When I saw how much I enjoy the Park, no one shares my enthusiasm for it, I find.'[102] He responded to some of Nan's queries about her son and gave advice on his summer plans.[103] When Nan worked out arrangements for a house in Eastbourne, he gladly followed her scheme.[104] He showed a touch of humour as she sent him a horseshoe on one occasion and a panda on another: 'I have put the horseshoe on my desk because it will bring me luck when I am working which I badly need.[105] Many thanks for the Panda, which has decided to sit beside the clock in my bedroom. I was astonished to find it but it is a very amusing animal.'[106] He wrote of his concerns about Mussolini and Hitler, about the inadequacy of Baldwin and Chamberlain.[107] Great issues of state often appeared in the same letter with daily issues of the household.

It is in these letters that Keith revealed some of his deep concerns about his deteriorating health. Often, he went to the Grange Cemetery to visit the grave of his wife, continuing the practice he had started earlier; he was attentive to whether or not flowers were there and in good order. When he wrote to Nan about such a visit, he sometimes added a note about how he was failing: 'Eyes not too good, indigestion very bad yesterday, a little better day, usually worst at night.[108]... I am too old and diseased to mind at all.'[109] He had little use for his doctor; he recognised the progressive nature of his circulatory problems by the illness and indicated that in several letters:

> I have written to the doctor to see if he can help, or rather prevent things from getting worse, which is what one needs at my age.[110]... I have seen my doctor

with no great results. My disease is worse, as I knew that it was, but not apparently desperate yet.[111]... I cannot get any better; it is only a question of trying to avoid rapidly getting worse.[112]

As the years went along, he was successful in that last hope: the disease moved reasonably slowly. He had a series of strokes. One episode put him in hospital for a period in the summer of 1942.[113]

From that time onward, he did get worse more quickly. While he survived another stroke in June 1944,[114] the one on Friday, 6 October 1944 led to his death. *The Scotsman* which Keith had used for thirty years as a principal forum for expressing his ideas, printed his picture and a lengthy obituary the next day under the banner: 'EMPIRE JURIST—PROFESSOR BERRIEDALE KEITH DEAD—BRILLIANT CAREER'.[115] Other papers throughout the kingdom carried notices of his death, as well. His funeral was held the following Monday at the Grange Cemetery where he was buried next to his wife. Other than bequests to Edinburgh University to add to the prize funds he had established in memory of his mother and his wife and to his secretary and servants, he left everything to Nan. She had cared for him for that final decade of his life and was clearly the nearest relative. She made the decisions on the disposition of his various effects, and, fortunately, placed many of his books and notes, together with a significant body of his correspondence and papers in Edinburgh University Library.[116]

Keith's death brought to a close a life that spanned slightly more than sixty-five years. That life had been lived essentially in the cities, universities, and institutions of Edinburgh, Oxford, and London. A brilliant mind, an extraordinary ability to pursue two different intellectual activities simultaneously, a scholarly career in several fields, any one of which would have satisfied most men, and an active advocate for justice and fairness, Keith lived a rich and productive life. If, in some ways, he did not realise the promise and potential he possessed as fully as he, and others, might have wished, he certainly left behind a body of significant and substantial work which must be examined to appreciate his perspectives, his knowledge, and his quite staggering achievements.

CHAPTER 14

'Wide Scope' and 'Detailed Exposition': Summing Up

When Leeds University awarded Keith the honorary degree of doctor of laws,[1] the writer of the citation found several significant phrases to characterise Keith's work. Certainly, two of those phrases provided an accurate summary of the range of that scholarship: it was, indeed, of 'wide scope', covering so many different academic disciplines plus so many different topics of current import, and it was, as well, subject to 'detailed exposition' as he put into words and print the results of his thorough research and his analytical thought. He read, studied, comprehended, and used a whole array of documents, law reports, manuscripts, books, journals, newspapers, reference materials,[2] and extensive correspondence to be certain that he had examined all aspects of a particular subject. The breadth of his interests, the exhaustiveness of his studies, and the detailed nature of his writings are symbolised in those phrases which are useful in summing up Keith's life.

During 1944 and 1945, many persons wrote appreciations about Keith's life and work. Those same themes of scope and of exposition ran through many commentaries. Keith was recognised as a 'tireless worker of vast learning and impeccable accuracy',[3] as one whose 'productivity was unapproached by any constitutional writer of his time',[4] as possessing a 'restless and scintillating mind' which 'roamed over virtually the entire field of Indic culture, and even entered that of Indo-European comparative grammar',[5] and as one who had 'such productive scholarship in several fields as has been seldom equalled and probably never surpassed in the combination of massiveness of output with authoritative quality'.[6] In addition to those themes, Sylvia Pankhurst in *New Times and Ethiopia News* called attention to Keith's tireless work for the cause of Ethiopia 'even when gravely ill' and acknowledged that he took his stand, rooted in international and national law, 'always firmly based on justice and a desire for the welfare of humanity the world over'.[7]

Yet, even as these themes were lifted up, some persons expressed qualifications and reservations about some of his work, a phenomenon which has continued. For instance, one writer commented, about the constitutional works, that the sheer volume 'will require sifting before its permanent value can be assessed'.[8] On his scholarship in Sanskrit and Oriental studies, another cautioned: 'it may fairly be said that no one, however brilliant (and Keith certainly was very brilliant), could possibly write so voluminously on so many and such diverse subjects, without laying himself open at times to the charge of lack of thoroughness.'[9] A similar point was made by K C Wheare in the entry he prepared for the *Dictionary of National Biography* when he referred to Keith's compulsion to keep material in his various books as current as possible, thereby, on occasion, leading to some undue haste.[10]

The energy he brought to his work was noted in the Special Minute adopted by his colleagues of the Senatus Academicus of Edinburgh University. Whoever prepared it had good knowledge of Keith and, in one portion of the resolution, acknowledged his unusual gifts:

> Berriedale Keith's equipment for all this mass of work was almost unique. He had a virtually infallible verbal memory for everything he read, and a hardly less fallible power of so arranging his stores that every item was immediately at his command when it was wanted. He had a gift of precision in the use of words, nurtured by his classical training and enriched by his studies in other languages, that enabled him to say exactly what he meant on the most intricate questions of legal and constitutional interpretation. Above all, he had enormous and unintermitted industry.[11]

Perhaps the form of appreciation he would most have enjoyed came in an article in the *Daily Worker* on 9 October 1944, just days after he died.[12] In that piece, the writer reported on responses that Keith, 'the great authority on international law in general, and on the Indian constitutional problem in particular', had given to several questions put to him by an Indian journalist about the Indian constitutional crisis. Keith's responses had arrived 'just as the news of the death ... reached us'. Among the questions raised was whether or not Britain should take the initiative in breaking the political deadlock; as may be expected, he gave a ringing response about Britain's responsibility to do that. What would be best for India, a division into two states or remaining united? 'Undoubtedly a united India is better.' Could India proceed to self-government under the present constitution without further delay? Keith assured his questioner 'that Indian self-government is possible under the present constitution'. The journalist concluded that answers on the deadlock had been given by the 'greatest constitutional expert' and, thus, there was no excuse for the British government to temporise further.

Scope, exposition; range, words; variety of subjects, lengthy writing; all these were true. But did Keith's work represent any sort of unity? Perhaps here Sir Isaiah Berlin's essay on the words of Archilochus may be useful: 'The fox knows many things, but the hedgehog knows one big thing.'[13] He reflected on those words to characterise intellectuals as being divided, broadly speaking, into two groups. He drew a distinction between those 'who relate everything to a central vision, one system less or more coherent or articulate' and 'those who pursue many ends, often unrelated and even contradictory, connected, if at all, only in some *de facto* way, for some psychological or physiological cause, related by no moral or aesthetic principle'. He described this latter group as having 'thought ... scattered and diffused, moving on many levels'. He saw the former group as hedgehogs who roll everything, or combine everything, into some coherent or grand philosophical, or other, system; he labelled the latter as foxes who know many things. By that definition, he identified Dante or Plato or Pascal as hedgehogs; Shakespeare

14   Arthur Berriedale Keith, *c.* 1942. Reproduced courtesy of the Sanskrit
Department, Edinburgh University.

or Aristotle or Erasmus as foxes. In the diversity of his work and the catholicity of his interests, Keith certainly was a fox, yet one who held as a consistent moral principle, the pursuit of justice as he understood it. There is nothing to indicate that he was ever troubled with his intellectual position. Rather, he seemed to relish the use of his powers of mind to master a wide range of material and, then, to write about it all. As a fox who knew many things, Keith was in good intellectual company.

Some felt, however, that Keith's life could be described more adequately as one of failed promise.[14] With the unquestioned brilliance of mind he possessed, with the extraordinary energy he exuded, and with the significance of the issues he addressed, why did he seem not to have had a greater effect on his times? There is some evidence in the later letters he wrote to his sister that he may have felt some of this concern. Yet, he wrote those letters which remain when his health was failing and when, as well, the world was moving swiftly towards the next great war.[15] While he wrote to officials in the government, worked with groups seeking to influence policy, and expressed his critical views in the press regularly, it must be said that, given the particular context of the 1930s, his was simply one among many voices speaking to a public and to a government which hoped the depression would disappear in a miracle and which wanted international peace at almost any price. Cassandras never are popular! Then, too, Keith's contentiousness alienated some people. He was too ready to argue a fine point, about which he may well have been correct, only, in that argument, to lose support for a more substantive one. The style of debate can often be crucial to carrying the point. From that view, he must have lost support. Moreover, Keith had no temerity about supporting unpopular causes. On, for example, relations with the Irish Free State or Eire, Keith certainly was out of step with popular thinking and conventional wisdom. In his times, few could conceive of Britain seriously addressing Irish aspirations to find some resolution to republican desires. Yet, he argued that the substance of Irish-British relationships was critical and vital to both parties while the form could be adapted in a pragmatic manner. On India where he invested great energy, he was out of step with officials in the India Office and the government. Arguing for extending responsible government to India on the basis of the Montagu-Chelmsford Reforms, he found gratitude and support from Indian leaders but not from public opinion in Britain. It would be hard to get a very sympathetic reception for criticising the government for its delay, hesitation, and unwillingness to move in any real or substantive sense to respond to Indian aspirations, especially when that policy of utter caution had editorial support from the major newspapers. Perhaps, too, he was just too brilliant and left less brilliant persons baffled or, merely, envious.[16]

Two Ways to Look at Keith's Works

If Keith can be characterised as a fox, as one who knew many things and demonstrated wide scope in his works, it may be helpful in summing up to indicate the categories into which those works fall.[17] There are, at least, two different ways to classify his works: by the various academic disciplines, or fields of knowledge, and by the type of books. In fact, in all the disciplines, he produced most of the various types of books.

To look first at the disciplines. He published, at various times during his life, in these: Classics, Sanskrit language and literature, Oriental Studies including philosophy, constitutional law of England and of the British Empire, history, geography, and international affairs both law and diplomacy. Simply to list these fields of knowledge is to suggest the breadth of Keith's learning and knowledge. While he wrote his major works in Sanskrit and Oriental Studies during the early part of his career, that is, through the 1920s, he continued to write shorter works, especially articles in the decades after that. He wrote major works in constitutional law of the British Empire from his initial edition of *Responsible Government in the Dominions* in 1909 throughout the rest of his life. As important developments emerged on the world scene in the 1930s, it is not surprising that Keith focused his attention on those matters.

To turn from that listing of disciplines to the sorts of works he produced. It is interesting to note, again, the wide scope here. He produced original works, scholarly studies of analysis and exposition in all the fields. These ranged from very brief pamphlets to very substantial, lengthy volumes. He undertook the task of translating and editing numerous manuscripts. Especially, the volumes he published in the Harvard Oriental Series represent an enormous investment of time to say nothing of the importance of the result. He compiled documents and edited them in a form that could be useful for scholars, students, political figures, lawyers, and the general public. In all cases, Keith's ideas can be found in the introductory essay. Often, his particular interests are reflected in the documents which he selected for inclusion. He compiled catalogues of manuscripts in the Bodleian Library, in the Indian Institute at Oxford, and in the India Office Library. He carried responsibility for the revision of several of the standard or classic treatises in aspects of English law and of international law, preparing some of those through several editions. In the subsequent editions, Keith invested time, not only in a revised preface or introduction in which he identified the particular new points of concern, but also in a revision of the text itself. He contributed chapters to works in series, to works on special topics, and to *festschriften*. He wrote letters, no one really knows how many, to the press, primarily in Britain but, as well, in Australia, South Africa, and elsewhere. Some portion of those letters, approximately two hundred and fifty, he collected into three volumes, organised topically, and published. He wrote articles for scholarly journals; again, there is no way to know what the actual number was.[18] Simply the range of journals indicates the many editors with whom he corresponded and the wide number of readers who knew his works. In addition, he wrote reviews of books in journals and newspapers so that he regularly contributed his critical appraisal of new studies in the several disciplines.

The areas of his interests are summed up in the inscription on his gravestone. Either he left the wording about himself, which seems likely since it parallels that used on the title page of his books, or his sister worked it out. It reads, in part:

In Memory of
Arthur Berriedale Keith
D.C.L., D.Litt., Hon. LL.D.
Barrister of the Inner Temple
And Advocate of the Scottish Bar,
Regius Profesor of Sanskrit and Comparative
Philology, also Lecturer
On Constitution of the British Empire
Edinburgh University 1914–1944[19]

Envoi

Keith's earliest reputation was made in Classics but, most importantly, as a Sanskrit scholar. In summing up his life, it may be appropriate to use two poems from that language to emphasise the primary themes that influenced him over the sixty-five years that he lived. Both come from *Poems from the Sanskrit*, edited by one of Keith's students, Professor John Brough of Cambridge. The first is from the 'outstanding poet Kālidāsa':

If a professor thinks what matters most
Is to have gained an academic post
Where he can earn a livelihood, and then
Neglect research, let controversy rest,
He's but a petty tradesman at the best,
Selling retail the works of other men.[20]

Clearly, Keith never saw his academic post as merely a place to rest and present lectures based on the past work of other people. Reared and educated in the best traditions of the universities of his age and taught by men who were themselves active, producing scholars, Keith had splendid direct experience and excellent mentors to emulate. He saw the academic post as providing him with the financial security, never sufficient in his view, to be sure, so that he could invest his energies in creating that new knowledge which he and other scholars could use. He recognised that time for scholarship was immensely important. In each negotiation he had with Edinburgh University, he made certain to protect time for his own scholarly work by restricting his teaching to two terms a year. He never neglected original research. Not only did he undertake remarkable new works, but he did not hesitate to engage in the somewhat arduous task of preparing catalogues of manuscripts so that other scholars might have access to materials. Any reader who simply handled one of his books whether in Sanskrit, English law, constitution of the British Empire, or international affairs was bound, indeed still is, to be impressed by the depth of knowledge that Keith displayed. And, it has to be said, again, that from his earliest days to his last, he lived in a household that was organised around his intellectual activities. Some credit for his enormous production, must be given, especially, to the three women in his life: his mother who nurtured his genius, likely sheltering and tying him too closely in the process; his wife of more than twenty years, Margaret Balfour Allan; and his younger sister, Nan B Keith Dewar, who dealt with the final decade of his life. His wife and his sister, especially, were important to his work. Keith always generously acknowledged the essential nature of their support with emphasis on sharing ideas with them, on their continual encouragement, and on their direct assistance in production of the works. Yet, they ran his daily activities so that he was completely free for his studies. Keith never neglected research!

The other poem from Sanskrit points to another theme in Keith's life.

> My lord, since you have banished Poverty
> From this fair land, I feel it is my duty
> To lay an information that the outlaw
> Has taken refuge in my humble home.[21]

Here, it is possible to imagine a man of impoverished circumstances undertaking the unpleasant and, perhaps, dangerous task of informing his lord that while poverty may have been banished by decree, it was scarcely gone in reality. Courageous statement, not necessarily oriented to win popularity, but, nonetheless, the clear truth! And that is the way in which Keith spoke to numerous issues, whether they were in the scholarly world where he engaged in debating some disputed point or in the public world where he felt an issue must be identified. Motivated by a strong conviction of the importance of due legal processes, Keith was neither hesitant nor repentant over the role he played in addressing Elgin and others over the actions of the government of Natal.[22]

Convinced of the rectitude of his analysis, Keith did not shy away from castigating successive prime ministers of Britain for their, in his view, ineffectual policies during the 1930s.[23] Committed to the sanctity of international agreements, he felt impelled to criticise Britain and France over their posture towards Abyssinia and over their, in his view, virtual destruction of the League of Nations.[24] Concerned over the ways in which Britain had successively withdrawn from its position of protecting natives in southern Africa, he could invest his own energy in seeking redress for a Swazi chieftain and could continually remind the British government of the Crown's responsibility for natives.[25] Often acerbic, sometimes appearing eccentric, frequently flailing out in too many directions, always assured, usually contentious, Keith, like the poor man in the poem, never hesitated about 'laying an information' to those in power where poverty, in whatever form that might take, was lodged. He stood for justice under law, for scrupulous scrutiny of evidence, for rational public discourse, for the rights of the oppressed, for the virtues and risks of responsible government, and for the effective use of the powers of the Crown.

Most assuredly, if there were a pantheon at the summit of Arthur's Seat to honour notable Scots, Arthur Berriedale Keith must deserve a special niche. Perhaps, he might even merit two niches as 'the chief ornament of Scottish learning'.[26]

Appendix

Arthur Berriedale Keith: Life and Work

Principal Events	*Books* (Abbreviated titles)

1879–1897 PORTOBELLO/EDINBURGH

1879   Birth, 5 April, Portobello
1887? Prize Book, Miss Douglas's
         Classes
1887–1894   Royal High School
1894–1897   Edinburgh University
1897   MA, 10 April

1897–1901 OXFORD

Balliol College
  Classical Scholar
  Boden Scholar
1899   1st Class, Classical Honours
           Moderates
1900   1st Class, Oriental Final School
           (Sanskrit & Pali)
1900   BA   1900   First article, JRAS
1901   *Literae Humaniores*
1901   Civil Service Examination,
           August; record score

1901–1914 LONDON

1901–1903   Colonial Office
1901   Entry, 21 October
           Nigerian Department
1902   North American and
           Australasian Department
1903–1905   Crown Agents for the   1903   *Catalogue of Sanskrit and Prākrit*
           Colonies   *MSS*
Secretary
1904   Called to the Bar, 17 November
1905–1914   Colonial Office
1905–1906   South African Department   1905   *Catalogue of Sanskrit MSS*
1905   BCL, Oxford
1906   Natal crisis, spring

Principal Events	*Books* (Abbreviated titles)
1906–1907 West Indian Department	
1907 Navigation Conference	1907 *Theory of State Succession*
German Measles, April	
Edinburgh University, Lecturer	
Ancient History, January–May	
With brothers, purchase of	
land in Dunbar for MSK	
1907–1912 Dominions Department	1908 *Śāṅkhāyana Āraṇyaka*
1909 St Margaret's, Dunbar completed	First article, JCL
'Scarlatinal rheumatism', ABK	1909 *Aitareya Āraṇyaka*
sick leave 67 days	*Catalogue of Sanskrit MS*
	Responsible Government in the
	Dominions
1911 Imperial Conference, May–	1911 *Catalogue of Prakrit MSS*
June	
DCL, Oxford, May	
MSK's death, 31 July	
1912 Marriage to Margaret Balfour	1912 *Responsible Government in the*
Allan, 11 June	*Dominions*
1912–1914 Private Secretary to Sir	*Vedic Index*
John Anderson,	1913 *Historical Geography*
December	1914 *Veda of the Black Yajus School*
1914 DLitt, Edinburgh University,	
July	
Named Regius Professor, October	

1914–1944 EDINBURGH

1914–1920 122 Polwarth Terrace	1915 *Sāṃkhya System*
1916–1924 Scottish Liberal	1916 *Imperial Unity and the Dominions*
Federation	*Indian Mythology*
	1918 *Selected Speeches and Documents*
	on British Colonial Policy
1919 India Office Study, March–June	Peace Handbooks, FO
1920–1944 4 Crawfurd Road	1919 *Belgian Congo and the Berlin Act*
	1920 *Rigveda Brāhmaṇas*
	1921 *Dominion Home Rule in Practice*
	War Government of the British
	Dominions
	Indian Logic and Atomism
	Karma-Mīmāṃsā
1922 Queensland Tramways Case	1922 [Dicey] *Digest of Laws*
	Speeches and Documents on
	Indian Policy
	1923 *Buddhist Philosophy in India*
	and Ceylon
	Classical Sanskrit Literature
	1924 *Constitution, Administration*
	and Laws of the Empire
	Sanskrit Drama

Principal Events		*Books* (Abbreviated titles)	
			Sāṁkhya System 2nd ed.
		1925	*Religion and Philosophy*
			Veda and Upanishads
		1927	[Dicey] *Digest of Laws*
			Responsible Government in the Dominions
			History of Sanskrit Literature
		1929	*Dominion Autonomy in Practice*
			[Wheaton] *Elements of International Law*
			Sovereignty of British Dominions
1930–1935	India Round Table Conference and Related Matters	1930	*Constitutional History*
			First British Empire
		1931	*Elements of Law of Contracts*
			Introduction to British Constitutional Law
		1932	*Speeches and Documents on British Dominions*
			[Dicey] *Digest of Laws*
1932–1933	Two Divorce Cases	1933	*Constitutional Law of the British Dominions*
1934	Death of Margaret Balfour Keith, 25 March		
1934–1944	Mrs Nan B Dewar, ABK's sister joins him to run household	1934	[Ridges] *Constitutional Law of England*
			Certain Legal and Constitutional Aspects of the Anglo-Irish Dispute
1935–1942	Concerns over Abyssinia	1935	[Anson] *Law and Custom of the Constitution*
			Catalogue of Sanskrit MS India Office
			Governments of the British Empire
			Letters on Imperial Relations
1936	Abdication Broadcast, 8 December	1936	*Constitutional History of India*
			King and the Imperial Crown
			Letters and Essays
			Privileges and Rights of the Crown
1935–1942	Assists various groups, NCCL	1937	[Ridges] *Constitutional Law* 6th ed.
1938	Malta Appeal, May–July	1938	*Dominions as Sovereign States*
			Speeches and Documents
			International Affairs
1939	Appeal, Sobhuza II	1939	*British Cabinet System*
			[Ridges] *Constitutional Law*
		1940	*British Commonwealth of Nations*
1941	Tanganyika Case		*The Causes of the War*
			Constitution of England, Victoria to George VI

Principal Events	*Books* (Abbreviated titles)
1942 Hospital summer	1942 *Constitution under Strain* *Federation: its Nature and* *Conditions*
1944 Stroke, June death, 6 October	1944 [Wheaton] *Elements of* *International Law*

Notes

Abbreviations Used in Notes

ABK   Arthur Berriedale Keith
Burton   Collection held by Mrs J Walcot Burton
CO   Colonial Office Files, Public Record Office
CSS   Civil Service Commission Files, Public Record Office
Dewar   Collection held by Professor Michael J S Dewar
FO   Foreign Office Files, Public Record Office
Gen   Arthur Berriedale Keith, Papers and Correspondence, Edinburgh University Library, Gen 140–153
JCL   *Journal of Comparative Legislation*
JRAS   *Journal of the Royal Asiatic Society*
OUP   Oxford University Press, Files on ABK

Acknowledgements

Materials in the Burton Collection and Dewar Collection appear with the permission of Mrs J Walcot Burton and Professor Michael J S Dewar.

All quotations from Crown-copyright records in the Public Record Office appear by permission of the Controller of HM Stationery Office. The copy of the CO file is also used by the same permission.

Quotations from Keith, Papers and Correspondence, 1896–1941, appear by permission of the Librarian, Edinburgh University Library.

Materials in the files on ABK held by the Oxford University Press appear by permission of the Press.

Quotations from the citation, 29 June 1936, appear with permission of the Vice Chancellor of the University of Leeds.

The two poems in Chapter 14 are from John Brough, *Poems from the Sanskrit* and are used with the permission of Penguin Books Ltd.

CHAPTER 1 pp 1 to 14

1   The words appear in the citation for honorary LLD awarded to ABK by the University of Leeds, 29 June 1936. See below p 252 for full text of citation.
2   The sketch given here rests upon lengthy conversations with Mrs J Walcot Burton, ABK's niece, and briefer ones with Professor Michael J S Dewar, ABK's nephew. Also, I was fortunate to spend a day at St John's, Cambridge University,

with Professor John Brough who learned his first Sanskrit at Edinburgh under ABK's tutelage, and to spend time, as well, with Mrs Neil Bayne of Edinburgh who, both in conversation and in writing, gave me some recollection of ABK's class in the Constitution of the British Empire. In addition, of course, I have drawn inferences based upon all of the materials that ABK wrote in the CO and in his extensive correspondence with persons. The numerous obituaries also provided clues about his character.

3   Burton, ABK to MSK, 18 May 1911.
4   Ibid., ABK wrote, 'As my boots are all very shabby, I have got as you bid a new pair chosen by Laura (I was too lazy to go to the shop) at 21/ patent leather. They look nice. Laura has found the necessary ties and I wore one today.'
5   Letter Mrs Neil Bayne to me, 20 August 1982.
6   'Peterborough', *Daily Telegraph* (11 October 1944).
7   This story was told to me by Mrs J Walcot Burton.
8   Letter of 8 October published in *The Scotsman* (10 October 1944), 4g.
9   CO 418/112, 16941.
10   CO 42/977/14536, 28.
11   CO 418/81/2095 10/11, 323.
12   CO 532/52, 17627.
13   CO 418/82/2994 10/11, 347.
14   Burton.
15   Patrick Ford, 'As Spring Draws Near', *The Scotsman* (26 February 1938), 11a.
16   Phrase used by Professor Dewar in conversation with me.
17   John Allan, the writer of the obituary of ABK in the journal of the Royal High School, *Schola Regis*, repeats this story (1943–5, p 52) so it had wide currency. In fact, I was told it by everyone with whom I talked about ABK! I have tried, with little success, to learn more about those rare persons who have this sort of 'double-track' mind. Some clues are in the intriguing book by Howard Gardner, *Frames of Mind: The Theory of Multiple Intelligences* (New York: Basic Books, 1983; London: Heinemann, 1984).
18   Mrs Bayne gave me a testimonial which ABK had written for her, 14 January 1936.
19   Letter from Ronald W Ferguson to Nan B Dewar, 7 October 1944. Burton.
20   'On Keith and Downing St. & Co', *Daily Sketch* (24 March 1923), 5.
21   Letter N Macnicol, 7 October 1944, in *The Scotsman* (9 October 1944), 4e.
22   This is well-sketched by R C K Ensor, *England, 1870–1914* (Oxford: Clarendon Press, 1936), Chapters 12, 13.
23   The longer, and well-considered, view on the gamble is N Mansergh, *South Africa, 1906–1961: The Price of Magnanimity* (London: Allen and Unwin, 1962).
24   The phrase, of course, is Rudyard Kipling's from his poem 'The White Man's Burden' (1899).
25   The concept and the phrase come from John Maynard Keynes' prophetic analysis, *The Economic Consequences of the Peace* (London: Macmillan, 1919).
26   The extension of suffrage to women as well as to all males in the Representation of the People Act (1918), the full effect of the Parliament Act (1911) limiting the power of the House of Lords, and the emerging power of political party organisation all illustrate the point. These, and much more, are dealt with by A J P Taylor, *England, 1914–1945* (Oxford: Clarendon Press, 1976) especially in Chapter 3, Note C, Chapters 4–6.
27   See any of ABK's books on the constitution of the British Empire after the Imperial Conference of 1926. Also, see R M Dawson, *The Development of Dominion Status, 1900–1936* (London: Oxford University Press, 1937); and W K Hancock, *Survey*

of British Commonwealth Affairs (London: Oxford University Press, 1937) where, in the initial chapter, he discusses the evolution of the term, British Commonwealth of Nations.

28 I developed this theme in *The Right of Secession in the Development of the British Commonwealth of Nations* (Ann Arbor, Michigan: University Microfilms, 1958).

29 See the discussion on domestic issues and on the range of dilemmas in Taylor, *op. cit.*, Chapters 9–11.

30 See Taylor, *op. cit.*, p 504.

CHAPTER 2 pp 15 to 40

1 Birth Certificate, Burgh of Portobello; Register of Births, Marriages, and Deaths, Scotland. ABK was born at '5 hr, 50 min. A.M.' Another copy, Dewar.

2 3 July 1872. Marriage Certificate, Dunbar; Register of Births, Marriages, and Deaths, Scotland. Witnesses were Peter Keith and Margaret Dewar. Another copy, Burton. Newspaper notice in *Haddingtonshire Courier*, 5 July 1872, 2d.

3 Information from Mrs J Walcot Burton.

4 Keith and Co, Correspondence, National Library of Scotland, MS 4361/19, MS 10595/86, MS 7544/722, MS 7545/673, MS 7547/146/548/826, MS 7548/261/289/653/873, MS 7549/576, MS 7550/244/890, MS 7551/460, MS 7552/178, MS 7553/61, MS 7554/36/120, MS 7622/386/409/454, MS 7623/123. See also advertisements for Keith and Co in Post Office, *Edinburgh and Leith Directory*, 1893–4, p 157. That directory indicates the range of the business that Davidson Keith was responsible for, by 1900–1: 'KEITH and Co, advertising agents, 59, George Street. Advertisements inserted in all newspapers at the publisher's prices. Special reduced rates quoted for frequent and continuous insertions. Intending advertisers are invited to apply for estimates. Birth, marriage or death announcements, and advertisements of situations wanted or vacant, houses, specific articles, etc., received at prepaid rates. Letters in reply may be addressed to a No at Keith and Co's office, to be retained till called for, or, if desired, they will be forwarded by post. Office hours, 9 A.M. to 9 P.M. Telegraph "Keith Edinburgh"; Telephone 286. KEITH and Co, newspaper and magazine agents, 68 Princes Street. Newspapers—daily and weekly, metropolitan and provincial—and magazines and periodicals of all kinds kept for sale, delivered to order throughout Edinburgh, or forwarded by post direct from places of publication to subscribers in the country at publisher's prices. There are numerous deliveries daily by a staff of careful and experienced deliverers of the Edinburgh, Glasgow, Aberdeen, Dundee, London, etc. morning, evening, and weekly newspapers, and the utmost care is taken to secure regular and early delivery.' Ibid., 1900–1, p 180.

5 *The Scotsman* carried the notices of births: William J Keith, 13 April 1873 (14 April 1873), 8f; Jeanie Ramsay Keith, 27 March 1874 (28 March 1874), 12f; Robert Charles Steuart Keith, 3 October 1876 (4 October 1876), 8h; Arthur Berriedale Keith, 5 April 1879 (7 April 1879), 8g; Annie Balfour Keith, 4 October 1880 (5 October 1880), 8g; Alan Davidson Keith, 19 May 1885 (21 May 1885), 8g.

6 Address on birth notices, also Post Office, directory; Census, 1881, 1891 give addresses, names of residents.

7 'To the *s* of the main road, here called ABERCORN TERRACE, a series of villas linking behind stone walls and illustrating the change from Georgian parade to

Victorian privacy ... the rest of *c* 1860 with variations on the theme of the canted bay beneath a steep gable.' John Gifford, Colin McWilliam, David Walker, and Christopher Wilson, *Edinburgh* in *The Buildings of Scotland* edited by Colin McWilliam (Harmondsworth: Penguin Books, 1984), p 659. See also an interesting contemporary book. William Baird, *Annals of Duddingston and Portobello* (Edinburgh: Andrew Elliot, 1898), especially Part II, 'Portobello'.

8   See n 5 above.

9   Robert Louis Stevenson, *Edinburgh: Picturesque Notes* (London: Seeley and Company, 1879), pp 26–8. For an appreciation of Edinburgh, see David Daiches, *Edinburgh* (London: Granada, 1980).

10 Comments by Mrs Burton and Professor J S Dewar. Also, I found confirmation in addresses on correspondence as well as in directories.

11 Mrs Burton's comment of her mother's recollection.

12 Davidson Keith died in London on 15 March 1921. He left an estate of personal effects of £30. 1*s*. 1*d*.; Scottish Record Office, Record of Inventory, vol 666, 7 July 1921 to 30 July 1921; SC 70/1/666,263.

13 Based upon views of Mrs Burton and Professor Dewar from what they had heard about MSK. I tried, without success, to find her case written in *The Lancet*.

14 Based upon conversations with Mrs Burton about her mother's recollections and also those of her aunt, Jean.

15 Sir William John Keith, 13 April 1873–22 January 1937, ICS, service in Burma; Jean Ramsay Keith (1) Adamson, (2) Groom, 28 March 1874–17 March 1949, lived in Burma many years, initially caring for Will's household, then married Robert Adamson who had interests in Burmah Oil; Robert Charles Steuart Keith, 3 October 1876–26 September 1919, ICS, service in Burma; Nan B Keith Dewar, 4 October 1880–17 January 1973, married Frank Dewar, ICS, many years of living in India; Alan Davidson Keith, 19 May 1885–22 February 1928, barrister and Professor of English, University of Rangoon.

16 Dewar.

17 In letter from Mrs Burton to me, 15 June 1985, she recounts the story again: 'When, as a child, he had read everything in the house and ended by reading the ABC of British Train times, the family jibed at him and worked out a most complicated journey, he, from memory, recited the trains with arrival and departure times and changes of trains where necessary!'

18 Royal High School, Matriculation Book, 1887–8; signatures of the brothers: #95, William J Keith, #96, Robert C S Keith, #97, Arthur Berriedale Keith.

19 J B Barclay, *The Tounis Scule: The Royal High School School of Edinburgh* (Edinburgh: Royal High School Club, 1974).

20 Ibid., passim.

21 The Royal High School of Edinburgh, *Prospectus of Sessions, 1893–1894*, p 4.

22 Ibid., passim. See also *Rector's Reports* for years when ABK was enrolled.

23 Application and testimonials, Arthur Berriedale Keith, for Professorship of Sanskrit, University of London. Keith Collection, U 14/36, p 8.

24 'Matriculation', *University of Edinburgh Calendar, 1894–1895*, pp 31–2; Edinburgh University, Matriculation Album, 1893–8, has ABK's signature, No 1,064, 15 October 1894; see also information he provided in, Edinburgh University, First Matriculation Book, 1894–5.

25 Judging from an examination of Matriculation Lists which give ages, I conclude that to be the case.

26 See the brief note in Daiches, *op. cit.*, Appendix. Also, *University of Edinburgh Calendar, 1894–1895*.

27 Gifford *et al.*, *op. cit.*, pp 188–91.

28 *University of Edinburgh Calendar, 1897–1898*, sets this out, p 103.
29 *Op. cit.*, for chairs, titles, and degrees.
30 Application and testimonials, Arthur Berriedale Keith, for Lectureship in Ancient History, University of Edinburgh. Keith Collection, U 12/14, pp 3–4.
31 Keith Collection, U 14/36, p 22.
32 Ibid., pp 8–9.
33 W R Hardie to ABK, 19 February 1897. Gen 144/5/19.
34 *University of Edinburgh Calendar, 1897–1898*.
35 Keith Collection, U 14/36, p 8.
36 Ibid., p 7.
37 Newscutting on Alan's award, Dewar. See Royal High School, *Rector's Report, 1895–1896*: 'the distinguished success of a number of our former pupils, notably of the brothers Keith, three of whom are now scholars in distinguished Colleges at Oxford', p 8.
38 'Balliol College', *Oxford University Calendar*.
39 See listing in Edward Hilliard, ed *Balliol College Register, 1832–1914* (Oxford: University of Oxford, 1914).
40 See notes on Balliol College in *Victoria History of the Counties of England: A History of Oxfordshire. III. The University of Oxford* (London: Oxford University Press, 1964), p 89.
41 'Balliol had completely established the reputation begun in the thirty-five years' reign of Jenkyns; its tutorial staff were the *elite* of the University; its undergraduates, drawn, since the opening of its scholarships to free competition, from a very wide field, with a preponderance from the great public schools and a strong stiffening of Scotsmen, were a microcosm of their own.' J W Mackail, *James Leigh Strachan-Davidson, Master of Balliol: A Memoir* (Oxford: Clarendon Press, 1925), pp 18–19.
42 *Victoria History, op. cit.*, p 87.
43 Burton.
44 Two different addresses appear in correspondence, #226 and #232. Both addresses also appear in JRAS of 1901 and 1902.
45 Balliol College, Records. Mr John Jones, Archivist of Balliol, when I talked with him, concurred that ABK was exceptional both in living out of College and in only subscribing to the Musical Society.
46 CSC 4/42.
47 Dewar.
48 Keith Collection, U 14/36, p 9.
49 Robinson Ellis, Keith Collection, U 12/14, p 19.
50 R W Macan, ibid., p 12.
51 L R Farnell, ibid., p 13.
52 J Wells, ibid., p. 14.
53 J S Smith, ibid., p 16.
54 Edward Caird, ibid., p 18.
55 JRAS, 1900, 127–36.
56 JRAS, list of members, 1900.
57 A A Macdonell, *A History of Sanskrit Literature* (London: Heinemann, 1900), Preface, viii.
58 Keith Collection, U 14/36, pp 12–13.
59 Ibid., p 10.
60 See Hilliard, *op. cit.*, for names of men at Balliol in ABK's time. The 'Oxford Connection' included many of ABK's colleagues in the CO, men who became governors in the colonies, Shadi Lal who became a judge in India, and so on.

61 Orders-in-Council, Civil Service Requirements, 15 August 1890, CSC 4/42.
62 ABK kept all these materials. Gen 144/3/88, 89, 90.
63 Gen 144/3/97, 98.
64 Dewar. Also CSC Report. Oxford University took note of ABK's achievement in an analytical supplement, *Oxford Magazine* (20 November 1901).
65 Letter from Sir Robert Armstrong, Permanent Secretary, Management and Personnel Office, to me of 7 July 1982: 'Our research confirms that in the 20 comparable years from 1895 to 1914 Keith's score of 5,382 marks was never bettered. Indeed, it was never really approached. Looking at the leading candidate for each of those years, no other topped 5,000, only three topped 4,000 (the best 4,556), and the rest scored 3,000 plus. A most remarkable achievement.'
66 46th *Report of HM Civil Service Commissioners*, CSC 4/44; another copy, Gen 144/3/99; copy of table of marks in Gen 144/3/85.
67 Ibid.
68 Cosmo Parkinson, *The Colonial Office from Within, 1909–1945* (London: Faber and Faber, 1947), pp 97–8.
69 Letter Sir William Muir to ABK, 30 September 1901. Gen 144/3/84.
70 Letter ABK to H Ross, 22 April 1912. Gen 144/1/26.
71 CO 323/472/35902, 280–1.

CHAPTER 3 pp 41 to 61

1 Post Office, *London Directory*, 1902–5. These addresses also appear on correspondence.
2 Civil Service Commissioners to ABK, 8 October 1901. Gen 144/3/92.
3 Civil Service Commissioners to CO, 7 October 1901. CO 323/471, 35124, 205–8; see also CO 378/15/35124.
4 ABK to CO, 9 October 1901. CO 323/472, 271 5; see also CO 378/15, 35279.
5 Ommanney to ABK, 12 October 1901. CO 532/472, 276–7; another copy, CO 323/472, 35279, 273 ff. ABK kept the letter. Gen 144/3/87.
6 ABK to Ommanney, 13 October 1901. CO 323/472, 35902, 280–1. The comment was by F R Round and was supported by W B Hamilton, 14 October 1901, in file cited, 278–9; see also CO 378/15, 35902. Letter H B Cox to ABK, 21 October 1901. CO 323/472, 35902, 282; ABK kept the letter. Gen 144/3/86.
7 The 'simply vast' phrase was used by Lord Carnarvon. Various sources describe the new office but one of the best is in Robert V Kubicek, *The Administration of Imperialism: Joseph Chamberlain at the Colonial Office* (Durham, North Carolina: Duke University Press, 1969). See also, WORKS 12/96/4 which contains details of relocating the famous mantelpiece; WORKS 12/96/2 has material about building the new office. George W Thornbury and Edward Walford, *Old and New London* (London: Cassell, Peter, 1879–85) describe the buildings, pp 392–3. I was kindly provided with a copy of the floor plans of the entire building as it was in 1914.
8 He certainly knew all corners of the office very well, simply on the basis of his varied assignments!
9 The best way to understand the CO is to study the successive editions of the *Colonial Office List*. But there are very helpful studies, as well: Brian L Blakeley, *The Colonial Office, 1868–1892* (Durham, North Carolina: Duke University Press, 1972); John Bramston, 'The Colonial Office from Within', *Empire Review* (April

1911), pp 279–87; John Arthur Cross, 'The Colonial Office and the Dominions before 1914', *Journal of Commonwealth Political Studies* (1966), pp 138–48; John Arthur Cross, *Whitehall and the Commonwealth: British Departmental Organisation for Commonwealth Relations, 1900–1966* (London: Routledge and Kegan Paul, 1967); Henry L Hall, *The Colonial Office* (London: Longmans, 1937); W S Baillie Hamilton, 'Forty-four Years at the Colonial Office', *The Nineteenth Century* (1909), pp 599–613; Kubicek, *op. cit.*; Cosmo Parkinson, *The Colonial Office from Within: 1909–1945* (London: Faber and Faber, 1947); R B Pugh. 'The Colonial Office, 1801–1925', in J H Rose *et al.*, eds, *The Cambridge History of the British Empire*, Volume III (Cambridge: Cambridge University Press, 1959), pp 711–68; R B Pugh, *The Records of the Colonial and Dominions Offices* (London: HMSO, 1964).

10   See *India Office List* for organisation and responsibilities.

11   D H E Butler and J Freeman, *British Political Facts, 1900–1968*, 3rd edn (London: Macmillan, 1969; New York: St Martin's Press, 1969), p 174.

12   CO 323/469, 1490; CO 323/487, 1470.

13   The analysis which follows is drawn mainly from materials in the third volumes of the *Cambridge History of the British Empire, op. cit.*, as well as a standard history which ABK had on his shelves: Howard Robinson, *The Development of the British Empire* (Boston: Houghton, Mifflin, 1922; 2nd edition, 1936). *Colonial Office List* gives details of acquisitions, area, population, resources, and the like.

14   'Lord Durham's Report', many places, but see ABK, *Speeches and Documents on British Colonial Policy, 1763–1917* (London: Oxford University Press, 1918), p 136.

15   Ibid., p 139.

16   Edward Marsh, *A Number of People: A Book of Reminiscences* (London: Heinemann, 1939), pp 123–4.

17   *Colonial Office List* included all the regulations needed!

18   This process is described in many places. I followed it out to understand ABK's role in getting Sir Thomas David Carmichael ready to go as Governor of Victoria in, 'The Dissolution of 1908—No. 1: A Governor Exercises His Power', *Journal of the Royal Historical Society of Victoria* (September, 1983).

19   Marsh, *loc. cit.*

20   For example, see ABK's work CO 446/17, 40722; CO 446/17, 44991.

21   Hall, *op. cit.*, p 24. ABK kept a copy of a summary done by the Chief Registry in January 1914 which summarises data for 1911, 1912, and 1913. Gen 142/3/93.

22   This is very well described and illustrated in Pugh, *Records, op. cit.*

23   Hartmann W Just, *Verses* (Cambridge: Heffer, 1930), p 15.

24   See definition of role of Crown Agents for the Colonies in 1881, C 3075, Papers re Functions of Crown Agents for the Colonies.

25   Ibid. Also, each edition of *Colonial Office List* contained a summary of their work and relationship to the Secretary of State for Colonies.

26   This change is discussed and analysed very well in J E Kendle, *The Colonial and Imperial Conferences, 1887–1911: A Study in Imperial Organisation and Politics* (London: Longmans, 1967).

27   For example, see CO 879, Confidential Print, Africa.

28   There are numerous illustrations: CO 879/65, No 640; CO 879/61, No 610, both contain many papers; CO 520/10, 44565; CO 446/21, 29344; CO 520/17, 28883. For a discussion of the evolution of the Committee of Imperial Defence, see Franklyn A Johnson, *Defence by Committee: the British Committee of Imperial Defence, 1885–1959* (London: Oxford University Press, 1960).

29   CO 885/8/156.

30 Correspondence with Treasury over the creation of additional positions in CO 323/468, 368–72.
31 See *Colonial Office List, 1901*.
32 Ibid., where the biographical section gives details of service.
33 The phrase is used in the description of the West African Frontier Force in *Colonial Office List, 1899*; see also Joseph Chamberlain, Memorandum to Governors of West African colonies, 26 June 1900 in CO 879/61, No 610.
34 At the end of 1899, an Order-in-Council created the Protectorate of Northern Nigeria and eliminated the Royal Niger Company. See *Colonial Office List, 1900*. On Lugard, see the great study of Margery Perham, *Lugard* 2 vols (London: Collins, 1956, 1960).
35 *Colonial Office List, 1901* gives a good sketch of Nigerian area including history, geography, resources, and the like.
36 By actually counting the files, I concluded that ABK handled that proportion once he started full-time work in the Nigerian Department.
37 Lugard gave special meaning to the concept of 'indirect rule'. See ABK minutes on CO 446/17, 41120; CO 446/21, 32771; CO 446/22, 3342/02.
38 CO 147/157, 43183.
39 Some examples: CO 520/10, 36263; CO 446/20, 36199. On CO role in appointing officers, see CO 520/12, 40498; CO 446/17, 40722; CO 147/157, 41367.
40 CO 520/9, 231–2.
41 CO 520/14, 25224.
42 Ibid.
43 CO 446/16, 30616.
44 CO 446/17, 39361.
45 CO 520/10, 37992.

CHAPTER 4 pp 62 to 90

1 See above p 7, and Chapter 1, n 17.
2 Gen 144/3/83.
3 Gen 144/3/82, 81.
4 This was the date suggested by Anderson and it is clear from the files that it was the date on which ABK commenced work.
5 Edward Marsh, *A Number of People: A Book of Reminiscences* (London: Heinemann, 1939), p 123.
6 *Colonial Office List, 1914*.
7 *Colonial Office List, 1902*.
8 *Report of HM Civil Service Commissioners, 1898*.
9 *Colonial Office List, 1902*, xiii.
10 CAB 18/10 for work of Colonial Conference, 1902. See also J E Kendle, *The Colonial and Imperial Conferences, 1887–1911: A Study in Imperial Organisation and Politics* (London: Longmans, 1967), pp 42 ff.
11 CAB 18/10; see also 1902, Cd 1299, Colonial Conference.
12 Donald C Gordon, *The Dominion Partnership in Imperial Defense, 1870–1914* (Baltimore: Johns Hopkins Press, 1965), passim.
13 1 Edw VII, c 15.
14 See ABK's minutes on CO 23 Bahamas, CO 37 Bermuda, CO 42 Canada, CO 67 Cyprus, CO 78 Falklands, CO 83 Fiji, CO 91 Gibraltar, CO 123 British Honduras,

CO 194 Newfoundland, CO 209 New Zealand, CO 225 Western Pacific, CO 418 Australia.

15 There are numerous illustrations but ABK handled the matter on CO 42/889, 46673.

16 63 and 64 Vic, c 12.

17 The filing system in the CO was reorganised so that separate files for each of the states were closed. All materials, after 1901, were filed in CO 418, starting with Commonwealth matters and then covering each of the states.

18 CO 418/26, 19125.

19 There is extensive material on the case. At least, a start would be found in CO 418/19, 41151, 43416, 43427. ABK discussed it, as well, in *Imperial Unity and the Dominions* (Oxford: Clarendon Press, 1916), pp 423–4.

20 CO 418/27, 10751.

21 From Tasmania, CO 418/28, 13510.

22 CO 67/131 holds 64 files from May to July 1902 of which ABK handled 13; CO 67/132 holds 58 files from August to December 1902 of which ABK handled 47; CO 67/133 covers the entire year of 1902 with 138 files of which ABK handled 33; CO 67/134 holds 40 files from January to April 1903 of which ABK handled 37; CO 67/135 holds 59 files from May to August 1903 of which ABK handled 28; CO 67/137 covers the entire year of 1903 with 58 files of which ABK handled 29.

23 See material on Cyprus in *Colonial Office List, 1903*.

24 ABK's minutes on CO 67/132, 1326 02/03, 37342.

25 ABK's minute on CO 67/133, 49961.

26 ABK's minute on CO 67/134, 8917.

27 Ibid.

28 He saved his notes, Gen 144/1/39.

29 For organisation in Bermuda, see *Colonial Office List, 1903*.

30 Gen 140/1/3. Other letters: Gen 140/1/6, 7, 8.

31 Gen 140/1/3.

32 CO 37/240, 13072.

33 For example, CO 78/103, 8453.

34 A copy of the circular despatch, CO 37/238, 44538.

35 See note on *Journal* in Bibliography below.

36 Bibliography below.

37 CO 42/891, 45137. See CO 42/891, 49860; also, George Johnson, ed *The All Red Line: the Annals and Aims of the Pacific Cable Project* (Ottawa: James Hope, 1903).

38 CO 209/264, 45215.

39 See above, Chapter 3, pp 59–60.

40 CO 147/161, 18453.

41 Ibid.

42 CO 885/8, No 149, p 1.

43 Ibid., p 12.

44 CO 23/258, 25872. There are numerous other files which ABK handled: CO 91/428, 39955; CO 83/75, 48182; CO 37/238, 50809; CO 83/75, 51198; CO 418/19, 53164; CO 123/241, 1690; CO 83/78, 9042; CO 37/239, 13694; CO 78/103, 27394.

45 CO 23/258, 25872.

46 Ibid.

47 Ibid.

48 J B Brebner, *The North Atlantic Triangle: the Interplay of Canada, the United States*

and Great Britain (New Haven: Yale University Press, 1945). Note also the separate set of files for Newfoundland and their antiquity.

49 There is a good summary of the Alaska Boundary Decision in *Annual Register, 1903*, pp 437–9.
50 The agreement is 1904, Cd 1472, Washington Convention on Alaska Boundary.
51 See ABK's minutes, and other staff, as well: CO 42/892, 1743, 7134, 7964.
52 CO 42/892, 8914. Anderson minuted: 'This is the end of the "judicial" tribunal. Senator Lodge is a fine piece of American humour'. 17 February 1902. CO 42/894, 6358.
53 CO 42/894, 10251 summarises the stages; CO 42/892, 2300; CO 42/894, 24298. ABK's notes from research at Gen 140/1/50; other materials Gen 140/1/34, 38, 44, 46.
54 Gen 140/1/45.
55 Gen 140/1/10.
56 Gen 140/1/47.
57 *Annual Register, loc. cit.*
58 Ibid.
59 CO 323/483, 1690. ABK made a copy, Gen 144/3/57.
60 Ibid.
61 Ibid.
62 Ibid. Also see details of offer to ABK and of his appointment in CO 323/483, 27470.
63 *Colonial Office List, 1904*, xv. See list, as well, in Arthur W Abbott, *A Short History of the Crown Agents and their Office* (London: Eyre and Spottiswoode, 1959), p 99.
64 Gen 144/3/25.
65 Gen 144/3/74. See, also, ABK's notes of 26 August 1904 on the assurances he received about becoming a Crown Agent. Gen 144/3/63.
66 See summary in Montagu Cox and Philip Norman, *Survey of London: London County Council, XIII. Parish of St. Margaret, Westminster, Part II* (London: Batsford, 1930), pp 198–203.
67 Gen 144/3/72.
68 CO 323/483, 16903. ABK kept copies. Gen 144/3/57.
69 Richard M Kesner, 'Builders of Empire: the Role of the Crown Agents in Imperial Development, 1880–1914', *Journal of Imperial and Commonwealth History* (May 1977), p 316.
70 Ibid., p 313. See Abbott, *loc. cit.*
71 Ibid., p 27–8 comments on this.
72 See 1904, Cd 1944.
73 CO 885/19, No 226, questions 307–17, 1710–13 all deal with ABK's transfer and pension status. See also 1909, Cd 4473.
74 The Archives of the Crown Agents contain nothing about personnel of this nature. ABK's notes are all in Gen 144/3 at various places as indicated.
75 Gen 144/3/67.
76 Abbott's terms in telling me stories about Blake.
77 ABK's letter to Mercer reflects their continuing discussions, Gen 144/3/66.
78 Gen 144/3/69.
79 Ibid.
80 Gen 144/3/70.
81 Gen 144/3/66.
82 Ibid.
83 Another phrase used by Abbott when he talked with me.
84 Gen 144/3/69.

85   Gen 144/3/62 and 68.
86   Gen 144/3/62. ABK's note: 'He [Carmichael] observed that he could not stand explaining things to Sir E Blake'.
87   Gen 144/3/61 and 64.
88   Gen 144/3/64.
89   Gen 144/3/59.
90   Gen 144/3/57. In addition, ABK made a long note of a conference he had with Blake and Mercer on 30 March. Gen 144/3/56.
91   Gen 144/3/54 and 56.
92   CO 323/509, 10925, CO 323/511, 12894, 14106.
93   CO 323/504, 11961, 12949, Gen 144/3/35, 52. See letter of Anderson from Singapore, 7 May 1905: 'I am very much disturbed by Fiddian's news that you have thrown up the CA and returned to the CO on account of incompatibility with Blake. He was not an easy man to live with in the old days but I had hoped he had mellowed especially when he had been gratified with a K.' Gen 144/3/24. There were more exchanges between Blake and ABK: Gen 144/3/28; Gen 144/3/29. The exchange did little to repair the breach!
94   *Intrants Book*, Faculty of Advocates, Scotland, 1921, ABK wrote in that as the date. W S S Breem, Librarian and Keeper of the Manuscripts, the Inner Temple, confirmed the date of ABK's admission, as 2 November 1899. See discussion above, Chapter 2, pp 33, 37, Chapter 3, p 42.
95   Council of Legal Education, *Calendar, 1904*. This was also summarised by W S S Breem in a letter to me. Note also the discussion by a Joint Committee on the Duties, Interests and Discipline of the Bar about considering special regulations for staff of the CO. CO 323/488, 21345.
96   Council of Legal Education, *Calendar, 1982*, p 2 where the various reforms are considered.

CHAPTER 5 pp 91 to 109

1   A V Dicey, 'The Extension of Law Teaching at Oxford', *Harvard Law Review* (1910), 24, pp 1–5.
2   Frederick H Lawson, *The Oxford Law School, 1850–1965* (Oxford: Clarendon Press, 1968), p 6.
3   *Oxford University Calendar, 1906*, pp 85–6. See summary in Lawson, *op. cit.*, pp 36–40, and Appendix II.
4   See Bibliography below for ABK's works.
5   Dicey, *op. cit.*, 2.
6   See above, pp 32–3.
7   See Bibliography below for ABK's works.
8   *Colonial Office List, 1905*.
9   *Colonial Office List, 1906*.
10   I did a count and concluded that ABK handled about one-third of the despatches from the Cape, CO 48; the bulk of the work for Natal, CO 179, including virtually every paper from January to April 1906, sixty-four out of sixty-nine despatches; the bulk of the work for Orange River Colony, CO 224; virtually every paper on Transvaal, CO 291. In addition, he handled an occasional paper from the High Commissioner and from the Inter Colonial Council.
11   This is all very well considered in R C K Ensor, *England, 1870–1914* (Oxford: Clarendon Press, 1936), Chapters 12, 13.

12   The best account of all this leading to unification is in Leonard M Thompson, *The Unification of South Africa, 1902–1910* (Oxford: Clarendon Press, 1960).

13   See Ronald Hyam, *Elgin and Churchill at the Colonial Office, 1905–1908: the Watershed of the Empire-Commonwealth* (London: Macmillan, 1968), pp 5–6. On the election, John Anderson wrote to ABK from Singapore: 'What a rout the Unionists have suffered! It looks as if the Liberal Majority over Unionists & Nationalists would be as large as the Unionist majority in 1900. *Sic transit.* I am anxious to see the returns.' Gen 140/1/41.

14   Ensor, *op. cit.*, p 38.

15   Quoted by Hyam, *op. cit.*, pp 42–3, from Violet Bonham Carter, *Winston Churchill as I Knew Him* (1965), p 15.

16   Hyam, *op. cit.*, p 545. This is the central thesis of his splendid book.

17   For example, see the long file on flogging of Chinese coolies which ABK minuted on 26 August 1905: 'It is I think deplorable that the Government should so flagrantly have overlooked the promises made no later than March 04 on information supplied by Lord Milner.' CO 291/84, 30852. Or, in October of the same year, on a report about prisons, ABK minuted: 'The Report reveals a most scandalous state of affairs and the Director of Prisons (as well as most of the officials) appears to me incompetent. I would not drop the matter but ? ackn receipt with an expression of grave regret at the disgraceful state of affairs: ask for a *detailed* report of the actions proposed to be taken with regard to the recommendations: ask whether he thinks that the Director should be continued in his post.' CO 291/84, 32459.

18   ABK understood the complexity of the scene but argued for native rights. For example, see these minutes: 9 June 1905, on restrictions in Orange River Colony: 'The provisions regarding natives & coloured persons are extremely drastic. The inclusion of everybody seems also unfair to educated or intelligent natives or Asiatics.' CO 224/19, 19161; 24 June 1905, on rights of Cape Coloured in Transvaal: 'say that no provision could be made for the grant of political rights in view of the terms of Peace, and that Mr L [Lyttelton] sees no reason to doubt that the Legislature of the Tvaal will ensure to the natives their civil rights in as full a measure as in the Cape.' Graham concurred with that, regretfully, 'No other answer is possible.' CO 48/580, 21875; 10 October 1905, on mortality among natives: 'The mortality among Tropical natives is disgraceful and their employment should I think be stopped.' CO 291/85, 35764; on 14 November 1905, on restrictive franchise in Orange River Colony: 'I confess I regret that we have not been able to do anything for the natives since annexation. But I fear that we cannot well take up the matter now.' CO 224/18, 40208; on 18 December 1905, still on franchise in Orange River Colony: 'I really think we must do something for those natives who are educated and well-behaved. The law of the ORC is a disgrace to any colony in that it lumps all persons together.' CO 224/18, 44693, and on this ABK got support from all his superiors who directed a despatch conveying those views.

19   ABK supported the idea of the appointment of a commission to examine the particular situation of Indians in South Africa, and felt it should go out from Britain rather than be composed mainly of South Africans. CO 291/83, 22829. See also CO 291/84, 26270. This concern was included in the inquiry set out in 1906, headed by Sir West Ridgeway. See CO 879/106, No 853, No 854.

20   For example, see letter from Aborigines Protection Society in regard to Swaziland on which ABK wrote lengthy minutes, 10 February and 26 February 1906. CO 291/92, 45264. Early in the Natal affair, ABK drafted response to the Society,

1 February 1906. CO 179/239, 3336. Later on, another, 19 April 1906. CO 179/239, 12589.

21 See Selborne's despatches in CO 291/83, 22918, 26882. ABK argued vigorously that there should be no reduction in medical staff for Chinese coolie labour. CO 291/84, 28877. See also file of Elgin-Selbourne exchanges. CO 291/88, 44878.

22 For example, see materials which include ABK's work in CO 879/106, No 801, No 807.

23 On a despatch which reported that some mine managers had engaged coolies in piece work contracts, ABK was angered and minuted to the effect that he opposed verbal agreements and that the terms of contracts must be honoured. CO 291/87, 41862.

24 See memorandum of Churchill, 15 March 1906, arguing for responsible government, a paper which went to the Cabinet. CO 879/106, No 834. Early in his time in the South African Department, ABK recognised the inevitability of granting responsible government as he minuted on 11 September 1905: 'We are bound to give responsible government—that is beyond doubt the meaning of self-government in the Terms of Surrender—unless the Boers agree to something else. I think it would be most unfortunate if we let any idea arise that we repudiated this obligation.' CO 224/8, 32383.

25 There are many examples; two will suffice in which ABK, on successive days, prepared an extensive response to constitutional proposals for Orange River Colony: 5 December 1905, CO 224/18, 42959; 6 December 1905, CO 224/18, 42856. Both were printed in CO 879/106, No 760, No 779.

26 Again, there are many examples: ABK minuted on 15 January 1906, 'Self-government must come soon. But despite defects of the franchise & of the principle—one man, one value—convenience & practically the universal practise in the Colonies points to a representative legislature being allowed to settle the lines of the Constitution.' CO 291/88, 1604 05/06; he drafted Letters Patent and Royal Instructions for Transvaal. CO 291/111, 3526. In the context of the grant of responsible government, he continued his concern for native rights; 10 March 1906: 'The grant of responsible government to the Orange River Colony renders it incumbent on us to consider what should be done for the natives in handing over the Govt. We cannot expect the Boers to do anything if we remain satisfied to all appearance with the status quo.   (1) As regards natives we should insist on the rule of equal rights for all civilised persons ...   (2) Then there is the question of Asiatics. The ORC law is a disgrace to a British colony.' CO 224/20, 8431.

27 Dated 1 September 1908 and reprinted in 1910, CO 886/1, No 10.

28 In addition to Hyam, op. cit., see the splendid study of the entire matter by Shula Marks, Reluctant Rebellion: The 1906–1908 Disturbances in Natal (Oxford. Clarendon Press, 1970). See also Thompson, op. cit., pp 44–7. A more contemporary account is James Stuart, A History of the Zulu Rebellion, 1906, and of Dinizulu's Arrest, Trial, and Expatriation (London: Macmillan, 1913) which, of course, does not rest upon an analysis of CO files. A great deal of material was prepared for Parliament: 1906, Cd 2905, Cd 2929, Cd 3027, Cd 3247; 1907, Cd 3563; 1908, Cd 3888, Cd 3889, Cd 3998, Cd 4001, Cd 4194, Cd 4195, Cd 4403, Cd 4404. The files of Natal, CO 179/233, for the spring of 1906 are almost exclusively given to the matter; thus, ABK handled material daily.

29 There are numerous illustrations. One will suffice here: 27 March 1906: 'We really ought to know under which laws the natives are to be dealt with as regards forfeiture etc. The S Afr rule appears to be that native lands can be forfeited for

rebellion, but who is to decide what rebellion is? The Courts or the Gov?' CO 179/233, 10386.

30 Marks, *op. cit.*, gives a detailed account of the sequence of events. Hyam summarises them, *op. cit.*, pp 239–41.

31 On martial law: CO 179/233, 4843, 4844, 7652. On censorship, CO 323/522, 5096.

32 CO 179/233, 5026.

33 Ibid. See also, CO 179/233, 4892, 5097, 5459.

34 CO 179/233, 5459, 5507; CO 179/234, 11450.

35 CO 179/233, 10712.

36 Ibid.

37 CO 179/233, 11034. Elgin accompanied this with a private telegram, Hyam, *op. cit.*, p 242. Both Elgin and Churchill responded to questions on 29 March 1906: HL, *Parl. Deb.*, 4th ser, 44, 1906, 1504; HC, *Parl. Deb.*, 4th ser, 44, 1906, 1646–50.

38 CO 179/233, 11545. ABK minuted, 2 April 1906: 'An unsatisfactory & to the Natal Govt discreditable ending of the affair.' To which Lambert added: 'That depends on the facts which are not fully known to us.'

39 CO 179/233, 10712.

40 Ibid.

41 Ibid.

42 CO 179/233, 11033.

43 Ibid.

44 CO 179/233, 11034.

45 The major one was 8 April 1906: 'The Rights of His Majesty's Government to Interfere in the Executive government of a Self-Governing Colony.' CO 179/233, 11034. He wrote a supplemental minute on 17 April 1906. CO 179/233, 11321.

46 ABK minuted, 31 March 1906: 'This proves conclusively that Natal is not in such a position as to justify executions under martial law. [Telegram reporting demobilisation of Mackenzie's column] ... They should not be executed without civil trial. I am rather surprised that no one has applied to the Supreme Court on behalf of the prisoners. The Marais' judgment besides being unintelligible could not conceivably apply in a case when there has been no actual fighting between whites and blacks. I think this should be pointed out to Ministers.' CO 179/233, 11321. He held to this position throughout the controversy and on 17 April 1906 pointed out that one of the reasons the Privy Council declined jurisdiction was that no appeal had been made to the Supreme Court in Natal. Ibid.

47 Ibid. His colleagues were unhappy about this comment. Cox minuted: 'I consider this statement an outrage on a population which is quite as humane as Mr Keith and has more knowledge of the circns.' Ibid.

48 CO 179/233, 11034, Memorandum, p 4.

49 CO 323/522, 5096.

50 Churchill indicated an outline for a despatch: 30 March 1906: 'Draft despatch as follows: 1. Prerogative of Crown is unquestionable, paramount, inalienable & persistent, 2. In practice good sense, circumstances, interest & power govern all relations between Mother country & colonies, 3. Though HMG had all through the *right* they had at no time the *intention* to interfere with resp of Natal govt, 4. The appeal for British troops however called a certain degree of their latent right into being, 5. The degree involved at cert time went beyond opportunities for friendly advice.' CO 179/233, 11034. In fact, Lambert prepared a text but it was never sent.

51 See n 41 above.

52   See Lambert's comments of 4 April 1906. CO 179/233, 11033. Also, his views on CO 179/234, 15015; CO 179/233, 11281.

53   ABK picked up the point in *Imperial Unity and the Dominions* (Oxford: Clarendon Press, 1916), p 81. Hyam, *op. cit.*, p 301, considered it.

54   *Responsible Government in the Dominions* (London: Stevens and Sons, 1909), pp 56–7 considered the matter but made no mention of Elgin's role; (Oxford: Clarendon Press, 1912), pp 291–6 but still no comment on Elgin; (Oxford: Clarendon Press, 1928), pp 193, 214–221, 828, 870 considered aspects of the matter and described Elgin as 'feeble and vacillating'. He maintained his views and, as late as 1939, commented that Asquith 'was able to rid himself of Lord Elgin, who had not managed colonial affairs with tact or distinction, and who on general issues maintained in Cabinet a discreet silence.' *The British Cabinet System* (London: Stevens and Sons, 1939). Hyam, *op. cit.*, pp 7–9 summarises the various views that historians and others have held of Elgin's work at the Colonial Office.

55   CO 179/233, 11321.

56   On tone, see Elgin's comment of 15 April 1906: 'I recognise Mr Keith's ability but the line he has taken here, not I think for the first time, detracts from the usefulness of his Minutes.' CO 179/233, 11321. On handwriting, see Churchill's comments, 9 April 1906: 'Great inconvenience is caused by this kind of writing to all who study it. I hope we may claim a little more consideration in future from Mr Keith.' ABK had a rejoinder: 'I hope it is not thought that I am not anxious to write clearly, tho' I admit I am not very successful in doing so.' CO 224/20, 10335; 2 May 1906: 'Almost illegible'. CO 291/98/15403.

57   Hyam, *op. cit.* See also Nicholas Mansergh, *South Africa, 1906–1961: The Price of Magnanimity* (London: Allen and Unwin, 1962).

58   Minute, 17 April 1906. CO 179/233, 11321.

59   Cited by Hyam, *op. cit.*, p 9, fn 1, p 10, fn 1, based upon correspondence in the Elgin Papers, 9 June 1906, 25 September 1907. Marks comments: 'Yet by the end of the disturbances there is every indication that most of the other members of the Colonial Office dealing with the disturbances shared his [ABK's] opinion.' *op. cit.*, p 243.

60   Gen 144/3/22.

61   Gen 144/3/21. Another copy in Dewar.

62   Epitaph composed by Henry Lambert, 28 May 1906

Memoriae sacrum
Illustrissimi viri
Omnium scientiarum periti
Sed praecipue in iurisprudentia
Inqua iuris consultos omnes officiales
Summa caede saepssime afflixit:.
A B Keith
Infantiam apud Americanos
Innocentissimam degit.
Adolescens visit Agentes Cormales,
Gentem missam,
Unde Gorgone quodam sacrissima insecuta
Vix incolumis effugit.
Postea inter Africanos adscriptus
Adeo in [Metulla, Seras, writing not clear], Gubernatores,
Nigrorum amicus,
Imperii oppugnator audax,

Saeviit
ut tremerent tyranni.
Necopinata eheu morte oppressus est.
Cadaver in litore Indorum
Occidentalium
ejectum
in longinqua et barbara terra sepultum est.
SIT TIBI JAMAICA LEVIS

Gen 144/3/18.

I am deeply indebted to my colleague and friend, Professor Jay W Gossner, for his assistance in suggesting ways to set this into English.

In ABK's papers, there are two other epitaphs, both in his handwriting:

Beneath this stone
is interred
R H Griffin
An elegant Homeric scholar
he was also
An excellent tennis player and a
successful golfer—
Alike in mind and body he was
adorned
by every virtue and every grace
which unfit a man for work on a fine Saturday afternoon
His health was shattered
by excessive devotion to BCA
and he ultimately died of a surfeit
of German SW Africa
As the base [? writing unclear] of his death which
occurred in his 59th year
he was a power in the SAD
Promotion cometh not from the north
Nor yet from the South.

Gen 144/3/19.

Here lies
All that is mortal of
Hartmann Wolfgang Just
for many years
a principal clerk in the SAD
The swiftest of men
No man living could ever catch him.
An ardent investigator of ancient history
He held [? writing unclear] one of the finest
collections of papers of his time
Whereby he inexpressibly endeared himself to
All his juniors.
He received the gratitude of successive
Secretaries of State
By a long series of LITTLE TELEGRAMS
But he will chiefly live in history

As the author of the immortal saying
I MUST SEE EVERYTHING
He died from a reduction of hours of work
to 11 1/2 per diem
consequent on a temporary failure of questions
due to the rising of the H of Commons
An institution for which he ever cherished
An extraordinary admiration.
'The memory of the Just is blessed'
(by his Juniors)

Gen 144/3/20.

CHAPTER 6 pp 110 to 126

1   For example, on 3 March 1907, he minuted on an Australian file. CO 418/52, 6961.
2   *Colonial Office List, 1906.*
3   *Colonial Office List, 1906,* p xiv.
4   ABK discussed this, *Responsible Government in the Dominions* (Oxford: Clarendon Press, 1912), pp 9–11.
5   See discussion in J H Rose *et al.*, eds, *Cambridge History of the British Empire* (Cambridge: Cambridge University Press, 1929–1959), Volume III, pp 470–2.
6   CO 23 Bahamas; CO 111 British Guiana; CO 123 British Honduras; CO 152 Leeward Islands; CO 295 Trinidad; CO 312 Windward Islands.
7   CO 137/655, 2972, 3942, 4574, 4970, 5607.
8   CO 137/655, 2972, 4574.
9   As I studied the files, I saw that his work tapered off towards the end of February.
10 The report is printed in 1907, Cd 3567.
11 See exchanges of August and September 1906: Gen 141/2/18, 19, 20, 21.
12 See ABK to Dicey, 7 February 1907: Gen 149/5/35.
13 JCL, 1908, 202.
14 *Imperial Unity and the Dominions* (Oxford: Clarendon Press, 1916), pp 215–16.
15 Keith Collection, U 14/36.
16 Ibid.
17 Ibid., pp 25–6.
18 Ibid., p 4.
19 Keith Collection, U 12/14.
20 See nn 15, 16 above.
21 Agendum XVIII. Meeting 18 February 1907. Appointment of Lecturer on Ancient History. Edinburgh University Court. Papers, 1907.
22 Edinburgh University Court. *Minutes.* 18 February 1907, p 56. A letter from Professor A S Pringle Pattison reported the recommendation of the Committee on the appointment of which he was convenor. He reported that they strongly recommended ABK although Professor Hardie 'seems to think that Keith might have defects of temper which might make him difficult to get on with.' The *Oxford Magazine*, 27 February 1907 reported ABK's appointment. A copy of that notice, Burton.
23 Edinburgh University Court. Papers, 1907.
24 Ibid.
25 Ibid.

26 Burton.
27 ABK kept a copy of a CO note on his sick leave. Gen 144/3/3. Cox wrote on 24 April: 'I am *so* sorry to hear you are laid up. You must be careful & not think of returning back till you are quite well.' Gen 140/1/1.
28 Edinburgh University Court. Papers, 1907.
29 Ibid.
30 Ibid.
31 Ibid.
32 'Feu ch by Mar Con Trustees of St Clair Cunningham of Westbains, now deceased, and Elizabeth Stewart Usher or Cunningham—To Margaret Stobie Drysdale or Keith residing at 2 Prince of Wales Mansions, London, in life rent, and William John Keith and Robert Charles Steuart Keith, both of the Indian Civil Service, Burma, and Arthur Berriedale Keith of the Colonial office, London, equally, and survivors and survivor, in fee—of 2 50/100 Acres of ground, bounded on south ...' Sasines, Haddington, 1901–1910, Lib 207. 20.
33 The house still stands and is used by the Winterfield Golf Club to whom I acknowledge their permission for me to go through the entire building. The property went to Will after MSK's death in 1911 and was held by Will's heirs until 1948.
34 An advertisement in an attempt to sell it, *The Scotsman*, 1 May 1937, 5.
35 *The Theory of State Succession with Special Reference to English and Colonial Law* (London: Waterlow, 1907), Preface.
36 Ibid., Chapters 2, 3.
37 Ibid., Chapter 6.
38 Ibid., p 38.
39 In New Zealand, the death of R J Seddon caused complications in the Liberal–Labour Party; in Australia, Deakin came back to power in May 1905. See Rose *et al.*, *op. cit.*, Volume VII, Part II, Chapter IX, and Part I, Chapter XVII.
40 Documents are in 1906, Cd 2785, Cd 2975; 1907, Cd 3337, Cd 3340, Cd 3404, Cd 3406, Cd 3523, Cd 3524. A summary of the recommendations is in CAB 18/11A.
41 See text in 1906, CD 2785.
42 The Round Table group were descendants of Milner's 'kindergarten'. Their work is thoroughly considered in J E Kendle, *The Round Table Movement and Imperial Union* (Toronto: University of Toronto Press, 1975).
43 See J B Brebner, *The North Atlantic Triangle: the Interplay of Canada, the United States and Great Britain* (New Haven: Yale University Press, 1945), pp 158–9.
44 The comment is Ronald Hyam's, *Elgin and Churchill at the Colonial Office, 1905–1908: the Watershed of the Empire-Commonwealth* (London: Macmillan, 1968), p 321.
45 Hyam, *loc. cit.*,
46 The first resolution. 1907, Cd 3523; also in CAB 18/11A.
47 CO 323/534, 29255.
48 Ibid.
49 CO 532/3, 34119. See 1908, Cd 3795.
50 I searched the South African files to see what he did and found nothing.
51 JCL, 1909, 40–92.
52 See notice and report in *The Times*, 21 and 29 January 1908. The lecture was printed in the *Journal of the Royal Society of Arts*, 21 February 1908, pp 332–47.
53 Clearly, he drew upon all the various papers he had written many of which, in one way or another, had become public through the Parliamentary Papers.
54 *The Athenaenum* (20 February 1909), 224. A copy, Burton.

55   Ibid.
56   Interestingly enough, the best biography of Smith is that of Professor Mary Dewar, ABK's niece-in-law: *Sir Thomas Smith: A Tudor Intellectual in Office* (London: Athlone Press, 1964).

CHAPTER 7 pp 127 to 152

1   This is described in R C K Ensor, *England, 1907–1914* (Oxford: Clarendon Press, 1936), pp 406–7.
2   See response of Elgin's son. Gen 144/3/12.
3   He was First Commissioner of Works, 1905–1910. Telegram to Dominions on Harcourt's appointment. CO 532/23, 34555.
4   ABK to Lucas, 2 September 1910. Gen 144/3/1.
5   Ibid.
6   A new set of files was created to reflect the Dominions Department, CO 532. ABK worked principally in that file as well as CO 42 Canada, CO 194 New-foundland, CO 209 New Zealand, CO 418 Australia.
7   Seely to ABK, 19 July 1909. Gen 140/4/37; CO 418/84, 10894, 10895.
8   CO 418/63, 13830, 30585.
9   CO 194/275, 8755, 11285.
10   CO 418/77, 12784.
11   MS Harcourt dep 468, 44. See also notes to ABK from George Cunningham, Privy Council Office, expressing Lord Beauchamp's appreciation for the memo-randum: 'Mr Keith's memorandum is *most* valuable. Would you mind thanking him very warmly for me? It is full of excellent material.' Gen 141/3/50; Gen 141/4/70.
12   CO 886/1, No 4; CO 418/68, 24667.
13   CO 886/1, No 6.
14   CO 418/68, 24667.
15   John A LaNauze, *Alfred Deakin: A Biography* (Melbourne: Melbourne University Press, 1965), II, p 488.
16   CO 418/68, 24667.
17   Ibid.
18   See n 13 above. See also CO 886/1, No 6, 'Memorandum on the Question of Treaties as Affecting the Dominions', 2nd edition.
19   ABK minuted on despatch in regard to Department of External Affairs Act, 3 June 1909: 'I confess that I think there is a great deal of fuss here about nothing. I am also a little afraid that Lord Grey will end by having a serious quarrel with Sir Wilfred Laurier if he presses him on all these matters.' CO 42/930, 18380. See also CO 42/936, 20802.
20   CO 532/6, 30802.
21   CO 532/20, 7180; CO 418/97, 7863.
22   CO 532/20, 33623.
23   CO 532/18, 34804.
24   CO 532/18, 34791, 36513.
25   CO 532/20, 35658.
26   CO 209/271, 39591.
27   CO 418/98, 24460.
28   ABK's appointment in CO 885/9, No 173; regular reports printed in CO 885/18, CO 885/19, CO 885/21; annual reports, for example, 1908, Cd 3992; 1909,

Cd 4476; 1910, Cd 4999; 1911, Cd 5514; 1912–1913, Cd 6024; 1913, Cd 6669.

29 CO 323/557, 2249; CO 885/19, No 224 for reports of 1908, CO 885/20, No 238 for 1909, CO 885/21, No 254 for 1910 and 1911.

30 See resolution of Advisory Committee, 11 December 1914 thanking ABK 'for the zealous and efficient way in which he had always performed the duties of secretary.' CO 885/23, 301, #85, p 53.

31 CO 885/21, No 265 for composition of Committee. ABK attended his first meeting on 6 December 1911.

32 ABK kept proof of despatch which included an outline of the syllabus for the lectures. Gen 142/1/40.

33 See above Chapter 3, n 18.

34 CO 42/956, 2546.

35 See discussion above, pp 69–70. There is extensive material in Keith, Papers and Correspondence, Gen 140, Gen 141.

36 Strickland to ABK, 10 October 1908. Gen 140/2/25.

37 Hutson to ABK, 26 December 1908. Gen 140/1/32.

38 Strickland to ABK, 28 December 1908. Gen 140/1/27.

39 Hutson to ABK, 20 February 1909. Gen 140/4/72.

40 MacGregor to ABK, 23 April 1909. Gen 140/3/9.

41 Williams to ABK, 12 July 1909. Gen 140/4/44.

42 Morris to ABK, 21 August 1909. Gen 140/4/22.

43 Ibid.

44 Strickland to ABK, 3 September 1909. Gen 141/2/45.

45 Carmichael to ABK, 15 September 1909. Gen 140/3/35.

46 ABK to Callan, nd January 1910. Gen 141/2/32.

47 ABK to MacGregor, nd May 1910. Gen 140/3/36.

48 Ibid.

49 CO 532/10, 22448.

50 Oppenheim to ABK, nd November 1908. Gen 140/2/16; 10 December 1908. Gen 140/2/17; 14 December 1908. Gen 140/2/18. Reeves to ABK, 19 December 1908. Gen 140/2/41; Oppenheim to ABK, nd January 1909. Gen 140/4/3.

51 Oppenheim to ABK, 14 December 1908, cited n 50.

52 For contributions to JRAS, see Bibliography. He served on various committees for the Royal Asiatic Society; see JRAS. ABK kept some notes about the African Society. Gen 142/1/39; Gen 141/3/56; Gen 141/5/76; Gen 141/5/74. For contributions to JCL, see Bibliography. See note from R Willcocks to ABK 7 February 1910 about his participating in the first meeting of Editorial Advisory Committee to JCL to be held at the CO. Gen 142/1/78.

53 Egerton to ABK, 3 January 1911. Gen 141/3/43.

54 Gen 141/4/30.

55 Responses in Gen 141/2/73–77. Bryce to ABK, 6 March 1911. Gen 14/3/51. ABK to Bryce, 24 March 1911. Gen 141/2/72. Bryce to ABK, 23 November 1911. Gen 141/4/30.

56 Washington to ABK, 22 August 1911. Gen 141/5/54.

57 Lucas to ABK, 7 November 1911. Gen 141/4/16; 18 November 1911. Gen 141/3/64; 21 December 1911. Gen 141/4/2.

58 Dicey to ABK, 19 January 1909. Gen 140/4/4.

59 ABK to Dicey, 22 January 1909. Gen 149/5/34.

60 Institut Colonial International. *Compte-rendu des séances, 1894–1928* 18 vols. (Bruxelles, 1894–1927). See report of 1894 for initial meeting.

61   Ibid.
62   Ibid.
63   Ibid., for successive meetings.
64   Ibid., Many of the papers were later published in *Bibliothèque coloniale internationale*.
65   Ibid.
66   *Catalogue de la bibliothèque* (Bruxelles: Institut colonial international, 1908).
67   See *Compte-rendu, op. cit.*
68   Letter of Janssen to ABK, 10 February 1909 makes reference to ABK's effective help in preceding year. Dewar.
69   Ibid., See also, *Compte-rendu* for the meeting of 1909.
70   In Gen 140, Gen 141, Gen 142. See letter of Reay to ABK asking 'English members of the Colonial Institute' to meet on 24 June 1912. Gen 141/1/10.
71   Deakin of Australia, especially, felt this way.
72   Lucas's memorandum on 'The Self-Governing Dominions and Coloured Immigration' was designed as the first of a series of publications in an Imperial Conference Secretariat Series. CO 532/9, 34812; published as CO 886/1, No 1. In the draft, Lucas acknowledged the 'great help' he received from ABK. Lucas went on a tour to Australia in 1909, in part, to help convey the reality of the secretariat.
73   CAB 18/12A,B. 1909, Cd 4475, Cd 4611, Cd 4948.
74   ABK kept a copy of the note summarising his illnesses. Gen 144/3/3.
75   From following the CO papers that went through the Dominions Department, I was clear about when ABK left and when he returned! On 18 December 1909, Just minuted to ABK: 'Now that you have returned, would you kindly draft ...' CO 532/16, 13700.
76   Both papers are in CO 532/23, 13535.
77   The Conference started on 18 May 1910. ABK shared secretarial duties with T W Phillips from the Board of Trade. CO 532/23, 19432. See ABK's minute reporting on the discussion he and Just had in seeking 'to secure for the self-governing Dominions the right of adherence to the Berlin Convention subject to a reservation excluding from the benefits of copyright all those who are not natives of, or in good faith residents in, Union countries.' CO 532/28, 13584. On 1 June 1910, ABK provided a summary of the work accomplished and the ways in which interests of the CO had been dealt with. CO 532/22, 15987.
78   The results were published in 1910, Cd 5272. See also materials in CO 532/33, 12936 on the model bill.
79   See Chapter 14 in Brebner, *op. cit.*, These matters are discussed, as well, in Chapter 30 in the Canadian volume in Rose, *op. cit.*, VIII. A good summary of the decision in the North Atlantic Fisheries Arbitration is in *Annual Register, 1910*, pp 458–9.
80   1909, Cd 4528, Cd 4558; 1910, Cd 5396; 1911, Cd 5803. There are extensive files on all this in CO. See ABK's work, for example, on CO 42/926, 8 08/09; CO 42/929, 1186, 7804; CO 42/934, 19488; CO 42/943, 38029; CO 194/278, 9443, 20021, 20482, 26851; CO 194/279, 20827; CO 194/278, 10936; CO 194/279, 8859.
81   'Copy of Berr's Letter to Sir F Hopwood, 23rd March, 1909,' likely made by MSK. Gen 144/3/9. Hopwood's response. Gen 144/3/8.
82   C T Davis went instead. See report of proceedings, 1910, Cd 5396. ABK knew about the details of the arbitration, not only from his colleagues in CO but also from discussions he had with Aylesworth. ABK wrote lengthy minutes on the decision, 18 and 21 September 1910, CO 194/281, 28811.

83   For documents made public, see 1911, Cd 5513, Cd 5513, Cd 5741, Cd 5745, Cd 5746.
84   CO 886/3, No 19 contains much of the correspondence.
85   1911, Cd 5745.
86   Ibid., also, CAB 18/13A.
87   Burton.
88   1911, Cd 5745.
89   CAB 18/13B, p 23.
90   All the premiers had had domestic issues and been through parliamentary crises: Fisher, Australia; Ward, New Zealand; Botha, South Africa; Morris, Newfoundland.
91   Gen 141/3/54.
92   See MSK's letter to ABK about taking the Lectureship in Ancient History; see above, Chapter 6, n 26.
93   Burton.
94   Burton.
95   Register of Births, Marriages, Deaths, Scotland. Dunbar.
96   Death notice, *Haddington Courier* (4 August 1911), 2c; *The Scotsman* (31 July 1911); *Dunfermline Journal* (8 August 1911), 4d, copy Dewar.
97   Scottish Record Office, Record of Inventories and Wills, SC 70. MSK's will was dated 28 July 1897 naming Jean as Executrix; she left a personal estate of £125. 11s. 8d.
98   Burton.
99   This reflects the impression that both Mrs Burton and Professor Dewar have of the sequence. They heard it from their mother.
100 There were cousins who settled in Australia. Apparently, when they visited in Scotland, ABK was attracted to one of them. Again, this rests upon recollections within the family.
101 Register of Births, Deaths, Marriages, Scotland. Bathgate. There was a notice, as well, in *The Scotsman*, 3 June 1912, 12h; also Dewar.
102 There seems to be nothing, although Mrs Burton can recall seeing a picture of her.
103 See Chapter 8 below, p 153, n 2.
104 'For help in compilation of the Indexes I am indebted to my wife.' ABK in Preface, *The Veda of the Black Yajus School: Tāittirīya Samhitā* (Cambridge, Massachusetts: Harvard University Press, 1914); 'I desire to repeat the thanks tendered in the last edition to my late wife for the assistance given in its preparation as in all my work ...' ABK in Preface, *Constitutional Law of England* 6th edition, E W Ridges (London: Stevens and Sons, 1937).
105 See below, Chapter 11, pp 243–5.
106 *University of Edinburgh Calendar, 1908–1909*, p 9.
107 See Bibliography, JRAS.
108 JRAS, 1909, 601.
109 JRAS, 1910, 892.
110 Ibid. The entire review runs 892–9.
111 Gen 152/6/84.
112 See above, Chapter 6, on *The Theory of State Succession*, pp 119–20.
113 Burton.
114 *Haddingtonshire Courier* (2 June 1911), 3d, recited ABK's various achievements.
115 Bibliography, JCL.
116 OUP, LB 3026. ABK to Chapman; Lucas to Chapman.

CHAPTER 8 pp 153 to 168

1   See his letter to Lucas, above, pp 127–8.
2   Gen 142/2/99.
3   See long, cordial letter from Anderson to ABK written probably in 1904 or 1905 from Singapore: 'There is somewhere on my table if I could only find it an unfinished letter to you begun a long time ago. Perchance it will be found when my papers are examined after my decease or my translation whichever happens first. ... I shall come back in a year's time and find all the boys I knew Seniors or Principals and much too big swells to condescend except in the patronizing & pitying fashion on a poor Colonial Governor who they are accustomed to order about in the most ruthless fashion. ... My kind regards to all of you and to the whole teaparty.' Gen 141/1/3.
4   Anderson to ABK, 7 May 1905, conveying distress that ABK had left Crown Agents especially since he had urged ABK to make the change. Gen 144/3/24.
5   Young to ABK, 23 January 1913. Gen 142/1/81.
6   *Colonial Office List, 1914*, p xvi.
7   See above, Chapter 3, p 45.
8   See above, Chapter 3, p 43.
9   CO 878/12, 62a; CO 878/12, 57.
10   Gen 142/1/16.
11   Gen 878/12/77.
12   CO 878/12, 73.
13   CO 532/71, 18544.
14   Ibid.
15   CO 532/63, 9191. 1914, Cd 7507.
16   Gen 142/2/4.
17   Gen 142/4/86, 87.
18   CO 532/3, 37699.
19   Gen 142/1/60.
20   Gen 142/2/64, 65.
21   Gen 142/2/62.
22   CO 428/117, 10414.
23   CO 878/12, 87.
24   Gen 142/4/42.
25   See minutes in CO 42, CO 194, CO 209, CO 418, CO 532.
26   ABK to Liverpool, nd [28] February 1913. Gen 142/1/83.
27   ABK memorandum, 1913. Gen 142/1/24. See also, CO 532/55, 4520.
28   See above, Chapter 7, pp 131, 133.
29   ABK to Watson, nd April 1913, suggesting that Newfoundland might subscribe to the extent of £5. 5s. 0d. Gen 142/1/28.
30   Lugard and ABK exchanges, June, July 1914. Gen 142/3/3, 4; Gen 142/4/88.
31   ABK to Janssen, 3 January 1913. Gen 142/1/109. ABK to Reay, 6 January 1913. Gen 142/1/108. ABK to Janssen, 16 January 1913: 'I desire to explain that my reason for resigning my membership was not that I was unwilling to do whatever was possible to provide the information necessarily required from time to time for the Institute, but because I had reason to believe that it would conduce more effectively to obtaining that information if it were applied for officially and dealt with in the ordinary official course. ...'; and he went on to explain that he had checked further with his superiors in the CO and found that it would be well for him to remain a member. Gen 142/1/102. He participated

in the sessions in London in May 1913; see note of appreciation from Jerningham to ABK, 9 May 1913. Gen 142/1/41.

32   Ridgway F Shinn, Jr, *Guide to Arthur Berriedale Keith, Papers and Correspondence, 1896–1941*, see listing of ABK's correspondents, pp 6–18.

33   Galway to ABK, Gen 142/2/1.

34   ABK to Stanley. Gen 142/2/5, 14, 19. Stanley to ABK. Gen 142/2/9; Gen 142/3/55.

35   ABK to Munro-Ferguson. Gen 142/3/69, 70. See CO 418/122, 4580, 4588. Munro-Ferguson to ABK. Gen 142/3/26, 69, 107, 110, 115, 116, 117, 121. In a note of 22 February 1914, Munro-Ferguson wrote: 'How you must hate being Governors' accoucher and undertaker.' Gen 142/3/115.

36   Buxton to ABK. Gen 142/4/73, 81, 83.

37   'I should be glad if you would put down for me what constitutional books you think it would be useful to take out with me.' Buxton to ABK, 6 July 1914. Gen 142/4/81.

38   CO 532/46, 24259; CO 532/51, 5663; CO 418/110, 14627; CO 532/52, 16432; CO 42/977, 18300; CO 418/117, 20159; CO 532/75, 12823.

39   Richard A Cosgrove, *The Rule of Law: Albert Venn Dicey, Victorian Jurist* (Chapel Hill, North Carolina: University of North Carolina Press, 1980), p 232.

40   See above, pp 137–8.

41   D H E Butler and J Freeman, *British Political Facts, 1900–1968* (London: Macmillan, 1969).

42   Cosgrove, *op. cit.*, p 233.

43   Ibid., p 232.

44   Ibid.

45   Dicey to ABK, 15 December 1911. Gen 141/4/32.

46   Dicey to ABK, 1 January 1912. Gen 141/1/74.

47   ABK to Dicey, 20 March 1912. Gen 141/1/34.

48   ABK to Dicey, 2 July 1912. Gen 141/5/129.

49   Cosgrove, *op. cit.*, p 247 for Dicey's analysis.

50   Dicey to ABK, 17 October 1912. Gen 141/5/72.

51   Cosgrove, *op. cit.*, p 247.

52   See discussion on ABK's views on Ireland, see below pp 169, 212–13.

53   The phrase was used by Eric Strauss as the title of a useful book, *Irish Nationalism and British Democracy* (New York: Columbia University Press, 1951).

54   See Bibliography.

55   ABK to Chapman, OUP, LB 3026.

56   *Responsible Government in the Dominions* (Oxford: Clarendon Press, 1912), 3 vols. Seventeen pages, double column, fine print are given to listing of statutes; thirty-two pages to listing of cases. ABK dedicated it: 'In Matris Memoriam'.

57   *The Morning Post* (3 June 1912), 2.

58   *The Fortnightly Review* (1 September 1912), 393–4.

59   Ibid., p 396.

60   *The Nation* (22 June 1912), 444; *The Glasgow Herald* (11 April 1912), 10c.

61   *The Morning Post, op. cit.*,

62   Comments of reviewer in *Journal of the Royal African Society* (1913–1914), 450–1.

63   A A Macdonell, ed, and ABK, *Vedic Index of Names and Subjects* (London: John Murray, 1912), comment in Preface, vi.

64   Ibid.

65   Reviewer in *The Saturday Westminster Gazette* (14 December 1912), p 10.

66   Comment of Professor John Brough, Cambridge University, to me.

67   See Bibliography.
68   See comments above, pp 149–51.
69   See above, p 151.
70   Lanman to ABK. Gen 152/3/159, 162, 164, 165, 166.
71   Comment of Professor Brough to me.
72   JRAS, 1916, 617–30.
73   Ibid.
74   See above, p 149.
75   Macdonell to ABK, 9 March 1913. Gen 152/6/71.
76   Eggeling to ABK, 4 October 1913. Gen 142/2/52.
77   *University of Edinburgh Calendar, 1913.*
78   ABK to Eggeling, 22 March 1914. Gen 152/6/57.
79   Ibid.
80   Resolution, 5 November 1914. University of Edinburgh. Senatus Academicus, Printed Minutes, Vol 1, pp 167–8. Macdonell expressed regret at Eggeling's situation: 'He, I was surprised to see by the papers, is in a concentration camp at present and is said to be engaged in teaching his fellow prisoners. ... There cannot be many demands to speak of for Sanskrit, and to teach German would be carrying coals to Newcastle.' Macdonell to ABK, 26 November 1914. Gen 145/2/244.
81   Letter from Mackinnon Wood, Secretary of State, Scotland, to Principal. Ibid., p 166.
82   A search of files in the Scottish Record Office yielded nothing on ABK's appointment. A report of 1925 listed ABK as being entitled to use the title, Regius Professor. ED 26/123/1925. On ABK's Commission, HH 29, Scotch Warrant Book, January 1914 to February 1922, #8, p 46.
83   n 81, above.
84   *The Glasgow Herald* (24 October 1914), 5f; *The Times* (24 October 1914), 9d; *The Scotsman* (24 October 1914).
85   Ibid.
86   ABK to Harcourt, 31 October 1914. CO 323/648, 42583. For his induction, Senatus Academicus, *op. cit.*, pp 166–7.
87   Anderson to ABK, 7 November 1914. CO 323/648, 42583.
88   Lanman to ABK, 10 November 1914. Gen 152/3/163.
89   Macdonell to ABK, 26 November 1914. See n 80 above.
90   Just to ABK, 30 December 1914. Gen 142/4/7.
91   ABK to CO, 19 November 1914. CO 323/648, 45732.
92   The Regius Chair of Sanskrit and Comparative Philology carried a salary of £600 when ABK went in 1914. He did improve his financial situation but still felt insufficiently rewarded.

CHAPTER 9 pp 169 to 191

1   A J P Taylor, *English History, 1914–1945* (Oxford: Clarendon Press, 1976), Chapter 1.
2   Ibid., pp 56–8.
3   Ibid., p 73.
4   Ibid., Chapters 3, 4.
5   Ibid., Chapter 4.
6   Margot Asquith to ABK, 12 August 1918. Gen 144/7/8.

7 See below, 'Scottish Liberal Federation', pp 185–7, 201–4.
8 Taylor, *op. cit.*, pp 132–8.
9 Post Office, *Edinburgh and Leith Directory.*
10 *University of Edinburgh Calendar, 1915.*
11 Some examination papers and other notes remain. Gen 152/1/254, 259; Gen 144/6/177, 178. Burton.
12 Recollections of Professor John Brough, Cambridge University.
13 ABK to Grierson, 2 May 1928: ABK troubled to hear about arrangements for an Assistant in Greek to teach Comparative Philology. Gen 144/6/35; the dispute went on. Gen 144/6/30.
14 This was also part of his negotiations when he applied for the post of Lecturer in Ancient History; see above, Chapter 6, pp 114–15.
15 *University of Edinburgh Calendar, 1915.*
16 Gen 144/6/145 where motion is restated. See also Senatus Academicus, Printed Minutes, 1915.
17 ABK to Smith, 29 November 1924 declining to attend a dinner for Lodge. Gen 144/6/142.
18 ABK to Jehu, 16 February 1917. Gen 143/4/55.
19 ABK to Brown, 30 May 1917. Gen 150/1/5.
20 University of Edinburgh, Senatus Academicus, Printed Minutes, Vol 1, pp 505–6.
21 Ibid.
22 Ibid., p 558.
23 Ibid.
24 Ibid., p 505.
25 Ibid., p 531.
26 ABK to Stubbs, 15 April 1917. Gen 143/4/67.
27 See Chapter 8 above, p 165.
28 ABK to Brown, 30 May 1917. Gen 150/1/5.
29 T Rajagopalachari, *The Indian Review* (February 1919), 127.
30 J Lindsay, JRAS (1923), p 479.
31 See Bibliography.
32 JRAS, 1916, p 355.
33 Ibid., 1920, pp 242–8.
34 Ibid., 1915, pp 545–6.
35 Ibid., pp 329–30.
36 ABK's initial salvo, ibid., 1916, pp 335–50.
37 Ibid., p 336.
38 Ibid., 1917, p 140.
39 Ibid., 1916, p 821.
40 Ibid., p 143.
41 Ibid., p 154.
42 Ibid., 1916, pp 143–6.
43 Ibid., p 561.
44 See above, n 18.
45 Dicey to ABK, 25 March 1915. Gen 144/2/36.
46 ABK to Dicey, 27 March 1915. Gen 144/2/37.
47 ABK to Dicey, 15 May 1915. Gen 144/2/41.
48 *Imperial Unity and the Dominions* (Oxford: Clarendon Press, 1916), dedication page.
49 ABK to Stanley, 1 August 1916: 'I am glad to have your letter of 12th June, as I am much interested in the matters on which you express your views and

I feel that you have exceptional advances [sic; likely, advantages] on forming an opinion on the questions at issue. One seldom meets any person with sufficient information to be able to form a correct judgment of the feeling of the Dominions, while you unlike many of your colleagues are not merely interested in all these matters, but have the necessary political experience.' Gen 143/4/13.

50   ABK to Stanley, 31 May 1916. Gen 143/4/6.
51   Munro-Ferguson to ABK, 24 July 1916. Gen 143/4/16.
52   ABK to Stanley, 19 November 1917. Gen 143/4/95.
53   All this is clearly discussed in J E Kendle, *The Round Table Movement and Imperial Union* (Toronto: Toronto University Press, 1975). Curtis was one of the 'kindergarten' and also played a role in negotiations creating the Irish Free State.
54   *Imperial Unity and the Dominions, op. cit.*, Part II, pp 418–588.
55   For views in Western Australia, ibid., pp 30–2.
56   Lecture, 27 November 1916, 'The Dominions and the Treaty Power', 28 November 1916, *The Scotsman* (28 November 1916), 6d; final session, 4 December 1916, ibid., (5 December 1916), 8c.
57   ABK to Dicey, Gen 143/4/27.
58   *Times Literary Supplement* (19 December 1918), 634c.
59   See Bibliography.
60   See below, 'India Office Study', pp 187–90.
61   Lal to ABK, 18 June 1917. Gen 143/4/70.
62   ABK believed in a greater role for Indians. ABK to Dicey, 13 August 1917: 'The Imperial Conference of 1911 was therefore held without any representative of India. The Secretary of State for India indeed spoke, but he acted in his capacity as a member of the imperial government, not as a spokesman of India. This position was clearly anomalous and wrong, and became impossible when the war showed the importance of India.' Gen 143/4/79.
63   See above, Chapter 8, pp 157–9.
64   ABK to Dicey, 30 July 1917. Gen 143/4/75.
65   ABK to Dicey, 10 August 1917. Gen 143/4/77.
66   Ibid.
67   ABK to Dicey, 12 August 1917. Gen 143/4/80.
68   Taylor, *op. cit.*, pp 154–61.
69   Ibid., p 133.
70   Structure for booklets, FO 373/5.
71   See exchanges in 1917: Prothero to ABK, 10 November 1917. Gen 145/2/218; ABK to Prothero, 13 November 1917. Gen 145/2/215; ABK to Prothero, 14 November 1917. Gen 145/2/216; Prothero to ABK, 20 November 1917. Gen 145/2/212.
72   *Journal of the African Society* (July 1918), 249–61. Prothero to ABK, 20 September 1918. Gen 145/2/196; 'I have sent the three copies of your paper on the Berlin Act to Sir Maurice Hankey, Secretary of the War Cabinet. Can you send me three more copies for certain members of the Foreign Office, to whom I think they might be useful?' 5 October 1918. Gen 145/2/195; 'Your paper about the review of the Berlin Act has apparently attracted some attention, and I shall be glad if you can send me six copies, to be given to the members of the War Cabinet.' 15 November 1918. Gen 145/2/193.
73   Gen 145/2/165. ABK to Prothero, 20 September 1919. Gen 145/2/170. Prothero to ABK, 14 October 1919.
74   *Journal of the African Society* (1919–1920), pp 74–5. See review in *Times Literary Supplement* (10 July 1919), p 371. G B Hurst reviewed it, *English Historical Review* (April 1920), pp 290–2.

75 Taylor, *op. cit.*, pp 73–5.

76 Gen 144/4/178, 179.

77 Ibid.

78 Ibid., All see letter, Murray to ABK, 29 September 1918. Gen 144/4/182.

79 Gen 144/4/178.

80 Ibid., p 6.

81 ABK to Murray, 28 October 1918. Gen 144/4/172.

82 Taylor, *op. cit.*, pp 125–32.

83 Margot Asquith to ABK, 24 December 1918. Gen 144/4/127.

84 For general nature of the Act, see Taylor, *op. cit.*, Note C, p 115. For specific changes on Scottish Universities, see *University of Edinburgh Calendar, 1919.*

85 The two MPs from Scottish Universities were W W Cheyne and Sir Henry Craik, both Unionist.

86 See report of Cowan's candidacy, supported by the Glasgow Local Association of Education Institute of Scotland, *The Scotsman* (9 November 1918), 6e.

87 Report of meeting, 6 December 1918, ibid. (7 December 1918), 8e.

88 The polling days were 20, 21, 23, 24 December 1918 as announced at a meeting in Scottish Universities Candidacy Session, 3 December 1918. Results came right after Christmas. See Cowan to ABK, 29 December 1918: 'I appreciate all you have done in support of my candidature—your kindly, & encouraging letter to begin with, your seconding of my nomination, your taking the chair at the Edinburgh meeting, & your sparkling introduction thereat. All these things were good assets & meant far to ensure the result.' Gen 144/4/136.

89 *Who Was Who, 1921–1930.*

90 On approaches to ABK, see ABK to Webster, 22 November 1918. Gen 144/4/135; Black to ABK, 20 December 1918. Gen 144/4/122; ABK to Black, 22 December 1918. Gen 144/4/123.

91 HC, *Parl Deb*, 5th ser, 97, 1695–6. ABK included it, *Speeches and Documents on Indian Policy, 1750–1921* (London: Oxford University Press, 1922), II, p 133

92 Ibid., pp 155–206. 1918, Cd 9109.

93 Taylor, *op. cit.*, pp 152–3.

94 Montagu to ABK, 29 November 1918. Gen 145/2/183.

95 Besides Crewe, the other members were: His Highness the Aga Khan, Viscount Esher, B N Basu, Sir J B Brunyate, Lieut-Col Godfrey Collins, Harry Gosling, Evelyn Murray; Lord Inchcape was named but did not serve and was replaced by W G A Ormsby-Gore.

96 ABK kept his copy, Gen 145/1/181. See India Office, L/P&J/9/1 File 36/1918 for drafting of terms of reference.

97 Ibid., Point 5.

98 Minutes of Evidence, Committee on India Office Organisation, 1919. India Office Whitehall.

99 Testimony in Minutes of Evidence conveys this impression. Also, see cautious letter, Brown to ABK, 17 June 1919. Gen 145/2/177.

100 ABK to Crewe, 8 May 1919. Gen 145/1/179; ABK to Montagu, 15 May 1919. Gen 145/2/180.

101 1919, Cmd 1909.

102 ABK's dissent, ibid., pp 36–60.

103 *Speeches and Documents on Indian Policy, 1750–1921, op. cit.*, pp 281 ff. It is interesting that, in selecting items from debates on the Bill, ABK included Lord Carmichael's speech in which Carmichael quoted ABK!

CHAPTER 10 pp 192 to 218

1   See Bibliography.
2   A J P Taylor, *England 1914–1945* (Oxford: Clarendon Press, 1976), Chapters 5–7.
3   Ibid., Chapter 6.
4   I developed this theme in *The Right of Secession in the Development of the British Commonwealth of Nations* (Ann Arbor, Michigan: University Microfilms, 1958).
5   I must express my deep appreciation to Mr and Mrs Harry Bull who purchased the house in the spring of 1945, the first owners from ABK himself. They have been most gracious in permitting me to go through the house several times and, as well, to take photographs.
6   See his note to Brown, pp 188–9.
7   Crawfurd Road is really a turning off of Craigmillar Park which going north leads to North Bridge, immediately behind Waverley Station. ABK to King, 23 November 1926: 'This house is only 10 minutes by taxi from the Waverley.' King Papers, MG 263, J 3, Box 92.
8   John Gifford *et al.*, *Edinburgh* (Harmondsworth: Penguin Books, 1984), pp 634–44 describe the district of Newington and indicate that the area of Craigmillar Park was laid out in 1877, p 633.
9   As used, that seems to have been the chief purpose. Mrs Bull commented that when they bought the house they concluded that ABK wasn't much of a gardener!
10 Gen 144/8/1.
11 Ibid., Some of the slips are part of the Keith Collection.
12 This was the description suggested to me by Professor Brough of Cambridge University.
13 P P S Sastri, 'Arthur Berriedale Keith', *Eminent Orientalists: Indian, European, American* (Madras: Nateson, nd [1922]), p 321.
14 University of Edinburgh. General Council, Printed Minutes. Minutes for 26 October 1923. ABK kept a copy of the resolution, Gen 144/6/161.
15 Nine in favour, twenty-one against. Minutes, *op. cit.*
16 ABK to [Smith], 29 November 1924. Gen 144/6/142.
17 *University of Edinburgh Calendar* for all the years indicates his classes.
18 ABK to W Wilson or A F Giles, 4 March 1924. Gen 144/6/155.
19 Ibid.
20 Ibid.
21 J Lindsay, JRAS, 1923, p 480.
22 *Times Literary Supplement* (1 September 1921), 567a.
23 Sisam to Chapman, 22 September 1925. OUP, 815411.
24 R L Turner on *Sanskrit Drama*: 'The title well expresses in epitome the contents of this last notable book from the hand of Professor Keith,' JRAS, 1925, 173–7. And numerous other reviews!
25 Professor Brough kindly indicated his judgement about the value of ABK's works, by indicating which had stood the test of time and continued of importance and which had become dated.
26 Lowell to ABK, 8 March 1926. Gen 144/6/126.
27 Ibid.
28 ABK to Ewing, 20 March 1926. Gen 144/6/125.
29 ABK to Lowell, 23 March 1926. Gen 144/6/124.
30 Lowell to ABK, 27 April 1926. Gen 144/6/121.
31 Lowell to ABK, 13 April 1927. Gen 144/6/91.

32   ABK to Lowell, 28 April 1927. Gen 144/6/92.
33   ABK to Ewing, 14 October 1926. Gen 144/6/115.
34   ABK to Farnell, 5 November 1926. Gen 144/6/104. Farnell to ABK, 8 November 1926. Gen 144/6/100.
35   ABK, Testimonial for F W Thomas for the Boden Professorship at Oxford, 17 December 1926. Gen 144/6/98.
36   Thomas to ABK, 19 December 1926. Gen 144/6/96. After he was elected, Thomas to ABK, 13 February 1927. Gen 144/6/94.
37   ABK to Ewing, 27 October 1926. Gen 144/6/84.
38   Ibid.
39   Williams to ABK, 29 October 1926, Gen 144/6/80; Whittaker to ABK, 21 December 1926. Gen 144/6/72. Ewing to ABK, 28 December 1926; 6 January 1927, DC 4.101–3.
40   Fleming to ABK, 25 March 1927. Gen 144/6/53; included 'Memorandum Meeting of the Principal and Professor Kemp Smith with Professor Berriedale Keith, Feb 25th, 1927' summarising the considerations and conditions. Gen 144/6/59; Senatus Academicus, Minutes of 24 March 1927, where approval is given. Copy of Minutes, Gen 144/6/47.
41   ABK to Hannay, 26 March 1927. Gen 144/6/51.
42   See above, Chapter 9, pp 186–7.
43   *The Glasgow Herald* (4 July 1922), p 9.
44   Asquith to ABK, 18 October 1920. Gen 145/2/130.
45   See above, Chapter 9, n 90.
46   ABK to Black, 28 July 1922. Gen 144/4/72.
47   ABK to Black, 29 August 1922 from Oban. Gen 144/4/65.
48   ABK to Black, 16 September 1922. Gen 144/4/60.
49   Black to ABK, 23 September 1922. Gen 144/4/51.
50   ABK to Asquith, 23 September 1922. Gen 144/4/52.
51   Asquith to ABK, 25 September 1922. Gen 144/4/48. See also the enclosure, repeating the arrangements. Gen 144/4/45.
52   ABK to Webster, 26 September 1922. Gen 144/1/49.
53   ABK to Webster, 17 October 1922. On reverse of Gen 144/4/33.
54   ABK to Webster, 3 November 1922. Gen 144/4/23.
55   ABK to Wood, 15 November 1923. Gen 144/4/11.
56   Webster to ABK, 2 April 1924. Gen 144/4/1.
57   Beeton to ABK, 14 May 1920. Gen 143/5/54.
58   With Munro-Ferguson, Stanley, Strickland, discussed above, Chapter 9, pp 179–80.
59   Brisbane Tramways Purchase Act, 1920.
60   ABK set all this out in letters to *The Times* (27 May 1920, 2 June 1920, 9 June 1920). See file, CO 418/193, 18986.
61   Ibid.
62   Ibid.
63   Petition, Gen 143/5/27.
64   Beeton to ABK, cited.
65   Gen 143/5/42. Note on the meeting with Milner, Gen 143/5/50. File on Theodore, CO 418/209, 31237.
66   See Robinson to ABK, 16 May 1920. Gen 145/5/55.
67   Petition, cited.
68   ABK to Beeton, [8?] July 1920. Gen 143/5/9.
69   ABK to Stanley, 25 June 1920. Gen 143/5/13; Stanley to ABK, 29 June 1920. Gen 143/5/12; ABK to Stanley, 30 June 1920. Gen 143/5/11.

70   *The Times* (9 June 1920), 12c.
71   ABK to Dicey, 30 September 1918. Gen 144/2/52.
72   Faculty of Advocates, Scotland. Minutes of Meeting approving Regulations based on action taken, 10 June 1921, 21 October 1921.
73   These were the Regulations, as adopted. Faculty of Advocates, Scotland. Intrants Book. ABK's petition recorded together with personal data.
74   Intrants Book. Minutes, 10 November 1921. *The Scotsman* (11 November 1921).
75   See below, Chapter 11, pp 231–4.
76   See above, p 179.
77   MS Bryce, 3, 270, 275.
78   *Times Literary Supplement* (3 February 1921), 791b.
79   Chapter 4 in Harold W V Temperley, ed *A History of the Peace Conference of Paris* (London: Henry Frowde and Hodder and Stoughton, 1924), Vol VI. Temperley to ABK, 31 March 1922: 'I have not yet assigned the British Dominions which is a very important Chapter for two reasons: one is that it is a very difficult one to write, and the other is that it is a very delicate one. ... I do not believe that the writing of this chapter would cause you much trouble, and it would certainly be a very great advantage to us.' Gen 148/8/16.
80   'Makers of the Constitution', in Hugh A Gunn, ed *Makers of the Empire*, Vol VIII in *The British Empire: A Survey* (London: Collins, 1924).
81   See Bibliography.
82   See Bibliography.
83   ABK, 'Dominion Treaty Powers', *The Times* (19 March 1923), 13e.
84   Ibid.
85   See Appendix for chronology of publication.
86   ABK, 'Imperial Relations', *The Times* (26 April 1921), 6e.
87   ABK, 'Treaty with Japan', ibid. (6 July 1921), 16g; 'The Disarmament Conference', ibid. (18 July 1921), 6c; 'Imperial Treaties', ibid. (26 April 1924), 6a; 'The Security Pact', ibid. (23 October 1925), 10d.
88   The point in letter on Canada and Lausanne, 26 April 1924.
89   ABK discussed these developments in public addresses: on the Imperial Conference, 1921, to Edinburgh University Historical Society, *The Scotsman* (13 October 1921); on India's changing role in 'India and the Empire' to the Edinburgh Indian Association, *The Scotsman* (9 February 1922); on issues for the Imperial Conference in 'Problems of the Imperial Conference, 1926' to Edinburgh University Philomathic Society, *The Scotsman* (16 October 1926). All also Dewar. It should be noted, as well, that former colleagues in the CO followed ABK's interpretations; CO 708/21, MT; CO 532/302. Hankey in February 1926, referred to ABK as 'a distinguished authority on constitutional law' in a minute, CAB 63/38, 84–5.
90   See above, pp 179, 186, 207.
91   See Chapter 9, 'India Office Study', pp 187–90.
92   *Speeches and Documents on Indian Policy, 1750–1921* (London: Oxford University Press, 1922), pp v, xxvii.
93   CO 886/1, No 1.
94   ABK, 'Indians in Kenya', *The Times* (3 August 1921), 4b.
95   Ibid. (4 May 1923), 13e.
96   Taylor, *op. cit.*, pp 154–61.
97   See above, p 158.
98   Articles of Agreement for a Treaty between Great Britain and Ireland, 6

December 1921. The basic principle was that the Irish Free State was to be analogous to Canada in its constitutional relations to Britain.

99   ABK, 'Minorities in Ireland', *The Times* (17 December 1921), 11e; 'The Irish Treaty', ibid. (10 March 1922), 8e; 'The Irish Constitution', ibid. (19 June 1922), 6c.

100 See letter cited below, p 243.

101 ABK, letter of 19 June 1922, cited. Figgis to ABK, 21 June 1922. Gen 145/2/83.

102 ABK to Figgis, 23 June 1922, the matter of appeals: 'In the case of Ireland, however, it is clear that it is not the intention—though this is not in my view effectively carried out in the Constitution—that there should be recognised the supremacy of the Imperial Parliament. What the Irish Free State demands is, I assume, that the Imperial Parliament shall renounce all power of legislation for Ireland. ... Personally I think the retention of the appeal a mistake and unworkable with the abolition of legislative supremacy, and that both sides would have been well advised to drop the appeal and substitute some agreed means of submitting to arbitration disputes on any point arising out of the interpretation of the treaty.' Gen 145/2/82.

103 Figgis to ABK, 21 September 1922: 'Will you allow me once again to make avail of your acknowledged pre-eminence in the matter of Constitutional provisions and practice respecting different parts of the Commonwealth of Nations?' Gen 145/2/77; ABK to Figgis, 23 September 1922. Gen 145/2/76.

104 Ibid.

105 See below, pp 240–3.

106 See above, n 4.

107 H Blair Neatby, *William Lyon Mackenzie King: the Lonely Years, 1924–1932* (London: Methuen, 1963).

108 All this is thoroughly developed in Philip Wigley, *Canada and the Transition to Commonwealth: British-Canadian Relations, 1917–1926* (Cambridge: Cambridge University Press, 1977).

109 MG 26 J 13, pp 162, 163.

110 Taylor, *op. cit.*, Note A, p 216; Wigley, *op. cit.*, pp 264–5

111 ABK, 'The Status of Canada: How Lord Byng's Action Challenges it', *The Times* (8 July 1926).

112 ABK to King, 30 June 1926. Gen 143/6/72.

113 ABK to King, 16 September 1926. Gen 143/6/68.

114 For example, King to ABK, 14 January 1927. Gen 143/6/65; ABK to King, 10 January 1928. Gen 145/1/81; King to ABK, 11 March 1931. Gen 145/1/47; King to ABK, 7 December 1931. Gen 145/1/37; King to ABK, 22 January 1933. Gen 145/1/18; King to ABK, 9 March 1937. Gen 145/3/56.

115 See above, n 4.

116 1926, Cmd. 2768.

117 An account of the workings of the Committee on Inter-Imperial Relations is in my article, 'Changing the King's Title, 1926: An Asterisk to "O'Higgins' Comma"', *The Irish Jurist* (1981), pp 114–40.

118 The Report was promptly printed in *The Times* (22 November 1926), 9.

119 ABK discussed this process in many places. See, for example, the brief passages in *An Introduction to British Constitutional Law* (Oxford: Clarendon Press, 1931), pp 163–72. See the accounts in K C Wheare, *The Statute of Westminster and Dominion Status* (Oxford: Clarendon Press, 1938).

120 ABK to King, 23 November 1926. King Papers, MG 26, J 3, Box 92; King to ABK, 24 November 1926. Gen 145/1/105.

121 ABK to King, 9 December 1926. Gen 143/6/66.

122 Ewing to ABK, 13 January 1927. Gen 145/1/98.
123 See above, p 201.
124 ABK to Ewing, 14 January 1927. Gen 145/1/97.
125 Ewing to ABK, 15 January 1927. Gen 145/1/96.
126 Balfour to ABK, 27 January 1927. Gen 145/1/95.
127 ABK to Chapman, 9 May 1924. OUP, LB 3026.
128 Milford to Chapman, 16 May 1924. OUP, LB 3026.
129 Chapman to ABK, 23 May 1924. OUP, LB 3026.
130 *The Nation and Athenaeum* (24 March 1928). Also Dewar.
131 *Responsible Government in the Dominions* (Oxford: Clarendon Press, 1928), Preface.

CHAPTER 11 pp 219 to 245

1 While there are many accounts to follow, I used two: A J P Taylor, *English History, 1914–1945* (Oxford: Clarendon Press, 1976); Sally Jean Marks, *The Illusion of Peace: International Relations in Europe, 1918–1933* (London: Macmillan, 1976).
2 The title of the book by Sidney and Beatrice Webb after they 'discovered' the new world of the Soviet Union; they later gained a more sober perspective on it. See Taylor's comments, *op. cit.*, p 348.
3 Lloyd George's appraisal, ibid., 54, n 1.
4 Ibid., pp 234–5. Chamberlain had urged that approach at the Colonial Conference, 1902.
5 JRAS, 1933, pp 949–50.
6 Ibid., 1932, pp 697–700.
7 Ibid.
8 Ibid., 1933, pp 486–91.
9 Ibid., 1934, pp 414–15.
10 Ibid., 1933, pp 813–20.
11 Ibid.
12 Ibid.
13 ABK review, B Churn, *A History of Pali Literature* in *Annals of Bhandarkar Oriental Research Institute* (XV, Parts I–II, 1934), pp 124–6.
14 See Keith. Gen 152.
15 'Daṇḍin and Bhāmaha', *Indian Studies in Honor of Charles Rockwell Lanman* (Cambridge, Massachusetts: Harvard University Press, 1929), pp 167–85.
16 'The Aryans and the Indus Valley Civilization', *Bharatiyanusilangranth, Festschrift for G. H. Ojha* (Allahabad: 1933).
17 'The Grouping of the Indo-European Dialects', *Commemorative Essays Presented to Sir George Abraham Grierson* (Lahore: Linguistic Society of India, 1933).
18 'The Home of the Indo-Europeans', *Oriental Studies in Honour of Cursetji Erachji Parry* (London: Oxford University Press, 1933), pp 189–99.
19 'The Etymology of Guṇa', *Commemorative Essays Presented to K. B. Pathak* (Poona: Bhandarkar Oriental Research Institute, 1934), pp 311–14.
20 ABK to Molson, 19 September 1931. Gen 146/1/38. See lengthy quotation from letter below. Also, see above pp 187–91 on ABK and India Office study.
21 Molson to ABK, 29 October 1930. Gen 146/1/86.
22 For exchanges, see Gen 146/1/63–86.

23 Gen 146/1/83, 108, 115, 117, 125, 189.
24 See ABK draft opinion, 2 July 1931. Gen 146/1/61; notes of Confer-
    ence, 4 September 1931. Gen 146/1/118; opinion, 19 September 1931. Gen
    146/1/137.
25 ABK opinion, 5 November 1931. Gen 146/1/17,h.
26 ABK, 'Indian Citizenship', 5 September 1931. Gen 146/1/48,a.
27 *A Digest of the Laws of England with Reference to the Conflict of Laws* (London:
    Stevens and Sons, 1932), 5th ed, pp 145, 149, 896–905.
28 W J Keith to ABK, 13 October 1931. Gen 146/1/95, 96; 'I enjoyed our talk and
    meeting you and Betty again,' 26 October 1931. Gen 146/1/94; 28 October
    1931. Gen 146/1/93; 4 November 1931. Gen 146/1/92; 6 November 1931,
    Gen 146/1/91. Apparently, Will came in on other occasions to join ABK,
    according to Mrs Burton.
29 ABK to Reading, 29 March 1933. Gen 146/1/170; Reading to ABK, 4 April
    1933; Gen 146/1/166; ABK to Reading, 27 June 1933. Gen 146/1/136;
    Reading to ABK, 7 July 1933. Gen 146/1/131; ABK to Cripps, 28 March 1933.
    Gen 146/1/168; Cripps to ABK, 29 March 1933. Gen 146/1/167; Rankeillour
    to ABK, 30 May 1933. Gen 146/1/155; ABK to Rankeillour, 2 June 1933. Gen
    146/1/150; Rankeillour to ABK, 8 June 1933. Gen 146/1/147; ABK to Samuel,
    29 March 1933. Gen 146/1/169; Samuel to ABK, 3 April 1933. Gen 143/8/14.
30 ABK to Molson, 19 September 1931. Gen 146/1/38.
31 Taylor, *op. cit.*, pp 277–8.
32 ABK to Colvin, 31 May 1933. Gen 146/1/153.
33 Sisam to Brierly, 11 March 1930. OUP, 6559.
34 ABK to Chapman, 31 March 1930. Ibid.
35 Sisam to Brierly, 6 June 1930. Ibid.
36 *The Solicitors' Journal* (11 June 1932), pp 412–13.
37 ABK to Edwards, 2 December 1928. Gen 143/9/84.
38 Ibid.
39 *The Constitutional Law of the British Dominions* (London: Macmillan, 1933).
40 Abrahams to ABK, 2 November 1932. Gen 149/4/77,
41 Decision of 24 November 1930, *Law Reports, Probate, Divorce and Admiralty
    Division, 1931*, pp 29–50.
42 See n 40 above.
43 Gen 149/4/109.
44 Gen 149/4/97.
45 Decision by Lord Fleming, Court of Session, Edinburgh, granting divorce to Lord
    Inverclyde, 22 December 1933. A full account of the proceedings, 'Judgment
    Against June', *The Scotsman* (23 December 1933), 14.
46 Gen 149/4/113,a.
47 Abrahams to ABK, 18 November 1932. Gen 149/4/67.
48 ABK to Abrahams, 24 January 1933. Gen 149/4/33.
49 ABK's draft. Gen 149/4/62.
50 See n 48. Also, ABK to Abrahams, 25 January 1933. Gen 149/4/31; Abrahams
    to ABK, 26 January 1933. Gen 149/4/29,c.
51 ABK to Abrahams, 27 January 1933. Gen 149/4/, 27, 28.
52 ABK to Campbell, 9 February 1933. Gen 149/4/14; ABK to Beaverbrook, 9
    February 1933. Gen 149/4/1; ABK to Campbell, 11 February 1933. Gen
    149/4/13; ABK to Beaverbrook, 11 February 1933. Gen 149/4/12.
53 Beaverbrook to ABK, 15 February 1933. Gen 149/4/6; 16 February 1933.
    Gen 149/4/5.
54 Decision by Lord Fleming, Court of Session, Edinburgh, 20 July 1933. *The Scots*

Law Times, Reports, 1934, p 45. The decision was noted in *The Times* (21 July 1933), 4e.

55   30 May 1934. Reported in ibid. (31 May 1934), 4c.
56   See above, Chapter 10, n 116.
57   The Union of South Africa, in 1928.
58   ABK traced this in his books after 1932. He collected the documents in *Speeches and Documents on the British Dominions, 1918–1931: From Self-Government to National Sovereignty* (London: Oxford University Press, 1932). K C Wheare, *The Statute of Westminster and Dominion Status* (Oxford: Clarendon Press, 1938).
59   See Bibliography, JCL. For letters, see the three volumes ABK published, Bibliography.
60   *Dominion Autonomy in Practice* (London: Oxford University Press, 1929), Preface.
61   *The Sovereignty of the British Dominions* (London: Macmillan, 1929), Parts III, IV.
62   Ibid., p 386, and elsewhere.
63   *The Times* (5 November 1929), 21a.
64   A consistent theme. See his letter to Figgis, 23 June 1922. Gen 145/2/82. Also, his views in the Queensland Case, above pp 204–8.
65   ABK to Chapman, 11 October 1929. OUP, 6505.
66   Chapman to Clark, 4 November 1929. Ibid.
67   Clark to Chapman, 8 November 1929. Ibid.
68   ABK to Chapman, 11 November 1929. Ibid.
69   *The Times* (5 December 1930), 20c.
70   See above, Chapters 4, 6, 7.
71   *The Times, loc. cit.*
72   King to ABK, 11 March 1931. King Papers. MG 26, J 3, Box 92.
73   *United Empire* (Volume 22, 1931).
74   K C Wheare and F W Thomas, 'Arthur Berriedale Keith', *Dictionary of National Biography, 1941–1950*, p 445.
75   ABK to Milford, 27 November 1931. OUP, 821294.
76   See note of Sandra Soderberg, Greenwood Press, 10 September 1975, in regard to reprint rights: 'I looked through countless Keith volumes. He must have written a book a year since he was born and sometimes two!' OUP, 821294.
77   'Constitutional Development of the British Empire in regard to the Dominions and India from 1887 to 1933', introductory chapter in G E H Palmer, *Consultation and Cooperation in the British Commonwealth* (London; Royal Institute for International Affairs, 1934).
78   See, for example, letters in *The Scotsman*: 'The Government and Russia', (13 July 1929); 'The Russian Negotiations', (3 October 1929); 'The Proposed Treaty with Egypt', (7 August 1929); 'The Egyptian Situation', (17 July 1930); 'The Palestine Mandate', (24 October 1930); 'Persia and the Oil Concession', (6, 9, 14, 20, 27, 31 December 1932); in *The Times*, 'Germans in South-west Africa', (31 May 1934), 'South-west Africa and the Mandate', (13 June 1934).
79   Ibid. (6 June 1934), 10c.
80   See his reputation in the CO; Lambert's phrase in the epitaph: 'Friend of the Blacks', Chapter 5, p 109.
81   South Africa Act, 1909, 9 Edw VII, c9, s151.
82   See above, Chapter 5, pp 103–4.
83   Harris to ABK, 3 July 1934. Gen 148/1/17. See also, Harris to ABK, inviting him to join group 11 June 1934. Gen 148/1/27; Harris to ABK, on using ABK's

letter in *The Morning Post* in draft Memorandum, Gen 148/1/21; Cripps to ABK, 9 July 1934, expressing thanks for materials that ABK sent him: 'I will try and see that this point of view is put during the course of the Debate on the 2nd Reading.' Gen 148/1/36.

84 See draft, ABK, nd [15 June 1934]. Gen 148/1/25.
85 Taylor, *op. cit.*, pp 357–9. ABK to DeValera, 15 June 1932. Gen 143/8/82.
86 ABK set this out briefly in letter, *The Manchester Guardian* (2 May 1932).
87 Ibid.
88 'On the other hand, Amendments Nos 20–22 of the Constitution, which were the occasion of the recent denunciation by Mr Thomas of the Free State, are manifestly and undeniably within the powers of a Dominion, as laid down by the Imperial Conferences of 1926–1930 and as provided in the Statute of Westminster, 1931. It is regrettable that the British Government should thus have cast grave doubt on the meaning and sincerity of the Conference declarations of 1926 and on the Statute of Westminster.' *Professor Arthur Berriedale Keith on Certain Legal and Constitutional Aspects of the Anglo-Irish Dispute* (London: Irish News and Information Bureau, 1934), p 11.
89 Taylor, *loc. cit.*
90 Ibid.
91 Amendments 20–22 to Irish Free State Constitution.
92 ABK to Inskip, 16 November 1933. Gen 143/8/70; ABK to Simon, 16 November 1933. Gen 148/8/72; ABK to Cripps, 16 November 1933. Gen 143/8/69. ABK to Samuel, 7 December 1933. Gen 143/8/61.
93 See above, *op. cit.*, n 88.
94 *The Scotsman* (15 November 1933).
95 Ibid. (6 December 1933).
96 Ibid. (15 November 1933).
97 ABK to Simon, 16 November 1933: 'After all Mr Cosgrove rejected the Crown from all reality in the Free State, and surely a respectable Republic would be preferable to the Crown as represented by Mr D Buckley.' Gen 143/8/72; ABK to *The Manchester Guardian* (6 December 1933): 'The flexibility of the Commonwealth Constitution should easily permit of Republican status with the recognition of the King as head of the Commonwealth, and it would be deplorable if the Free State were lost to the Commonwealth through lack of constructive thought and narrow legalism, as were the American colonies.'
98 *The Scotsman* (15 November 1933).
99 ABK to Simon, 16 November 1933. Gen 143/8/72.
100 Obituary notice, *The Scotsman* (26 March 1934), 18g.
101 The Latin words: QUIS DESIDERIO SIT FUDOR AUT MODUS TAM CARI CAPITIS? I am indebted to my colleague and friend, Professor Jay W Gossner for suggesting an English setting of these words.
102 ABK to Nan Dewar, 26 March 1937. Burton.
103 Ibid., 8 January 1939: 'I went to the Grange today. The wreath was not bad, and the flowers —1/9— were poor.' Burton.
104 Professor Dewar indicated that his mother was surprised at the invitation, but did not hesitate about going so long as she could maintain a home in London.

CHAPTER 12 pp 246 to 264

1 Sir George Waters, *The Scotsman* (7 October 1944), 4e.
2 A J P Taylor, *England, 1914–1945* (Oxford: Clarendon Press, 1976), Chapters 10–13.

3 Ibid., p 405. ABK described the Cabinet, thus created: 'In May, 1937, Mr Chamberlain became head of a ministry which, as the figures of the election of 1935 show, depends essentially on Conservative votes; there is essentially no distinction between the Conservative members and others, and the organisation of the latter are without substantial backing, and no doubt will disappear as soon as their futility is fully appreciated.' *The British Cabinet System, 1830–1938* (London: Stevens and Sons, 1939), p 74.

4 Taylor, *op. cit.*, pp 398–404.

5 This is the thrust of ABK's entire argument; see Chapter 13, p 275 ff, 'Critic of Foreign Policy'.

6 Taylor, *op. cit.*, pp 384–5.

7 Ibid., pp 449–50.

8 ABK acknowledged her assistance in the Prefaces to his various books as, for example: 'In the preparation of the Fifth Edition (1934) I had valuable assistance from my late wife, and in this, which at the suggestion of the Publishers, appears under a new style, I owe aid to my sister, Mrs N B Dewar.' E W Ridges, *Constitutional Law of England*, 7th edition (London: Stevens and Sons, 1939), p xx.

9 ABK to Nan Dewar, 31 March 1937, approved arrangements for Eastbourne. Burton.

10 Ibid., 26 March 1937. Burton.

11 The points were in letters: ibid., 30 March 1937; 13 April 1937; 26 March 1937. Burton.

12 ABK, 'The Issues at Stake', *The Student* (XXXVI, New Series, 1939–1940, 17 October 1939), pp 10–12.

13 This was the impression of Mr Jennings, Matriculation Officer, Edinburgh University when I talked with him.

14 ABK to Nan Dewar, 10 October 1938. Burton.

15 These were the recollections of Professor John Brough of Cambridge University when I talked with him.

16 Letter from Mrs Neil Bayne to me, 20 August 1982.

17 Phrase used in testimonial he wrote for Mrs Bayne, then Margaret W Burns, 14 January 1936.

18 ABK to Nan Dewar, 8 December 1936. Burton.

19 Mr Peter W H Brown, Secretary of the British Academy, in a letter to me of 23 July 1985 stated that there was no indication in their files about the reasons: 'I can find no correspondence of any kind with Keith, and so there is a mystery.' My hunch, in view of the date, is that someone in the British Academy had made statements in defence of Chamberlain and that irritated ABK, but I have no evidence to support this view. The Diploma of the American Philosophical Society is in Gen 144/1/1.

20 ABK to Nan Dewar, 7 May 1936. Burton. The invitation, Sir James Baillie to ABK to be present in the autumn when a new library would be dedicated, 23 April 1936. Archives, University of Leeds; ABK to Baillie, indicating an obligation for 6 October 1936, 7 May 1936. Ibid., Baillie to ABK, invitation, then, for 29 June, 8 May 1936. Ibid., ABK to Baillie, accepting, 9 May 1936. Ibid., Baillie to ABK, confirming date, 11 May 1936. Ibid. It is important to note that this was the only honorary degree which ABK accepted; Harvard University had offered one in 1935 as part of its Tercentenary Conference, but ABK declined to participate. Gen 145/1/7.

21 Sir James Baillie to ABK, 30 June 1936. Burton; also Archives, University of Leeds. ABK to Baillie, with thanks for the citation, 2 July 1936. Ibid.

22   Citation, University of Leeds, 29 June 1936. ABK kept a copy. Burton. The Office
     of the Vice Chancellor very kindly supplied me with a copy of the programme
     for the academic proceedings.
23   *Letters on Imperial Relations, Indian Reforms, Constitutional and International Law,
     1916–1935* (London: Oxford University Press, 1935), p vii. Mackenzie King
     expressed his appreciation to ABK for sending a copy of *The King, the Constitution,
     the Empire and Foreign Affairs: Letters and Essays, 1936–7* (London: Oxford Uni-
     versity Press, 1938): 'Treating as it does the questions which have been of most
     concern to those who, during the last two years have been in positions of
     responsibility in different parts of the Empire, its personal as well as its political
     interests would be hard to exaggerate. ... Each year places all parts of the British
     Empire increasingly under an abiding obligation to yourself.' King Papers, MG
     26, J 3, Box 92.
24   *The Times* (20 December 1935), 19a.
25   ABK, letters, *The Morning Post* (15 March 1935; 9 June 1935); Harris to ABK,
     24 May 1935. Gen 148/1/52. ABK continued the theme, 'Crown Protection of
     Native Tribes and the British Mandates', *The Scotsman* (23 April 1936). Thomas
     delivered an Aide-Memoir to Hertzog, 15 May 1935 (1935, Cmd. 4948) which
     restated the principles of transfer; see also, HC, *Parl. Deb.*, 5th ser, 20 June 1935,
     594–650.
26   Draft of resolution. Gen 148/1/48; Report of meeting at Caxton Hall, *The Times*
     (19 June 1935), 9b; Roberts to ABK, expressing appreciation, 19 June 1935.
     Gen 148/1/46.
27   ABK phrase, *The Morning Post* (15 March 1935).
28   ABK to Carr, 13 February 1935. Gen 146/1/121; ABK to Molson, 7 March
     1935. Gen 146/1/4; Carr to ABK, 25 July 1935. Gen 146/1/188.
29   ABK to Sinclair, 23 October 1939. Gen 145/4/150.
30   ABK to Crozier, 12 February 1942. Gen 148/4/6.
31   See Chapter 11 above, pp 240–3.
32   ABK, 'The Privy Council and the Irish Free State', *The Spectator* (21 June 1935).
33   Ibid.
34   ABK, 'An Irish Paradox', *The Morning Post* (22 June 1935).
35   Ibid., ABK to Fitzgibbon, 18 June 1935. Gen 143/8/41; ABK to Fitzgibbon, 20
     June 1935. Gen 143/8/40; Fitzgibbon to ABK, 21 June 1935. Gen 143/8/39;
     ABK to Fitzgibbon, 23 June 1935. Gen 143/8/38; Fitzgibbon to ABK, 5 July
     1935. Gen 143/8/37.
36   ABK, 'The Privy Council and the Abrogation of Treaties', *The Scotsman* (13 June
     1935).
37   ABK, 'The Free State Problem', *The Morning Post* (11 July 1935).
38   ABK, 'Britain and the Free State', *The Scotsman* (11 July 1935).
39   ABK, 'The Free State: A Possible Republic', *The Morning Post* (19 July 1935).
40   ABK, 'Irish Citizens Resident in Great Britain', *The Sunday Times* (19 July 1935);
     'Irish Free State "Nationals" ', *The Spectator* (12 February 1937).
41   Under terms of the Constitution (Amendment No 27) Act, 1936 and the Executive
     Authority (External Relations) Act, 1936, 'accepting in the latter Act from
     December 12, 1936, the transfer of the throne to George VI'. Ridges, *op. cit.*,
     p 124.
42   In the Executive Authority (External Relations) Act, 1936.
43   Fitzgibbon to ABK, 31 December 1937. Gen 145/3/114; ABK to Fitzgibbon, 3
     January 1938. Gen 145/3/115.
44   Taylor, *op. cit.*, p 406.
45   Ibid., p 453.

46   Ibid., p 406.
47   This was so, even to the extent that Ireland maintained diplomatic relationships with Germany through an envoy accredited by George VI.
48   See above, p 134.
49   He had been successful in achieving a peerage, in 1928.
50   ABK to Strickland, 10 January 1938. Gen 147/1/144; Strickland to ABK, 30 March 1938. Gen 147/1/142.
51   See text of ABK's Pleadings. Gen 147/1/152.
52   ABK to Blount, Petrie & Co, 12 May 1938. Gen 147/1/133. ABK's materials on the case in Gen 147.
53   See Gen 147/1/151.
54   There was considerable discussion about who would actually present the case between 15 May 1938 and 31 May 1938 when ABK agreed to present it himself. Gen 147/1/108, 122, 129, 131. The daily proceedings were reported in *The Times* (22 June, 24 June, 1 July, 26 July 1938). See report of 'Sammut and Another, Appellants v Strickland, respondent on Appeal from the Court of Appeal, Malta', Judicial Committee of the Privy Council, 25–30 July 1938. *Law Reports*, 1938, pp 678–707. In preparation for *Law Reports*, see letter Clayton to ABK, 9 September 1938. Gen 147/1/33.
55   Chapman to Brierly and Milford, 21 July 1938. OUP, 4539.
56   ABK to Strickland, 24 June 1938. Gen 147/1/69.
57   Gen 147/1/2–17.
58   29 July 1938, HC, *Parl. Deb.*, 5th ser., 338, 3472–3.
59   Strickland to ABK, 15 July 1938. Gen 147/1/53.
60   Mabel Strickland to ABK, 12 August 1938. Gen 147/1/36.
61   McRoberts to ABK, 17 September 1941. Gen 150/1/12.
62   ABK to McRoberts, 14 October 1941. Gen 150/1/14.
63   Ibid.
64   McRoberts to ABK, 18 November 1941. Gen 150/1/6.
65   ABK to Crozier, 12 February 1942: 'No British minister has so far committed himself to the doctrine that Dominion Status implies the right of unilateral secession.' Gen 148/1/6.
66   *The British Commonwealth of Nations: its Territories and Constitutions* (London: Longmans, 1940), p 8. This pamphlet was translated into Finnish, *Brittilainen Kansainyhteiso* (Helsinki: 1946); copy in Keith Collection, U 5/14.
67   *The British Commonwealth of Nations*, *op. cit.*, p 19.

CHAPTER 13 pp 265 to 290

1   OUP, 4539.
2   ABK to Chapman, 27 July 1938. Ibid.
3   ABK 7th edition of E W Ridges, *Constitutional Law of England* (London: Stevens and Sons, 1939), repeated his concerns over MacDonald, p 150. He developed this theme throughout his analysis in *The British Cabinet System, 1830–1938* (London: Stevens and Sons, 1939).
4   A J P Taylor, *England, 1914–1945* (Oxford: Clarendon Press, 1976), Chapter 10.
5   Ridges, *op. cit.*, pp 147–8.
6   *The Causes of the War* (London: Thomas Nelson, 1940), p 271.
7   Ibid., pp 361, 363.

8   Ibid., p 186.
9   Taylor, *op. cit.*, pp 379–81.
10 *Causes, op. cit.*, p 271.
11 Ibid., p 280.
12 Taylor, *op. cit.*, pp 384–5.
13 ABK, 'The Policy of Sanctions', *The Scotsman* (27 December 1935).
14 *Causes, op. cit.*, p 280.
15 ABK, 'The King's Death: Monarchy and People, Changes since Victoria', *Manchester Guardian* (25 January 1936).
16 Ibid.
17 See response of DeValera and the Irish Free State, above, pp 258–9.
18 See text of ABK broadcast, n 21 below.
19 Taylor, *op. cit.*, pp 398–402.
20 ABK, 'The Marriage of the Sovereign', *Manchester Guardian* (4 December 1936). ABK was contacted by numerous organisations for his opinion and analysis; see Gen 145/3, 27–38, 62–69.
21 Text of telegram from National Broadcasting Corporation to ABK, 8 December 1936. Gen 145/3/38. The text of the broadcast, in copy, Burton, Dewar, and also Gen 145/3/62, has 8 December 1937, but clearly that is a typographical error. He sent the text to the *Manchester Guardian*. These were his remarks:

The Problem of the Royal Marriage Project Broadcast.

The popularity of our King is unparalleled in our history and in his present position he commands unstinted sympathy.

Under our law the only restriction of the King's right of marriage is that, for historic reasons, he may not marry a Roman Catholic. His choice is otherwise absolutely free. But that freedom is qualified by one consideration. His wife becomes our Queen, and her character and conduct have a vital interest for all of us. It was the example of Queen Victoria and the Prince Consort which rescued society from the laxity of the Regency period, and Queen Alexandra and Queen Mary have set noble examples of devotion to their private and public duties alike. It is the standard which they have set which makes the present situation so difficult.

Of Mrs Simpson we know that she is charming, cultured, and a hostess tactful and distinguished. That she is a commoner means nothing whatever to us. Our Duchess of York was in law a commoner before she married the Duke, and marriage to a commoner would cause great pleasure to us all. That she is of American origin is equally unimportant. For America we have a feeling of admiration, and many American women have married in our country and have been warmly welcomed. No imagination but would have been fired by the thought of the wedding of the monarch of the greatest of Empires and a daughter of the greatest of Republics.

The obstacle to the marriage lies in the fact alone that the lady has twice divorced her husbands. To her marriage with the King grave objections have been raised on religious grounds. The Roman Catholics who number some three millions in England and Scotland, who constitute nearly a half of the people of Canada, and are strongly represented in Australia and other parts of the Empire, regard marriage with a divorced person as contrary to the tenets of their religion, and this view is shared by a large number of members of the Church of England and even of other Churches. They would feel deeply wounded if such a marriage were contracted, and to the Roman Catholics the rule which excludes one of their faith as Queen would appear more than ever intolerable. Those who are not bound by Church doctrines yet feel that the sanctity of marriage is the foundation of civil society, and that to make Queen a lady whose conduct shows that she does not share this view would be to set an example which would injure gravely the moral tone of British society and to undo the noble work of Queen Mary, to whom our sympathy is fully extended in this time of trial. To these religious and moral grounds may be added a legal objection which some of us lawyers feel. Our law is far less catholic in recognising the effect of divorces by Courts out of England than are the Courts of many American States, and we are afraid that in the eyes of our law the first divorce of Mrs Simpson may not be effective so as to render marriage with the King legal.

These are the reasons which perplex us and our King, and they explain His Majesty's enquiry whether a morganatic marriage might not be possible, so that Mrs Simpson might become his wife, but not his Queen, and her children might not be heirs to the throne. It has been found impossible to entertain his suggestion, and it is important to understand the reasons. In the first place we feel that the idea of a morganatic marriage is foreign and un-English. Matrimony for us means complete equality between wife and husband and anything short of that we dislike nor do we deem it fair to any issue of the marriage. Secondly, even if we in our deep regard for our King should be ready to acquiesce, we know that the solution would not be accepted by the people of the Dominions, who are entitled equally with ourselves to decide the issue. Under the Statute of Westminster 1931 which defined imperial relations, any change affecting the succession requires united action by the Dominions as well as the British Parliaments, and even if we could by a form of words evade the necessity of such assent, none the less the principle is clear that without Dominion assent such a status could not properly be created even for the United Kingdom alone.

There remain therefore three possible courses of action. In the first place the King might insist on marriage with Mrs Simpson, despite the advice which would be formally tendered him by all his Governments against such a marriage if he announced such a decision. In that case his ministers in Britain, in Canada, Australia, and New Zealand would resign and he would be compelled to find ministers to take their place. Were such ministers forthcoming, which is most unlikely, they would be defeated in Parliament. The result of such a dissolution would be a disaster to the nation. It would expose it to the utmost peril in a time of grave crisis in Europe when democracy is menaced on every side. It would discredit constitutional monarchy, and, whatever the result, would divide the country into monarchists and anti-monarchists. That our King would take such action, the vast majority of us absolutely disbelieve.

Secondly, His Majesty may place his affection above his throne and people and abdicate. If so it would be without precedent in our history. Our Kings have had troubled times to face and sacrifices to make. Queen Victoria felt at times that the burden of Empire was too great for her widow-hood, King Edward felt deeply the responsibility imposed on him by the strife between Lords and Commons. But neither abdicated and our late King bore steadfastly the trials of a reign full of public anxieties. Abdication we feel is not in the tradition of British Kingship; we expect now as in the past the courage which sacrifices self for the public welfare. Moreover the constitutional position created by abdication would be very difficult. The Dominions must accept the British proposal, and we can rely on Canada, Australia, New Zealand and even South Africa following our lead. But the case of the Irish Free State presents a grave problem.

The accession of King Edward has been accepted there, but a change in the succession would give the Free State Government the opportunity which it could hardly avoid taking of raising the whole issue of the connection of the State with the British Crown. That, we feel, is a problem which should be allowed to solve itself with the passage of time and with the dying down of ancient enmities due to wrongs of no longer living, and we are most anxious that the issue should not now be raised in such unauspicious circumstances.

There remains therefore the third course, and it is that which is unquestionably desired by the people of Britain and the Dominions, of India and of the Crown Colonies, with the utmost unanimity. They trust that it may please the King to relinquish the thought of a marriage which they cannot welcome. They respect and admire Mrs Simpson for her generosity in leaving the King free to decide as the interests of his Empire as opposed to the dictates of his heart suggest. They do not reckon lightly the sacrifice they ask him to make, but they can assure His Majesty that, while they will understand and sympathise if he cannot meet their hopes, they will feel themselves under the greatest debt of gratitude to him if he can grant their prayer, and in the meantime their petition is God save and guide our King.

ABK discussed the abdication in Ridges, *op. cit.*, pp 123–4; in *British Cabinet System*, *op. cit.*, pp 366 ff.

22 Taylor, *op. cit.*, p 402.
23 Ridges, *op. cit.*, p 162.
24 See above, pp 258–9.
25 Ridges, *op. cit.*, p 126, fn x.
26 ABK, *The Scotsman* (16 February 1937, 5 April 1937, 16 April 1937).
27 Ridges, *op. cit.*, p 162.
28 ABK, *The Scotsman* (4 February 1937, 6 February 1937).
29 Ridges, *op. cit.*, pp 128–30; p 129, fn z, ABK notes the Regency Act, 1937, 1 Edw VIII & 1 Geo VI, c 16, incorporated his advice.
30 Taylor, *op. cit.*, pp 393–8; *The Causes of the War*, *op. cit.*, pp 287–311.
31 Ibid., pp 297–8.
32 Ibid., pp 306–7.
33 Ibid., p 307.
34 Ibid., p 359.
35 *The British Cabinet System*, *op. cit.*, p 559.
36 *The Causes of the War*, *op. cit.*, p 427.
37 ABK to *The Scotsman* (30 September 1938). It was Munich which prompted the chapter, 'The Constitution under Strain' in *The British Cabinet System* and the expanded version in 1942.
38 *The Constitution under Strain: its Working from the Crisis of 1938 down to the Present Time* (London: Stevens and Sons, 1942), p 5.
39 *The Causes of the War*, *op. cit.*, Postscript, p 501 ff.
40 Ibid., pp vii–viii.
41 Taylor, *op. cit.*, on causes, pp 453–4; ibid., pp 633–5 for comments on literature; see also Taylor, *The Origins of the Second World War* (London: Hamish Hamilton, 1961).
42 J M Keynes, *The Economic Consequences of the Peace* (London: Macmillan, 1919).
43 See, for example, the Index to *The Causes of the War*, *op. cit.*, Keith Feiling reviewed it, quite negatively, as might be expected: 'Professor Keith lays about him with the gusto of an Edinburgh Reviewer of a hundred years ago. ... His

points are taken too arbitrarily, and his indignation diffuses heat without light.'
The Observer (1 September 1940). Burton.

44 *Monthly Summary of the League of Nations* (1936), pp 155–8.
45 *The Causes of the War, op. cit.*, pp 263–87.
46 Ibid., p 285.
47 Ibid., p 282.
48 Ibid., p 283.
49 Ibid., p 228.
50 Ibid., p 283.
51 Ibid., pp 284–5.
52 Ibid., p 284.
53 For example, see Taylor, *The Origins of the Second World War, op. cit.*
54 Gen 145/4/47–54, 103, 104, 135, 136; Gen 150/3/1–26.
55 Gen 150/3/3.
56 *New Times and Ethiopia News* (3 April 1943), 4.
57 Ibid. (3 September 1937) and on.
58 Italy controlled Abyssinia and Haile Selassie was in exile in Britian.
59 *New Times and Ethiopia News* (20 September 1941).
60 FO 371/27522.
61 Ibid.
62 *New Times and Ethopia News* (14 February 1942).
63 Taylor, *op. cit.*, makes this same point, p 414.
64 *The Causes of the War, op. cit.*, pp 359–60.
65 ABK to Strickland, 5 October 1938. Gen 147/1/31.
66 ABK, *The Scotsman* (1 October 1938), 15a.
67 ABK to Nan Dewar, 10 October 1938: 'This has been a busy day for me. In the morning I received a confidential letter from the King's Private Secretary asking me what I thought George VI could have done, with reference to my letter in The Scotsman of October 1, which I sent to you in a copy. I replied to him at some length. I shall show you the letter when you come. It is private but I know you would like to know.' Burton.
68 *The Causes of the War, op. cit.*, p 187.
69 Ibid., pp 1–2.
70 Ibid., p 2.
71 Ibid., p 171.
72 Ibid., p 175.
73 Ibid., pp 186–7.
74 Ibid., p 248.
75 Ibid., p 264.
76 Ibid., p 278.
77 Ibid., p 299.
78 Ibid., p 320.
79 Ibid., p 357.
80 Ibid., p 371.
81 Ibid., p 432.
82 Ibid., p 428.
83 Ibid., p 500.
84 Ibid., see Index.
85 See above, pp 59–60, 103–4, 239–40.
86 *The Times* (24 February 1938), 8c.
87 Sobhuza II to Harris, 8 November 1938. Burton.
88 ABK's revision of petition. Gen 148/1/96.

89   National Council of Civil Liberties, statement of purpose, 1934. See note in *The Guardian* (15 April 1985), 17.

90   Kidd to ABK, 6 March 1935. Gen 151/1/9.

91   Ibid., 25 July 1939. Gen 145/4/184; ABK to Kidd, 27 July 1939. Gen 145/4/183; Kidd to ABK, 28 July 1939. Gen 145/4/177; ABK to Kidd, 31 July 1939. Gen 145/4/178; Kidd to ABK, 2 August 1939. Gen 145/4/182.

92   Kidd to ABK, 26 April 1940; Gen 145/4/100; ibid., 6 May 1940. Gen 145/4/95.

93   Kidd to ABK, 2 February 1940. Gen 145/44/159; ABK to Kidd, 5 February 1940. Gen 145/4/158; Cooper to ABK, 15 May 1940. Gen 145/4/91; Kidd to ABK, 28 May 1940. Gen 145/4/86; ABK to Kidd, 30 May 1940. Gen 145/4/87; Kidd to ABK, 3 June 1940. Gen 145/4/85.

94   Kidd to ABK, 6 July 1940. Gen 145/4/83; But the letter, 'Let Public Opinion Have its Say: Battle of Ideas', was handled by *Reynolds News* (21 July 1940).

95   ABK to Kidd, 25 July 1941. Gen 150/3/17.

96   Ibid.

97   Ibid.

98   ABK statement to Kidd, nd [December 1941]. Gen 145/4/26.

99   Bell to ABK, inviting him, 26 September 1941. Gen 145/4/28; but there is no response from ABK to this in the files, only a notation 'D 29.ix.41' which likely indicates that he dictated a response. He did, however, prepare a brief statement for publication.

100   He maintained his concern about emergency powers during war.

101   ABK to Nan Dewar, 21 December 1938: 'I am afraid I cannot help about amounts. If you want you buy, buy what you like. I never keep any intelligible accounts of what you pay out, I grieve to say.' Burton.

102   Ibid., 21 July 1939. Burton.

103   Ibid., 15 July 1939, in regard to her son's summer plans: 'It is no doubt easy to go to Finland from Sweden and it is safer than travelling via Germany. But it all seems so funny to me, because wandering to foreign countries where you do not know that language seems rather absurd. It is bad luck that they could not go in August but one cannot help what will be.' Burton.

104   Ibid., 20 July 1939, in regard to taking a typewriter to Eastbourne. Burton.

105   Ibid., 3 January 1939. Burton.

106   Ibid., 2 July 1939. Burton.

107   Ibid., 11 January 1938: 'But what is amazing is the bitterness of Italy against Britain. They feel that we did our best against them over sanctions and they believe they beat us, whereas the truth was that the influence of Chamberlain was always thrown against sanctions and that when the feeble Baldwin disappeared from the scene as an active agent he had full control long before B. actually handed over office. B. should never have been PM. Now that it is too late, it is widely admitted that we made a complete muddle of the Ethiopian affair.' Burton.

108   Ibid., 2 April 1937. Burton.

109   Ibid., 12 January 1939. Burton.

110   Ibid., 2 July 1939. Burton.

111   Ibid., 4 July 1939. Burton.

112   Ibid., 15 July 1939. Burton.

113   *New Times and Ethiopia News* (1 August 1942), 1.

114   Professor and Mrs Dewar recall this occurring near the time they were married in June of 1944.

115   *The Scotsman* (7 October 1944), 6f.

116   See note on Keith Collection and Keith, Papers and Correspondence, in Bibliography.

CHAPTER 14 pp 291 to 297

1   See above, p 252.
2   See 'Keith Collection' in Edinburgh University Library; the variety within some 5,000 items illustrates the point.
3   'Arthur Berriedale Keith', *University of Edinburgh Journal*, 1944–1945, p 47. The obituary notice in JCL called attention to ABK's wide learning and interests: 'His knowledge was encyclopedic, and extended far beyond the subjects with which his name is known in his works. He could supply, for example, particulars of cricket and bowling averages, and in such matters he kept his information up to the latest available date.' JCL (1944), 61–2.
4   Obituary notice, *Times Literary Supplement*, 14 October 1944.
5   Franklin Edgerton, 'Arthur Berriedale Keith', *Yearbook of the American Philosophic Society*, 1945, p 377.
6   Edinburgh University, Senatus Academicus, Printed Minutes, 8 November 1944, p 44.
7   *New Times and Ethiopia News*, 14 October 1944, 3.
8   *Times Literary Supplement, op. cit.*
9   Edgerton, *op. cit.*
10   K C Wheare and F W Thomas, 'Arthur Berriedale Keith', *Dictionary of National Biography, 1941–1950*, p 445.
11   Senatus Academicus, *op. cit.*
12   Walter Holmes, 'Questions on India', *Daily Worker*, 9 October 1944. Burton, as well.
13   Isaiah Berlin, *The Hedgehog and the Fox: An Essay on Tolstoy's View of History* (London: Weidenfeld and Nicolson, 1953), p 1.
14   This is the phrase used by the Hon Lord Cameron in a letter to me of 16 July 1983: 'He was a man of promise whose future career disappointed others as well as himself.'
15   ABK to Nan Dewar; 13 April 1937: 'I despatched the book yesterday, and I do not feel eager about doing another one, but I shall have to carry it out, no doubt. It is all waste energy, as I am quite indifferent to what people say of my books, having nothing to gain or lose'; ibid., 30 December 1938: 'I cannot enjoy anything and my judgment of what is worth enjoying is decidedly out.' Burton.
16   This is the point made by Mr W W S Breem, Librarian and Keeper of Manuscripts, Inner Temple, in a letter to me of 6 July 1982: 'The English are always suspicious of multi-talented persons.'
17   See listing below, 'Keith's Works', in Bibliography.
18   See note and listing below in Bibliography.
19   Gravestone, Grange Cemetery, Edinburgh.
20   John Brough, *Poems from the Sanskrit* (Harmondsworth: Penguin Books, 1968), #165, p 113.
21   Ibid., #56, p 67.
22   See above, Chapter 5, pp 103–4.
23   See above, Chapter 13, pp 275 ff.
24   See above, Chapter 13, pp 278–9.
25   See above, appeal of Sobhuza II, pp 286–7.
26   See above, p 252.

Bibliography

This bibliography is organised in the following manner:

PRIMARY MATERIALS
  Manuscript Sources
    Of Primary Importance
    Of Secondary Importance
  Public Records
  School and University Records
  Keith's Works
    Printed Books and Pamphlets
    Contributions to Other Works and to *Festschriften*
    Articles in Journals
    Letters to Newspapers
  Other Printed Materials

SECONDARY WORKS
  Books
  Articles

PRIMARY MATERIALS

Manuscript Sources

Of Primary Importance

BURTON COLLECTION

These materials are held privately by Mrs J Walcot Burton, daughter of Mrs Nan Dewar, in her home in London. They include correspondence between ABK and his sister Nan Dewar, with other persons; photographs of the family; clippings of reviews of ABK's books; newspaper cuttings of ABK's letters to the press; copies of some of his books; typescript of some articles and letters; an essay from his days at Royal High School.

DEWAR COLLECTION

These materials are held privately by Professor Michael J S Dewar, son of Mrs Nan Dewar, in his home then in Austin, Texas when I used them. They include copies of some correspondence; photographs of ABK, of St Margaret's, Dunbar, of MSK's grave in Dunbar Parish churchyard, of the Imperial Conference, 1911; a notebook of cuttings, notes, newspaper articles, and other items of family interest, started by MSK since it carries her initials, and continued by Margaret B Keith and Nan Dewar; a notebook of ABK's obituary notices; some of the prize medals which ABK won; various items which belonged to ABK such as his walking stick, desk ruler; a nearly complete collection of his books.

KEITH, PAPERS AND CORRESPONDENCE

This collection of some 4,800 pieces is held by Edinburgh University Library, Special Collections, as Gen 140–53. The contents, both in general terms and in detail for each piece, are described in: Ridgway F Shinn, Jr, *Guide to Arthur Berriedale Keith, Papers and Correspondence, 1896–1941*, October, 1981. In addition, there is a manuscript, 'Historical Syntax of Classical Greek' that ABK prepared, E 511128; letters to and from John Ewing, Lecturer in Indian and Colonial History, DC 4.101–3; letters to and from Charles Sarolea, Professor of French, Sar coll 140, 229; autograph note to Father D Manning (Liberia), Gen 863/8/41. Further, Keith, additional MSS, includes four boxes of materials, mainly about courses and lectures in the Constitution of the British Empire and in Sanskrit.

OXFORD UNIVERSITY PRESS

Several files at the Oxford University Press contain correspondence between ABK and officers of the press about the publication of various of his books. The files are: LB 4615, 4539, 821294, 815411, 6559, LB 3026, 6505, LB 3400.

Of Secondary Importance

BODLEIAN LIBRARY, OXFORD UNIVERSITY
James Bryce Papers, MS Bryce.
Lewis Harcourt Papers, MS Harcourt.
Sir Louis Stuart correspondence with ABK, MS Eng. Hist. C 612.

NATIONAL LIBRARY OF SCOTLAND
Materials used include copies of orders by the Church of Scotland with Keith and Company, advertising agents.

NATIONAL LIBRARY OF WALES
This contained one letter from ABK to Stanley Jevons.

SCOTTISH RECORD OFFICE
This contained limited correspondence of ABK and Lord Lothian (Philip Kerr) from 1932–1933 about Indian affairs.

Public Records

ARCHIVES OF THE CROWN AGENTS
Presently held in the Offices of the Crown Agents at 4 Millbank, Westminster, London; materials were useful for seeing the range of work carried out for the colonies.

INDIA OFFICE LIBRARY
Files in connection with Lord Crewe's Committee of 1919 to examine the Home Administration of India: L/P&J/9, V/26/220/19, L/R/4/8.

LIBRARY OF THE FOREIGN AND COMMONWEALTH OFFICE
Materials used include items from the Colonial Office Library, pamphlets, and photographs of the Colonial Office staff in 1904.

PARLIAMENTARY DEBATES, 4th, 5th Series, selected 1900–1944

PARLIAMENTARY PAPERS
1881   C. 3075, Papers re Functions of Crown Agents for the Colonies
1902   Cd. 1299, Colonial Conference, 1902

Cd. 1056, Report of Interdepartmental Committee on Cable Communication

1903   Cd. 1433, Northern Nigeria

Cd. 1434, Cyprus, Correspondence on Drought

Cd. 1465, Cyprus Blue Book, 1901–1902

Cd. 1472, Washington Convention on Alaska Boundary, 24 January
1903

1904   Cd. 1785, Colonial Marriage and Divorce Laws

Cd. 1877, Cd. 1878, Correspondence, Alaska Boundary

Cd. 1940, On Metric Weights and Measures

Cd. 1944, Crown Agents, Office Despatch on Commerical Business

1905   Cd. 2246, Anglo-Chinese Convention on Employment of Chinese Labour
in British Colonies

1906   Cd. 2785, Colonial Conference, 1907. Preliminary Correspondence I

Cd. 2975, Colonial Conference, 1907. Preliminary Correspondence II

Cd. 2905, Papers on Native Disturbances in Natal

Cd. 2927, Petition to His Majesty in Council of the Twelve Natives
Recently Executed in Natal and the Affidavit in Support of the Petition
and the Judgement

Cd. 3027, Further Correspondence Relating to Native Disturbances in
Natal in Continuation of Cd. 1905

Cd. 3247, Further Correspondence Relating to Native Disturbances in
Natal in Continuation of Cd. 3027

1907   Cd. 3337, Colonial Conference, 1907. Agenda

Cd. 3340, Colonial Conference, 1907. Further Papers

Cd. 3404, Colonial Conference, 1907. Summary of Proceedings

Cd. 3406, Colonial Conference, 1907. Precis of Proceedings

Cd. 3523, Colonial Conference, 1907. Minutes of Proceedings

Cd. 3524, Colonial Conference, 1907. Papers Laid before the Colonial
Conference

Cd. 3563, Correspondence Relating to the Removal of Certain Native
Prisoners from Natal in Continuation of Cd. 3247

Cd. 3567, Proceedings of Conference on Merchant Shipping, 1907

1908   Cd. 3795, Despatch [Elgin] on Colonial Office Reorganisation

Cd. 3888, Further Correspondence Relating to Native Affairs in Natal

Cd. 3889, Natal Native Affairs Commission, 1906–1907, Report and Evidence

Cd. 3992, Report of the Advisory Committee of the Tropical Diseases
Research Fund for 1907

Cd. 3998, Further Correspondence [Natal] in Continuation of (Cd. 3888
of 1908)

Cd. 4001, Further Correspondence [Natal] in Continuation of (Cd. 3998
of 1908)

Cd. 4194, Further Correspondence [Natal] in Continuation of (Cd. 4001
of 1908)

Cd. 4195, Despatch from Governor of Natal forwarding a Bill to
make Special Provision for the Trial of Natives accused of Certain
Crimes

Cd. 4328, Further Correspondence [Natal]

Cd. 4403, Papers Relating to the Case of Mr Alfred Mangena [Natal]

Cd. 4404, Further Correspondence [Natal] in Continuation of (Cd. 4195,
Cd. 4328)

Cd. 4325, Correspondence Relating to the Naval Defence of Australia and New Zealand

1909   Cd. 4473, Organisation of Crown Agents Office

Cd. 4475, Correspondence relating to the Proposed Formation of an Imperial General Staff

Cd. 4476, Report of the Advisory Committee of the Tropical Diseases Research Fund for 1908

Cd. 4528, Anglo-American Agreement Arbitration, North Atlantic Fisheries

Cd. 4554, Correspondence re International Naval Conference, 1908–1909

Cd. 4555, Proceedings, International Naval Conference

Cd. 4558, Anglo-American Treaty, Boundary Waters with Canada

Cd. 4585, Correspondence Relating to the Trial of Dinizulu and Others

Cd. 4611, Memorandum by the Army Council on the Existing Army System and the Present State of Military Forces in the UK

Cd. 4948, Conference on Imperial Defence, Papers

1910   LXVI (129), Correspondence with Foreign Powers on Constitutional Position of Dominions and Colonies in Treaties

Cd. 4999, Report of the Advisory Committee of the Tropical Diseases Research Fund for 1909

Cd. 5153, Report of Dominions Department, Colonial Office, 1909–1910

Cd. 5272, Imperial Copyright Conference, 1910. Memorandum of Proceedings

Cd. 5273, Further Correspondence Relating to the Imperial Conference, in Continuation of Cd. 3524 of 1907

Cd. 5396, North Atlantic Fisheries Arbitration

Cd. 5418, Correspondence Respecting, Declaration of London

1911   Cd. 5513, Cd. 5741, Cd. 5745, Imperial Conference, 1911, Correspondence, Precis, Minutes of Proceedings, Papers

Cd. 5514, Report of the Advisory Committee of the Tropical Diseases Research Fund for 1910

Cd. 5582, Report of Dominions Department, Colonial Office, 1910–1911

Cd. 5718, Correspondence Relating to the Declaration of London

Cd. 5746-I, -II, Imperial Conference, 1911, Papers Laid

Cd. 5777, Paper Relating to the Financial Relations in the British Self-Governing Dominions between Central and Local Governments

Cd. 5803, Anglo-American Agreement for Settlement of Outstanding Pecuniary Claims

1912–13   Cd. 6024, Report of the Advisory Committee of the Tropical Diseases Research Fund for 1911

Cd. 6091, Report of Dominions Department, Colonial Office, 1911–1912

Cd. 6451, Cd. 6585, Cd. 6645, Anglo-American Correspondence, US Panama Canal Act of 1912

Cd. 6560, Committee of Imperial Defence, Despatch on Representation of Self-Governing Dominions

1913   Cd. 6669, Report of the Advisory Committee of the Tropical Diseases Research Fund for 1912

1914   Cd. 7506, Correspondence Relating to the Recent Political Crisis in Tasmania

Cd. 7505, Report of Dominions Department, Colonial Office, 1913–1914

1918   Cd. 9109, Report on Indian Constitutional Reforms [Montagu-Chelmsford Reforms]

1919   Cmd. 207, Report of the Committee Appointed by the Secretary of State for India to Enquire into the Home Administration of Indian Affairs

1926   Cmd. 2768. Summary of Proceedings. Imperial Conference, 1926

1930–32 Cmd. 3778, India Round Table Conference Proceedings
         Cmd. 4238, India Round Table Conference Proceedings

1935   Cmd. 4948, High Commission Territories in South Africa. Aide-memoire handed to the Prime Minister of the Union of South Africa by the Secretary of State for Dominion Affairs on 15 May, 1935

PUBLIC ARCHIVES OF CANADA
Correspondence of ABK and Mackenzie King was used as well as King's diaries.

PUBLIC RECORD OFFICE, LONDON
The following classes of material were used:

CAB, Cabinet
CAB 17/77, Papers Prepared for Colonial Conference, 1902; Colonial Preferential Tariffs, Naval and Military Subjects
CAB 17/79, Papers relating to Defence Questions, Imperial Conference, 1911
CAB 18/10, Proceedings. Colonial Conference, 1902
CAB 18/11, Proceedings I. Colonial Conference, 1907; Papers laid before Conference
CAB 18/12, Imperial Conference on Defence of the Empire, 1909
CAB 18/13, Minutes of Proceedings of Imperial Conference, 1911 and Papers Laid before the Conference
CAB 32, Contains Papers for Imperial Conferences: 1928, 1929, 1930, 1932, 1933, 1935, 1937
CAB 37, Cabinet Papers, 1907–1914

CSC 4, Civil Service Commission, Reports, 1870–1914

CO, Colonial Office Files
CO 23, Bahamas, 1902–1903, 1906–1907
CO 28, Barbados, 1906–1907
CO 37, Bermuda, 1902–1903, 1906–1907
CO 42, Canada, 1902–1903, 1907–1914
CO 48, Cape, 1905–1906
CO 67, Cyprus, 1902–1903
CO 78, Falklands, 1902–1903, 1906–1907
CO 83, Fiji, 1902–1903
CO 91, Gibraltar, 1902–1903
CO 111, British Guiana, 1906–1907
CO 123, British Honduras, 1902–1903, 1906–1907
CO 137, Jamaica, 1906–1907
CO 147, Lagos, 1902–1903
CO 152, Leeward Islands, 1906–1907
CO 179, Natal, 1905–1906
CO 194, Newfoundland, 1902–1903, 1907–1914
CO 209, New Zealand, 1902–1903, 1907–1914
CO 224, Orange River Colony, 1905–1906
CO 225, Western Pacific, 1902–1903
CO 291, Transvaal, 1905–1906

CO 295, Trinidad, 1906–1907
CO 312, Windward Islands, 1906–1907
CO 323, Colonies (General), 1901–1914
CO 378, Registers of Correspondence, 1901–1915
CO 379, Colonies, Register of Out-Letters, 1901–1905
CO 417, South Africa, High Commission, Bechuanaland and Rhodesia, 1905–1906
CO 418, Australia, 1902–1903, 1907–1914
CO 429, Patronage, 1908
CO 431, Accounts, 1908
CO 445, West Africa Frontier Force, 1901–1902
CO 446, Northern Nigeria, 1901–1902
CO 449, Governors Pensions, 1901–1914
CO 520, Southern Nigeria, 1901–1902
CO 523, Chief Clerk, 1908–1914
CO 527, Inter Colonial Council, South Africa, 1905–1906
CO 532, Dominions, 1907–1914
CO 878, Office Minutes, 1899–1914 [1903–1907 missing]
CO 879, Confidential Print, Africa, #677, 695, 703, 706, 712, 730, 751, 779, 796–
     801, 808–830, 833, 848, 849–852, 857–860A, 887
CO 885, Confidential Print, Miscellaneous, #112–287
CO 886, Confidential Print, Dominions, #1–63

FO, Foreign Office Files
FO 371, 627, 800, Foreign Office Files, letters of ABK to FO
FO 375/5, 11, 12, 14, 15, 16; /6, 2–10. Peace Handbooks.

WORKS
12/96/2, File on Building New Colonial Office and Home Office
12/96/4, File on Removal of Marble Chimney from Old Colonial Office to the New
   Buildings

PUBLIC RECORDS, SCOTLAND
Census, 1881, 1891
Records of Inventories. Record of Wills. SC 70
Register of Births, Marriages and Deaths: Bathgate, Dunbar, Portobello
Sasines, Haddington
Scottish Office
   ED. 26/123/1925. Regius Professors
   HH 29, Scotch Warrant Book, January 1914 to February 1922, #8, p 46

School and University Records

Council of Legal Education, London
   Calendar
   Examination, 1904
Faculty of Advocates, Edinburgh
   Intrants Book, 1921
   Minutes, 1921
Oxford University
   Balliol College
      Records of Balliol College
   Oxford University Calendar, 1897–
   1913

Statuta Universitatis Oxoniensis,
   1904–1912
The Royal High School of Edinburgh
   Annual Report and Course of Study
   in the High School, 1883–1894,
   1895–1909
   Matriculation Book, High School,
   Edinburgh, 1887/8–1897/8
   Prospectus for Sessions, 1894–1894
   Rector's Reports, 1894–1909

The University of Edinburgh
  First Matriculation Book, 1894–95
  Matriculation Album, 1893–1898
  Matriculation Lists, 1894–1897
    [lists all students and degree,
    alphabetically, by year]
  General Council,
  Printed Minutes

Senatus Academicus, Printed
  Minutes, 1913–1944
University Court, *Minutes*, 1907,
  1914–1944
University of Edinburgh Calendar, 1894–
  1944
University of Edinburgh Journal, 1944–
  1945

Keith's Works

Printed Books and Pamphlets

Aitareya Āraṇyaka Anecdota Oxoniensia, Aryan Series, Part 9 (Oxford: Clarendon Press, 1909)

The Belgian Congo and the Berlin Act (Oxford: Clarendon Press, 1919)

The British Cabinet System, 1830–1938 (London: Stevens and Sons, 1939) 2nd edn ed N H Gibbs (1952)

The British Commonwealth of Nations: its Territories and Constitutions. British Life and Thought Series (London: Longmans, 1940). (Translated into Finnish and published Helsinki, 1946)

Buddhist Philosophy in India and Ceylon (Oxford: Clarendon Press, 1923)

Catalogue of Prākrit Manuscripts in the Bodleian Library, with a preface by E W B Nicholson (Oxford: Clarendon Press, 1911)

Catalogue of Sanskrit Manuscripts in the Bodleian Library Appendix to Volume I, Theodore Aufrecht's Catalogue (Oxford: Clarendon Press, 1909)

Catalogue of Sanskrit Manuscripts in the Bodleian Library Volume II Begun by M Winternitz (Oxford: Clarendon Press, 1905)

Catalogue of Sanskrit and Prākrit MSS in the Indian Institute Library, Oxford (Oxford: Clarendon Press, 1903)

Catalogue of Sanskrit (and Prākrit) Manuscripts in the Library of the India Office Volume 2 Brahmanical and Jaina Manuscripts (Oxford: Clarendon Press, 1935)

The Causes of the War (London: Thomas Nelson, 1940)

Classical Sanskrit Literature Heritage of India Series (Calcutta: Association Press; London: Oxford University Press, 1923)

The Constitution, Administration and Laws of the Empire. Volume 3 in *The British Empire: A Survey* (London: W Collins, 1924)

Constitutional History of India, 1600–1935 (London: Methuen, 1936)

Constitutional History of the First British Empire (Oxford: Clarendon Press, 1930)

The Constitutional Law of the British Dominions (London: Macmillan, 1933)

Constitutional Law of England E W Ridges. 5th edn revd 'and largely rewritten' by A B Keith, 1934; also 6th edn, 1937; 7th edn, 1939 (London: Stevens and Sons)

The Constitution of England from Queen Victoria to George VI (London: Macmillan, 1940) 2 volumes

The Constitution under Strain: its Working from the Crisis of 1938 down to the Present Time (London: Stevens and Sons, 1942)

A Digest of the Law of England with Reference to the Conflict of Laws A V Dicey. Editions by A B Keith: 3rd edn 1922; 4th edn 1927; 5th edn 1932 (London: Stevens and Sons)

Dominion Autonomy in Practice, revd edn of *Dominion Home Rule in Practice* (London: Oxford University Press, 1929)

Dominion Home Rule in Practice, The World of Today (London: Humphrey Milford, 1921)

The Dominions as Sovereign States: their Constitutions and Governments (London: Macmillan, 1938)
Elements of International Law. Henry Wheaton. Revised and edited by A B Keith, 1929; also 7th edn, 1944 (London: Stevens and Sons)
Elements of the Law of Contracts (Oxford: Clarendon Press, 1931)
Federation: its Nature and Conditions Historical Association Pamphlet No. 123 (London: Wyman and Sons, 1942)
The Governments of the British Empire (London: Macmillan, 1935)
The Historical Geography of the British Colonies: Volume III, West Africa. Volume IV: South Africa. Charles P Lucas. 3rd edn A B Keith (Oxford: Clarendon Press, 1913)
A History of Sanskrit Literature (Oxford: Clarendon Press, 1928)
Imperial Unity and the Dominions (Oxford: Clarendon Press, 1916)
Indian Logic and Atomism: An Exposition of the Nyāya and Vaiçeşika Systems (Oxford: Clarendon Press, 1921)
Indian Mythology Volume 6, in L H Gray, ed, *The Mythology of All Races* (Boston: Marshall Jones, 1916)
An Introduction to British Constitutional Law (Oxford: Clarendon Press, 1931)
The Karma-Mīmāṁsā Heritage of India Series (Calcutta: Association Press; London: Oxford University Press, 1921)
The King, the Constitution, the Empire and Foreign Affairs: Letters and Essays, 1936–7 (London: Oxford University Press, 1938)
The King and the Imperial Crown: the Powers and Duties of His Majesty (London: Longmans, 1936)
The Law and Custom of the Constitution W R Anson. 4th edn of Volume II, *The Crown*, A B Keith (Oxford: Clarendon Press, 1935)
Letters and Essays on Current Imperial and International Problems, 1935–6 (London: Oxford University Press, 1936)
Letters on Imperial Relations, Indian Reforms, Constitutional and International Law, 1916–1935 (London: Oxford University Press, 1935)
Professor Arthur Berriedale Keith on Certain Legal and Constitutional Aspects of the Anglo-Irish Dispute (London: Irish News and Information Bureau, 1934)
Privileges and Rights of the Crown (London: C A Pearson, 1936)
The Religion and Philosophy of the Veda and the Upanishads. Harvard Oriental Series, Volumes 31, 32 (Cambridge, Massachusetts: Harvard University Press, 1925)
Responsible Government in the Dominions (London: Stevens and Sons, 1909)
—— (Oxford: Clarendon Press, 1912) 2nd edn, 3 volumes
—— (Oxford: Clarendon Press, 1928) 2nd edn, revised to 1927, 2 volumes
Rigveda Brāhmanas: the Aitareya and Kauşītaki Brāhmaṇas. Harvard Oriental Series, Volume 25 (Cambridge, Massachusetts: Harvard University Press, 1920)
The Sāṁkyha System: A History of Samkhya Philosophy. Heritage of India Series (Calcutta: Association Press; London: Oxford University Press, 1915) 2nd edn, 1924
The Śāṅkhāyana Āraṇyaka with an Appendix on the Mahāvrata Oriental Translation Fund, New Series, Volume 18 (London: Royal Asiatic Society, 1908)
Sanskrit Drama in its Origin, Development, Theory and Practice (Oxford: Clarendon Press, 1924)
Selected Speeches and Documents on British Colonial Policy, 1763–1917. World's Classics Series (London: Oxford University Press, 1918) Reprinted in 1933, 1948, 1953
The Sovereignty of the British Dominions (London: Macmillan, 1929)
Speeches and Documents on the British Dominions, 1918–1931: From Self-Government to National Sovereignty. World's Classics Series (London: Oxford University Press, 1932) Reprinted 1938, 1948

Speeches and Documents on Indian Policy, 1750–1921. World's Classics Series (London: Oxford University Press, 1922)

Speeches and Documents on International Affairs, 1918–1937. World's Classics Series (London: Oxford University Press, 1938)

The Theory of State Succession with Special Reference to English and Colonial Law (London: Waterlow, 1907)

The Veda of the Black Yajus School: Tāittirīya Samhitā. Harvard Oriental Series, Volumes 18, 19 (Cambridge, Massachusetts: Harvard University Press, 1914)

Vedic Index of Names and Subjects, ed A A Macdonell. Indian Texts Series (London: John Murray, 1912)

War Government of the British Dominions Economic and Social History of the World War, British Series (Oxford: Clarendon Press, 1921)

Contributions to other Works and to Festschriften

This list represents titles found mainly in the Keith Collection. There are undoubtedly many more such contributions to be found if the list were to be fully inclusive of everything that ABK did.

'The Age of the Ṛg-veda', *Woolner Commemorative Volume* (Lahore: Mehar Chand Lachhman Das, 1940) pp 137–56

'The Aryans and the Indus Valley Civilization', *Bharatiyanusilangranth, Festschrift for G H Ojha* (Allahabad: 1933)

'The Authenticity of the *Arthaçastra*', *Sir Asutosh Memorial Volume* (Patna: Samaddar, 1926–1928) pp 8–22

'Babylon and India', *Kuppuswami Sastri Commemoration Volume* (Madras: G S Press, nd [1936?]) pp 67–72

'The British Dominions', Chapter IV, Part I in Volume VI, ed Harold W V Temperley, *History of the Peace Conference of Paris* (London: Henry Frowde and Hodder and Stoughton, 1924)

Cambridge History of India, E J Rapson, ed. Volume I, Chapter IV, 'The Age of the Rigveda', and Chapter V, 'The Period of the Later Saṁhitās, the Brāhmaṇas, the Āraṇyakas, and the Upaniṣhads' (Cambridge: Cambridge University Press, 1922)

'Constitutional Development of the British Empire in regard to the Dominions and India from 1887 to 1933' Introductory chapter in G E H Palmer *Consultation and Cooperation in the British Commonwealth* (London: Royal Institute for International Affairs, 1934)

'Daṇḍin and Bhāmaha', *Indian Studies in Honor of Charles Rockwell Lanman* (Cambridge, Massachusetts: Harvard University Press, 1929) pp 167–85

'Dominions, Colonies, Possessions', in *Halsbury's Laws of England*, Volume II, 2nd ed (London: Butterworth and Company, 1931–42) pp 71 ff

'Early History of the Indo-Iranians', *Bhandarkar Commemorative Volume, 1917* (Poona: Bhandarkar Oriental Research Institute, nd [1918?]) pp 81–92

'The Etymology of Guṇa', *Commemorative Essays Presented to K.B. Pathak* (Poona: Bhandarkar Oriental Research Institute, 1934) pp 311–14

'Foreword', in N N Law *Aspects of Ancient Indian Polity* (Oxford: Clarendon Press, 1921)

'The Grouping of the Indo-European Dialects', *Commemorative Essays Presented to Sir George Abraham Grierson* (Lahore: Linguistic Society of India, 1933)

'The Home of the Indio-Europeans', *Oriental Studies in Honour of Cursetji Erachji Parry*. (London: Oxford University Press, 1933) pp 189–99

'India in the Empire' Volume I in F M Houlston and Pyare-lal Bedi, *India Analysed* (London: Victor Gollancz, 1933)

'Makers of the Constitution', in Hugh Gunn, ed *Makers of the Empire* (London: Collins, 1924)

'A New Explanation of the Gandharvas', in Coomaraswamy Volume, 1937. *Journal of the Indian Society of Oriental Art* (Calcutta)

'New Theories as to Brahman', *Jha Commemoration Volume: Essays on Oriental Subjects* (Poona: Oriental Book Agency, 1937) pp 199–215

'Pāṇini's Vocabulary', *Bhārata-Kaumudī: Studies in Indology in Honour of Dr Radha Kumud Mookerji* (Allahabad: The Indian Press, 1945) pp 343–5

'The Sanctity of Treaties', *Czechoslovak Yearbook of International Law* (London: Czechoslovak Branch, International Law Society, 1942)

'The Vedic Mahāvrata', Volume II, *Transactions of the Third International Congress for the History of Religions* (Oxford: Clarendon Press, 1908) pp 49–58

Articles in Journals

It is difficult to compile a full list of ABK's contributions to journals since many of them are not indexed and there is no full listing of his work among any of his papers.

For this study, all his articles and notes in the *Journal of Comparative Legislation* and in the *Journal of the Royal Asiatic Society* were used; they are cited. In addition, so far as it is possible to do so, journals to which he made a contribution are listed by title, and, where readily available, many of those articles were used in the preparation of this study as indicated in the footnotes.

Journal of Comparative Legislation [*Journal of the Society of Comparative Legislation*, 1896–1917]

'Merchant Shipping Legislation in the Colonies', 1908, pp 202–22

'Judicial Appeals in the Commonwealth', 1908, pp 269–80

'South African Union', 1909, pp 40–92

'British Ships and the Jurisdiction of the Commonwealth', 1909, pp 123–5

'The Legal Interpretation of the Constitution of the Commonwealth, Part I', 1910, pp 220–42

'Merchant Shipping Legislation of the Empire', 1910, pp 294–9

'The Legal Interpretation of the Constitution of the Commonwealth, Part II', 1911, pp 95–134

'The Commonwealth Referenda', 1912–1913, pp 526–41

'Recent Cases on the Canadian Constitution', 1914, pp 351–80

Review of A Lawrence Lowell, *The Governments of France, Italy and Germany*, 1915, pp 255–6

Review of C Reis, *The Government of Trinidad* and A H F Lefroy, *Leading Cases in Canadian Constitutional Law*, p 87, 89

'The Constitutions of India and Canada', 1916, pp 199–219

'Ministerial Responsibility in the Dominions', 1917, pp 277–32

'Initiative and Referendum in Canada', 1920, pp 112–15

'Notes on Imperial Constitutional Law', 1920, pp 328–32

Review of *Journal of the Parliaments of the Empire*, 1920, pp 367–8

'Notes on Imperial Constitutional Law', 1921, pp 132–4, 306–14

'Notes on Imperial Constitutional Law', 1922, pp 71–83, 104–8, 233–41

'The Canadian Constitution and the Company Legislation', 1922, pp 201–9

'Notes on Imperial Constitutional Law', 1923, pp 120–7, 274–81

Review of W P M Kennedy, *The Constitution of Canada*, 1923, pp 321–2

'Notes on Imperial Constitutional Law', 1924, pp 135–42, 193–209

'International Status of the Dominions', 1924, pp 161–8

Review of W Renwick, *The Canadian Constitution: in Form and in Fact*, 1924, pp 174–5

'Privy Council and the Canadian Constitution', 1925, pp 61–8

'Notes on Imperial Constitutional Law', 1925, pp 101–9, 195–211

Review of Charles Warren, *The Supreme Court and Sovereign States*, 1925, pp 121–2

Review of Sir Valentine Chirol, *The Occident and the Orient*, 1925, p 128

'Note on the Personality of an Idol', 1925, pp 255–7

Review of David Kerr, *The Law of the Australian Constitution*, 1925, p 267

Review of K P Jayaswal, *Hindu Polity*, 1925, pp 274–6

Review of J Stoyanovsky, *La théorie générale des mandats internationaux*, 1925, pp 279–81

'League of Nations and Mosul', 1926, pp 38–49

'Notes on Imperial Constitutional Law', 1926, pp 125–35, 275–91

'Note on the Cabinet and the Attorney General', 1926, pp 136–7

'Imperial Conference, 1926', 1927, pp 68–94

'Notes on Imperial Constitutional Law', 1927, pp 123–9, 241–59

'Notes on Imperial Constitutional Law', 1928, pp 100–23, 293–310

'Claims By and Against the Crown', 1928, pp 186–95

Review of *Great Britain and the Dominions*, Harris Foundation Lecture, 1928, pp 326–9

'Notes on Imperial Constitutional Law', 1929, pp 113–31, 250–67

Review of E E Buchet, *Le 'Status' des Dominions britanniques en droit constitutionnel et en droit international*, L L M Minty, *Constitutional Laws of the British Empire*, Dr Stoyanovsky, *The Mandate for Palestine* 1929, pp 142–5

Review of P E Corbett and H A Smith, *Canada and World Politics*, P J Noel Baker, *The Present Juridical Status of the British Dominions in International Law*, John Murtagh Macrossan Lecture, *The Australian Constitution: its Interpretation and Amendment*, 1929, pp 287–90

'Notes on Imperial Constitutional Law', 1930, pp 94–108, 278–98

Review of Michael Rynne, *Die volkerrechtliche Stellung Irlands*, 1930, pp 308–13

'Imperial Conference, 1930', 1931, pp 26–42

'Notes on Imperial Constitutional Law', 1931, pp 114–27, 246–65

Review of W P M Kennedy, *Treaties and Documents of the Canadian Constitution*, Norman Bentwick, *The Mandate System*, Nathan Feinberg, *La Juridiction de la Cour Permanente de Justice Internationale dans le Système des Mandats*, S D K Sen, *The Indian States*, 1931, pp 138–41

Review of W P M Kennedy and Gustave Lanctot, *Reports on the Laws of Quebec, 1767–1770*, W P M Kennedy and D C Wells, *The Law of the Taxing Power in Canada*, Harold W Stokes, *The Foreign Relations of the Federal State*, 1931, pp 278–82

Review of Leo Gross, *Pazificmus und Imperialismus*, E C Stowell, *International Law*, W N Hibbert, *Leading Cases in Conflict of Laws*, Leo Raape, *Einführungsgesetz. 2 Teil: Art. 7-3, Internationales Privatrecht*, 1931, pp 298–305

'Notes on Imperial Constitutional Law', 1932, pp 101–24, 255–82

Review of H Hughes, *National Sovereignty and Judicial Autonomy in the British Commonwealth of Nations*, E F W Gey van Pittius, *Nationality within the British Commonwealth of Nations*, 1932, pp 134–7

'Notes on Imperial Constitutional Law', 1933, pp 117–23, 255–64

Review of R P Mahaffy, *The Statute of Westminster*, Hans Walter, *Die Stellung der Dominien in Verfassungs-system des Britischen Reiches im Jahre 1931*, Mr Justice Terrel, *Malayan Legislation and its Future*, 1933, pp 129–31

Review of W P M Kennedy and J Finkelman, *The Right to Trade: An Essay on the Law of the Tort*, 1933, pp 134–7

'Report of the Newfoundland Royal Commission', 1934, pp 25–39
'Notes on Imperial Constitutional Law', 1934, pp 131–9, 289–300
Review of K C Wheare, *The Statute of Westminster*, W P M Kennedy, *Some Aspects of the Theories and Workings of the Constitutional Law*, 1934, pp 152–3
Review of Paul Roubier, *Les Conflits de Lois dans le Temps*, 1934, p 165
Review of E Salant, *Constitutional Laws of the British Empire*, 1934, p 320
'Notes on Imperial Constitutional Law', 1935, pp 109–12, 269–80
Review of A C V Melbourne, *Early Constitutional Development in Australia: New South Wales, 1788–1856*, 1935, pp 134–5
Review of W P M Kennedy, *Essays in Constitutional Law*, 1935, pp 139–40
Review of D G Karve, *Federations: A Study in Comparative Politics*, 1935, p 149
Review of W P M Kennedy and H F Schlosberg, *The Law and Custom of the South African Constitution*, Otto W A Hoops, *Der Status der Sudafrikanischen Union*, F Apelt, *Das Britische Reich als volkerrechtsverbundene Staatengemeinschaft*, Frank Pakenham, *Peace by Ordeal*, 1935, pp 291–2
'Notes on Imperial Constitutional Law', 1936, pp 110–26, 277–88
Review of *The Australian Digest, 1825–1933* Vol IV, Compensation to Costs, W A Wynes, *Legislative and Executive Powers in Australia*, 1936, pp 307–9
Review of H V Evatt, *The King and His Dominion Governors*, 1936, pp 309–11
Review of M Venkatarangaiya, *Federation in Government*, and K V Punnaiah, *India as a Federation*, 1936, pp 311–13
'Notes on Imperial Constitutional Law', 1937, pp 105–20, 264–79
Review of K R R Sastry, *International Law*, 1937, pp 324–5
'Notes on Imperial Constitutional Law', 1938, pp 105–18, 251–61
Review of W P M Kennedy, *Constitution of Canada*, J E Tyler, *The Struggle for Imperial Unity*, R A MacKay and E B Rogers, *Canada Looks Abroad*, 1938, pp 283–7
'Notes on Imperial Constitutional Law', 1939, pp 98–108, 251–64
Review of K V Punnaiah, *The Constitutional History of India*, 1939, pp 127–8
Review of H E Read, *Recognition and Enforcement of Foreign Judgments in the Common Law Units of the British Commonwealth*, 1939, pp 134–7
Review of E C S Wade, *Dicey's Introduction to the Study of the Law of the Constitution*, 1939, pp 279–80
Review of John A Hawgood, *Modern Constitutions since 1787*, 1939, pp 280–82
'Notes on Imperial Constitutional Law', 1940, pp 77–92, 209–25
Review of W I Jennings, *Parliament*, 1940, pp 115–17
'Note in Legitimation by Adoption', 1940, pp 231–4
'Note on Foreign Guardianship and English Control of Wards', 1940, pp 234–5
'Note on Loss of Expectation of Life', 1940, pp 238–40
'Notes on Imperial Constitutional Law', 1941, pp 75–87, 177–84
'Note on Loss of Expectation of Life', 1941, pp 99–101
'Notes on Imperial Constitutional Law', 1942–43, pp 63–7, 130–3
'Note on Privy Council on *Renvoi*', 1942–43, pp 69–70

Journal of the Royal Asiatic Society

'The Nīti-mañjarī of Dyā Dviveda', 1900, pp 127–36
'A Nītimañjarī Quotation Identified', 1900, pp 796–8
'Date of Kumāradāsa', 1901, pp 578–82
'A Nītimañjarī Quotation', 1902, p 956
'The Metre of the Bṛhaddevata', 1906, pp 1–10
Review of *Vedic Metre*, 1906, p 484
Review of *The Philosophy of the Upanishads*, 1906, 490

Review of *Some Sayings of the Upanishads*, p 495
'Use of the Gerund as Passive in Sanskrit', 1906, p 693
'Vedic Metre', 1906, pp 718–22
'Negative *a* with Finite Verbs in Sanskrit', 1906, p 722
'Use of the Passive Gerund in Sanskrit', 1907, p 164
Review of *Die Apokryphen des Ṛgveda*, 1907, p 224
'Śāṅkhāyana Śranta Sūtra', 1907, p 410
Review of *Vier Philosophische Texte des Mahâbhâratam*, 1907, p 462
'Modern Hinduism and the Nestorians', 1907, p 490
'Denarius and the Date of the *Harivaṃśa*', 1907, p 681
'Some Modern Theories of Religion and the Veda', 1907, pp 929–49
'The Child Kṛṣṇa', 1908, pp 169–75
Review of *A Vedic Concordance*, 1908, p 200
'The Śāṅkhāyana Āraṇyaka', 1908, pp 363–88
'Date of Udayanācārya and Vācaspati Miśra', 1908, pp 522–6
Review of *A Short History of Indian Literature*, 1908, p 574
'Game of Dice', 1908, pp 823–8
'Battle between the Pāṇḍavas and Kauravas', 1908, pp 831–6, 1138
'Vedic Religion', 1908, pp 844–7
'Bhagavant and Kṛṣṇa', 1908, pp 847–8
Review of *Beiträge zur indischen Kulturgeschichte*, 1908, p 868
Review of *The Religion of the Veda*, 1908, p 883
'An Unusual Use of the Nominative', 1908, pp 1124–7
'The Pāṇḍavas and the Kauravas', 1908, pp 1138–42
Review of *Ausgewählte Erzählungen aus Hemacandra's Pariśiṣṭaparvan*, 1908, p 1191
'Date of the Bṛhatkathā and the Mudrārākṣasa', 1909, pp 145–9
'Tenses and Moods in the Kāṭhaka Saṃhitā', 1909, pp 149–54
'Buddhist Era in Ceylon', 1909, p 176
Review of *Mysterium und Mimus im Rigveda*, 1909, pp 200–9
'Amitrochates', 1909, pp 423–6
'Notes on Syntax', 1909, pp 428–32
'Vikramāditya and Kālidāsa', 1909, pp 433–9
Review of *Le Védisme*, 1909, pp 469–73
'Baudhāyana Paribhāṣāsūtra, Khaṇḍa VII', 1909, pp 752–5
'A Quotation from the Aitareya Āraṇyaka', 1909, pp 755–6
'On the Antiquity of Vedic Culture', 1909, pp 1100–6
'Pythagoras and the Doctrine of Transmigration', 1909, pp 569–606
'The Antiquity of Vedic Culture', 1910, pp 464–6
'Āpastamba Mantra Brāhmaṇa ii, 8, 4', 1910, pp 466–8
'Grammatical Notes', 1910, pp 151–9, 468–74
'Bhu with the Accusative', 1910, pp 151, 873–4
Review of *Der Rigveda im Auswahl*, 1910, p 921
Review of *Zum Andenken für seine Kinder und Enkel*, 1910, p 930
Review of *Aus dem Alten Indien*, 1910, p 932
Review of *Das Vaitānasūtra des Atharvaveda*, 1910, p 934
'Peculiarities in the Use of Iti', 1910, pp 1317–21
'Archaisms in the Rāmāyaṇa', 1910, pp 1321–6
'Some Irregular Uses of *me* and *te* in Epic Sanskrit', 1911, pp 177–9
Review of *The Suffixes mant and vant in Sanskrit and Avestan*, 1911, pp 254–6
Review of *Das Śāntiśataka, mit Einleitung, Kritischem Apparat, Übersetzung und Anmerkungen*, 1911, pp 257–60
Review of *Die Wurzeln der Sage vom Heiligen Gral*, 1911, pp 261–4

'The Planet Bṛhaspati', 1911, pp 794–800
Review of *The Sāhityadārpaṇa of Viśvanātha Kavirāja*, 1911, pp 848–50
'The Vedic Ākhyāna and the Indian Drama', 1911, pp 979–1009
Review of *The Vedas and their Anyas and Upangas*, 1911, pp 1157–8
'The Origin of Tragedy and the Ākhyāna', 1912, pp 411–38
'Cremation and Burial in the Ṛgveda', 1912, pp 470–4
'Notes on Vedic Syntax', 1912, pp 721–6
'Age Criteria in the Rigveda', 1912, pp 726–9
'The Suffix *sat*', 1912, pp 729–34
Review of *The Pariśiṣṭas of the Atharvaveda*, 1912, pp 755–76
'Authenticity of the Ṛtusaṃhāra', 1912, pp 1066–70
Review of *Kāṭhaka Saṃhitā, Book III*, 1912, pp 1095–1103
'The Vratyas', 1913, pp 155–60
Review of *Ethische Probleme aus dem 'Mahābhārata'*, 1913, pp 194–7
Review of *Ṛgevda, VII–X. Textkritisch und exegetische Noten*, 1913, pp 197–201
'Authenticity of the Ṛtusaṃhāra', 1913, pp 410–12
'Birth of Purūravas', 1913, pp 412–17
'The Alcmanic Figure', 1913, pp 677–81
'Brahmanic and Kṣatriya Tradition', 1914, pp 118–26
'The Vedic Calendar', 1914, pp 627–40
'Bhavabhūti and the Veda', 1914, pp 729–31
'Meaning of Jāmi, Māya, and Devagavā', 1914, pp 731–4
'Earliest Indian Traditional History', 1914, pp 734–41
'Age of the Purāṇas', 1914, pp 1021–31
Review of *Reden und Aufsätze vornehmlich über Indiens Literatur und Kultur*, 1914, pp 1071–8
Review of *Bhāradvāja Gṛhya Sūtra: the Domestic Ritual*, 1914, pp 1078–89
Review of *Introduzione allo Studio della Filosofia Indiana*, 1914, pp 1089–99
Review of *The Study of Sanskrit*, 1914, pp 1099–1100
Review of *Vāsavadattā* [translation by L Gray], 1914, pp 1100–4
Review of *Hariścandra il virtuoso, (Satyahariścandra), Dramma indiano di Rāmacandra*, 1914, pp 1104–6
'Two Notes on Vedic Religion', 1915, pp 127–33
'The Saturnalia and the Mahāvrata', 1915, pp 133–8
'The Date of the *Rāmāyaṇa*', 1915, pp 318–28
'Dynastics of the Kali Age', 1915, pp 328–35
'Āpastamba and the Bahvṛca Brāhmaṇa', 1915, pp 493–8
'Notes on the *Kauṣitakī Brāhmaṇa*', 1915, pp 498–504
'The Denarius as a Proof of Date', 1915, pp 504–5
Review of *History of Religions, I*, 1915, pp 545–51
'Indian Origin of the Greek Romance', 1915, pp 784–90
'The Magi', 1915, pp 790–9
'Dynasties of the Kali Age', 1915, pp 799–800
Review of *Indian Theism*, 1915, pp 833–41
Review of *The Heart of Jainism*, 1915, pp 842–7
'The Authenticity of the Kauṭilīya', 1916, pp 130–7
'The Zoroastrian Period of Indian History', 1916, pp 138–43
'Day and Night in India', 1916, pp 143–6
'Beginnings of the Indian Drama', 1916, pp 146–51
Review of *Indian Thought, Past and Present*, 1916, pp 167–71
'Professor Ridgeway's Theory of the Origin of Indian Drama', 1916, pp 335–50
'The Unlucky Number 13', 1916, pp 350–5

Review of *The Prābhākara School of Pūrva Mīmāṁsā*, 1916, pp 369–76
'M Reinach's Theory of Sacrifice', 1916, pp 542–55
'The Indian Day', 1916, pp 555–61
'The Order of the Nakṣatras in the Epic, and the Epic Month', 1917, pp 135–9
'Professor Ridgway's Theory of the Origin of Indian Drama', 1917, pp 140–3
Review of *Comparative Administrative Law*, 1920, pp 242–8
Review of *An Outline of the Religious Literature of India*, 1920, pp 627–9
Review of *Pañcaviṁśa-Brāhmaṇa*, 1932, pp 697–700
Review of *Vedic Variants, Vol II*, 1933, pp 486–91
Review of *Brahman*, 1933, pp 949–50
Review of *The Individual and the Community*, 1933, pp 950–1
Review of *Matériaux pour l'étude du système Vijñaptimātra*, 1934, pp 414–15
Review of *Story of Kālaka*, 1934, pp 563–5
Review of *Ṛgveda-Saṃhitā, Part I*, 1934, pp 850–1

Other Journals to which ABK Contributed

Annals of the Bhandarkar Oriental Research Institute, Poona
Bulletin of the Linguistic Society of India, Lahore
Bulletin of the School of Oriental Studies, London
Canadian Bar Review, Toronto
Canadian Historical Review, Toronto
The Classical Quarterly, London
The Cosmopolitan, Edinburgh
Elder Dempster Magazine, London [*Elder's Review of West African Affairs*, the *West African Review*]
Indian Culture, Calcutta
Indian Historical Quarterly, Calcutta
The Indian Review, Madras
Journal of the African Society, London
Journal of the Society of Oriental Art, Calcutta
Juridical Review, Edinburgh
The Near East and India, London
Royal Society of Arts, Journal, London
University of Toronto Law Journal, Toronto
Zeitschrift für ausländisches u. internationales Privatrecht, Berlin
Zeitschrift für Volkerrecht und Bundesstaatsrecht, Frebnitz

Letters to Newspapers

ABK wrote extensively to the press. He edited and organised some 250 of the letters he wrote from 1916–37 into three volumes published in 1935, 1936, and 1938, cited above in the list of printed works. How many that represents of the total is difficult to tell.

In preparation of this study, all those letters were used plus all other letters and notes in the *Glasgow Herald* and *The Times* which, fortunately, are indexed, plus a large number of other letters and notes in *The Manchester Guardian* and, particularly, in *The Scotsman* which, unfortunately, lack an index. In addition, all issues of *New Times and Ethiopia News* were used. Certain other newspapers were used: *Daily Union* 2 July 1945, 'Truth about Cabinet Secrets'; *Daily Worker*, 9 October 1944, 'Questions on India'; *Dunfermline Journal, 1911*; *Edinburgh Citizen and Portobello Advertiser, 1897–1938*; *Evening News* (Edinburgh); *Haddington Courier*; *West Lothian Courier and Lanarkshire, Stirlingshire, and Mid-Lothian Herald, 1912*.

The newspapers, so far as can be determined, to which ABK contributed are listed below.

Cape Times, Capetown
Daily Despatch East London, Union of South Africa
Daily Mail
Edinburgh Evening Dispatch
Glasgow Herald
Irish Independent
Manchester Guardian
Morning Post [after 1937, *Morning Post and Daily Telegraph*]
Natal Mercury, Durban
The Near East and India
New Times and Ethiopia News
Outlook
Opinion, Durban
Reynolds News [Australian news service]
The Scotsman
The South Pacific Mail, Valparaiso
The Spectator
The Sunday Times
Sydney Daily Telegraph
The Times
The Times of India
The Times Literary Supplement
West Africa

Other Printed Materials

Annual Register
Baird, William, *Annals of Duddingston and Portobello* (Edinburgh: Andrew Elliot, 1898)
Colonial Office List, 1898–1915
Dail Eireann, *Debate on the Treaty between Great Britain and Ireland* (1922)
Dail Eireann, *Constituent Assembly* (1922)
Dail Eireann, *Debates* Sessions, 1922–1938
Dicey, Albert Venn, *Introduction to the Study of the Law of the Constitution* (London: Macmillan, 1885) [Reprinted with editorial notes by R E Michener from 8th edition, 1915, Minneapolis: Liberty Classics, 1982.]
——, 'The Extension of Law Teaching at Oxford', *Harvard Law Review*, 1910, pp 1–5
——, *Lectures on the Relation between Law and Public Opinion in England during the Nineteenth Century* (London: Macmillan, 1905)
Harrison, Henry, *The Partition of Ireland: How Britain is Responsible* (London: Hale, 1939)
Hilliard, Edward, ed, *Balliol College Register, 1832–1914* (Oxford: University of Oxford, 1914)
Institut colonial international, Brussels, 1894–1948
   Bibliothèque coloniale internationale, sér 6, 1902, 1903; sér 7, 1906–1909; sér 8, 1906–1927; sér 9, 1909–1910; sér 10, 1911
   Catalogue de la bibliothèque, 1908
   Compte-rendu des séances, 1894–1927, 18 vols
   Recueil international de législation coloniale, 1911–1914
Jebb, Richard, *The Imperial Conference* (London: Longmans and Company, 1911)

Johnson, George, ed, *The All Red Line: the Annals and Aims of the Pacific Cable Project* (Ottawa: James Hope, 1903)

Keith Collection, Edinburgh University Library

> This includes approximately 5,000 books, journals, pamphlets, collections of documents from ABK's working library, given to Edinburgh university by Mrs Nan B Dewar, his sister. It is not possible to determine what fraction of the total that he had this represents. It includes a copy of each of his published books. In addition, many of the slips which he used to indicate where the books should be shelved in his house were given as part of the collection. In the preparation of this study, these materials from ABK's library were used extensively. However, they are not all entered as separate items below.

Law Reports, Probate, Divorce, and Admiralty Division, 1931

Law Reports, Judicial Committee of the Privy Council, 1938

Lucas, Charles P, ed, *Lord Durham's Report on the Affairs of British North America*, 3 vols (Oxford: Clarendon Press, 1912)

Macdonell, Arthur A, *A History of Sanskrit Literature* (London: Heinemann, 1900; Delhi: Lal, 1958, 1961). Reprinted from initial edition of 1899

The Monthly Summary of the League of Nations (Geneva: Information Section, League of Nations, 1936)

Oppenheim, L, *The Panama Canal Conflict between Great Britain and the United States of America: A Study* (Cambridge: Cambridge University Press, 1913)

The Oxford Magazine

Post Office, *Edinburgh and Leith Directory*, 1878–1940

——, *London Directory*

Rait, Robert S, ed, *Memorials of Albert Venn Dicey: Being Chiefly Letters and Diaries* (London: Macmillan, 1925)

Sastri, P P S, 'Arthur Berriedale Keith', in *Eminent Orientalists: Indian, European, American* (Madras: G A Natesan and Company, nd [1922])

The Scots Law Times Reports, 1934

Seeley, John R, *The Expansion of England* (London: Macmillan, 1888)

Shepherd, Thomas H and John Britton, *Modern Athens, Displayed in a Series of Views of Edinburgh in the Nineteenth Century* (London: Jones and Company, 1829)

Steven, William, *The History of the High School of Edinburgh* (Edinburgh: Maclachlan and Stewart, 1849)

Stevenson, Robert Louis, *Edinburgh: Picturesque Notes* (London: Seeley and Company, 1879)

Stuart, James, *A History of the Zulu Rebellion, 1906, and of Dinizulu's Arrest, Trial, and Expatriation* (London: Macmillan, 1913)

Thornbury, George W and Edward Walford, *Old and New London* 6 vols (London: Cassell, Peter, 1879–1885)

Todd, Alpheus, *Parliamentary Government in the British Colonies* (London: Longmans and Company, 1880)

Turner, Henry G, *The First Decade of the Australian Commonwealth: A Chronicle of Contemporary Politics, 1901–1910* (Melbourne: Mason, Forth, McCutcheon, 1911)

SECONDARY WORKS

Books

Abbott, Arthur W, *A Short History of the Crown Agents and their Office* (London: Eyre and Spottiswoode, 1959)

Aggarwal, H R, *A Short History of Sanskrit Literature* (Delhi: Lal, 2nd edn, 1963) [1st edn, 1940]

Asquith, Margot, *The Autobiography of Margot Asquith* 2 vols (London: Thornton Butterworth, 1920)

Barclay, J B, *The Tounis Scule: The Royal High School of Edinburgh* (Edinburgh: Royal High School Club, 1974)

Barker, Nicholas, *The Oxford University Press and the Spread of Learning, 1478–1978* (Oxford: Clarendon Press, 1978)

Beaverbrook, *The Abdication of King Edward VIII* ed A J P Taylor (London: H Hamilton, 1966)

Berlin, Isaiah, *The Hedgehog and the Fox: An Essay on Tolstoy's View of History* (London: Weidenfeld and Nicolson, 1953) (New York: Simon and Schuster, 1953)

Blakeley, Brian L, *The Colonial Office, 1868–1892* (Durham, North Carolina: Duke University Press, 1972)

Brebner, J B, *The North Atlantic Triangle: the Interplay of Canada, the United States and Great Britain* (New Haven: Yale University Press, 1945)

Butler, D H E and J Freeman, *British Political Facts, 1900–1968* (London: Macmillan, 1969)

Brough, John, *Poems from the Sanskrit* (Harmondsworth: Penguin Books, 1968)

Carmichael, Baroness [Mary H E], *Lord Carmichael of Stirling: A Memoir* (London: Hodder and Stoughton, 1929)

Catford, Edwin F, *Edinburgh: the Story of a City* (London: Hutchinson, 1975)

Chamberlain, Austen, *Politics from Inside, 1906–1914: An Epistolary Chronicle* (London: Cassell and Company, 1936)

Cohen, Emmaline W, *The Growth of the British Civil Service, 1780–1939* (London: Allen and Unwin, 1941)

Cordeaux, E H and D H Merry, *A Bibliography of Printed Works related to the University of Oxford* (Oxford: Clarendon Press, 1968)

Cosgrove, Richard A, *The Rule of Law: Albert Venn Dicey, Victorian Jurist* (Chapel Hill, North Carolina: University of North Carolina Press, 1980)

Cox, Montagu and Philip Norman, *Survey of London: London County Council, XIII. Parish of St Margaret, Westminster, Part II* (London: Batsford, 1930)

Cross, John Arthur, *Whitehall and the Commonwealth: British Departmental Organisation for Commonwealth Relations, 1900–1966* (London: Routledge and Kegan Paul, 1967)

Daiches, David, *Edinburgh* (London: Granada, 1980)

Dangerfield, George, *The Strange Death of Liberal England* (London: Constable and Company, 1936)

Dawson, Robert M, *The Development of Dominion Status, 1900–1936* (London: Oxford University Press, 1937)

Dewar, Mary, *Sir Thomas Smith: A Tudor Intellectual in Office* (London: Athlone Press, 1964)

Driberg, Thomas E N, *Beaverbrook: A Study in Power and Frustration* (London: Weidenfield and Nicolson, 1956)

Earle, Lionel, *Turn Over the Page* (London: Hutchinson, 1935)

Eden, Anthony, *The Memoirs of the Rt. Hon. Sir Anthony Eden. Vol. 2: Facing the Dictators* (London: Cassell and Company, 1962)

Ensor, Robert K, *England, 1870–1914*, Oxford History of England (Oxford: Clarendon Press, 1936)

Fage, John D, *A History of West Africa*, 4th edn (Cambridge: Cambridge University Press, 1969)

Feiling, Keith, *The Life of Neville Chamberlain* (London: Macmillan, 1946)

Fieldhouse, David K, *The Colonial Empires: A Comparative Survey from the Eighteenth Century* (London: Weidenfeld and Nicolson, 1966)

——, *Economics and Empire, 1830–1914* (Ithaca, New York: Cornell University Press, 1973)

Fitzroy, Almeric, *The History of the Privy Council* (London: John Murray, 1928)

Furse, Ralph, *Aucuparius: Recollections of a Recruiting Officer* (London: Oxford University Press, 1962)

Gardner, Howard, *Frames of Mind: The Theory of Multiple Intelligences* (New York: Basic Books, 1983) (London: Heinemann, 1984)

Gifford, John, Colin McWilliam, David Walker, and Christopher Wilson, *Edinburgh* in *The Buildings of Scotland* edited by Colin McWilliam (Harmondsworth: Penguin Books, 1984)

Gordon, Donald C, *The Dominion Partnership in Imperial Defense, 1870–1914* (Baltimore: Johns Hopkins Press, 1965)

Hall, Henry L, *The Colonial Office* (London: Longmans, 1937)

Hancock, W K, *Survey of British Commonwealth Affairs* 2 vols (London: Oxford University Press, 1937, 1940)

——, *Smuts*, 2 vols (Cambridge: Cambridge University Press, 1962, 1968)

Hanbury, Harold G, *The Vinerian Chair and Legal Education* (Oxford: Basil Blackwell, 1958)

Hardie, Frank, *The Abyssinian Crisis* (London: Batsford, 1974)

Harkness, David K, *The Restless Dominion: the Irish Free State and the British Commonwealth of Nations, 1921–1931* (London: Macmillan, 1969)

Hazlehurst, C and C Woodland, *A Guide to the Papers of British Cabinet Ministers, 1900–1951* (London: Royal Historical Society, 1974)

Henige, David P, ed, *Colonial Governors from the Fifteenth Century to the Present* (Madison, Wisconsin: University of Wisconsin Press, 1970)

Hughes, Colin A and B D Graham, *A Handbook of Australian Government and Politics, 1890–1964* (Canberra: Australian National University, 1968)

Hyam, Ronald, *Britain's Imperial Century, 1815–1914* (London: Batsford, 1976)

——, *Elgin and Churchill at the Colonial Office, 1905–1908: the Watershed of the Empire-Commonwealth* (London: Macmillan, 1968)

——, *The Failure of South African Expansion, 1908–1948* (London: Macmillan, 1972)

Hynes, Samuel, *The Edwardian Turn of Mind* (Princeton: Princeton University Press, 1968)

Johnson, Franklyn A, *Defence by Committee: the British Committee of Imperial Defence, 1885–1959* (London: Oxford University Press, 1960)

Joyce, R B, *Sir William MacGregor* (Melbourne: Oxford University Press, 1971)

Just, Hartmann W, *Verses* (Cambridge: Heffer, 1930)

Kendle, J E, *The Colonial and Imperial Conferences, 1887–1911: A Study in Imperial Organisation and Politics* (London: Longmans, 1967)

——, *The Round Table Movement and Imperial Union* (Toronto: University of Toronto Press, 1975)

Kennedy, W P M, *The Canadian Constitution* (London: Humphrey Milford, 1922)

Keynes, J M, *The Economic Consequences of the Peace* (London: Macmillan, 1919)

Koss, Stephen, *Asquith* (London: Allen Lane, 1976)

Kubicek, Robert V, *The Administration of Imperialism: Joseph Chamberlain at the Colonial Office* (Durham, North Carolina: Duke University Press, 1969)

LaNauze, John A, *Alfred Deakin: A Biography* (Melbourne: Melbourne University Press, 1965) 2 vols

Lawson, Frederick H, *The Oxford Law School, 1850–1965* (Oxford: Clarendon Press, 1968)

Lyons, F S L, *Ireland since the Famine* (London: Fontana, 1973)

Macardle, Dorothy, *The Irish Republic* (London: Victor Gollancz, 1937)

Mackail, J W, *James Leigh Strachan-Davidson, Master of Balliol: A Memoir* (Oxford: Clarendon Press, 1925)

Mackintosh, John P, *The British Cabinet* 3rd ed (London: Stevens and Sons, 1977)

Madden, A Frederick, ed, *Imperial Constitutional Documents, 1765–1952: A Supplement* (Oxford: Blackwell, 1953) [A supplement to ABK's collected documents on colonial policy and dominions.]

Mansergh, Nicholas, *The Irish Free State* (London: Allen and Unwin, 1934)

——, *South Africa, 1906–1961: The Price of Magnanimity* (London: Allen and Unwin, 1962)

Marks, Sally Jean, *The Illusion of Peace: International Relations in Europe, 1918–1933* (London: Macmillan, 1976)

Marks, Shula, *Reluctant Rebellion: The 1906–1908 Disturbances in Natal* (Oxford: Clarendon Press, 1970)

Marsh, Edward, *A Number of People: A Book of Reminiscences* (London: Heinemann, 1939)

Martin, Ged, *The Durham Report and British Policy: A Critical Essay* (Cambridge: Cambridge University Press, 1972)

——, and Ronald Hyam, *Reappraisals in British Imperial History* (London: Macmillan, 1975)

Mowat, C L, *Britain between the Wars, 1918–1940* (London: Methuen, 1956)

Millin, Sarah Gertrude, *General Smuts* 2 vols (London: Faber and Faber, 1936)

Mullett, Charles L, *The British Empire-Commonwealth, its Themes and Character: A Plural Society in Evolution* (Washington, D.C.: Service Center for Teachers of History, 1961)

Namier, Louis B, *Diplomatic Prelude, 1938–1939* (London: Macmillan, 1948)

Neatby, H Blair, *William Lyon Mackenzie King: The Lonely Heights, 1924–1932* (London: Methuen, 1963)

——, *William Lyon Mackenzie King: The Prism of Unity, 1932–1939* (Toronto: University of Toronto Press, 1976)

Nimocks, Walter, *Milner's Young Men: The 'Kindergarten' in Edwardian Imperial Affairs* (Durham, North Carolina: Duke University Press, 1968)

Pakenham, Frank, *Peace by Ordeal* (London: Jonathan Cape, 1935)

Pakenham, Thomas, *The Boer War* (London: Weidenfeld and Nicolson, 1979)

Pankhurst, E Sylvia and Richard K Pankhurst, *Ethiopia and Eritrea* (Woodford Green: Lalibela House, 1953)

Pankhurst, Richard K, *Sylvia Pankhurst: Artist and Crusader: An Intimate Portrait* (London: Paddington Press, 1979)

Parkinson, Cosmo, *The Colonial Office from Within, 1909–1945* (London: Faber and Faber, 1947)

Perham, Margery, *Lugard* 2 vols (London: Collins, 1956, 1960)

Petrie, Charles, *Scenes of Edwardian Life* (London: Eyre and Spottiswoode, 1965)

Priestley, J B, *The Edwardians* (London: Heinemann, 1970)

Pugh, R B, 'The Colonial Office, 1801–1925', in J H Rose *et al*, eds *The Cambridge History of the British Empire* Volume III (Cambridge: Cambridge University Press, 1959)

——, *The Records of the Colonial and Dominions Offices* PRO Handbooks No 3 (London: HMSO, 1964)

Robinson, Howard, *The Development of the British Empire* (Boston: Houghton, Mifflin, 1922) 2nd edition, 1936

Rose, J H, A P Newton, and E L Benians *et al*, eds *The Cambridge History of the British Empire* 8 vols (Cambridge: Cambridge University Press, 1929–1959)

Ross, William, *The Royal High School* (Edinburgh: Oliver and Boyd, 1934)

Sackville-West, Vita, *The Edwardians* (London: L and V Woolf, 1930)

Seely, J E B, *Adventure* (London: Heinemann, 1930)

Shinn, Ridgway F, Jr, *The Right of Secession in the Development of the British Commonwealth of Nations* (Ann Arbor, Michigan: University Microfilms, 1958)

A Short History of the Office of the Crown agents for the Colonies together with a Description of its Functions and Character, prepared on the occasion of its Centenary, 1st April, 1933 (London: Crown Agents for the Colonies, 1933)

Skelton, Oscar D, *Life and Letters of Sir Wilfred Laurier* 2 vols (Toronto: S B Gundy, 1921)

Sutcliffe, Peter, *The Oxford University Press: An Informal History* (Oxford: Clarendon Press, 1978)

Sweetman, Edward, *Australian Constitutional Development* (Melbourne: Melbourne University Press, 1925)

Tarring, Charles J, *Chapters on the Law Relating to the Colonies* (London: Stevens and Haynes, 1913)

Taylor, A J P, *Beaverbrook* (Harmondsworth: Penguin Books, 1972)

——, *The Origins of the Second World War* (London: Hamish Hamilton, 1961)

——, *English History, 1914–1945*, Oxford History of England (Oxford: Clarendon Press, 1976) [Originally published in 1965; this printing contains revised bibliography.]

Thomson, David, *England in the 19th Century, 1815–1914* (Harmondsworth: Penguin Books, 1957)

——, *England in the 20th Century* (Harmondsworth: Penguin Books, 1965)

Thompson, Leonard M, *The Unification of South Africa, 1902–1910* (Oxford: Clarendon Press, 1960)

Trotter, James H, *The Royal High School, Edinburgh* (London: Pitman and Sons, 1911)

Turner, A Logan, ed, *History of the University of Edinburgh, 1883–1933* (Edinburgh: Graduates Association, 1933)

Victoria History of the Counties of England: A History of Oxfordshire. III. The University of Oxford (London: Oxford University Press, 1954)

Wheare, K C, *The Statute of Westminster and Dominion Status* (Oxford: Clarendon Press, 1938) numerous subsequent editions

——, and F W Thomas, 'Arthur Berriedale Keith'. *Dictionary of National Biography, 1941–1950*, pp 443–5

Wigley, Philip, *Canada and the Transition to Commonwealth: British-Canadian Relations, 1917–1926* (Cambridge: Cambridge University Press, 1977)

Articles

[Allan, John] 'Obituary of Arthur Berriedale Keith (1894)', *Schola Regia*, 1943–1945, pp 51–2

Bramston, John, 'The Colonial Office from Within', *Empire Review*, April 1911, pp 279–87

Bruce, Sir Charles, 'The Colonial Office and the Crown Colonies', *Empire Review*, July 1906

Burton, Ann, 'Treasury Control and Colonial Policy in the Late Nineteenth Century', *Public Administration*, 1966, pp 169–92

Cross, John Arthur, 'The Colonial Office and the Dominions before 1914', *Journal of Commonwealth Political Studies*, 1966, pp 138–48

——, 'Whitehall and the Commonwealth', *Journal of Commonwealth Political Studies*, 1963–1964, pp 189–206

Dictionary of National Biography, all entries dealing with persons who were ABK's correspondents, who were on the staff of the Colonial Office, or who were involved in some way with ABK

Fieldhouse, David K, 'New Zealand, Fiji, and the Colonial Office, 1900–1902', *Historical Studies*, May 1958, pp 113–30

Ford, Trowbridge, 'Dicey's Conversion to Unionism', *Irish Historical Studies*, September 1973, pp 552–82

——, 'Dicey as a Political Journalist', *Political Studies*, 1970, pp 220–35

Hamilton, W S Baillie, 'Forty-four Years at the Colonial Office', *The Nineteenth Century*, 1909, pp 599–613

Harkness, David K, 'Mr DeValera's Dominion: Irish Relations with Britain and the Commonwealth, 1932–1938', *Journal of Commonwealth Political Studies*, 1970, pp 206–28

Kesner, Richard M, 'Builders of Empire: the Role of the Crown Agents in Imperial Development, 1880–1914', *Journal of Imperial and Commonwealth History*, May 1977, pp 310–30

Koss, Stephen, 'The Dissolution of Britain's Last Liberal Government', *Journal of Modern History*, 1968

Kubicek, Robert V, 'Joseph Chamberlain, the Treasury, and Imperial Development, 1895–1903', *Canadian Historical Association Report*, 1965, pp 105–16

Lucas, Charles P, 'Want of Vision', *Canadian Historical Review*, 1922, pp 343–50

MacLeish, Roderick, 'The Mystery of What Makes a Prodigy', *Smithsonian*, March 1984, pp 70–8

Mansergh, Nicholas, 'Ireland: From British Commonwealth towards European Community', *Historical Studies*, October 1968, pp 381–95

McGill, Barry, 'Asquith's Predicament, 1911–1918', *Journal of Modern History*, 1967, pp 283–303

Penson, Lillian M, 'The Origins of the Crown Agency Office', *English Historical Review*, April 1925, pp 196–206

Shinn, Ridgway F, Jr, 'Arthur Berriedale Keith (1879–1944)', *University of Edinburgh Journal*, December 1982, pp 281–3

——, 'The Dissolution of 1908—No 1: A Governor Exercises His Power' and 'The Dissolution of 1908—No 2: "What an Ass You Must Think Me!" ', *Journal of the Royal Historical Society of Victoria*, September, December 1983

——, 'Changing the King's Title, 1926: An Asterisk to "O'Higgins' Comma" ', *The Irish Jurist*, 1981, pp 114–40

——, 'The King's Title, 1926: A Note on a Critical Document', *English Historical Review*, 1983, pp 349–53

Steiner, Zara, 'The Last Years of the Old Foreign Office, 1895–1914', *Historical Journal*, 1963, pp 59–90

Index

Abbreviations used: ABK, Arthur Berriedale Keith; MSK, his mother, Margaret Stobie Drysdale Keith; CO, Colonial Office; *JRAS, Journal of the Royal Asiatic Society*. Only ABK's books mentioned or discussed in the text are indexed; see Bibliography for full listing of ABK's books and for his contributions to *Journal of Comparative Legislation, JRAS*, and *festschriften*.

Asquith, H H, 8, 127, 146, 157–8, 164, 170, 185–6, 193, 202–3, 221
Asquith, Margot, on Churchill, 96; on Lloyd George, 170; on election 1918, 186
Asquith, Raymond, 33
Associated Chambers of Commerce of India and Ceylon, 224–5, 227, 229, 255
Athenaenum, review of *Responsible Government in the Dominions*, cited, 124
Atholl, Duke of, 185
Atlantic Charter, 282
Atlantic Triangle, 74, 143
Aufrecht, Theodor, 32–3
Australia, 9, 46, 64–6, 71; states of in re CO, post-1901, 66; and merchant shipping, 112–13; and Colonial Conference, 1907, 120; and imperial defence, 1911, 121; files in Dominions Department, 128; and Foreign Office, 131, 155, 169, 179–81, 201, 204, 209, 211–12
Austria, 247, 276
Aylesworth, Sir Allen B, and Alaska Boundary Commission, 76–7

Bagehot, Walter, 125
Bahamas, 47, 68, 73–4, 110
Baillie-Hamilton, Sir William A, 56
Baldwin, Stanley, 193, 215, 221, 246, 265, 268–70, 272, 278–80, 289
Balfour, Arthur J, 8, 94–5, 215–17, 234
Balliol College, Oxford, 27–33, 63, 151, 200
Barbados, 74, 110
Basu, B N, 190
Basutoland, 93–4, *see also* Protectorates and Union of South Africa
Batterbee, Harry F, 122
Battersea Park area, London, 41
Beaverbrook, Lord [Max Aitken], 221, 232–4
Bechuanaland, 93–4, *see also* Protectorates and Union of South Africa
Beeton, H R, 205
Belgian Congo and the Berlin Act, 1919, 178, 184–5
Bell, Sir Hesketh, 281

Bell, Nancy, 287
Benthall, E P, 224–5
Bentham, Jeremy, 92, 125
Bering Sea, 63
Berlin, Sir Isaiah, 292
Bermuda, 68–9, 72, 110
Berne Convention, 142
Beveridge, William, 33
Bhārata-Kaumudī: Studies in Indology in Honour of Dr Radha Kamud Mookerji, 251
Bikaner, Maharaja of, and Edinburgh University, 174
Black, James, 187, 202–3
Black, Margaret, *see Campbell v Campbell*
Blackstone, Sir William, 125
Blake, Sir Ernest, Senior Crown Agent, 1903, photo, 80; argues to create post of Secretary, 78–9; actions, 81, 83, 85; ABK's difficulties with, 85–9; 107
Blount, Petrie & Co, 260–1
Blundell, Muriel, 281
Boden Professor of Sanskrit, Oxford, Macdonnell and, 28, 31, 32, 113–14; ABK deputy for, 1907–8, 114, 124; and ABK, 1926, 200–1
Boden Scholarship in Sanskrit, Oxford, 27
Bond, Sir Robert, 105
Borden, Sir Robert, and Edinburgh University, 173–4
Bracton, Henry, 124
Brazil, 111
Brebner, J B, and concept of North Atlantic Triangle, 74, 142–3
Brett, F W, 56
Brierly, J L, 229
Brisbane Tramways case, 204–7, 226
British Academy, ABK Fellow of, 252
British Cabinet System, 1830–1938, 1939, 267; 2nd edn N H Gibbs, 1952, 268
British Commonwealth of Nations, emergence in 1920s, 11–12, 210; and Irish Free State, 212; ABK and possibility of republic in, 213, 243, 257–8; and Imperial Conference, 1926, 213–16; 219, 226–7, 240–1, 247–8, 253–9, 263–4, 267
British Commonwealth of Nations: its Territories and Constitutions, 1940, 263–4